Turkeyfoot:

What is Our BIG Problem?

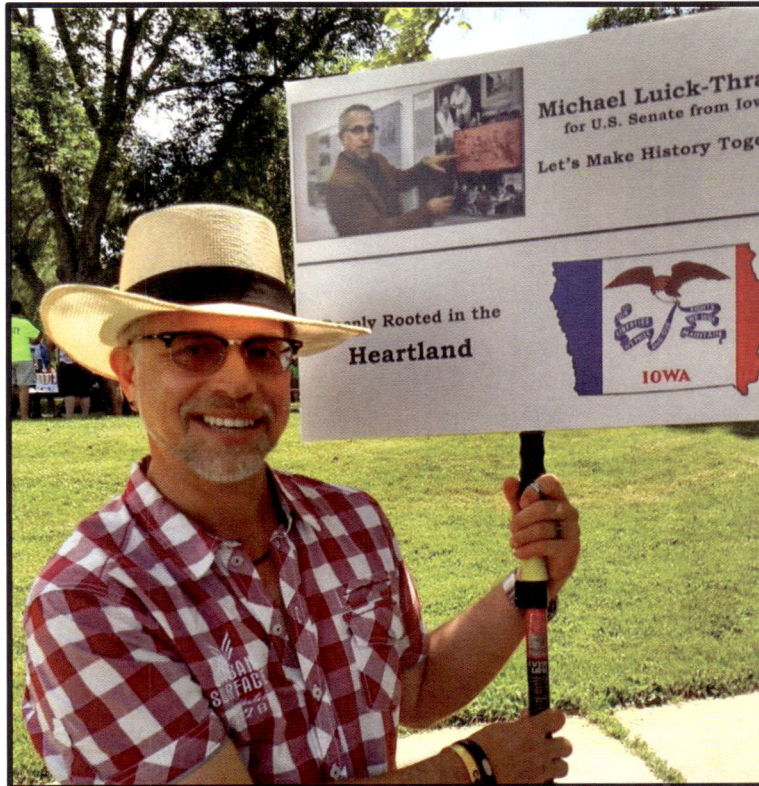

by Michael Luick-Thrams

copyright 2020

about this book:

An eccentric gay-Quaker historian living in Germany decides on a quixotic whim—for deeply idealistic and quasi-spiritual reasons—to run for the US Senate in his native Iowa. To his consternation, he soon finds himself hip-deep in the moral quicksand of Midwestern Trumpism. Unexpectedly, he discovers that his Trump-drunk relatives embody the very electorate he has to woo. This story tells how this onetime farmboy got into this swamp, how he escaped, and how other residents of Trump Nation—if they truly care about our country and the larger world—might punch their way out of political paper bags as well. This book—two tomes woven into one, each uniquely pertinent to this historical moment—provides all Americans (as well as other mortals beyond our shores) a way out. Book One explores the cynical, two-party electoral system that both feeds and embodies the social-political deadlock our country faces; Book Two concludes with fifteen strategies for how to bridge the chasms that currently divide us: Combined, they outline how to rediscover compassion for each other at a juncture in our national and global history when either we find each other again or we all will be lost, together, forever.

about its author:

Michael Luick-Thrams (Ph.D. in 1997, Humboldt Universität in Berlin) directs two non-profit educational organizations, the TRACES Center for History and Culture in Iowa (founded 2001; www.TRACES.org) and Spuren in Germany (2011). Single, he divides his time between Iowa and Germany, where his two Hausmates consist of a goofy Swabian professor of religious history and a stuffed-toy Spaniel, Sparky.

the cover photo:

The author holds a handmade campaign placard, which reads as follows, in-full:

> **Michael Luick-Thrams**
> **for U.S. Senate from Iowa**
> **Let's Make History Together!**
>
> **Deeply Rooted in the**
> **Heartland**

for our mother,
in thanksgiving

contents

*

introductions

"What is the use of a house if you haven't got a tolerable planet to put it on?"

— the New England Transcendentalist
Henry David Thoreau, *Familiar Letters*

Introducing the Thesis

Today, my torn family is at war with itself. At the same time, our divided country is, too. Inadvertently, I ignited the spark that unleashed our family's current ugly, tragic warfare. Unpredictably, the flaying of our own flesh has given me insight into America's social stalemate:

Deadlock occurs when movement becomes blocked because one person (or a group of people) is holding an expectation of another—of one's "opposite," a.k.a. "The Other"—and is awaiting a "concession" to be granted by his or her opposite, who expects a concession from *their* Other. With neither party willing to extend or expand its Self on behalf of The Other, movement is not possible. An anticipated concession might involve a belief, a behavior, a pledge of loyalty, a job, money or other tangible resources, a favor or a vote, forgiveness, praise, sex, etc., *ad infinitum*.

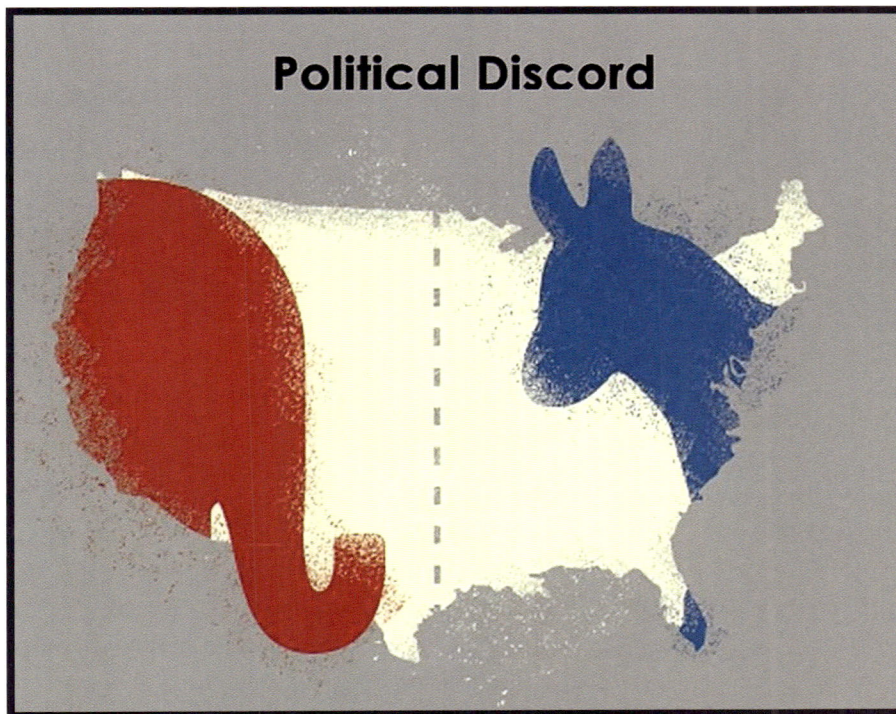

a political-art exhibit sponsored by *https://www.laslagunagallery.com/political*

How deadlock occurs:

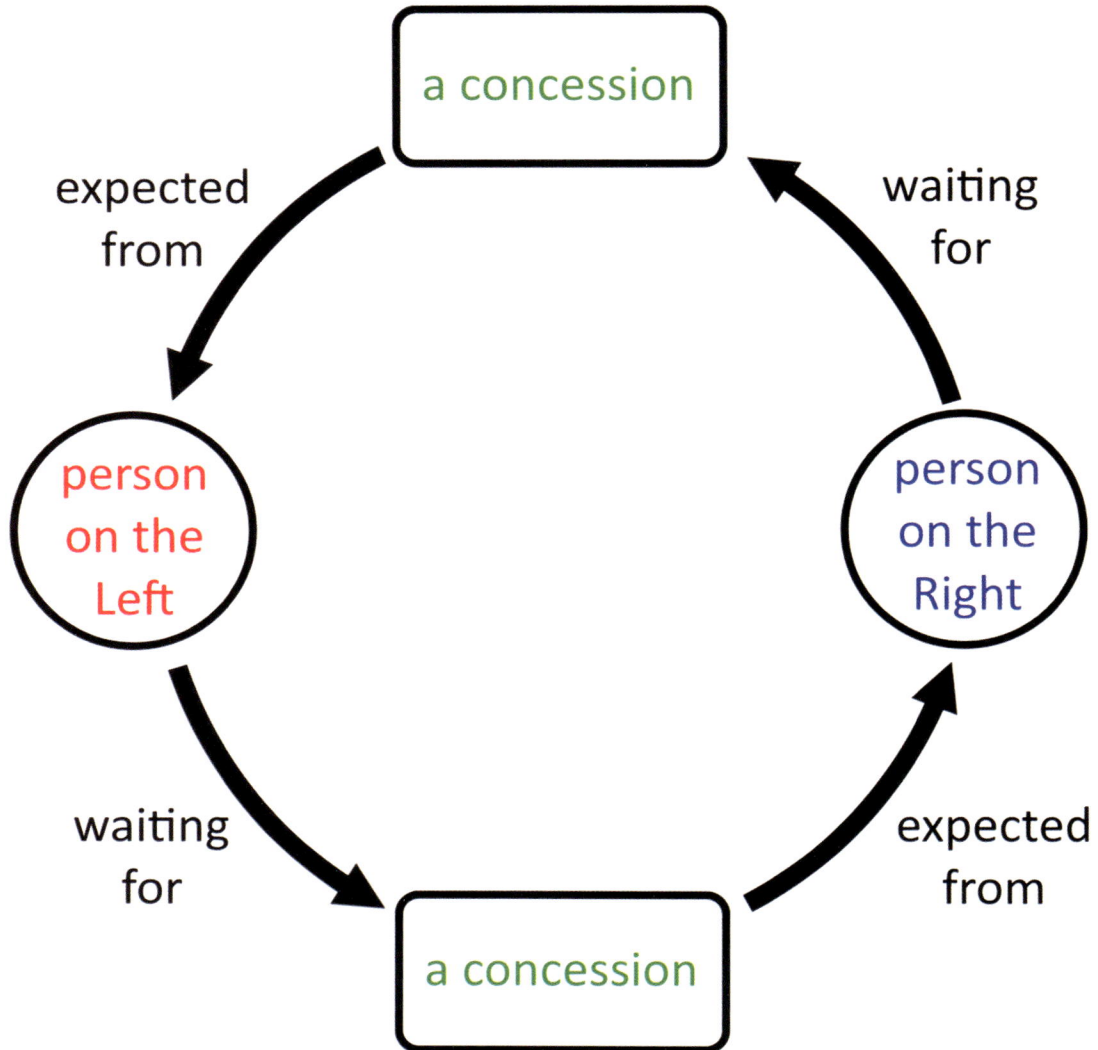

An example: Two trains are coming toward each other on the same track; as there is only one track, neither of the trains can advance once they are in front of each other. Thus: 1) the moving trains ram into each other; 2) each train stops, then stays in place, in an unyielding standoff—not unlike when family members or neighbors break all contact with each other; or 3) one of the trains brakes, then backs up to allow The Other passage, at which point, having conceded, the train that first breaks stalemate could then, in theory, proceed—IF the train granted passage a) leaves the track passable and b) does not block or otherwise hinder the initially-yielding train's ensuing passage.[1]

The endless war I've been fighting with most of my family for four decades has been over beliefs (they'd likely say "non-belief")—not only religious but also social and political beliefs. Because such beliefs represent core parts of each one's Self identity, we are loathe to concede that The Other's beliefs, behaviors, work, expressions of love, etc. might be as (or worse, *more*) valid or honorable as our own. Note: Each of these elements of identity is an **ideal**, *not* physically real.

Similarly, our nation—indeed, much of our interconnected world—is now split along **ideol**ogical fronts. In the United States, those who adore Donald Trump and those who abhor him embody opposing sides of a deep rift that presently cuts through the heart of American society. [As I write this, similar dynamics tear away at Great Britain (*vis-à-vis* "Brexit"), Germany (AfD Partei), France ("Yellow Vests"), Italy (the "Five Star" movement), Poland (PiS), Russia (Putin), Turkey (Erdoğan).] Folks on polarized, diametrically-opposing fronts struggle to understand those on the other. It seems we have lost each other. In effect, too many of us say, too often and reflexively, "I don't agree with what you say—and, by the way, everything else you do is wrong, bad and idiotic."

By the sheer randomness of genetic lottery, my relatives' beliefs and behaviors represent for me the norm in a camp I find foreign and distasteful. I encountered their socio-political co-travelers in most of the electorate I tried to reach in my 2016 US-Senate campaign. To understand that mainstream, I had to attempt to understand them better—which I have done, in small ways.

How can we ever bridge the gaps that have formed between us if we cannot feel compassion for one another? After all, the passions fueling our estrangement involve basic pillars of life: Our divisions include differing **ideals** about systems that dictate how humans "should" live and work, love and play, make art, worship—or not—and govern or be governed. In each case, our beliefs give rise to a system or set of systems that have the potential to liberate or to enslave all of us.

Currently, most Americans—regardless of political stripes—complain "The system is broken" but then shrug and go about our daily routines. Therefore, we seem unable—or outright refuse—to see something fundamental:

- We remain trapped in a system that does not serve the majority of our people optimally.
- For our willful blindness, we fail to demand systemic change, which is possible and long overdue.
- Our nation's psychological makeup fuels our shared strengths even as it casts ideological straightjackets that keep us from re-evaluating our values and updating our beliefs.
- Out of mental laziness, we habitually reduce those who don't share our beliefs as stupid or "evil."
- Fearing change, we refrain from making better lives than the ones we have now, for ourselves and those who will follow.

We *must* cease our self-imprisonment if we're to restore a world reeling from our abusing it, let alone save ourselves. To do that, we must renew our minds and stop conforming to sick systems.

Human beings create systems. Like us, systems vary in degrees of being healthy or ill, clever or unwise, efficient or inept. Humans (like families, communities, nations) evolve—or devolve—

over time: Our fortunes and abilities wax, just as they also wane. So do systems: Even once-healthy, robust systems become sick and unfit. As with a person with cancer, much of a given system's decline takes place internally, invisibly, latently: Often, decay is visible only when the chance for remedy, for a return to vitality, has passed. As with cancer, systemic rot spreads first from within, in the most essential, minute parts of an organism. All might appear "all right" on the outside, but on the inside atrophy has become the norm—and final fate. As with terminally ill human beings, end-stage systems no longer can attain equilibrium: Renewal or replacement *must* occur if Life at all is to continue. Is it not this place, then, where we presently find ourselves?

What follows is a record of journeys that brought us to this unworthy, fractured present. While it often isn't a pretty process, we must wade through an at-times uncomfortable, unflattering review of our shared as well as individual paths if we're to reach a worthwhile, united future. Such cautionary tales are invitations to search for deeper understanding, to find new strategies. Without reflection, we stay stuck; with it, we might find a way forward at this eleventh hour.

*

Introducing the Theorist

It takes nerve for an author-historian to take on an entire system, to focus on what does not work, then to dare to suggest what is to be done to fix it. I, Michael Luick-Thrams, possess that chutzpah. Who am I? I am the offspring of ordinary farm folk who tilled the North American soil for 355 years—as of 1630 in Puritan Massachusetts, until 1985 on the Iowa prairies. I remain a dedicated son, an irritating brother guilty of "historical obnoxiousness" (per my brother); I am a devoted partner and a loyal friend, a daring next-door neighbor and caring global citizen. I am a gay man who once was a Young Republican engaged to Beth. Then, I wanted to be a farmer and a Methodist minister, who at the time planned to spend extended stints of time serving refugee camps in Thailand. Soon, however, Life conspired to have me do other things, in other places.

the author in TRACES' early days, 2003; the BUS-eum displayed at the University of Iowa, spring 2016: Over a third of a million people have toured our various mobile exhibits; we know, as we have a counter. By making history and culture mobile, we reach populations that otherwise might never visit a museum. We have shown the BUS in Western Nebraska cowtowns, Northern Minnesota logging camps, on South Dakota's Pine Ridge Reservation and South Chicago's inner-city streets. A video tour is possible here:[2]

I am a Midwesterner from the American Heartland, who lives much of the year in the heart of Germany—the homeland of half of my emigrant ancestors, a country I love like the land of my birth. My calling consists of organizing programs that explore historical and current connections between those two cultures: lectures, school visits, university courses and internships, exhibits, publications, conferences, concerts, films, theatrical pieces, student exchanges and more. Part of such work involves TRACES' staff and me living for months on end in retrofitted school buses, plying the byways of rural America as we show exhibits and give presentations about them.[3] Out of stories about events involving ties between Germany (or Austria) and the Midwest, 1914-'48, I help people of various ages, of differing social and ethnic origins better comprehend not only these shared historical legacies, but the lessons they offer us in being wiser, kinder people today.

Like a poet, I am complex in how I think and love, yet modest in my aesthete way of life, built on voluntary simplicity: In two weeks I'll be 57, yet owned a private car for only eight of those years; I got a credit card at 33 solely to rent cars. I have traversed the world, but never strayed far from Home in my heart. I care deeply about my land and suffer the more for its current naughtiness, egotism and spiritual drift. I am a Wendell Berry conservative and a Walt Whitman liberal, neither truly Left nor Right, but always up front. A radical centrist, I tap insights from all corners of the world, regardless of from what culture they hail. I chase wisdom in any form, anywhere, all of the time. I try to judge my brothers and sisters of all lands more on the content of their characters, less the color of their burka or sombrero. I ache for justice and well-being, everywhere, forever.

My global travels and deepest reflections have convinced me that we could do—and deserve—better; however, we are stuck in dysfunctional systems that diminish and threaten to destroy us. Thus, I write this account of what happened to me as a candidate for public office in 2016, that my experiences might shed a piercing light on sick dynamics that are killing us all. My story of the election that surprisingly produced the Trump administration can't be understood in its totality without my delving into the psyches of my closest of kin, who eagerly elected him. "They" are us.

My tale can only have value to the extent that it offers detailed maps out of our societal cul-de-sac. Where one front might feel an impulse to dig containment walls against perceived threats from the other, we must try to build bridges. When we might most wish to extract retractions from "them," we first must offer concessions of *our* roles in having gotten stuck in ideological gridlock. We can ask for apologies, but can hope to receive them only after we have owned our failures. We may not enjoy taking these steps, but we cannot move forward without doing so.

*

"...Iowa is not a chunk of Midwest cut out by arbitrary lines from the enormous map of farmland that extends interminably through twelve states. It is a unit of consciousness, and it has a culture of its own. It exists in a way that Pennsylvania or New York do not. It is a state in the way that, say, Norway is a nation."

— Philadelphia-born Iowa historian
Laurence Lafore in *Iowa, a Celebration*[4]

Introducing the Topography

Much of the year I live in Thüringen, in the middle of Germany. My adopted home was once the westernmost province of the communist-ruled East. Now, I'm just as quickly in Berlin via high-speed train as I am in Munich or Frankfurt—and just as quickly amongst my Thrams relatives in Brandenburg, along the Polish border, as I am among my Lui[c]k ones near Stuttgart, not far from the French one. Although the Berlin Wall fell three decades ago, and Germany's two halves have been reunited for almost 30 years, it amazes me how relatively little the two sets of Germans know about each other—and how what they *think* they "know" is often fragmented and flawed.

As an Iowan, I know this dynamic too well: I come from "Flyoverland" and countless times have endured the ignorance and arrogance of my East- and West-coast compatriots, who have taken those of us from the Heartland for granted far too long—at their own peril and real costs. Although Iowans endorsed Obama twice, we voted for Trump in droves, angry and eager to be finally heard. While coastal elites engineered global trade, offshored most manufacturing jobs and used mid-continent farmers as political pawns, we in the center unraveled—and still suffer.

In 2016, I ran for public office, seeking a platform from which to critique the systems that both blind and bind us. Assuming I would never win, I was the "un-candidate candidate," a maverick from the prairie as native yet odd as the tall "Turkeyfoot" greenswards that once covered the Great Plains. An exceptional, unwieldly and concurrently stunning grass, Turkeyfoot is a noble form of life—even more special because of its distinctiveness and rarity in a vast, diverse world.

a sward of "Big Bluestem" prairie grass, known for its three-pronged seed heads as "Turkeyfoot:"
It is a perennial warm-season bunchgrass that blooms in summer and seeds in fall. It grows in dense
stands that can out-compete other plant species and grow until disturbance interrupts their spread.[5]

Now, in 2019, I am writing about that campaign and my concerns which fueled it, to serve as a roadmap as well as warning to the many ascending stars hoping to illuminate our nation's way forward. As my writing progressed, I realized I needed to broaden its scope as my campaign led me to better understand the things that divide us. That led me to consider our divisions, both on the individual and the national level, and to question how those divisions might be overcome.

A fellow refugee from what once was an intact and proud Middle America, my friend Marcellus (from Iowa City but living in Berlin) reviewed an early draft of this book. Despite our shared Midwestern roots, he warned "Why you using Iowa as your setting? You're whittling away any marketable audience: Your tome will appeal only to gay-Quaker farmboys from Iowa!"[6] My urbanized, globalized pal resists realizing that in the pages to come, our Iowa is a stand-in for Anywhere Rural USA. With some sand, cows and Native Americans, it could be New Mexico; add water, palms and baying hounds, it would be a bayou in Louisiana or the Southeast's Tidewater. Venture beyond Seattle, you'll find Des Moines; west of Portland, Oregon, lie the Hills of Iowa. Outside of booming Boston's endless Exurbia, rural New England's social ills resemble our own.

a 2008 topographic map of Iowa showing the Hawkeye State's 99 counties and major waterways

Beyond the poetic qualities of focusing on a waning Iowa, are practical ones: If we are to "lock in" carbon on a scale large enough to mitigate the most extreme effects of global warming, that project won't take place primarily in cities but rather in rural areas; only actions like Restorative Agriculture, reforestation and similar efforts will make an adequate difference, soon enough. We cannot reinvent our world if we do not include land outside city limits: Doing so is requisite. As Kansas native-son Dwight Eisenhower said, "Whatever America hopes to bring to pass in the world must first come to pass in the heart of America."

The relatives with whom I again find myself at war also are stand-ins: While they likely will take what I'm about to reveal about our broken family as familial treason, our misery could be that of many millions of American families, as the core of our feud is about values and experiences. Textbook irreconcilable differences continue to tear us apart. If "liberal" city folk wish to finally comprehend "What's wrong out in the Heartland," they need first to truly understand—and care about—those of us who populate and love rural America. There is no "country" separate from those of us *in* the country. A nation consists of communities, which consist of families; familial micro-systems mirror macro- ones: To heal a nation, we must heal its families and their homes. What better place to begin both our autopsy as well as our rebirth than in America's **Heart**land?

Upper-Midwest literary figure Hamlin Garland called Iowa "the Middle Border." One-time Iowa State University writing instructor Michael Martone says in *Iowa, a Celebration* that "On one level, we sense that somewhere within the borders of Iowa, the East ends and the West begins. The Middle Border also implies that Iowa is the setting for transformation and change, even while it embraces stability and calm. The Middle Border (like all borders) divides even while it connects." Perhaps here, then, lie the roots of a new national understanding—our homecoming.

*

> "From everyone to whom much has been given, much will be required; and from the one to whom much has been entrusted, even more will be demanded."

— Luke 12:48, the New Testament of the Bible

What is Our BIG Problem?

When, in 2016, I announced my running for the US Senate from Iowa, I had not been born the day before; I brought a slew of experiences that guided me as I waded into the political foray:

Thursday, July 4th, 1985—summer in the Ukrainian capital, Kyiv.

The room buzzed with anticipation. Our Chicago-born tour guide looked at us, her American college-student charges, for signs of unease. Seeing none, she nodded to the stout Ukrainian kindergarten teacher, already beaming with pride, to proceed. She, in turn, opened a door to the right of a wall-tall painted portrait of Vladimir Lenin, who looked down upon the unfolding scene with an approving, fatherly smile as some dozen to twenty kids marched into the room.

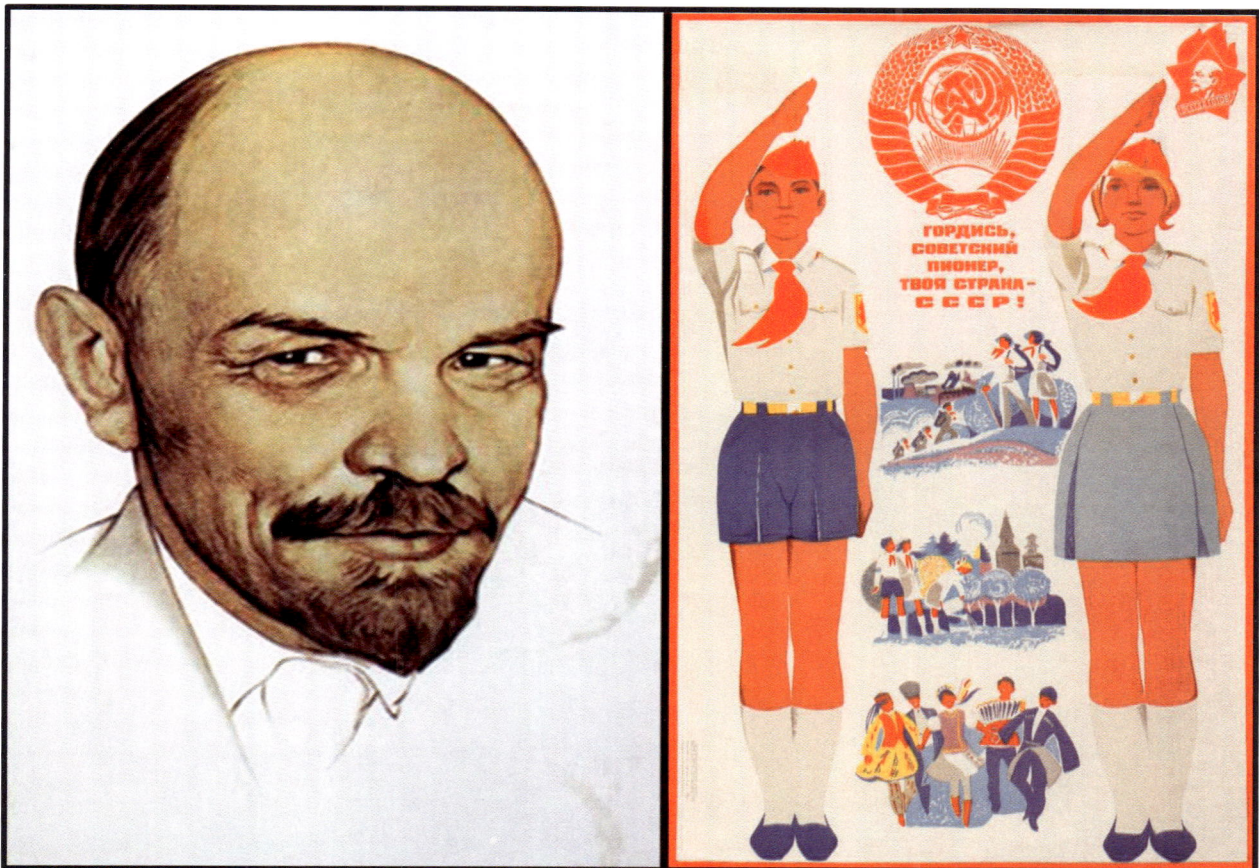

the image of Vladimir Ilych Ulyanov Lenin that hung in that Ukrainian kindergarten; a poster touting "Гордись Советский Пионер Твоя Страна СССР: Be a Proud Soviet Pioneer of Your Country, the USSR"

Both genders wore Party-red kerchiefs around their little necks. The girls' hair boasted ribbons atop their heads that looked like satellite antennae; the boys wore white sleeveless undershirts. All had donned indigo-blue shorts and bright-red tennies. They looked smart, but their nifty outfits paled compared to the perfectly timed and executed dances and calisthenics they then performed for us. I, for one, left that demonstration of Soviet-style pedagogy deeply impressed by those tykes' ability to set aside their own egos and move in flawless unison, as a fluid body.

"Our kids could *never* be able to pull off such concerted choreography" I remember noting. "We're too individualistic, too welded to our own rigid ideas of how we think a gig should go down—too unwilling to listen to others without feeling offended by differing opinions. We are too busy doing our own, isolated thing to accomplish much of real greatness as a group." For over half a decade, I touted what I had seen that morning in Kyiv as an example of how "Not everything behind the Wall is rotten." I thought it accentuated America's failure to generate enough citizens capable of acting effectively as a whole, in concert, to reach shared goals.

While I was never an apologist for a People's Republic of Anything, I did strive during the Reagan years to build bridges between my country and those we said we were poised to blow to smithereens—just as the Soviet Union, in turn, promised to annihilate the United States. In the name of forging grassroots links in an era both government heads and peace activists deemed "MAD—mutual assured destruction," in a world of then more than 50,000 nuclear weapons, I ventured onto "enemy soil." I visited the Soviet Union twice (in 1982 and 1985; I toured post-Soviet Russia in 1994) and Cuba once; I sojourned in Vietnam for a month in 1998.

Each time I slipped behind what Winston Churchill had coined an "Iron Curtain" in a speech he gave in Iowa's southerly neighbor, Missouri, I felt as if I'd landed on Mars. There were no private businesses or independent craftspeople. There was no for-profit advertising, no TV spots or billboards, scarcely any buildings with fresh coats of paint, and endless mostly-empty store shelves. The people bearing the dull weight of "dictatorship by the proletariat" seemed not only drably dressed, but as if their souls were gray and frayed, too.

Then, at the end of each such trip, I quietly returned to the capitalist West and oddly felt, at least initially, as out of place "at home" as I had "over there." Slipping between systems entailed such psychological disconnects that both took on surrealistic undertones for me. The distance that I gained by exposure to diametrically opposing systems helped me see both with new eyes.

*

"Now Fatherland, Fatherland, show us the sign
Your children have waited to see
The morning will come
When the world is mine
Tomorrow belongs to me
Tomorrow belongs to me
Tomorrow belongs to me
Tomorrow belongs to me."

— John Kander, *Cabaret*

Entire Worlds in a *Schnapsglas*

The late '90s found me living in Berlin, in what the Germans already then were calling their "New-Old Capital" on the Spree. 'Twas a heady time in freshly-reunited Germany—and I loved it!

My partner, Andres, had been raised in what had been West Berlin, but his mother had family in the former East. Her aunt, *Tante* Herta, resided in Satow, an archetypical Prussian village a hundred miles northwest of the bustling city. It might as well have been a day or even a planet away, for the erection of the Berlin Wall in August 1961 had cut the surrounding countryside from not only the big city, but the world at large. A hamlet of less than a hundred families, its railway line had long been truncated, its people pressured by lack of opportunity to drift off.

a period postcard of a typical Prussian village, showing: (top) Hans Böge's "Restaurant of the Sun;" "church and parsonage;" "Greetings from Satow" and "Main Street"

When the *alte Dame* died, she was in her 90s, frail yet sharp-of-mind. I had never met her, but when I trekked to Satow with Andres and his father, Achim—who'd been a West Berlin cop despite having been also a hippie sympathizer and later a Green Party activist—I felt as if I had. We rifled through her musty apartment—a large room with a couple of alcoves carved off a larger thatched-roof farmhouse, like in a Teutonic version of a scene from *Dr. Zhivago*. Her half-century old, thread-bare dresses, pre-war furnishings and myriad other relics chronicled almost a century of modern German history. As I helped sort through the earthly remains of a long life in the rushed course of a short morning, I could literally see not only a seamless flow of historical evolution, but astonishingly-well-preserved watermarks of shifting systems over time.

Herta Karras had spent her entire life in a tiny village, yet lived that life under serial systems. From sticking drawers and long-forgotten jars on back shelves, we dug out seven currencies:

1) During the *Kaiser*'s era, imperial Prussia's booming economy demanded potent potato *Schnaps* from backwaters newly opened by the spreading *Reichsbahn* lines that tied the swelling capital to its provinces. As we later explored the ruins of the *Schnapsbrennerei*, the distillery decaying across from the rail line that once carried its high-octane brew to Berlin, we marveled at how a single industry could dominate the lives of those around it. Its workers had loyally served the *Brennerei*'s owners, Herta's *Vater* Wilhelm and—until the firm fell victim to the times—her heir self, who in turn took over local acts of charity.

2) The unexpected (and by most imperial-era Germans unwanted) arrival of the wobbly *Weimarer Republik* ushered in a new currency, along with newfangled ways of living and working. Although never stable, that experiment in democracy midwifed modernity, for it severed the Germans from Hohenzollern rule that stretched back for centuries. In the ensuing vacuum, *Tante* Herta's family and neighbors scrambled to cope as the village's largest economic engine, the *Schnapsbrennerei*, hit hard times. Then, darkness fell.

3) Overnight, the Nazi-imposed "Third Reich" recast the area's economy again, this time pushing all production to support Hitler's insatiable appetite for armed expansion. In the process, it forced the realignment of Satow's values and social structures. Yes, *Schnaps* might embolden lagging troops in their slogging conquest of Europe, but foodstuffs once fermented into booze became more critical to the system in edible, not drinkable forms. Yes, during war full employment reigned, but many of the jobs sowed death, not life.

4) Post-war Russian occupation brought an interim social order that mirrored both martial rule and centrally-planned, Soviet-style economics. Strong-armed into swallowing a new order imposed from outside and above, *Tante* Herta's life changed forever. Like so many yoked into an artificially-driven economy, she took a token job in a token post. Paid enough to survive but not to thrive, she found the scope of her daily world shrank and stank. As the fates of the "Hertas" of the Soviet-occupied east sank, despair spread.

5) The introduction of the (so-called) German Democratic Republic's *Ost-Mark* in 1949 embodied the social ideals of the ruling dictatorship proclaimed that same year. Old capitalistic ventures like the *Schnapsbrennerei* were seized and subjugated to central planning; their very existence depended on their ability to erase their roots and morph into inflexible units of production that soon began to entropy and later turn moribund. Workers were assigned and reassigned, based not on skills or passions, but head counts.

6) The fall of the Berlin Wall in 1989 saw a "Wild-East" fever erupt among West-German speculators. Economic as well as political opportunists cannibalized what remained of the GDR's collective farms and state-held factories, which disappeared quickly, leaving both rural and urban workers not only unemployed, but socially shell-shocked. Yes, *Tante* Herta's purse briefly boasted the much-touted Federal Republic's *Mark*, but she reeled under new economic conditions she could neither control nor cope with. It was in this disorienting fog of yet another systemic shift that Herta Karras lived her last days.

7) The European Union's much-heralded new currency, the chic *Euro*, was adopted by most EU countries on New Year's Day in 1999. By now feeble and sick, *Tante* Herta nonetheless knew that beyond the door of her large room within a larger thatched-roof farmhouse, the people of her village had weathered seven systems in order to see this momentous day. While hers was drawing to a quiet end, their lives would never be the same. Since the emperor's reign, she'd witnessed systems rise and then fall. Except for brief spells, she had had little say in those systems—and had mutely accepted that.

Tante Herta never moved once from her *hinterland* home, yet several markedly different systems came to her. Each time a new system replaced a currency, existing ways of living and working, spending free time and experiencing *Kultur*, as well as forms of being governed totally changed overnight. In that moment, staring at ruins of a defunct Prussian *Schnapsbrennerei*, I realized **no** system is inevitable, **none** lasts eternally, and **all** can be changed—**IF** an ensnared people wills it.

*

Book One: How I Fell Down Fast

"Nobody has the intention of building a wall."

— Walter Ulbricht, head of the "German Democratic Republic," on 15 June 1961,
59 days before the unannounced erection of the Berlin Wall on 13 August 1961

My Family's Wall

Soon after launching my campaign, I realized that much of the Iowa electorate I had to win over to win consisted of archetypes embodied by my own kin. As I was to find, the majority of Iowans not only staunchly stood behind the incumbent but also was in love with a new guy, Don Trump:

Monday, July 4th, 2016—summer in the Iowa countryside.

The terrace table already groaned under the swelling weight of masses of food. Never mind: Lucy[7] kept bringing waves of plates stacked with grill-fresh burgers oozing with pink juice, steaming cobs of corn, an array of pickles. Close behind, her dutiful daughters-in-law trotted up to the crowded table in frantic succession, juggling bowls sloshing with marinated veggies, icy sheet-cake pans lined with frozen desserts, and sweating pitchers of fluorescent-colored Kool-Aid.

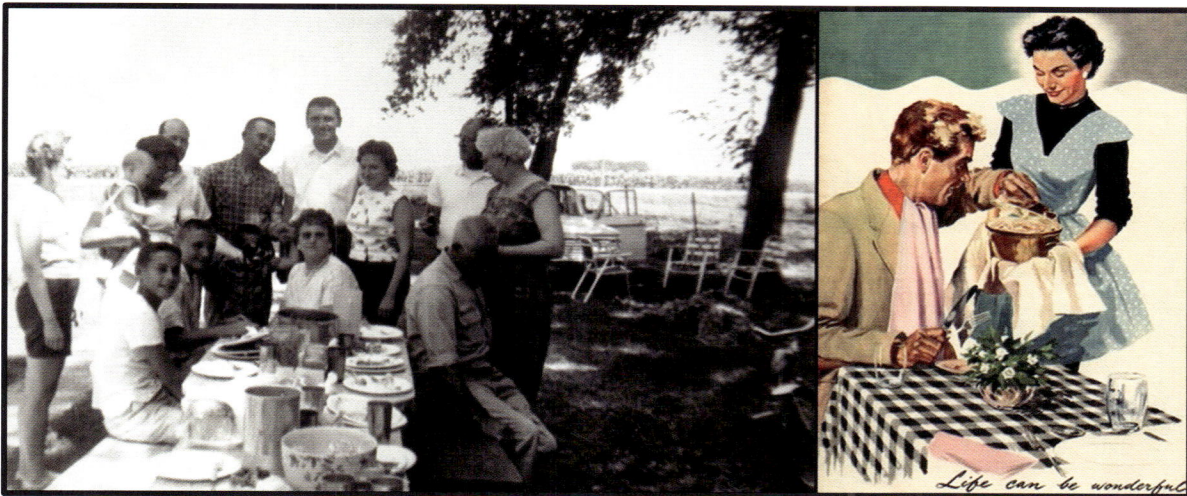

The Thrams family resided at Ashlawn Farm for 105 years; Grandpas' mother's people (the Ehrhardts in Wisconsin) and Grandma's father's (the Falcons in Eastern Iowa) lived on my great-greats' farms about 150. Such uninterrupted residences allowed my family to acquire a couple thousand photos dating from the 1850s to 2002—the year my parents sold Ashlawn Farm. As a whole, these captured moments show our people at work, play, school, church... and at various picnics that spanned more than a century, such as this one at Ashlawn Farm, summer 1963: standing (l. to r.) Irene (Thrams) Floyd, me as an infant...[8]

The whole while pondering what topics we might safely brave, we half-dozen men sat staring at the artificial lake along the lot's edge. Green cattails swayed occasionally as faint breezes stirred under azure prairie skies, offering us brief but penetrating whiffs of putrefying plant matter.

Finally, Linus leaned his stout torso forward and, lazily tugging at his graying beard, chided his new brother-in-law. "The algae's sure growin' a heck of a lot worse this year than last."

"Yeah" Curly mumbled, nodding. "Gotta do something 'bout it real soon. It's jus' takin' over this year, like all git out. Your sister keeps gittin' on me, but—" his voice faded off.

Wedging a pan of apple pie into a space half its size, Lucy plopped down in a rickety lawn chair on the far corner of the table—clearly uncomfortable but cozily distant from me, the queer black sheep. "Grace, honey?" she cued her three adult sons' deceased dad's recent replacement.

Dropping his head hammer-like, "Heavenly father" he began, but I stopped listening and simply peered out over the jade-hued water. Out of the twenty or so souls present, only I, the family's eternal disgrace, sat eyes open and chin raised, wondering what hot seat in hell would be mine. Having spent most of my adult life in self-imposed exile in Germany after being sentenced to blanket banishment in the early '80s for having dared to be honest about whom I wish to love, I knew too well the dull yet deep pain of always being the odd man out at every family gathering.

Despite a clumsy start, our gathered extended family then eased rather smoothly into a shared meal that for once didn't just hang in our tightening throats but slid down to our churning guts.

Until, that is, Lucy's oldest, Jared, asked "So, what ya doin' in Germ'ny these days, Mike?"

Surveying the faces around the table, I timidly replied "Working mostly with refugees who—"

"You mean with Mus-s-slims?" Lucy hissed, as if suddenly an angry bee. "You're workin' with—"

Knowing where we were headed, having followed each other over a cliff countless times before, I noted quietly "Yes, with people who share the same god as Jews and Christians."

"That's *not* true!" Lucy glared as everyone else busied themselves by chasing evasive morsels around slippery plates. "They worship a *different* god! Who is it, again—Buddha or sompthin'?"

Immediately I had to wonder *So, how many Americans have such little real knowledge about Islam, the beliefs of Buddhists or Hindus—or even what practicing Jews believe?* My mind reeled.

Inwardly I groaned but outwardly only flashed a hollow grin as I bid "Pass the pepper, will ya?"

Recognizing the emotional landmine he'd exposed, Jared offered "Last week Amy and I took the boys to—" as I looked out over the big, pungent pond and plotted how to exit this scene, fast.

Like most little boys, I had learned not to tangle with big girls. Once, when I didn't jump fast enough to her barking to pick up my toys atop the upstairs landing, Lucy opened a laundry room window and began throwing them to the yard below, where I rushed to retrieve them. I never forgave her the cuts Johnny West's chiseled cowboy face thereafter bore, or Geronimo's broken hip. Although only some seven years older than me, even then Lucy acted as if she were Mother.

As we matured, Lucy's sharp-tongued reprimands took less physical forms. When I was a junior at Clear Lake High School, in 1979, and she was a young mother, she took me aside one day and said in no uncertain terms I had "better stop spendin' time with Cong Cam Li," a young Laotian refugee who I'd volunteered to tutor in English and, after school, help wade into American life.[9]

"Why?" I was baffled. "We've become good friends. I enjoy working with Cong and his family."

"Because they're heathens, Mike" Lucy scowled. "They will *never* enter the Kingdom of God."

Although I was still a devout, practicing Christian, already then her extremist stance galled me.

Now, decades later, it didn't surprise me when over dessert Lucy bubbled with praise for "her" candidate, xenophobe Donald Trump. Her adamancy over his rightness for the office fit Lucy to a "T[rump]," but I didn't get it. Her first husband, Gerry, had battled prostate cancer for four years. Lucy took excellent, flawless care of him—as she does of my aging mother. Pitiably, the poor man kept working for a food-service supplier until the end, as losing his job-tied health care wasn't an option. Even though he succeeded in staying insured until he died, he failed to conquer his creeping cancer—or the enormous related costs. Unending financial worries kept Lucy under constant stress, which taxed the strength she needed to face Gerry's agonizing demise with him.

"Trump's gonna overturn Obama Care, big time" she promised from the other end of the slowly emptying table, "once and for all!" As she beamed, the rest of the table nodded, hope-filled. "And, he's gonna build a high, long wall to keep out all them who would harm or take from us."

I couldn't imagine then, how so many Americans could so enthusiastically rally behind those who day in, day out work against their own interests—and of all people, this young widow should know the perils and crushing weight of inadequate health-care funding. Once, stumped by her rabid hatred of all things Barack Obama, I asked Mom why Lucy so fervently railed against our then-President as if he were the anti-Christ. Herself having had African-American and Hispanic friends as a girl in the 1940s and '50s in a lily-white Iowa where doing so wasn't a given, she lowered her voice to dare speculate "I'm not sure, but I suspect his race plays a role in it."

Was this so? Was the dynamic at work here racism or rather fear of The Other? I hoped the latter. Presuming she has had few experiences with minority groups and is an ardent Republican, I assumed Lucy follows the patterns she takes as gospel, bolstered by what she hears from fellow fundamentalists, who seem simply anti-anything a Democratic President might say or do. I felt sure she would have been equally fervently critical were Hillary Clinton to become President.

*

"My country, right or wrong; if right, to be kept right; and if wrong, to be set right."

— German immigrant Carl Schurz' remarks in the US Senate on 29 February 1872

Our National Emergency

Trumpism, supported by my own relations and so many others, is not just a problem; more, it's a symptom of a much larger crisis: It is neither the cause of nor the cure for what ails America. The roots of our national emergency long predate him and lie in each of us.

Similarly, the mass shooters who for years claimed first tens, now hundreds of victims (e.g., the Las Vegas massacre) in a single spree of deadly madness are not only problems *per se*, but also indicators. They are thermometers gauging how decayed our nation's sickest souls have become. It also speaks volumes that more Americans have died from gunfire since 1968 than those killed during all US wars since the Revolution—moreover, that we tolerate such insanity, for what we tolerate, we condone. What sort of nation allows mass-scale murder to continue unchecked?[10]

Simply shaking one's head, wagging one's finger or wringing one's hands won't exorcise our collective rot, nor will it build viable alternatives with which to replace the dysfunctional system we have now. To change things, we must name the sources of the dysfunction and confront the self-serving elite who sustain our unjust system. We must challenge the narratives they peddle to perpetuate that system, and craft new visions of how we might better get our needs met even as we (re-)learn to live well with each other. We must acknowledge our shared stakes in resettling what our pioneering ancestors so quickly erected.[11] We must mature as a people to the point where we can weave a sustainable culture where all of us can not only survive, but thrive.

To that end, for eight months, from March to November 2016, I ran for the US Senate from Iowa. I did it to raise issues mainstream candidates wouldn't easily dare, to expand the scope of topics given collective attention, and to offer new narratives or alternative possible cures.

To my mind, doing so was imperative. For one thing, for me the incumbent personified some of the most diseased aspects of America's moribund "democracy." Not only has Charles Grassley comprised half of Iowa's Senate presence in Washington since 1980 (he was first elected when I was 17) and held that seat all of my adult life (at that point, I was 53), but few Iowans have seriously considered challenging his monopoly on the state's Congressional delegation. One person having so much power, for so terribly long, embodies the antithesis of democracy.

"Uncle Chuck" Grassley's official portrait (left), October 2017; Chuck Grassley, then-US Representative, later US Senator from Iowa, as shown in the 1977 Congressional Pictorial Directory, 96th US Congress: It boggles my mind to think that one person could hold the same public office, from so young to so ancient.

That Iowans continue to re-elect politicians they know over those they don't baffles me when—as in this case—the incumbent is no longer at the top of his game. "Chuck" would have been 83 if elected to yet another term—89 at the end of it. Such necrophilia keeps the Hawkeye State's political culture calcified and trapped in the realm of aged white men—make that, "aged RICH white men." (Iowa's governor during my campaign was Terry Branstad, who had held the same office in the 1980s, when I was a college kid at Iowa State. In fact, on 13 December 2015—his 7,642nd day in office, during his sixth term, which ended on 24 May 2017—Branstad became the longest-serving governor in the history of the United States. The 73-year-old now serves as Trump's ambassador to China; his son Eric served as Trump's campaign manager in Iowa.[12])

On top of all the rest, there is a recurring rumor that Charles Grassley is grooming grandson Pat to take over his Senate seat.[13] Allergic to family-based dynasties dominating the political stage—be they Kennedys or Bushes, Clintons or now Trumps—I cannot bear the thought of Iowans further endorsing the Grassley-family brand. (How can it be that a state of three million or, worse, a country of 330 million can muster top-ranking leaders from only a handful of families?[14])

More than trying to break up political syndicates in Iowa as well as Washington, in my campaign I sought to shake up the Midwest's political status quo. As a cultural historian, I'm keenly aware of how the mess we are enduring at present is the product of America's past: It is the aggregate outcome of our individual as well as collective experiences, values, wishes, choices... our successes and failures, our private as well as public strengths and weaknesses. To recognize the way out of our current quandary, we have to truly comprehend how we got into it. We have to recognize connections between what we have done and who we have been, to what we are doing and who we are now. And, we *must* stop following losing strategies, for if we always do what we've always done, we'll always get what we've always got. Just as all of us are the children of our biographies, America today is the sum of what it's been in the past—which imprints its future.

*

> "In the end, the American dream is not a sprint, or even a marathon, but a relay. Our families don't always cross the finish line in the span of one generation. But, each generation passes on to the next the fruits of their labor."
>
> — Mexican-immigrant descendent Julian Castro, Democratic National Convention speech on 4 September 2012

Their Dreams Betrayed

As I first wrote this introductory section (one year after Trump's unexpected election), I sat five kilometers [three miles] from Kallstadt, the Trump family's geographical genesis. It sits on the Weinstrasse, a ribbon road that ties together the Rhine Valley's western slopes. Its postcard-perfect appearance, however, quietly hides the President's grandfather's secrets: A trained barber, 16-year-old Friedrich Trump had skipped town in 1885 without official permission and thus avoided military service; his marrying a local girl, Elisabeth Christ, upon returning in 1901, ended up in his being banned and threatened with deportation by a Bavarian prince. In New York, the couple built a real estate empire—until Friedrich died at 49, in the 1918 flu pandemic.[15]

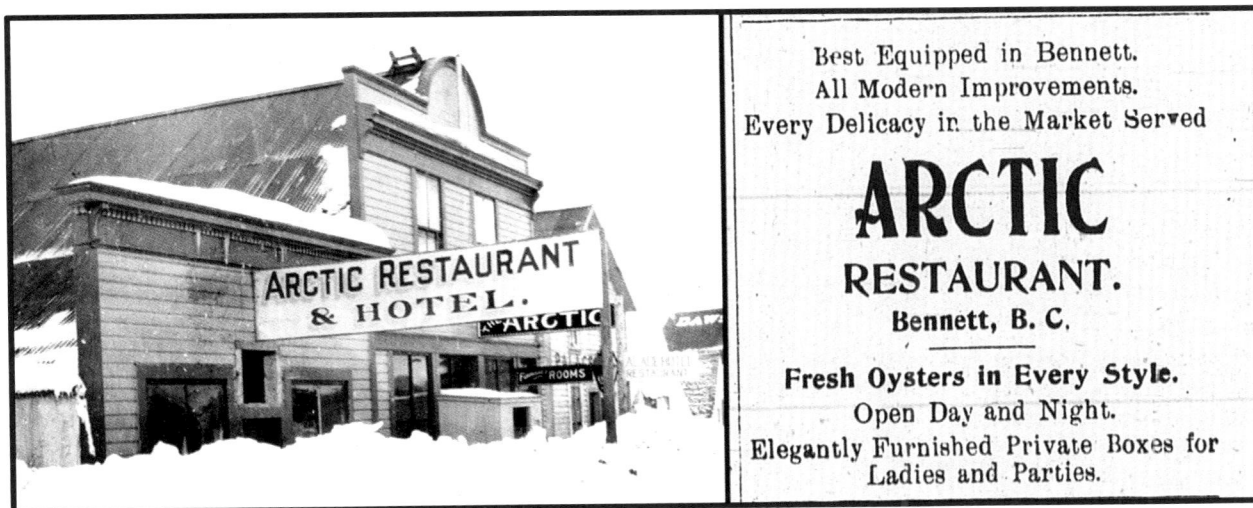

I find Donald Trump so distasteful, I do not wish to acknowledge one more shared commonality with the man than undeniable but, in truth, there are several. For one, his grandfather, Friedrich Trump, and my 3xgreat-grandfather Heinrich Luick (both German immigrants) once owned hotels. The Trump patriarch set up the Arctic Hotel in 1899 in the goldrush-era Klondike. He left the frozen North within three years, having amassed the seed money he later would use to plant the Trump family's fortune. According to the Times Colonist, "The Arctic Hotel was open 24 hours a day and boasted 'private boxes' for ladies, which included a bed and a gold scale so customers could pay in nuggets." In contrast, "Henry Jr" likely did not offer such "amenities" at the Luick House Hotel in Eddyville, Iowa, in the 1870s. His project also involved a fortune—not the making of but the losing of one, as meticulously documented in this footnote.[16]

The idyllic, vineyard-laced village was so close I could set off for it after lunch by foot, enjoy mid-afternoon *Kaffee und Kuchen*, then stroll back to Bad Dürkheim in time for dinner. I thrice visited Trump's Kallstadter ancestral home, a humble little hovel, unassuming and not sympathetically renovated. As my hiking comrades and I gawked at it from across the street, I marveled that such an immense contemporary figure could hail from such a modest Old World nest. But, then again, most Americans with European roots do, too—especially the Germans. In the main, it wasn't the well-to-do, nor even professionals who emigrated: 'Twas the poor by far.

If we break "Hispanic" into "Mexican-American," "Cuban-American," "Guatemalan-American" and so on, German Americans still constitute the largest ethnic group (by nation) in the United States, with every fifth of us claiming German ancestry.[17] In my native Iowa, two out of every five do—and in some communities, it's three out of five.[18] Like The Donald's granddad Friedrich, Heinrich Luick Sr fled Germanic lands due to a criminal offense—in 1833, having thrashed a royal cavalry officer who took exception to the way my 4xgreat-grandfather was currying the king's horses. Friedrich's and Heinrich's reasons for setting sail, however, were far from being rarities.

Heinrich "Henry" Luick Jr (left, circa 1880s) and Friedrich "Frederick" Trump Sr, circa 1900[19]

Our national mythos, of rank-and-file white Americans having arisen from "huddled masses yearning to breathe free,"[20] belies a beguiling tale in lieu of embracing a deeper truth: Our ancestors were mostly running from, more than marching to, something—be it poverty, lack of social mobility, military service, war, etc. Fleeing Home is, at its core, a desperate act: If one doesn't perceive a need to ditch one's current life, doesn't a person stay put and bask in the circle of family, friends, mother tongue, native culture and sustaining work? Folks who have it good stay home; those who don't, don't. Historical facts expose the contention that most of our ancestors came to the US for religious freedom, as being a self-serving yet hollow exaggeration. Where to better start disabusing ourselves of national mistruths that hinder moving forward if not with a primal one, about what led non-natives to traverse the globe in search of new lives?[21]

What is true is that the early Trumps, as well as my New World-bound ancestors—and most likely yours, too—set off on packed ships in pursuit of a dream, a vision, a goal. Is the country we have now worthy of their efforts? Would they be at least disappointed in what we've made out of what they built, if not genuinely shocked and dismayed by our mess? I suspect so.

Perhaps, however, I'm projecting a partial point of view. Still, it sobers and saddens me to think Trumpism might be a likely, if lamentable, culmination of Friedrich's... of Heinrich's... of most of our ancestors' profoundest desires for self-advancement at any price—the consequences to others, to the planet, or even the ultimate costs to ourselves be damned. Is our current collective state a detour, a bizarre blip in the American Dream, or an expression of core cultural values of individualism and personal gain writ large? If so, are we morally damned as a people? I fear so.

Are we not the product of generations of millions of fortune seekers, always settling but never settled? Isn't our current state a predictable consequence, the plausible result of who we've been as a people all along?[22] If so, is our inability to "dance" together in concert, to perform functional political "calisthenics" an indelible part of our shared DNA? Are we destined to eternal stalemate and, ultimately, helplessness—of all things now, when our survival depends on cooperative mass-action? Can we still somehow grab the national steering wheel and save ourselves? I hope so.

*

31

"Make the impossible possible."

— Mark Strickland, *Make the Impossible Possible: One Man's Crusade to Inspire Others to Dream Bigger and Achieve the Extraordinary*

Bringing the Whole Thing Down

When I returned to the States in March 2016 to run for the US Senate, I had lofty visions and goals: I wanted to sideswipe the political culture, delivering an ultimately fatal blow that might bring the whole thing down—even if only long after the ballots had been counted. I assumed I couldn't trounce Grassley—or, for that matter, even collect a decent number of votes—but such damning prospects dampened my feverish enthusiasm not in the least. Still, if I wanted my campaign to have any lasting value at all, I had to conduct it seriously and strategically:

- First, I had to get on the ballot—under Iowa's election laws do-able, but not for the half-hearted. By 19 August 2016, I'd have to submit to the Secretary of State's office in Des Moines at least 1,500 signatures, coming from at least ten of the state's 99 counties.
- Next, I'd have to find individuals (or even better, groups) who'd support my project of waging a campaign from the outset not to win office, but to win converts to a new, radically unconventional political consciousness—in unadventurous Iowa, no small feat.
- To persuade would-be supporters to "waste" their vote on my candidacy, I'd have to distill my profoundly different perspective in a way that was concise yet convincing. My platform had to compensate for the fact that I wasn't a politician wanting to set policy, but a historian wanting to make history: For supporters, the latter had to be overriding.
- Once I secured supporters, I'd have to raise at least minimal funding for outreach—a massive undertaking, "How to massage loose 'real' donations for a *symbolic* campaign?"
- And, I'd have to continually—but successfully—scale the wall of yawning uninterest the US media erects against non-mainstream-party candidates, since no exposure = no impact.

Naysayers immediately demanded, "How the hell ya gonna git so many sig'tures, Mike?" At first as defiant as ever, my initial bravado swiftly evaporated as the enormity of the task settled in.

"Ya, who'd support such a wild hair?" I asked myself. Then, it occurred to me:

"Who's served least by the way things are, and thus gain most from changing the status quo at its core? And, who's most invested in keeping things the way they are, with a stake in securing a rigged gig? How do we take power from, or at least weaken, elites?" How can I facilitate that?

Having distilled what sort of people most plausibly would populate my support base, I began to seek them out. I bought a clipboard mounted on a thin, page-sized box, which included a lidded pen-and-business-card tray above the clip. Taking it wherever I went, I buttonholed anyone who

the author standing in front of Hickory Grove Friends Meetinghouse, built 1865 near West Branch: Not only does this meetinghouse resemble Bear Creek's, the two were part of a chain of Quaker communities once spread across not just Iowa, but the Midwest; many Southern Friends went west to shun slavery.

I even remotely suspected might give me their signature, if not also their vote.

One windswept early-spring Saturday, I attended the memorial service of a Des Moines activist, held at Bear Creek Meetinghouse, home to a rural Quaker community dating from the 1850s.[23] At first, even I cringed at my own nerve, the raw cheekiness of quietly soliciting signatures at the basement luncheon afterwards. But, after a first few awkward minutes of doing so, most folks' eagerness to add theirs to my effort convinced me that the deceased would have approved: Dee had spent decades working for social justice and the fundamental change needed to realize it.

Emboldened by having gathered over a hundred signatures in about 3/4ths of an hour out in the countryside, that night I raided (first, buying a ticket) a pre-concert reception for the Des Moines Gay Men's Chorus at the Unitarian-Universalist Church. Again, *Bingo*! The moment in my *Spiel* I mentioned "...running against Chuck Grassley..." concertgoers and singers alike couldn't sign my petition fast enough. I ran out of photocopied forms before I had worked the entire crowd, so I went back the next night and repeated the same, wildly effective procedure.

Both nights, after trawling for signatures among gay guys and their mostly liberal supporters, I went crawling through Iowa's capital-city queer bars until the wee hours. An equal-opportunity opportunist, I didn't care who signed my petition sheets as long as they claimed to be Iowa residents of voting age. Still, some of the characters in those bars were… "questionable" at best. At first, aging yuppies and college students, former hippies and closeted farmers alike wanted to discuss politics, almost all unified in their refrain "Chuck's been there *way* too long!"

The later it got to be, however, the more increasingly impossible real, serious discussion with passing patrons became. Their speaking grew slurred, they swayed wider and wilder as they attempted to stand still long enough to sign their names, and their signatures became ever less legible. Especially the bosomy drag queens suffered as the night waned: Their stilettos turned torturous to wear, their wigs wilted, their fake eyelashes drooped and, as they tried to scribble what often were stage names, their glued-on fingernails would stick to my pen as they handed it back to me. A few of the signees offered me a bed for the night or at least for a "hot hour"— propositions I politely declined. As a group, their mostly caustic comments about those in the Statehouse or in DC's Capitol reflected how deeply disenfranchised many sexual minorities feel. My bid to take on the status quo offered a cause they could join by proxy, simply with a scrawl.

Like sexual minorities, some student minorities also are prone to support dark-horse candidates. (In this case, it's more an ideological classification than simply a racial one, even if non-whites often belong to both categories.) Problem is, administrations purposely make policies related to accessing private-college campuses so stringent that doing it is nigh impossible. Still, leveraging a few faculty invitations to speak to their classes as "official sanction" to do so, on left-politicized campuses like Coe or Cornhill Colleges', I harvested pages of signatures until being caught.

[Iowa's state colleges and universities are, as a norm, non-compliant in providing "free access" to political candidates, as most require student groups to sponsor and accompany candidates on-campus. This is in violation of the Iowa Election Commission's guidelines about "public access."]

Even if much more mainstream, the most heterogeneous sources of signatures for me were the thriving farmers' markets in Des Moines, Cedar Rapids, Iowa City, Decorah and a handful of other communities across the state. Many expressed staunch support for the sitting senator, but the majority aired marked frustration with what they saw as Grassley's unwillingness to move—not only from his office *per se,* but in his position as chair of the Senate Judiciary Committee. In that position, he refused to call hearings to consider the nomination of Merrick Garland, President Obama's choice to fill an empty US Supreme Court seat. Even many of the Senator's long-time supporters were furious over his intransigence, which resulted in a "hung" court. Both in-state and nationally, Grassley's refusal to budge from his party's line drew him bad press. That issue alone promised for a while to become Chuck's political Waterloo, but, alas, it wasn't to be.

> "Democracy is more than a ballot box."
>
> — Egyptian democracy activist Mohamed ElBaradei

More than Names on Ballots

By April, I felt confident I could collect sufficient signatures in enough counties to place my name on November's ballot. That bolstered my conviction in not just the validity but viability of my crusade. At the same time, I realized while it was one thing to tap mounting dissatisfaction with an interminable incumbent long enough to land protest signatures on a non-committal petition; it would prove quite another to transform disgruntled compatriots' short-term displeasure into their endorsing long-term change. To succeed, I'd have to offer inarguable logic why supporting my campaign would do more to advance our state's, moreover our nation's political fortunes than reflexively voting an umpteenth time for a stalwart defender of the status quo. I'd have to appeal not only to the electorate's heads but also to their hearts, as social scientists have long documented that voters' minds bend more to emotional than rather to solely rational appeals. I'd have to offer an alternative worldview which they would buy into.

New York polling place circa 1900, voting booths on the left

So, knowing I would soon have to formally announce my candidacy, to commit publicly to running a race to the end, I began to weigh possible positions that might most effectively sway staunchly risk-avoidant Iowans. How could I best touch my fellow Hawkeyes' hearts even as I turned their heads? In an attention-deficit age like ours, which pithy pleas could best lure them to invest a few more moments in considering supporting a most unorthodox movement? The press release volunteers and I crafted to announce my candidacy outlined its initial motifs; here are excerpts:

PRESS RELEASE for immediate release:
Date: April 12th, 2016
www.HeartlandParties.US

Iowa Cultural Historian Seeks Senate Seat:
Michael Luick-Thrams to Run as Independent for the US Senate

CEDAR RAPIDS, IA —Iowa cultural historian Michael Luick-Thrams has announced his candidacy for the US Senate from Iowa, a seat currently held by Charles Grassley, R-Iowa.

Luick-Thrams grew up between Mason City and Clear Lake on a Century Farm operated by his family, which has been in Iowa since the 1830s. He directs two non-profit cultural-history organizations—one since 2001 in the United States, the other since 2011 in Germany.

The author or editor of 14 books about Midwest cultural history, he earned degrees in history from Iowa State University (B.S., 1985), Vermont's Goddard College (M.A., 1991) and Berlin's Humboldt Universität (Ph.D., 1997). He has organized innumerable exhibits, programs and other projects across the region.

As a scholar of human behavior and of nations over time, Luick-Thrams will bring a unique perspective to this year's complex and conflicted political process. "In Iowa, we need a deep, swift shift from outdated ways of dealing with our problems to a change of perspective that says 'yes' or at least 'maybe' but not always 'no.' In the US, we need a social recalibration, a rethinking of the practices and policies of the past 35 or so years that have led us to the crisis in which we currently find ourselves."

"I'm really not running 'against' Charles Grassley, because he has become irrelevant. He is blocking movement forward; he is keeping Iowa locked in 1980s ideology. My candidacy is about Iowans as a community of inter-dependent people sharing a rich and beautiful land, seeking a decent life. If the majority of us re-elects him, it says we are content with the status quo, and I don't believe we are, based on what I'm hearing. I'm 53, yet one man has occupied half of Iowa's senatorial team in Washington my entire adult life—and our current governor was in office when I was an undergrad student in Ames."

"As terrifying as the process might seem at times, what's really happening is the old status quo is breaking up and dissolving. The Republican Party is on its last gasps; if we're lucky, the world's oldest surviving political party, the Democratic, will go down with it. Both parties are calcified syndicates, whose sole purpose is to divide, then grasp onto power at whatever cost to Iowa and to the nation. This election provides Iowans an opportunity to lead the way into a new direction—to real, lasting change."

"The door is ajar—but will we hostages bolt? That is the central question of this political season and especially of this senatorial race. What will Iowa's profile on the national stage be: vital, relevant and open, or irrelevant and obstructionist? Our current political landscape makes us relevant only every four years. The only way to change that situation is to be bold, to be creative and to cast a new political landscape. This is why Charles Grassley won't still be sitting in Washington ten months from now."

#

To learn more about what Washington or Adams thought about a two-party system, see this footnote.[24]

Having co-drafted, then revised this press release uncountable times, I excitedly sent it out, expressly to Iowa's largest newspapers and wire services active in the region, but also to the editors of hometown papers in every county. It went to all of the state's radio and television stations; I sent it to friends, family and any acquaintances who might be willing to forward it.

Then, I waited—and prayed.

*

Eating Humble Pie

On the big day of my big announcement, I drove into the parking lot of the Cedar Rapids Public Library, took a breath, then sauntered through the spanking-new building's vast glass and metal atrium to the meeting room a volunteer had reserved for this occasion. My palms sweating and my heart racing, I mentally prepared for a room full of reporters with grilling questions and photographers with clacking cameras, of eager supporters and testy protesters. It would be hot, loud and intoxicating. I loved it—even before I'd arrived. I had long awaited this moment.

Then, I opened the door—and crashed. The nearly empty room was cold, silent and sobering. From the scores of media outlets and organizational reps we had invited to attend my formal announcing, there sat one solitary (but broadly smiling) cub reporter from the *Cedar Rapids Gazette*, Mitchell Schmidt. In one of the most deflating moments of my life, I instantly had to recalibrate—*sigh*—everything: My expectations, my hopes, my approach, my tone... the works.

Humble pie rarely tasted so humiliating to me as the crow I ate that day, in that dire moment.

newspaper caption: "Michael Luick-Thrams, independent candidate for Iowa's open US Senate seat, photographed at the Gazette office in Cedar Rapids Tuesday, Oct. 11 2016. (Liz Martin)"[25]

Only after I'd distributed my first campaign-related press release across the state did I quickly learn from immediate feedback from others some key lessons—about both effective as well as counterproductive strategies. For starters, I intuitively understood Iowans would want to know who I am, and about my connections to them and our shared homeland. In rural society, if a person wants to be accepted in the community, it's primary that s/he has local ties. As most Iowans have direct connections to the land only one, perhaps two generations back, citing my family's long tradition as farmers seemed essential; that we'd worked our last farm for over a hundred years means even more in the Midwest than elsewhere. And, by mentioning my own professional credentials and achievements, I touted ongoing association with Iowa and Iowans.

Some of my audience would write me off out-of-hand, while others would remain open to being convinced. In my one-shot text, I showed this race had implications beyond our state and this particular political cycle. In referring to issues reflecting voters' then-current concerns, I distinguished myself from the venerable "Chuck" and hinted that upsetting Iowa's US-Senate seat would be of watershed importance. In one of my few commonalities with his would-be Democratic challengers, I alluded to what others tagged as Grassley's "intransigence" in Congress and his reflexive, drumbeat "no-ism"—and how both feed Federal-government-level deadlock. As even strong opponents of his warned me against "playing his age," I pointed to my own and how his "keeping Iowa locked in 1980s' ideology" was part of "blocking movement forward." I brandished words like outdated, irrelevant, blocked, calcified and "the old status quo" as often as I felt I could without sounding excessively negative. Attempting to forge my own brand, I bandied about terms like "swift shift," recalibration, rethinking, bold and creative.

Less effectively, while generating campaign texts I found it virtually impossible to "dumb down" my language. As critics charged, my inability to do so alienated many—"Michael, your readers' eyes will glaze over as they drown in this dense stuff!" they protested. But, what to do? The few times I invited volunteers to take an editing knife to my drafts, their revisions cut either too much or too little; some versions barely resembled what I wanted to communicate, while others added content which embodied someone else's campaign platform, not mine.

Doesn't every candidate face this dilemma: To what degree do I (or you) morph into some one, some *thing* that we're not in order to bait votes; or, to what extent, at what cost do we insist on maintaining personal integrity? In my case, on one hand, as a historian and academic but also as a person dedicated to what I do, it goes fully against my nature to speak in anything but exact, differentiated terms. On another, why feed some of the same social dynamics I decry as culturally cancerous? If one of the causes of our current collective demise is the gradual trivialization and vulgarization of our people over the past three or more decades, will stooping to its victims' nadir help them—*any* of us—regain intellectual ground? Won't insisting on higher standards slowly but ultimately midwife our nation's sorely needed renaissance? In any event, despite others' repeated pleas to "tone it down," I couldn't bring myself to more than a token simplification. "To raise the highest common denominator, we gotta quit playin' to its lowest" I scolded those on the campaign trail who pushed a "populist approach" to politics.[26]

A glaring failure of my announcement was its emotional dearth. Even while conceding from the git-go the indispensable importance of appealing to my fellow citizens' hearts, my feeble attempts to do so were only that—a flaw born of ambivalence. Look, I'm a historian—as were Winston Churchill; Kansas-born, disgraced 1988 presidential candidate Gary Hart; Chancellor Helmut Kohl, who watched the Wall fall and presided over German reunification; and Slobodan Milošević, who oversaw the disintegration of Yugoslavia, then drove it into barbarity. Besides them, the majority of politicians in the Western world are lawyers—the vast majority of whom have studied at least some legal history. So, like both career as well as hobby historians, I know the importance of understanding how lands and peoples change over time—or not—and how change is facilitated or, conversely, hindered by public policies. Historical understanding, therefore, is key to honing the body politic. (It's also potentially lethal, as it lends itself to the emotional exploitation by those who master it, of those who don't.) My concern not only with myself but also with my supporters and with the public was how "real" I could ru: Should it be as a quasi-anonymous pusher of new-wave policies, or would I "have to" run as "Michael Luick-Thrams, a social historian with a notable background that qualifies me to earn your vote."

the candidate as a tourist in Prague, summer 2013: This became one of my standard campaign images.

Cedar Rapids (Iowa) *Gazette*; 13 April 2016

Independent Luick-Thrams to challenge Grassley

Mitchell Schmidt
for the *Gazette*

CEDAR RAPIDS — At 53 years old, Michael Luick-Thrams has spent the majority of his life with U.S. Senator Chuck Grassley in office.

But the cultural historian is hoping to make history himself by unseating the 36-year incumbent and Republican.

"With all due respects, I would have hoped Grassley would have been gracious enough to realize his time has passed—but, he is running again," he said. "One of the reasons I'm running is because he's running and we have to stop this, we have to change the narrative."

As an Independent, Luick-Thrams won't run in the June 7 primary. He'll have to file during the general election period from Aug. 1-19 to be placed on the November ballot with Grassley.

Luick-Thrams said he would advocate for term limits of no more than 12 years for legislators, more transparency in government and campaign donors, and a 10 percent pay cut for those in congress, according to the release.

Also in the November election will be the victor of the Democratic primary. Former lieutenant governor Patty Judge, former lawmaker Bob Krause, bankruptcy lawyer Tom Fiegen and state Sen. Rob Hogg are vying for the Democratic nomination.

Luick-Thrams acknowledged the challenge of running not only against a long-term incumbent like Grassley, but doing so as an independent candidate.

He said he's hopeful there are enough voters who also want to see a change.

"If there's a chance at all that American democracy still is vital and not comatose, people like me should be able to win. If I can't win, you can't win, nor your uncle, nor your neighbor, nor your girlfriend," he said. "I'm running for all of us who are the 99 percent."

Luick-Thrams, who grew up on a Century Farm between Mason City and Clear Lake, directs two non-profit cultural history organizations and is the author or editor of 15 books about Midwest cultural history, according to a Tuesday news release.

*

> "We are not here to curse the darkness, but to light the candle that can guide us through that darkness to a safe and sane future."
>
> — John F. Kennedy, presidential nomination acceptance speech, delivered on 15 July 1960 to the Democratic National Convention

Midwifing New Models

There is no comparison between the practical process of becoming a candidate for any office in the US and a corresponding position in, say, Germany. As modern Teutons would literally say, doing so in a place like Iowa is "Easy peasy." (Did our occupying troops teach them to say that?)

Still, there are requisite hands-on steps to becoming a candidate, which are many and minute:

> Core volunteers had to agree to populate my election committee (the minimum of which had to consist of a secretary and treasurer), who then had to register me with the Federal Election Commission. Both steps required our getting an identifying number for our entity and issued same—but to pay the fee for applying for an official status required our not-yet-registered body to open a provisional bank account, which necessitated creating a name: We coined "Heartland Parties." Doing so was not mandatory but asked for on the application form, so it seemed wise to create both a website and corresponding email addresses—speaking of which, we also had to have a physical address (a PO Box would not have sufficed) as well as someone to monitor post coming to it. Parallel to controlling mail, we had to keep immaculate, accurate accounts of all donations (including a close record of the sources) as well as all expenses, and report same monthly to our committee and quarterly to the Federal Election Commission… and so on and on.

Having a name, an address and unassailable accounting, however, would keep us going, but it would not get us to where we wanted to go—or any votes. To advance, we had to go beyond the practical and forge a philosophical framework from which to work. Any durable ideological engine would have to be built on constant research, reflection and revision of both goals and the messages to encapsulate as well as communicate our aims. In short, my volunteers and I had to juggle the pragmatic with the theoretical at every step of our campaign, every day, in every way. What we crafted would have to have real-world relevance to voters' everyday lives, even as it spoke to the essence of the governance needed to both facilitate and regulate same.

A Vision for Iowa's 3rd Century

Transforming the Heartland's Social, Economic, Cultural, Political and Natural Landscapes

Friends, we have ten years to reform our world — *period*.

Despite calls for real solutions to wars, poverty, weather disasters of biblical proportions, and the poisoning of our precious world, politicians of both parties play us against one another while offering meaningless platitudes and gestures. But "they" are not the fundamental problem: *We* are; we are the sole solution, as well.

We must stop looking for a great leader to govern us from the top, and restore Iowa's future from the bottom, up. We must take responsibility and act — *together*.

Heartland Parties' project committee suggests three ways to reverse Iowa's current decline by 2046, our bicentennial:

#1: Reconnect

To turn things around, we must reconnect to **true health** and **true wealth**.

True health is more than "I feel fine", more than turning to medicine and technology when disease or illness strikes. It arises from fresh, pure air, water and food; it stems from sustaining family and community relationships; and, it comes from meaningful work and social lives. Mental health depends on a grounded sense of well-being and hope, free from fear of "the other". All forms of health require sustainable wealth to make them last.

True wealth is more than the size of your wallet, car, home or bank account. Our early pioneers came to America's Heartland looking not for jobs but for ways to transform the region's resources (e.g., rich topsoil) into useable products (crops, livestock, lumber). Others came to transform their knowledge and time to serve those working the land, as shopkeepers, teachers, pastors and others. Wealth arises from adding value to what one has. It reflects inner, not only outer resources.

We must reconnect to deeper, true health, sustained by expanded wealth generation for ALL, not just those few at the top.

#2: Revitalize

In the Hawkeye State, abundant agriculture spawned towns, not vice-versa. What made Iowa spiritually, culturally and monetarily rich was its family farms and small towns.

Urban Iowa cannot flourish if rural Iowa continues to decline. In the last census, 71 of Iowa's 99 counties continued to lose population. If we wish to turn Iowa around, we have to revive its rural areas. Above all:

We need more people — *now*.

How? Each of Iowa's 100 county seats must serve as anchors, a dynamic means to hold their area's inhabitants as long-term residents. By 2046, each county should have:

- A stable, well-funded school system
- A comprehensive medical/fitness center
- A state-of-the-art community center
- Year-round farmers' and hand-crafted-goods' markets; centrally-located cafés
- A forestry program, and a recycling and clean-energy coordination center
- An ample, trail-connected park system
- A conference or convention center

Todd, a Quaker-librarian friend and volunteer, designed the inside of my primary campaign flyer—one of a couple.

For guidance in calibrating an effective balance between being too pedestrian and too pie-in-the-sky, I surveyed the main types of republican governance. In a proportional-representation, typically parliamentary system, parties—usually, a palette of parties representing the spectrum of values and agendas—adopt specific platforms reflecting a party's members and those willing to run for office. Once an overall, agreed-upon platform and a roster of candidates emerges, voters study parties' platforms before voting for the candidates to see if they align with their own values and visions of desirable change. If those elected don't, rogue candidates can expect a pummeling at the polls at the end of that term. In short, in such electoral systems, one votes for policies, not personalities *per se*. In those lands where this system works, it works well—my adopted Germany being one of the most convincing examples.

Not so in the United States' two-party system. Parties say they support specific policies yet, on the ground, all campaigns are driven by "their" candidates' biographies, by those women's and men's values, goals and character—not to mention naked self-interest—but less so by partisan orthodoxy. Pursuing the New Order I want to usher in, I resisted further using a tired template.

Disdaining politics based on the whims of individuals who come and go was easy; chipping away at the political culture that keeps churning them out proved deflatingly difficult. Still, I remained convinced: To effect lasting change, we must build groups with lasting goals, which members hone over time and do not abandon 'til they've had a chance to leverage real change.

The majority of people with whom I spoke at length similarly decried the paralysis-prone pitfalls of candidate-driven elections. Few, however, were prepared to translate their frustration into voting for an alternative contender, one who represented consensus-derived platforms over opinions-for-hire public personas. Everyone speaks about the aching need for a new model; almost no one is willing to do what it will take to graft that model onto the existing system.

#3: Realign

Forget the Republicans (founded in 1854) and Democrats (world's oldest surviving party, from 1828)! They have devolved into pawns of big-money donors, whose sole mission is to broker power. As such, they no longer point the way forward; instead, they block progress and hold us all back. Solutions are closer to home.

We share biospheres (watersheds, aquafers, air, flora and fauna species) with our most immediate Midwest neighbors. As global weather and climate patterns shift in coming years, the need to coordinate environmental actions and safeguards will increase: We can't solve such problems alone.

For our own physical health and sustainable material wealth, we are best served by importing more of our foodstuffs from regional sources and exporting the same to regional markets—for example, Chicago, the Twin Cities, Denver, Kansas City, St. Louis, etc.

And, we must strengthen our international ties through (for ex.) teacher-student exchanges; we must welcome all individuals who come to live peacefully and productively among us.

We must shift our focus from Federal to regional power levels, while remaining part of both the Federal and global communities.

How can I get involved?

To donate or volunteer:

Online at: http://bit.ly/MLT4usSenate

Or send a check made out to
Friends of Michael Luick-Thrams to:

Heartland Parties US
PO Box 1127
Mason City, IA 50401

641.420.9118   HeartlandPartiesUS@gmail.com

www.HeartlandParties.US

www.Facebook.com/MichaelLuickThrams

MICHAEL LUICK-THRAMS
for
U.S. SENATE

...the great cities rest upon our broad and fertile prairies. Burn down your cities and leave our farms, and your cities will spring up again as if by magic; but destroy our farms and grass will grow in the streets of every city in the country.

-- William Jennings Bryan, 1896

affix stamp here

paid for by Friends of Michael Luick-Thrams

Here is the flip side of my primary campaign flyer, designed to be folded as well as ready to be mailed per post.

My task, then, even as I ran as a sovereign adult citizen and a reasonable, experienced person, was to push concurrently a radically different approach to politics. Instead of running a classic campaign focused on a poll-preened candidate, I'd concentrate on flawed-but-enduring parts of our system, those which prolong impasse and block midwifing a new political culture to replace our dysfunctional one. Already feeling incomplete as a "convincing political package," I sought to compensate for my, for *any* candidate's inadequacy in serving as a "perfect" catalyst for lasting change. Instead of perpetuating the charade of being all things to all voters, I'd de-emphasize my person and instead [re-]turn the onus of democratic governance back to the people. I would peddle direct-action self-governance; I would offer a new political structure—one reflecting not a new party *per se*, but a "non-party" that, in fact, didn't yet exist.

To win acceptance, a new model not only would have to overcome ideological divisions causing our country's gridlock, it would have to compensate for historical inadequacies in our national character. Instead of shouting each other down as we do now—whether on-air or in our living and city-council rooms—we would *have* to listen to each other if all of us are to move forward. Rather than excluding others—especially those who initially might seem quite "Other-ish" from ourselves—we'd need to include others in order to succeed.[27] Rather than a few ramrodding policies over the heads of the many, it would have to reflect seasoned, widely-based consensus. Instead of consisting of self-serving agenda generated by squawking politicos in narrow echelons at the top, then sold to the masses, it would be comprised of socially-serving agreement arising from local smaller bases, then sent to broader bodies for their consideration.

This all sounded worthy, but utopian. Thus, I needed to find a time-tested template—for which I turned to the quiet yet persistent Quakers, whom I'd joined at age 17 and continue to attend.

*

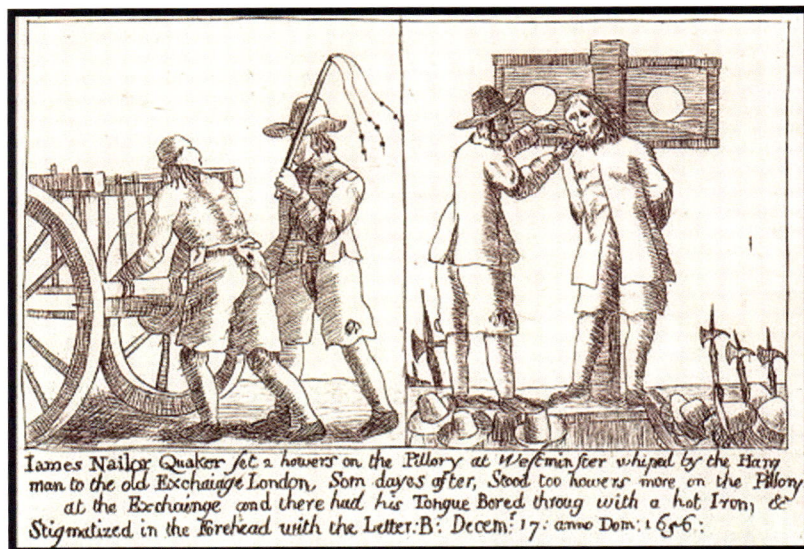

prominent Quaker James Nayler being pilloried and tortured in 1656

"There is a principle which is pure, placed in the human mind,
which in different places and ages hath had different names; it is,
however, pure, and proceeds from God. It is deep and inward,
confined to no forms of religion, nor excluded from any,
when the heart stands in perfect sincerity."

— early American Quaker John Woolman, in his *Journal*[28]

Drafting a Map to Utopia

Quakers had existed for almost 350 years before I came to them in 1981.[29] Arising from the religious (mirroring socio-political) strife and tumult of early-1600s England, the self-named Religious Society of Friends took the era's anti-clerical movement to its farthest degree. So radical [from *radix*, Latin for "root"] was these heretics' drive to speak to the faith, to the heart of each "Seeker" that even the Puritans felt threatened by those among them who were first known as "Publishers of Truth." This earth-shaking movement came not from the top, but from the bottom of society: It arose from the yearnings and expectant meetings of farmers, shepherds, laborers... and, to this day, it organizes itself primarily at the local level, not at national or global ones.

In Friends' worldview, there is something divine and sacred, something we deem "that of god" in each individual. Because an inextinguishable spark lies inalienably in every person, all have access to that spirit or "Inner Light." Pole-vaulting past any pretense of "needing" a priest or pastor or other intermediary in order to tap "that still, small voice within," Quakers (as early Friends were scornfully nicknamed by detractors) embodied an intolerable threat to their fellow rebels, Puritans—and much later to my suspicious family, who assumed I'd joined a cult; in any case, they concluded that the "mystics of Christianity" certainly could *not* be Christian—right?

an early American Friends Service Committee emblem:
In 1947, the AFSC—along with Britain's Friends Service Council,
—was awarded the Nobel Peace Prize on behalf of all Friends.

The author speaks at a Young Friends retreat convening in the Hickory Grove Meetinghouse, spring 2019. My campaign had relied on small-group encounters to reach rural and special-interest urban audiences.

As I wanted to craft a body politic that arose from a free people [the root of the word "democracy"], grassroots-organized Quakers provided a practical model for self-governance. Friends have no clergy and only rarely local executive administrators. Committees execute all "business" of the meeting. [Quakers don't gather in churches, but in "meetinghouses."] As with all decisions regarding collective matters, committee members are confirmed by consensus. And, as ever more Americans balk at elites' pretense of our "needing" politicians or other governmental intermediaries in order to secure our shared, essential needs, Friends' staunch egalitarianism embodies a perfect, proven model for pure democracy. But, how to translate such a model from an otherworldly, personal realm into an earthly, political one? And, how to tailor, then market it in such a way that folks other than those already in my choir might accept, practice and eventually sustain it? A Friendly model would serve no use, let alone survive, if they didn't.

As daunting and difficult as I found it, I had to turn to my own family to test my model—even if, ultimately, doing so wasn't about two known stand-in mortals *per se*, but rather the third or so of all Americans they represent for me, who seem to *not* be in "my choir" at present but whom I need to be. My relatives' beliefs and biographies—seemingly vastly different from my own or my friends'—spoke promisingly for key aspects of my community-based approach to social change.

For decades, Lucy passionately and tirelessly invested in the well-being of Boulder, Iowa, the little *Burg* where Gerry and she raised their three sons. Lucy long ran the Latchkey program there, assuring that its children had a "safe" place to congregate during weekdays when they weren't in the nearby school. For some time, she also served on Boulder's emergency-response unit, rushing to accident scenes and health crises throughout her community. For his part, Linus sat for several years on the town council of his "safe" Minneapolitan suburb, Laketon. Although it cost him frayed nerves, he often took controversial stands on core local issues and interacted with disagreeing individuals whom he found disagreeable. Still, he served all as best he could.

For those two siblings, the idea of being "safe" has long been vital. Linus—who said he fled his Saint Paul neighborhood after he saw parochial schoolgirls smoking on their way home from class—once told me his sister Lucy suffers from "agoraphobia," an intense fear of leaving home or being in crowds. Certainly, Lucy chose to "safely" reside in Boulder, a bedroom town a half-hour drive from Waterloo, the race-and-class-divided city where Gerry worked for years at the John Deere factory—until, that is, that venerable pioneer in agricultural equipment followed other manufacturers' examples and cynically relocated much production to low-wage regions in the South and south of the border. The couple of times I rode with Lucy through Waterloo, she always insisted we roll up the car's windows and lock its doors as she barreled through "bad areas," which each time consisted of African-American neighborhoods. I sighed, but complied.

I have never experienced Lucy to be genuinely welcoming of "The Other"—not of the Soviet Jews I befriended in Queens and who once spent a week with my parents at Ashlawn Farm; not the Latino boyfriend I had for six months and fetched from Uruguay to spend Easter with us in Iowa one spring; not the Japanese graduate-student couple I met at Iowa State and brought to her house on our way to hike in hilly Little Switzerland... of *none* of my "other" friends, including the charming (and *tres* white!) French newlyweds and Gabriela, a German *au pair* girl I "adopted."

Lucy's self-chosen insularity, however, took an involuntary hit when her eldest son, daring Jared, moved his young, burgeoning family into South Minneapolis. While I find problematic the missionary nature of this evangelical pastor's "inner-city witness," I'm proud of his willingness—along with Amy's and their three boys'—to work and live in an urban milieu that for decades has been home to race- and class-fanned unemployment... its subsequent despair-driven substance abuse... the ensuing drug- and gang-violence misery... and all the resultant dangers. Although I assume she has to mentally (if not literally) hold her nose each time she ventures there, Lucy is forced by circumstances—her deep love for her offspring—to wade into what for her must be an extremely threatening environment: Doing so can't help but stretch her world.

Things had to change for Linus, "safely" tucked away in Laketon, after a "Muslim guy" moved in next door to the house I had helped him secure by co-signing loan papers. He found the arrival of the man and his growing family on the same cul-de-sac didn't usher in the demise of the neighborhood—nor property devaluation. And, Linus seemed to come to like the gainfully-employed, devoted father. For sure, Linus' shielded world was cracked open when a female engineer in his department at Bullseye's national headquarters turned out to be a lesbian... who played on their corporate softball team... and whom he grew to like—along with her partner.

The key lessons that I take away from my two relatives' evolution are that they deeply care about their families and their communities, despite their distrust of forces greater than either one—say, state or Federal, not to mention global or NGO governing bodies. IF they can *see* and *touch* the people inhabiting their chosen spheres of "safety," then they untiringly invest and donate, assist and defend. But, ask them to find a bit of empathy for a dark-skinned mother fleeing with her teenagers from voracious gangs in Guatemala or compassion for a traumatized couple who had walked across the Balkans with babies in their arms in order to escape bombs falling on *their* once-"safe" residential streets in Damascus, good luck: They don't always seem to care, despite paying lip service to playing Samaritans to "the least of these"—the hungry, the naked, etc.[30]

So, if the only way to get Americans who are cut from the same psychological cloth as my fear-driven relations to address the ever more frequent flooding of their town's baseball field because of "100-year" cloudbursts that now happen, oh, about every half decade, is to include them in locally organized and active community groups—then so be it. If the only way to get a third of our nation's population behind adequately funding their local library or replacing their school's broken playground equipment is to come together for community-based efforts, then OK. Since statewide or national projects (regulating immigration, codifying abortion, legislating civil rights for sexual minorities, agreeing upon controls over corporate capitalism, combating global warming) seem "too crowded" with dissonant voices or perhaps too abstract for some of us, then so be it: The model I pushed every day of my campaign was meant for them, too, as I was not running this campaign for my own edification. Rather, it seemed to me a uniquely effective platform from which to say "There's something wrong here—and we *need* to change it, fast, together." My campaign was a mirror for everyone who was able to see what, alone, we did not wish to see. And, it was meant to offer practical ideas and proposals for real and lasting change.

Imperfect as the embryonic product was at that point, in my crafting a model I attempted to codify not just the structure but the spirit behind unprogrammed Friends' peculiar culture.[31] In the process, I coined an umbrella name for it, "Heartland Parties." Yes, it reflected my Midwest roots, but moreover my conviction that any viable new political body must echo the deepest stirrings in the hearts of those driving it. Alluding to "land" evokes the paramount issue of our times—our world's unraveling environment; and, the plural "Parties" in the name reflects the movement's decentralized nature. Armed with an alternative model for reorganizing America's dysfunctional political culture, I returned to the task of putting legs under lofty wings—once, that is, I had up-loaded onto the web my draft blueprint for new political structures, posted at:

http://heartlandparties.us/parties/

It helped me to have drafted a description of utopia, but even the loveliest dream did not alter the fact that I had to face a skeptical, change-resistant electorate to get that dream broadcast, then debated. Just as I had had to identify those who had a stake in my succeeding in collecting enough signatures to be on the fall ballot, I realized that in order to overcome the obstacles to my being heard and taken seriously, I had to identify those who would seek to scuttle my bringing up the very issues that motivated me to run in the first place. What surprised me, however, was the group I swiftly learned wanted most to silence me—and it wasn't the Right.

*

altered, colorized "pop" version of Johan Froben's woodcut
map of Utopia as it appears in Thomas More's Utopia, 1518

51

Blindsided by the "Liberal" Left

Operating on a budget [largely candidate-financed] that was just a fraction of what the mainstream nominees had at their disposal,[32] I depended on word-of-mouth, social media, an on-line presence and other low-cost forms of publicity. Primarily, it meant my supporters and me striking up conversations with people we encountered every day, mentioning my campaign and our wish for their support. We distributed our brochures and promoted our website. Typically, Republicans smiled, bemused by our quixotic, austere crusade, but also assured that no political pipsqueak like me could wrestle even a smattering of GOP votes from Uncle Chuck's fans.

Not so among Iowa Democrats.

When I began my campaign, three men[33] had already campaigned long and exhaustively to challenge Grassley's iron grip over half of the Hawkeye State's US Senatorial presence in our national capital. Although I'd never heard of any of them before launching my campaign, I quickly liked and much admired two of them. The third one, however, proved—at least in my case—to be a Black Widow to my dark-horse candidacy. Ironically, though a straight, suburban-family man, he shot his venom at me at Cedar Rapid's Gay Pride celebration in June that year.

I'd come down for the day from my mobile campaign headquarters—then temporarily parked in the college town of Decorah—to stump among the rainbow crowd gathering in Eastern Iowa's "secret capital." I had brought with me to the cozy hometown of Quaker Oats, Grant Wood and Elijah Wood, a young and promising political activist from Detroit, Bryan Hill, who lived in Decorah while serving as an Ameri-Corps home-energy auditor/outreach coordinator.

During the long car drive from Northeast Iowa's wooded anomaly, the Driftless Area's Little Switzerland region,[34] 23-year-old Bryan-Bryan (as I called him, evoking what for me seemed his split personality) spoke about his generation's "non-binary" approach to sexuality—and what he called his own "queer" identity that he said didn't necessarily equate being "gay." Although I listened intently and with genuine interest to his somewhat diffused, at times self-contradicting monolog, I found what he shared disorienting. That feeling in the car of being perplexed by things I could not easily grasp, however, was nothing in comparison to what awaited me in Cedar Rapids.

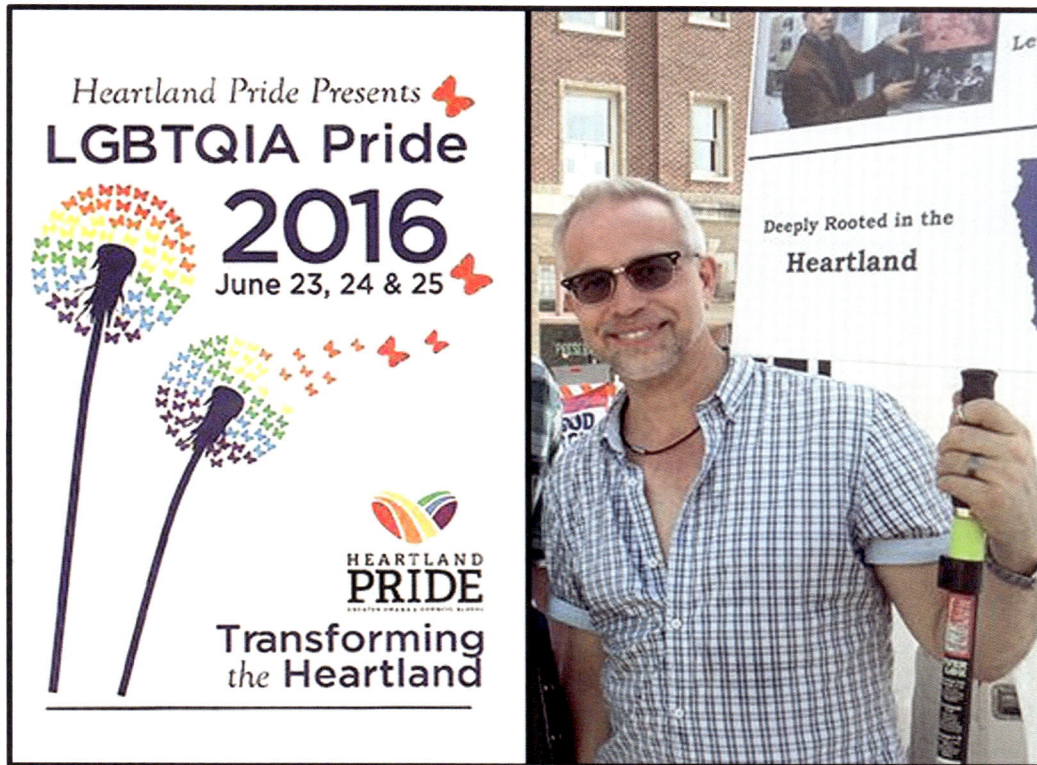

Omaha/Council Bluff's Heartland Pride 2016 poster; the candidate at Des Moines' Gay Pride, June 2016

The Gay Pride organizers granted us candidates only a few minutes to introduce ourselves and present our *Spiel*, in a block of run-'em-through rapidity, which seemed begrudgingly conceded during what otherwise was meant to be one big party. Glad for any exposure, the handful of us pursuing various public offices took our turns at trying to funnel mountains of information into what seemed to be a few fleeting moments as we delivered our tailored elevator pitches.

Afterwards, I began to work the crowd, starting at the awning-covered booth nearest the stage where we'd all just spoken. As I stretched out my hand to those behind the first table, fellow US-Senate candidate Bob Peigg appeared from behind me and extended his hand to the same folks, but closer to their out-stretched arms than mine. Confused, they awkwardly took his as he dove into a hearty rendering of "Good mornin'! I'm Bob Peigg, and I'm runnin' for—" .

I had never met this man, but had heard from the majority of Democrats whom I had informally polled that he was the candidate they preferred by far out of the three Iowa men seeking the Democrats' US-Senate nomination. My sources also warned me that his name was pronounced "peg" like a hook, rather than how it might sound with a rural drawl, like another word for "swine." As I was to find, however, his sabotaging me suggested the latter, not the former.

Choosing to think Peigg had not seen me, I shrugged and went on to the next booth. Again, I smiled as I offered "Hi, I'm Michael Luick-Thrams, running for—" but, once again, blustering Bob blindsided me. This time, he even lightly brushed my hand aside as he shoved his towards the stunned man staffing that booth. Surely, there was no way he couldn't have seen me.

At this point, it seemed the two incidences were not coincidental. As I was neither absolutely sure nor wanting a confrontation commensurate to the outrage which Peigg had perpetrated, twice, I crossed the walkway between the two rows of facing booths and once more greeted…

When Bob Peigg then shadowed me again, his trying literally to elbow me out of the race was not a wild supposition but a judicious conclusion. I felt floored—and conceded to my lack of will to strongarm my way past my Democratic detractor's antics. Standing nearby, Bryan-Bryan only shook his head and agreed that I best simply withdraw from an ugly duel I had not sought.

This whole time, I had watched Willy Hawk watching me as I stumped among our fellow homos[35] for their political backing. Given his weighty presence among Linn County Democrats, I then walked over to my cousin, staffing the queer-Democrats booth, to inquire if he'd seen what "his" candidate had just done. He simply shrugged and asked "What did you expect?"

To that, I replied quietly, shaking my head sadly from side to side, "More—and much better."

*

William "Hawk's" US naturalization certificate, signed 17 October 1860 in Linn County, Iowa

> "Behold the work of the old; let your heritage not be lost, but bequeath it as a memory, treasure, and blessing. And, pass it down to your children."
>
> — Amana Colonies spiritual leader Christian Metz, from a testimony given on 1 November 1846

Betrayal from Within: Type I

Willy Hawk and I go back—*way* back. Although we share a familial heritage we both hold dear, we hardly could have hailed from more differing backgrounds. This I saw nearly every summer as a boy, when Grandma Thrams took me along on her annual pilgrimages "back home" to visit relatives or childhood friends in Central City, Mount Washington, Marion and Cedar Rapids.

the "Hawk" farm, near Central City, circa 1880—not far from the Quaker settlement of Whittier

Born Florence "Erma" Hawk, my mother's mother was a granddaughter of Wilhelm Habicht—a German settler with a surname meaning "Hawk," to which "William" anglicized his name soon after he became naturalized in 1860. Born on a prosperous farm, her father—Wilhelm's son Clemence—later became president of Mount Washington's Citizens State Bank and owner of the town's lumberyard, coal company and grain elevator. Grandma's older and only brother—also "Will"—had five children, one of whom was Jim, husband to JoAnn and adoptive father to Willy and Janelle. Jim and his wife loved their acquired offspring dearly, but also (so it seemed to our branch of the family) spoiled them terribly—perhaps to compensate for Jim's demanding position in the Johnson White House and later work in the nation's Federal machinery. In any case, Jim and Czech-descended Hawkeye JoAnn made a point of bringing their family to Iowa every year.

Clemence (the author's maternal and Willy's paternal great-grandfather) at Citizens State Bank, 1910s

On those lazy summer jaunts "down East" from the Thrams-Luick farm on the windswept open prairies of Northcentral Iowa, Jim and his family often also appeared at the cramped Central City home of Uncle Will's widow, Aunt Jennie—Jim's mother, Willy and Janelle's grandmother, whom I loved almost as much as my own. My grandmother fawned over her nephew Jim, even as she and her South-Dakota-born sister-in-law, Aunt Jennie, seemed locked in a running battle marked by low-level but caustic verbal sparring. Perhaps it was their unintended doing, but no matter what I did or how hard I tried to do it differently, I always had the feeling Willy and Janelle saw me as an interloping hayseed competitor for their granny's attention and affection.

Although I had not seen him for three or four decades, at some point early in this current century, Willy appeared at one of my programs about Iowa social history, held at Cedar Rapids' National Czech & Slovak Museum & Library, which his parents enthusiastically supported for years, even if from halfway across the country. At first, I did not recognize the once-pretty, ebony-haired boy until Willy lumbered over to me after the Q-and-A and outed himself as my long-lost cousin. I felt dumbstruck yet also excited to reconnect. When we hastily made a dinner date, I was thrilled.

Later, as he dug into a heaping plate of fried food and a super-sized sugary drink, Willy brought me up-to-date, even as I could sense that he also kept me at emotional arm's length during our entire reunion meal. As much as I tried (perhaps, *because* I tried?) to pry out of reticent Willy a fuller account of his life over the intervening years, he offered only vague, partial summaries. Unhappily fielding my eager questions, he abruptly concluded with a scant sketch of how he'd ended up scuttling a hectic DC life and trekked "out West" to take over his mother's people's white-clapboard "American four-square" home, now full of books and PBS-esque videos. Although he once studied political science, Willy told me he presently is a theater manager in a Cedar Rapids mall "to pay bills," but most passionately volunteers in Democratic-party politics.

At Willy's last revelation, I erroneously thought to myself *Finally—and hurrah: an interest we have in common, left-of-center social policy!* My euphoric relief, however, was to be short-lived.

As an East Coast kid, Willy seemed to us staid, restrained Midwestern youth to be a shameless brat. Like his sister's, his snarly responses to his doting parents were constantly whiney and rebuffing. Even as an undifferentiating farmboy, I concluded these two urban terrors both despised their unfazed parents—and yet: That night, sitting in an "in" eatery in a former auto garage across from Coe College, decades later, the values which informed Willy's political worldview and fueled his activism seemed consistently compassionate and accommodating to those in need, to those in other—especially developing—countries and to the planet. Several times as he sat across from me, I imagined Willy was channeling Mom's sweet cousin, dear Jim.

Willy's clever father—whom I'd always liked and as an adult enjoyed visiting in JoAnn's and his plushy retirement refuge on Maryland's pricey shore—had built a career on the coattails of Kennedy's Camelot and LBJ's Great Society. Willy's grandfather—besides being his namesake, a Great-Plains cattleman—had been a staunch Republican. His father, Jim, however, had grown into personhood during the reign of a New-Deal Democrat, when it seemed only the likes of a Roosevelt offered the sole way to conquer a Great Depression, later Hitler and ultimately Joe Stalin. Given such ingrained social sensibilities in his political pedigree, I assumed Willy had been weaned on and positively integrated Democratic tenets, despite his youthful orneriness. What I only realized a couple of years later, though—on a sun-soaked spring day at Gay Pride in 2016— was that Willy's partisan allegiances trumped any hereditary ones.

"So, Willy" I had asked over the growing hubbub of Gay Pride hullabaloo, my fingers drumming the table, "how do you explain Bob Peigg's just now pushing me out of running for public office"?

As Willy had always been an intelligent lad, and as my short inspection after our reunion dinner of his inherited hermitage had revealed the trappings of an exceptionally well-read man with an engaged and discerning mind, I expected a thoughtful, peacemaking response. Instead, Willy clenched his jaw and curtly demanded "What did you expect?" Then, he added "Why do you insist on stealing votes from the real candidates? *You* are gunna be the one to return Grassley back in the Senate!" Then, he snorted, turned around, wobbled off and pretended to be busy restocking Iowa-Democrat T-shirts to lay out on the booth's big table for passersby to grab.

Stunned, I turned and set off. I pretended to seek Bryan-Bryan, but I really wanted to vanish. Not wanting to confront bomb-waiting-to-go-off Willy, I mouthed "More—and much better."

After having been sideswiped, I'd hoped for at least a smattering of support from this related man, yet I got not even a grain of gratitude for investing my all in engaging in and sustaining the democratic process. Sadly, I was to find my cousin's political as well as personal snubbing to be the norm among Iowa's relatively few dyed-in-the-wool "liberals." That, I had not expected.

*

Will (Willy's paternal grandfather, standing) and Erma (the author's maternal grandmother, with the ribbon in her hair) were siblings: Their parents were Willy's and my shared ancestors; circa 1910

> "Turning and turning in the widening gyre
> The falcon cannot hear the falconer;
> Things fall apart; the centre cannot hold;
> Mere anarchy is loosed upon the world,
> The blood-dimmed tide is loosed, and everywhere
> The ceremony of innocence is drowned;
> The best lack all conviction, while the worst
> Are full of passionate intensity."
>
> — William Butler Yeats, "The Second Coming" in *The Dial*

Mapping a Rainbow

My feeling alienated from the Near-, let alone Far-Left grew as spring turned into summer. It hurt sorely to have my idealism-stoked goals and efforts rejected by people I'd known most of my life, but it also stung when folks I hadn't known long or deeply, yet already liked, turned their shoulder to me—politically but socially as well. As my campaign dragged on, it began to drag me down. Turning searchingly to anyone I thought might be an ally, serial rebuffs battered my spirits.

Fearing constantly the pained awkwardness of reaching out while misreading others' comments or actions, I practiced detecting nuances in their apparent values, along with their willingness (or not) to act upon those values in tangible forms in the "real" world. Out of self-protection, I began to assign people I met—at least temporarily—spots on a graduated mental map I devised. Having this evolving circular graph in my mind, I modified the dosage of "political medicine" I gave to people in audiences I addressed, as well as to individuals I cornered, as I pitched Sea Change.

General Political-Rainbow Graph:

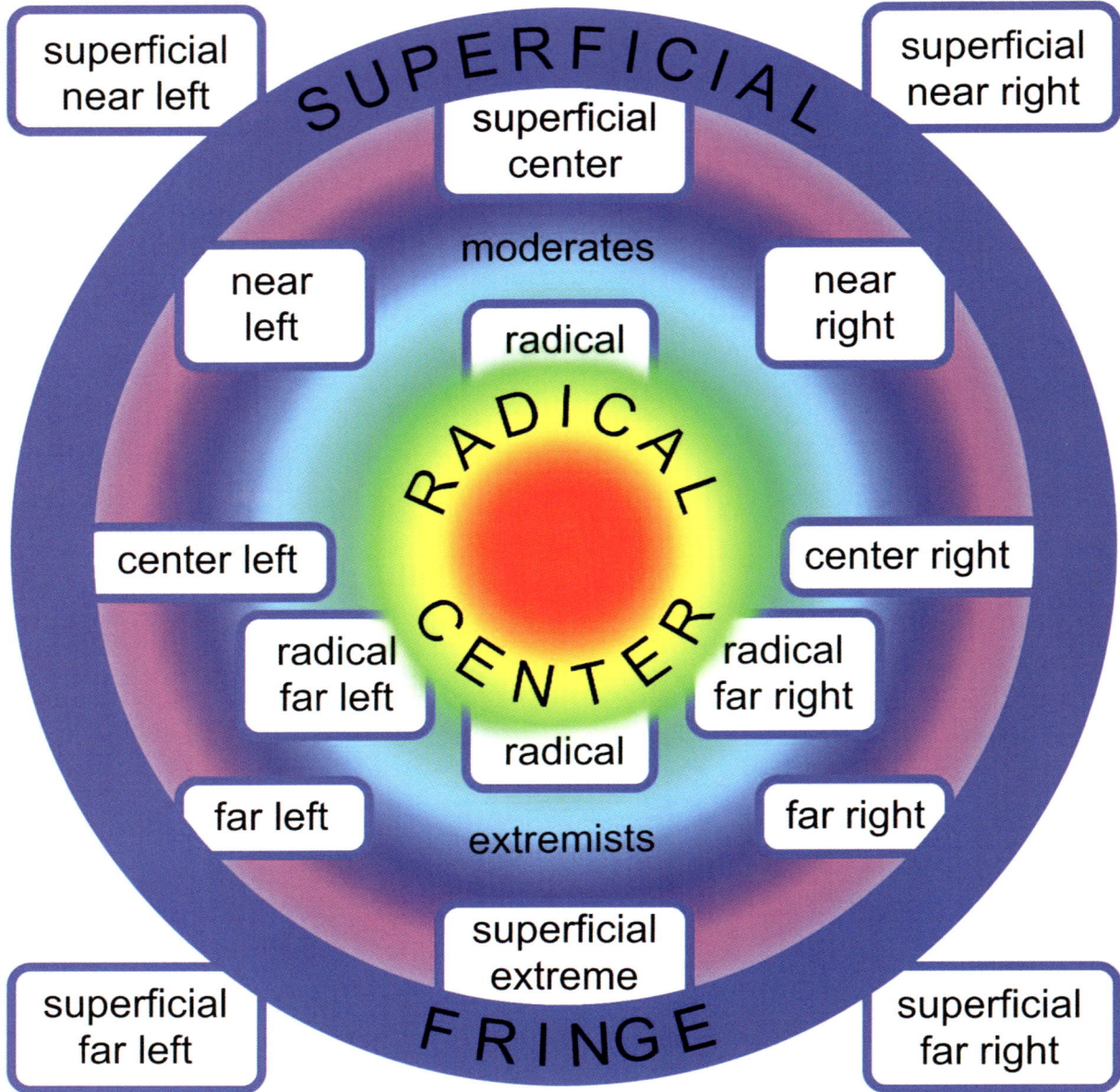

As it took recognizable form, I named it my "General Political-Rainbow Graph." As a tool, it was not perfect; in fact, it represented gross generalities—and yet, as usual, it seemed the generalizations upon which it was built contained countless germs of truth. And, its greatest strength (the graph put invisible dynamics into visible form) was also its greatest weakness: It was stuck in language; it depended on ideas trapped in imperfect, inadequate words assigned meanings by me that others may or may not share, let alone understand in the same ways I do.

Still, I crafted this instrument because I wished—no, I *had*—to have greater clarity in my world.

To start, I deemed those at the top of it the Superficial Center—people who claim on surveys or dating profiles to be "independents" yet have neither truly studied today's most pressing issues nor taken a clear stand on same, or (to me, even sadder) both. Their philosophical cousins in the Radical Center (to which I strive to belong) also resist being self- or externally-labeled as being reflexively Left or Right. Beyond that, however, Radical Centrists insist on studying and reflecting on some of our day's most pressing issues in order to arrive at thoughtful, unscripted responses, open to revision as new information avails itself. Typically, once we do, we seldom shy from taking public, if at times loud,`` stands based on our findings. At the same time, ideally Radical Centrists genuinely wish to hear others' perspectives, from which we might lift material with which to update our own. We Radical Centrists often seek open, civil discourse; we can listen— and, we can ask. Unlike too many of our compatriots, such Americans care to know and dare to inquire: To us, the process of learning and gaining insight is invigorating, not intimidating.

I named the act of diving into one's soul in order to research and reflect upon important issues "acting inward," whereas taking action in the public realm by seemingly uninformed, unreflective people as "acting out." Despite the risk of its being tainted by a residual bad taste lingering from a former use by HIV/AIDS activists in decades past, I recycled the term "acting upward" to represent all who take direct action to the public as a means to embody values or goals in visible, concrete ways. We see examples of these three kinds of "acting" all around us:

- Those people who spew toxic, non-negotiable positions in public are "acting out:" They don't care about the impacts of their often outrageous, offending remarks and aren't open to having their beliefs updated by input from others—to whom they hardly listen.
- Those who step back from the emotionality of social issues long enough to research the deeper aspects of an issue, then reflect on various stands they could take before re-emerging and sharing their current perspectives are "acting inward." We *want* them.
- Those who've done their homework as well as the "emotional work" around an issue, then take action—solo or in tandem with others—are "acting upward" on behalf of all. These individuals believe in real exchange and cooperation with others. We *need* them!

Increasing numbers of people in North America, Europe and Oceania may like to think they are political "independents," yet the majority of "Centrists" fit the Superficial more than the Radical classification; their penchant for acting out hardly masks their frequent failure to act upward. Growing the size and standing of the second group while eroding those of the first is a vital step in wresting power from those who continue to block collective movement forward, toward meaningful change, then conferring it to those thoughtful ones willing and ready to act upward.

Human beings are complex creatures. We exist and move through Life as hybrid constellations, cast in infinite spectrums; each is unique, like any snowflake or fingerprint that has ever existed in the history of the universe. Despite that being the case, those qualifying as true "Centrists"—

either of the Superficial or Radical ilk—can still be more exactly sorted. Based on the aggregate sums of their individual values, choices and impact, in actuality they are either Center Left or Center Right. So, as I met individuals on the campaign trail, I often intuitively assessed them as, for example, "Superficial Center Right" or "Radical Center Left." A kind of Myers-Briggs Model of Political Personality Types,[36] these initial assessments—which I often adjusted as I spoke with a person—helped in calibrating my message. To be completely useful, however, my model's General Political-Rainbow Graph had to be wider and deeper in terms of differentiation. In order to accommodate those who truly aren't Centrist at all, I couldn't overlook the majority.

As a historian, I know that at given times, in most societies, public opinion has broken down into approximate thirds. At one time, for example, British America consisted of forty colonies or territories. When thirteen of them chose to rebel and later to form a confederation, roughly a third of their collective population supported independence, and another third remained loyal to the ruling monarchy; the last third reportedly was undecided or did not care. As time passed, those proportions shifted as the "undecided" third began to choose and Loyalists caved in to growing rebel sentiment or they fled to Maritime Canada or even back to Mother England itself.

We see similar breakdowns at various points in history, in—for instance—Germany's *Weimarer Republik* as the Nazis legally manipulated their way into power; liberalization movements in the Arab world during recurring waves of a short-lived "Arab Spring"—to the current day, including, at times, President Trump's approval ratings. Public-opinion polls about a given matter almost never initially score "supermajorities" (e.g., "3/5ths-" or "2/3rds-majorities" of respectively 60% or 66%); if anything, they may indicate "absolute majorities" of 51% or more—but then expect miseries like Brexit. (Do note: Garnering a "simple majority" does *not* constitute "democracy."[37]) What is key in each case, is what becomes of the initial sentiments of the "undecided" crowd— those who, if pressed, mostly would take (at least in that moment) stances others could clearly label as being "Left wing" or "Right wing." These are the swayable people I call the Near Left or Near Right, those who can determine an election by cross-voting, but then "return home." While Center-Left/-Right voters yield "swing votes," Near voters' votes constitute "crossover votes."

A distinguishing trait of "Near" partisans is that while they usually claim affiliation with a Right- or Left-leaning party, they can be persuaded—either through the promise of personal gain or threat of personal loss—to support an opposing movement, which under normal conditions they would not do. Most so-called Founding Fathers of the young United States, for example, once had been "loyal sons of England," had studied or at least traveled in the "home country" and subscribed to "English" values, norms and behaviors. Ditching the crown symbolized less a shift in cultural and political worldviews, more momentary career goals and personal ambitions: If it had been monarchical rule *per se* that they had come to disdain, then why did many rally a few years later around the proposal to install George Washington as their new "King George"?

Similarly, millions of Germans who in the *Weimarer Republik* had supported "socialist" tenets suddenly had no visible qualms living under a fascist system... until, that is, after that twelve-year Nazi experiment imploded; then, abruptly, most Germans swore they had been "anti-Nazi all along." In a related development, with the founding of Israel, socialist idealism drove the creation of Kibbutzim and welfare-state egalitarianism; now, after the arrival of about a million once-secular Soviet Jews, Israel's political fabric has become unrecognizable by earlier, mostly Western-European Jews—some of whom dare to apply "fascistic" as an adjective to describe the Netanyahu regime. In both cases, when so many individuals "flip" so does a whole country.

During my stay in Czechoslovakia, I winced to see the most ardent "new capitalists" had just been top "old-guard communists." Today in Italy, former *"Internationale"*-singing communists have flipped into migrant-bashers; East Germans weaned on "socialist fraternity" can't vote fast enough to embolden the rabidly xenophobic *Alternativ für Deutschland* party's serial outrages. What drives individuals—worse, mass groups of them—to shift convictions out of convenience? Per my fellow Midwesterner, John Cougar Mellencamp, "Ya gotta stand for something, or yer gonna fall for anything:" What has to happen for a person to take a stand—and *stand* by it?

To cite examples of the "flipping" dynamic closer to home, the majority of Iowa voters blessed Barack Obama's candidacy at the polls—twice, in 2008 and 2012—but in 2016 lent their seal of approval to Donald Trump's presidential ambitions. Stalwart "union states" like Pennsylvania and Michigan[38] jumped partisan ships and helped rocket-drop Trump into the White House. But, not only groups of voters can flip their partisan alliances; individual candidates do, too: Donald Trump was once a registered Democrat, as was former New York mayor Michael Bloomberg [currently, once again a Democrat]; both became prominent Republicans—at least in public. In the other direction, onetime Democratic VP-nominee Joseph Lieberman—then a US Senator from Connecticut—defected from the Democratic Party when he endorsed a McCain-Palin ticket during the 2008 National Republican Convention. ('Twas truly a disgusting stage event to watch!)

"Near" partisans are capable of relatively casually flipping party affiliations based on shifting political winds. Those of the Far Left and Far Right, however, rarely do. To most of them, doing so would be repugnant, let alone inconceivable. Ironically, while their particular stances might seem those of irreconcilable opposites, the ideological fervor characteristic of "Far" partisans of all stripes is something they share more with each other than they do with, say, their "Center" or even "Near" political cousins. In addition, while "Superficial Far" partisans might prance about, spewing nonsense or hawking immoral screeds, "Radical Far" ones at least go through the motions of researching and reflecting on the issues about which they usually passionately care. In this respect, I respect (admittedly, grudgingly) the considered positions of "Radical Far" ideologues. At least, they make up with conviction a bit of what they lack in "convincibility."

Following the Right/Left trajectory of my graph farther, we reach extremes—literally. For lack of a more tasteful metaphor for the differences between Superficial and Radical Extremists, think of qualitative distinctions in the cultural makeup of Ku Klux Klan members since World War II. Some poorly-educated, day-wage hick eager to "kick a nigger" might be attracted to join the KKK as a vent for accumulating resentments and pent-up rage. Ask that same rube, however, to explain in detail the Klan's historical origins and structure, or to rationally defend illogical contradictions in the Klan's positions, past or present, and s/he likely will verbally stammer as they mentally fumble. Still, give that dupe a torch or gun—and enough booze—and you've got a quick recipe for disaster, a Superficial-Extremist patsy willing to terrorize innocent victims.

An equally distasteful but illustrative parallel:

Many of the Radical-Extremist Klan leaders of all three waves[39] of America's hydra-headed "white cancer" actually hailed from educated, [at least lower-]middle-class backgrounds. Those in charge behind the scenes or even out front might be able to appear charming, even charismatic—as long as their audiences don't think too long, too deeply about their verbal poison. Still, such individuals obviously have invested considerable time and thought in mapping out a complex mental map of the world—one which I likely would not agree with in any way, but at least I could "see," then dissect and ultimately disassemble.

Sadly, however, even coherent, semi-intelligent Extremists also are capable of committing truly heinous acts against their fellow human beings—be those individual members of the Klan, ISIS, fundamentalist-Hindu nationalist movements or any other of the numerous Extremist groups active around the globe today. As objectionable and unacceptable as the inhabitants of the last category in my graph might seem, don't we have to be willing and able to name their behavior and understand it in its wider complexity, so that we can counter it? Doesn't remaking our world have to include transforming the vile contents of the most wounded hearts and warped minds among us? Is there any way forward, without trying to take each kind of person with us?

*

On the Ground

Neatly dividing folks into supposed categories of political sentiments or affinities, however, would not win me votes. Beyond the theoretical, I had to understand those populating my would-be constituency as individuals, with biographies particular to each one. I had to try not just to *think* about what was on their minds, but *feel* that in their hearts—then imagine how it got there.

As a road map for my journey into the hearts and minds of fellow Iowans, I scrutinized the words we otherwise so casually brandish about without thinking about what they really imply. For one, the Greek word *polis* means "city": "Policy," "politician" and "political" all come from the root idea that how one moves "within the city" determines one's "politics." Similarly, the Latin *civitas* refers to "city-state": "Citizen," "civilization," "civil" and "civics" all derive from it. Again, the root idea has to do with how one lives "in the city," in concert with others. To some degree, then, we are *all* "political" creatures—an unavoidable state, as we all live and move in social contexts.

Like nuancing political positions, splitting terminological hairs may sow greater understanding, but as head-heavy stuff, it also can yield mental numbness. In the end, how each of us lives and moves in our social surroundings isn't determined decisively by etymology—the origins of our words—but by genealogy, the origins of our personhood. While my General Political-Rainbow Graph granted me clarity during my campaign, my own classification—like yours—is based not on abstract intellectual constructs in the air but specific emotional experiences on the ground.

How—where, from whom—did I learn to be a human being, to live and move within "the city"? How did you—and *how* do you know? Of course, you and I gleaned most of our cues from those around us soon after we arrived on the planet. According to behavioral scientists, by the time we got on that bus or were walked to our first day of school, our base characters were set, cast by myriad "others" we encountered in our first years on Earth, yet we mostly have forgotten.

little Iowans with farm friends near Rosenort ["Place of Roses" in German], Manitoba, circa 1962: For us "pale skins" growing up on the Great Plains then, such scenes were "normal;" for the Natives who had roamed those prairies for ten thousand years before our families arrived, we were invaders' offspring.

As I reconstruct the social environment of my impressionable first half-decade of life—for a historian, an instinctual thing to do—I recall Draper Long, the bushy-eyebrowed pediatrician in Mason City who delivered me at 8:06 on a cold Tuesday morn, 18 December 1962, then cared for me into my elementary-school years. I remember Agnes, a big-bosomed lady who still wore Depression-era crimped curls, print-cotton dresses and arched shoes 30 years on. She babysat me while Mom was browsing at a sparkling new Sears store in the postwar-era shopping center opened on what had been the old fairgrounds, where my parents met showing calves in '52.

A parade of folks passes through my mind when I dredge up the faces. Even the obscure names of those who had slipped out of my consciousness decades ago with effort again take primary places in my childhood memories: fruit-market Earl, an ever-smiling but frantic man who always brought stingy Grandma Thrams "ripe-but-edible" (read: "cheaper") peaches; Mrs. Short, the

Sunday school teacher whom I admired all the more because of her classy-yet-aloof demeanor; Wayne down at the Burchinal Farmers Co-op, who used to scoop me up in his giant arms as Dad unloaded corn into the elevator—and Phyllis Nelson at the nearby general store, whose Cruella-streaked ebony-and-snow hair made her seem all the more intimidating as she handed me the candy Dad let me have on the way to call on Gene Tannehill, our ever-chatty hog-feed peddler.

I was born mostly a blank slate, yet didn't all of those personalities leave marks on me? (Didn't their counterparts in your pre-conscious world do the same for you?) Hadn't Draper Long been a Doughboy in France, Agnes a telephone switchboard operator during the Dust Bowl? Was Earl wounded as, with his battalion, he hunted Hitler; didn't Mrs. Short attend college in "the Cities" during lunch-counter sit-ins? And Phyllis Nelson—did her sternness have to do with her and her never-talking husband's slowly losing their store, year-by-ever-more-meager-year? Didn't Mom say Gene Tannehill had been a POW in Nazi Germany, along with so many other Hawkeyes—Carroll Bogard, Mason City's high-school principal, and Leonard Juhl, Gramma Luick's amiable, crew-cutted cousin who for years drove the school bus that carried us kids to and from school?[40]

Of course, each of those long-gone souls left lingering impressions on me—if not, I could not recall them today. Clearly, we learn how to be people—and how to "dance" with people, either in concert or in discord—from those around us. At the same time, who touches our lives more, deeper and longer, than our families of origin—above all, our parents and siblings, even cousins? More than the happy or unfortunate influences of those outside my childhood home, my inner cosmos—like yours—was most colored by those closest to me. As such, I long ago concluded that anything soft and warm, joyous and affirming in me came from the Thramses, my mother's people. My father's folk, the Luicks, were harder, colder, rarely joyous and seldom affirming.

Yes, my three maternal aunts—Eleanor, Irene and Dorothy—could obsess for hours about the most inane aspects of postwar household materialism: the latest window treatments, shag rugs and plush recliners, stick-proof pans and yo-yoing hemlines. On the other hand, Mom and her sisters laughed a lot, hugged and touched habitually, could say sweet things—and *mean* them.

The Thrams girls had grown up in a colorblind home: Grandpa and Grandma dined in Hispanic homes in the late '40s when doing so wasn't the norm; Grandma frequented Doc Martin, the podiatrist whose wife was the first African-American nurse in Northcentral Iowa. My mother bunked with their daughter, Cynthia, at Methodist Camp, on the shores of Clear Lake, and after school would go to Ardith Millard's farm to play jazz piano with Cynthia's brother, Anthony. She once confided that he didn't always return sheet music, like her favorite, *Boogey Blues*. When I asked her why she didn't press him to do so, she replied "Well, he played it better than I did, anyway." She'd never admit it, but I suspected Mom had a crush on Anthony—as she once had on Marco, a Puerto Rican friend of her visiting North Carolina cousins, the three Pedelty boys.

The Luick kids, in contrast, came from a very different world. Unlike the land-owning Thramses, their parents were for decades tenant farmers who moved often. Unlike the Thrams family's, none of the Luicks' kin had studied beyond high school. When they were forced to find off-farm employment, they didn't pursue professions: Great-Grandpa George and his four brothers drove buses, drayed freight, graded gravel roads, pumped gas and the like. Perhaps it was their competing with other poorly-educated, unskilled workers for low-wage jobs that in the 1920s led George Michael Luick—my namesake, whom I knew and loved—to join the Iowa Ku Klux Klan. Rather than particularly anti-black, the three or so million "Second Wave" Klansmen and -women—at least in the Midwest—were rabidly anti-Catholic… but more on that later.

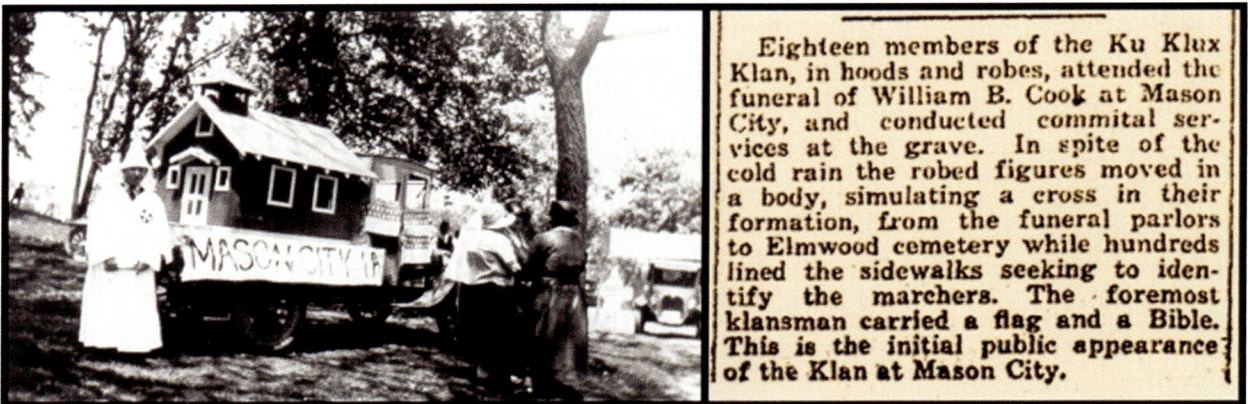

Eighteen members of the Ku Klux Klan, in hoods and robes, attended the funeral of William B. Cook at Mason City, and conducted commital services at the grave. In spite of the cold rain the robed figures moved in a body, simulating a cross in their formation, from the funeral parlors to Elmwood cemetery while hundreds lined the sidewalks seeking to identify the marchers. The foremost klansman carried a flag and a Bible. This is the initial public appearance of the Klan at Mason City.

Postville [Iowa] Herald *article of 10 April 1924 detailing Klan rally George Luick attended in Mason City: When I was a child, we watched on the news as inner cities went up in flames. Too young to understand the dynamics behind the riots, I was sensitive enough to perceive some underlying sentiments. That race played a role was clear; that we in the North held Southern whites to be backwards racists did not have to be verbalized: I absorbed my elders' prejudices wholly. What a shock, then, when some half-century later I discovered that in the 1920s the Midwest was home of hundreds of thousands of KKK members.*

How we perceive, how we treat and interact with those who seem different from us not only informs our worldviews but gives form to our daily lives. For those of us whose personhood formed in homogenous environments (I was twelve before I got to know an African-American or Hispanic person, 20 before I met a Jew), "The Other" embodied both mystery and dread. As a child I was curious, even fascinated by individuals who were anything other than white-skinned, Anglo-Saxon Protestant Midwesterners, yet I had absorbed from those around me fear of them.

Due to the schizophrenia I experienced for almost two decades, in me reside today two opposing impulses. One is to comfort, encourage, embrace—to love. The other is to scold, criticize, reject—to hate. These irreconcilable instincts, locked in a constant contest, arise from two inherited, opposing parental lineages. I neither created nor chose them; I only can counter or choose them anew, every day, in each moment. It's an exhausting task, but I have no choice if I prefer that the spirits of my better ancestors prevail over my lesser ones. I'll keep ya posted.

"Tell me who are your friends, and I'll tell you who you are."

— a Spanish proverb

By Second Nature

Primary relationships—those with parents, siblings, partners and perhaps the most intimate of friends—play primal roles in forming our basic personalities, then help determine not only the outcomes but lasting impact of our experiences for the rest of our lives. The number of primary relationships we enjoy—or endure—vary in each biography, yet typically are limited to a few.

Secondary relationships—those with almost everyone other than the above-cited—in contrast, can occur in infinite numbers and settings, yet they also influence the outcomes and impact of our experiences, as well as imprint our ever-evolving personalities. During my fast-paced and statewide campaign for the US Senate, they both fed and diminished my soul. A few examples:

I'd met Raul Nutting of Decorah early in my socio-political crusade—and liked him immediately. A starting wood-arts teacher in a high school across the border in Southeast Minnesota, in what little "spare" time he has outside the classroom, Raul chases the rare hobby of locating and dismantling, then rebuilding frontier log cabins. Sometimes with the help of young Amish men from Canton or Harmony, Minnesota, Raul has breathed new life into a dozen or more cabins.

On top of that, Raul serves on the board of Decorah's peculiar Porter House museum (featuring a quirky collection, housed in a fussy Italianate-towered mansion, tucked behind odd coral-reef-and-geode walls), along with Widge Tjome. Happy to have inherited a unique nickname (short for "Winifred"), as a young woman Widge lived in Norway for 22 years; today, she personifies a Norsk lady who speaks straitlaced English. Half of Widge's pioneer ancestors were among the first Norwegians to settle in Iowa's Little Switzerland in the early 1850s, yet her mother's people were Germans out on the open prairie—a heredity she rarely and barely acknowledges. Widge long proved, repeatedly, to be a loyal, patient, supportive friend—even if she also can be doggedly stubborn and at times her earlier training to be a prim Lutheran pastor's wife bleeds through. Still, between them, Raul and Widge came to serve as point people for my campaign.

Dunnings Spring Park and Vesterheim Norwegian-American Museum in Decorah: "Oneota" is Iowa's answer to Utopia—a rolling landscape marked by grazing dairy herds, thick woods and tidy villages, with a flourishing counterculture built around a vibrant food coop, too many funky cafés and fusion eateries to count, live music of various beats, community-action groups galore and even a Lutheran liberal-arts college that dares once and a while to be different from its ilk. It was this region's quirkiness that offered me a lifesaver when, as an awakening teen, Northcentral Iowa wasn't colorful or broadminded enough.

One night, Widge asked if I'd like to join her for dinner at the red-brick Greek Revival house Raul and his partner, Thom Lee, are restoring. "Sure" ever-lonely me replied gratefully. Over much red wine, I soon learned about Raul's family, which also had come to the area in the 1800s and is deeply rooted in the local community. During Raul's long and involved discourse, though, I noticed his partner—who I'd not met before that evening—watching me guardedly. Suddenly, he turned to me and said out of context "So, I heard you're running for the US Senate"—at which point I nodded affirmingly yet timidly—"as an independent." As that last word crawled its way over Thom's lips, he seemed to be on the verge of choking or perhaps even vomiting. Thankfully doing neither, he glared at me a piercing moment as he waited for an account of what I sensed he already had deemed to be my impertinent folly and unpardonable subversion.

a 1908 panorama of Decorah; Raul and Thom's house is below the hill in foreground on the right panel

70

Smelling the tense stink in the air, Raul switched from explaining his family's olden times to his partner's present projects, noting "Oh, by the way—Thom's active in the Winneshiek County Democrats," an affiliation which explained the wiry Oklahoman's cold stare and barebones comment. Having already come to adore driven-yet-delightful Raul, I hoped his politically-passionate partner might at least accept, if not celebrate, my deeply committed exercise in the democratic process. Wiry Thom, however, clearly was neither impressed nor moved, not even as I reported Bob Peigg's then-recent sabotage stunt, which I recounted in detail, sure that it would win some sympathy from skeptical Thom. But, his stoic response mirrored Willy Hawk's.

Today I consider Thom a friend, but during the entire summer of 2016 his partisan ties trumped any friendship we might have formed at that time. He now admits disillusion with the current Democratic Party, but then his protected allegiance to it blocked his seeing my project in a wider context. When I argued that the way to slay the two-party system is to sidestep its tight monopoly over American politics, he said he agreed with my goal, yet "It's more important right now to reinforce the Democrats' containment walls against the worst of Republican attacks."

And so, the madness continues…

That night as I sat in Raul and Thom's 170-some-year-old house, I felt the weight of our nation's calcified political structure. On one hand, many Americans complain about two parties' inability to represent the diverse backgrounds and to advance the complex needs of our country; on the other, with few exceptions we not only continue to shoehorn almost all contenders into two political corsets, but most of us vote solely for GOP- or Demo-endorsed candidates. After each election, some in our two-faced electorate grouse about the lack of truly alternative voices on the political field, yet hardly any citizens run on independent or third-party tickets—or cast ballots for same. Almost equally fatal to fostering partisan reform, within the two parties constant wrangling takes place—mostly behind closed doors—to support one set of candidates while sabotaging others. This blocks change, but both big parties' big wigs must like it that way.

Betrayal from Within: Type II

By the time I arrived in Iowa in March 2016 to launch my campaign, three male Democrats had long been hitting all corners of the Hawkeye State. They had meticulously, relentlessly worked the ground wherever they went. As I casually chatted-up Iowans I met during my campaigning, I heard various degrees of enthusiasm regarding all three. Still, it seemed most Iowa Democrats strongly favored one of the three; as a bloc, they had generated copious optimism that "Uncle Chuck" at long last could be chased into forced retirement. That is, until the DNC stepped in.

'Twas a great shock when the Democratic National Committee—faraway from Ioway, safely concealed in the partisan echo chamber that is "the District"—secretly sent scorched-earth letters to the men. In them, it pushed aside not only those three individuals' tireless efforts but their personal passions, and installed Patty Judge as the DNC's favored gal to face Grassley. The geniuses in DC apparently didn't care one dot that few ordinary folks in-state supported her; the lack of enthusiasm among Iowa Democrats was immediate and palpable. One example:

That political season, I attended a handful of Gay Pride events across Iowa, at which I rarely saw signs pushing Patty Judge. In fact, at the Iowa City gathering, the Johnson County Democratic Party's float conspicuously lacked (as far as I could see) a single Judge poster stapled to a trailer otherwise literally wallpapered with those of candidates for every other conceivable office, at all levels. In asking Hawkeyes about their political leanings, not a single person I encountered spoke favorably about Judge's candidacy; at best, I heard lukewarm acceptance that she was "our *only* choice if we want to unseat Chuck." Betraying Willy Hawk or Thom Lee's loyalties, such tepid "support" for her spoke volumes about how distant machineries of both mainstream parties again trumped not only local political passions, but the wisdom of party activists on the ground.

Sadly, the DNC's strongarm tactics in 2016's Iowa US-Senate race weren't an isolated incident:

That same year, Bernie Sander's shooting-star campaign put a spotlight on a central yet stifled fissure in the *façade* of our two-party political charade. Even as a non-Democrat in Iowa, I could clearly see the deep, increasingly bitter divide between the Sanders and Clinton camps within the Demos' rank and file. Bernie's and Hillary's respective followers embodied very different, hardly reconcilable worldviews—each with their particular social sensibilities, convictions and goals. As these competing factions vied for predominance, the non-democratic, behind-the-scene stunts of the Debbie Wasserman Schultzes at all strata of the "Democratic" Party became increasingly and undeniably apparent. And, they confirmed my unbending critique of the two "syndicates" I sought to overturn—which I repeatedly stated publicly, as in this opinion piece:

PRESS RELEASE for immediate release:
Date: April 19th, 2016
www.HeartlandParties.US

Letter to the Editor/Op-Ed Piece: What's Wrong with Patty Judge
Independent Candidate Michael Luick-Thrams critiques the Would-be Senator

Des Moines, IA — This weekend a Des Moines TV station ran a featurette about Patty Judge's come-lately campaign to be the Democratic nominee to run against GOP stalwart, Senator Grassley. As I watched it, it reminded me of the driving reasons I'm running as in Independent. First, I don't like being snowed by unsubstantiated claims—"spin". Having gotten in the past two weeks a third of the 1,500 signatures I need to run myself for the US Senate from Iowa, I'm perplexed by Judge's claim that support for her run has been "overwhelming." Not only have I heard—with one notable exception—blatantly negative or at least lukewarm response from Iowans about the specter of her running in November, I also have heard rank-and-file of the Iowa Democratic Party pointedly support Bob Peigg's or Tom Fiegen's runs over hers.

Second, I don't like what it says that despite Peigg's, Fiegen's and Bob Krause's months' of preparations to run for the US Senate, the moment Patty utters the slightest interest to run, the DC Democratic Party machinery and part of the Iowa Democratic one begins to salivate and float into a state of euphoria. Not only is such support for the 72-year-old unfair, even disrespectful to the dedicated preparation of the other three, but it betrays how undemocratic the "Democratic" echelon has become. Don't be surprised, folks, if the Democratic bigwigs in DC ram Patty's nomination to the fore at the expense of her hardworking competition.

Third, I don't like Judge's indelible loyalties. Long an ally of Big Business (think Monsanto), Judge has repeatedly flouted the interest of the elderly on behalf of the state's nursing-home moguls. She has sided with the Farm Bureau so often—and with the rising yet fragile organic-agriculture movement so seldom. Recently, she joined forces with those who would block Polk County's efforts to advance the issue—if symbolically—of ultimate responsibility for Iowa's increasingly contaminated water sources. Patty Judge embodies the Good-Ol'-Boys clique, but in a skirt.

Fourth, the issues Judge cites as her most urgent reflect the failure of liberalism, not just conservatism in this country. While conservatives generally wish to conserve the existing social order, liberals would toy with reforming but never replacing it. That's a pity, for at present America faces a systemic failure in most areas of public life: Which sub-system of contemporary America would you patent and peddle abroad if you could—our "justice" or penal system? Our rigged economic model; our healthcare system, perhaps—or senior-care system? The systems we use to supply the nation with and distribute fuel, food or other essential resources? Our educational system? How could we herald any of those? I wouldn't.

As a member of the oldest surviving political party in the world (the Democratic founded 1828—the Republican sixteen years its junior), Patty embodies The Establishment. She claims to be "Progressive," yet that label looks very different than siding, repeatedly and with such loyalty, to the elite that ramrods special interests over those of the non-elite. Iowa deserves better.

#

Because Iowa Democrats never "owned" Patty Judge's puppet candidacy, they never truly got behind it. For the zillioneth time *ad nauseum*, party elites in DC crafted another local defeat. In this way, a mummified system continues to deny Americans a vital, diverse political culture. Doing so doesn't serve the people, but it perfectly suits the elites who sustain—and bankroll—the very scheme that for over two centuries has protected the interests of an invisible few.

*

"The Best Democracy Money Can Buy"

— Greg Palast's title for a book and later film

Passing the Plate

Shortly after Thom had castigated me for "helping to re-elect Grassley," a friend from my ISU days invited me to attend a Democratic-Party fundraiser in Des Moines. It took place in an upscale sports bar in the first-tier suburb, not far from John's sleek mid-century, perched majestically above a wooded stream. The moment we walked into the crowded joint one summer afternoon, at the end of a workday, I could smell the money: Older women with carefully coiffed hairdos had donned their finest seasonal attire, accentuated with many clinking, blinking gold and silver clunkers. Their male peers boasted posh golf-club fashion, draping down from their padded paunches to the top of their luxurious loafers. The younger set sported trendy, costly garb—and all held pricey drinks in their manicured hands; some slammed their way through serial shots.

Excitement hung in the air like sparks from shorting wires. I could barely hear John ask me what I wanted to imbibe, let alone his answer to my question "So, like, what's everyone waiting for?" Before I could ask him to repeat the name of the guest speaker, perfectly-tailored, tanned and trim Martin O'Malley appeared at the far end of the packed room. A sudden and complete hush descended upon what had been a raucous audience as Maryland's former governor began to tout the virtues of the Democratic Party's previous First Lady. Apparently having forgiven the acerbic words she'd uttered before she secured the party's primary's nomination for president, the eloquent, also-ran O'Malley gushed with praise for Hillary Clinton. Then, having whipped up his well-lubricated listeners, the exquisitely-coached man buttonholed them into opening their pockets or purses and dropping a few shekels into the Des Moines Democratic chapter's coffers.[41]

O'Malley spoke only a few minutes before rushing off to another fundraiser—a steeply-priced dinner in nearby Ankeny, I heard. The festive atmosphere he swiftly exited, however, seemed to suffer little from his sudden absence. By now quite tipsy, those present showed no visible qualms in shucking out dough; checkbooks flew open and credit cards coursed about the room as eager

Martin O'Malley's family en route *to his inauguration in January 2011; inset: the governor, 2014*

party reps passed through it several times to harvest a windfall of willing cash. Always keen to vacuum up edifying impressions and useful information, I eavesdropped on those nearest to me long enough to confirm what I expected: Des Moines' most monied were all around—and they hesitated not one millisecond before donating heavily to those oh-too-keen to do their bidding.

As I recall that sloshing sea of ritzy cocktails being sipped by cool cats wearing high-priced haircuts, three years have passed and the likes of those present in that flush crowd of influence buyers currently are represented by another "Uncle Chuck" (US Senator Charles Schumer) and his equally meek co-chair, Aunt Nancy Pelosi. Given my political passions, I can only wag my head when I meditate too long on the lack of opposition coming from America's "opposition." But, what oppositional alternatives for our country's future can we expect from agents of a separate-but-similar set of big-party politicos? An "opposition" has to offer a differing vision, an alternative model from that of a ruling party in order to muster genuine opposition: The career-minded Debbie-Wasserman-Schultz ilk of "liberal" Democrats, however, hardly intend to do more than tweak a status quo that caters to the nation's thin percentile that owns most wealth.

*

"Where there is no vision, the people perish…"

— Proverbs 29:18, the Old Testament of the *Bible*[42]

Passing Out Band-Aids

For the rest of my life, I will be deeply grateful to Barack Hussein Obama for having forever shattered the color line at the White House. Our nation will *never* be the same: "Thank <u>you</u>!"

Barack and Michelle Obama with daughters Sasha (l.) and Malia in the White House's Green Room, 2009

At the same time, let us not be blinded by the lure of our own dreams of a better land to the fuller truth about the Obama administration, nor victims to our hunger for happier narratives. Truth is, the man was created, groomed and zoomed into the public eye by the same hidden kingmakers who yield the baton that directs the likes of Debbie Wasserman Schultz. From his stellar speech at the 2004 Democratic National Convention to his spectacular sweep into the presidency in 2008, this talented, inspiring, persuasive man pursued a calculated-for-success playbook. Still, he didn't reach those improbable goal posts by himself, nor did he hold bake sales to fund the journey: He owed if not literal millions then tangible favors to whomever those wealthy wizards were who stood behind the curtain, pulling levers and blowing whistles.

Catapulted from being a nobody-knows-me South Chicago community activist to an everybody-loves-me Nobel prize laureate in no time, he promised us "Change we [could] believe in." Right out the gate, however, he failed to fire even one of the major banksters who caused the 2008 economic collapse which marred the lives of tens of millions of Americans, for years. Similarly, one of his first acts was to turn a blind Department of Justice eye to his predecessor's war grimes. Instead of having Attorney General Eric Holder prosecute war criminals such as sinister Dick Cheney, disturbed Donald Rumsfeld or lying Colin Powell [there never was any "yellow cake" uranium, the sham rationale for war he presented in United Nations testimony], Obama perpetuated the moral outrage (and fiscal blackhole) that is Guantanamo Bay. Were that not damning enough, he ordered more drone assassinations of terrorist "suspects" than did killer George W. Bush, whose having been a dim-witted, willing puppet of Cheney's intrigues was no excuse for not being accountable for having signed off on premeditated war crimes. And, Obama let his appointees harass, arrest and deport more Latin immigrants than any of his predecessors.

Although he reigned over two Democrat-controlled chambers in Congress for the first half of his first term, Barack Obama proved to be a smooth-talkin' underachiever: He could have passed almost any legislation his whims might then have fancied—sensible, fair healthcare among the most pressing. (Hadn't Hillary Clinton already created—at least on paper—a template during husband Bill's administration?) He left G. W.'s No Child Left Behind model of education intact, despite its gutting our children's intellectual capacities generally, and despite reports showing it did little to bring more students to grade level proficiency.[43] Worst of all, he repeatedly reassured us that he "Had [our] backs"… but he did *not*. (In America almost no one has anyone else's back: It's a dog-eat-dog system—and always was so. It will remain that way until we change it.)

Why *did* Obama usher in so little lasting change, relative to what both he promised and we, his supporters, expected? Well, what did I say about "opposition" having to offer a differing vision, an alternative model in order to deserve its name? In the end, Obama's cheap refrain of change proved as hollow as many of his grand gestures because, truth be told, like too many "liberals" he did not truly wish to jettison the status quo; he sought/they seek only to slap a fresh coat of paint on the rusting, cracked frame of our broken system: Where the removal of malignant rot is called for, from "liberals" the sick and dying can expect, at most, a big Band-Aid to cover it up.

That is not to say that there aren't sincere liberals—but do you recall my General Political-Rainbow Graph? There *are* "radical liberals" but they tend to belong to the hardcore *laisser-faire* class—hobbyist economists who eat, breath and shit the stuff. The lesser kind, the more superficial sort, frequent chic sports bars in well-heeled Midwest suburbs, looking for a favor to buy from politicians desperate to raise a few slick grand. If elected, cads among them shift their stances on key issues based on expediency or cynical deals. Whereas "radical liberals" will have studied and thought deeply about lofty constructs like free trade and uncensored media, their "superficial" cousins are there for the Bloody Marys and flirty gossip with bleach-bottle blonds.

The ugliest, most wicked sin committed by "liberal" Democrats [and "liberal" Republicans?] is that their shallow politicking gives sincere, caring individuals like Thom the illusion of a chance for change where no real, deep-reaching change can be realistically expected. Intelligent and articulate, the Thoms [and Thomasinas] among us volunteer endless hours and their most fiery energies on behalf of fake messiahs who, in the end, will have had a good run, shot sexy selfies and left behind citations in the yellowing annals of history. Then, there are the Widges of the world—traveled, savvy global citizens who know what it's like *not* to be an American and that there are other, more effective ways to organize a society; yet, they, too, land in our two-party madhouse and soon resign themselves to going through the motions of cheering on line-towing partisans even as they long for an alternative. Both Thom and Widge (the latter likely sucked into it by her would-be suitor, the "liberal" elderly widower, Floyd) dabble in Democratic Party politics, even as each secretly yearns for something else, something better. The Democrats as a species, then, hold out eternal hope to working, to minority, to non-wealth-holding Americans that someday, some way things might change—but they *never* will... at least not enough... not fast enough, not long enough so long as we all keep dancing to the tune of the current system.

The present state of things is unbearably cruel and *must* change. But how? I've tried for years, yearning for quick, easy recipes—yet I know only this: Our existing system can't give us what we need in the world we have today. That being the case, don't we *need*, then, to change systems? How do we build new shared ways of living, however, when we are so divided as we are now?

*

"Love is patient and kind. Love is not jealous or boastful or proud or rude.
It does not demand its own way. It is not irritable,
and it keeps no record of being wronged.
It does not rejoice about injustice but rejoices whenever the truth wins out.
Love never gives up, never loses faith, is always hopeful,
and endures through every circumstance."

— 1st Corinthians 13:4, the New Testament of the *Bible*

The Great Divide

My family and I have always "moved through the city" differently. It's unavoidable, because we're so different—or at least we seem to be on the surface, although we share not only genes but also formative experiences, underlying temperaments and even still today some shared values.

Oddly, despite having in theory grown up near each other (Linus was four years old when I was born, Lucy seven), I have few conscious memories of Linus before he reached adolescence. In my mind, I can recall mostly images of him as a teenager—and most of those as an older high schooler. Lucy stands out more clearly in my memory—typically in scenes of her scolding me.

As a child, I didn't have close ties with either of them. For me, they were "there" but *not* there. Linus was outdoors serving as my father's default farmhand during almost every waking hour that he wasn't at school. For her part, Lucy got serial off-farm jobs as soon as she could drive: as a bank teller, as a waitress at Mason City airport's restaurant, or cleaning house for "Old Furleighs," grandparents of my chum Dwight, who lived on a farm a few miles away. And, as Dad sensed something different about me early on, he was happy to have me in the house, playing on my own or, as I got older, helping Mom—but, most of all, *not* being "in the way."

This paternally-imposed house arrest suited me fine: While downstairs Mom busied herself with baking or canning, cleaning or sewing, or… I had a swell time reading (Laura Ingalls Wilder was my favorite author and main hero) or play-acting (if not as Laura, then as Timmy of *Lassie* fame), building Western towns and German castles with prefab sets Santa showered upon me, or dressing up in old clothes (of either gender), listening to Disney movie-music LPs, drawing, etc. For the first decade of my life left mostly alone, save for being the charge of one of three women, the world of ideas not only took on fantastic dimensions, it was the only realm allowed me.[44]

Still, if I got bored I had two options. I could badger Mom until she spirited me off to one of two libraries we frequented, where I devoured books primarily with historical American themes: the lives of Washington, Franklin, Lincoln—but also of Harriet Tubman, George Washington Carver, Sequoyah. Or, I could wander over to Grandma Thrams' cottage, where she would scoop me to her huge, calico-dressed lap and tell stories of "our people" coming down the Ohio on flatboats, crossing the Mississippi on the first train to do so (in 1856, for free!), then creeping out onto the prairie in covered wagons.[45] As she rocked with me for hours, I trailed after her into history, rapt. For the child I was, there was no past, just an earlier present, still all around and visible to me.

Meanwhile, in sobering and resentment-sowing contrast:

At eighteen, Lucy married Gerry, a mechanic. Although we'd never truly bonded before she left her parental home, she continued to boss me around every chance she got, which she seemed to relish. As newlyweds, Gerry and she lived first in a cute-but-tiny chauffer's apartment above a garage behind a posh house on Clear Lake, later in three different homes in Charles City after lucky Gerry landed a job "on the line" in what was then Oliver Tractor Company. As my parents were eager to help the young couple get established, we often called on the Wassons, who around that time were "finding God" as they underwent what they called "being born again."

By this time, although just becoming a teenager, I was forming my own religious sentiments. A pious Methodist bent on becoming a pastor, like my parents I found Lucy's intense zealotry and increasingly doctrinaire stances alarming and alienating. The "relationship" between us that arose after that was an uneasy one: It was about then when she informed me that I had "better stop spendin' time with Cong," the young Laotian refugee who I'd taken on as a project. As Lucy's world was becoming increasingly divided between "born-agains" and everyone else, I objected to her chastising me for who I chose as friends. Later, I felt infuriated when she—and later Linus— told me my parents weren't "true Christians" because they were not born-again. That offended the Methodist I was then; it still sickens and outrages the Quaker I became soon thereafter. And, our relationship never recovered; it only worsened as we grew further apart.

Meanwhile, Linus and I only had a one-on-one relationship after he had earned an undergrad degree in environmental engineering at Iowa State and I—freshly returned from a life-changing year at Ermysted's Grammar School in North Yorkshire—had just began liberal-arts studies in Ames. For some reason, Linus—then working for a large engineering firm in faraway Brainerd, Minnesota—stopped by his alma mater one day. That night, he visited me at the Mennonite Student Center, where as a new Quaker I felt much at home. As we sat in my quiet, candlelit room, I felt like I was meeting him for the first time—as a person in each our own rights.

As rector Peter Toller's will of 1492 confirms that he already had founded a school in his chantry of St Nicholas, the parish church, Ermysted's marks that year as its founding date. Lawyer Sylvester (shown before †1719) and brother William Petyt bequeathed the school generously, with the former endowing it with £30,000—then a fortune. Ermysted's "boys" belong to one of four "Houses:" I belonged to Petyt— and so accordingly wore its tie. The National Portrait Gallery's painting is from 1710, an oil portrait on canvas by Richard van Bleeck; Thomas Wales' photo shows the Main School as it appeared in 2006.

One of the few topics where we connected that night—to a point—was the environment. In August of the previous school year, 1981, my geography instructor at Ermysted's—Ian Douglas, a thick-thighed rugby player from Cornwall, with a stout accent that reflected his being both a "rugger" and Cornish—had presented a unit about global warming. The unfamiliar "greenhouse effect" he chillingly diagramed on the chalkboard—as he shook his head and pounded his pointer into his free palm—left me in a panic. As I relayed Master Douglas' teachings to Linus, I warned him of subsequent droughts and floods, increases in forest fires and avalanches, more frequent and intense tornadoes and hurricanes, resultant species' extinction, etc. He, in turn, shrugged dismissively and let the issue die, after noting that President Reagan had appointed a commission to "explore the matter"—a sure way to relegate any issue to obscurity in no time. I cautioned him to take the threat seriously, but he would hear none of it. So, I dropped it.

What Linus and I *could* discuss was pollution and soil erosion—the latter the focus of a speech contest I had won in high school that first sensitized me to environmental matters and led me to read Rachel Carson's groundbreaking expose on the dangers of farm chemicals, *Silent Spring*. My guest nodded his head in acknowledging the problems we reviewed per duo and a need to address them—but then, in his last statement about the matter, he cited Ronald Reagan's fundamentalist Secretary of Interior James Watt, who reasoned—in effect—that we may "use up

81

this world" because Jesus would return soon and herald a new one. I had a massive problem with Linus' seeming to have no problem with the Secretary's stance, which left me confounded. *Doesn't being an environmental engineer* I thought to myself, *demand that one takes care of it?* It seemed that Linus' overriding rationale for nature conservation was to secure enough game for his annual pheasant, turkey, deer and other fishing or hunting sprees. Anything else was a "bonus," a good deed done as time might allow, in the course of taking "dominion over the fish of the sea, and over the fowl of the air, and over every living thing that moves upon the Earth."[46]

When Linus left the MSC later that night, I felt disappointed that he was willing to see humans' damage to the planet only so far, then quickly veer away from agreeing on measures to counter it. Less emotive in his approach to worldly matters than Lucy's, Linus did try to break apart issues into what he sensed were their logical components. Still, his mind—or rather, his ideological auto-pilot—applied a stubborn brake to his reaching conclusions warranting change.

Of course, we are all evolving—we *have* to: In lab dishes, those cultures which don't grow, die. At the same time, over the intervening thirty-five years, I have witnessed little to suggest that my older relative's ability or willingness to separate his religious worldview from his real-world interactions regarding our worn and weary planet has grown. It was during the summer of my 2016 campaign, for example, that his (to my mind) equally religiously-blinded wife, Cherry, and he drove from Minnesota to Alaska and back—a journey long on Linus' wish-list of experiences.

Committed to carrying on with my campaign to reform the world through attacking the systems that I see as diminishing it, I could not accompany them yet offered to carry their bags if they would take me along. Linus smiled as he declined my jesting offer, but he did promise to tell me about their trip when they returned. After they did, I felt as disappointed with their take-aways as I had with Linus' resistance to taking global warming seriously the first time we discussed it.

As Cherry pushed another forkful of pie into her mouth, she reported on their trek onto a retreating glacier. With the rest of us sitting around Lucy's packed breakfast-nook table, she recounted how a guide they met purported that "glaciers melt anyway—they *always* have."

"Yeah, it's nothing new" Linus chimed in. "Al Gore's fulla hooey if he sees a climate catastrophe behind every shrinkin' patcha ice. The Earth goes through phases" he noted casually, "with warming and cooling periods. We just happen to be in a warming one." As my fingernails dug into my thighs, I said nothing as Linus and his wife set off their intellectual ammo as they shot down any arguments—mine or others'—why we should be alarmed and take mitigating action now, before doing so is too late. With nasty images of James Gaius Watt dancing in my exploding head, as they spoke I worried for their two daughters and *their* offspring to come.

Temperature Change in the Last 50 Years

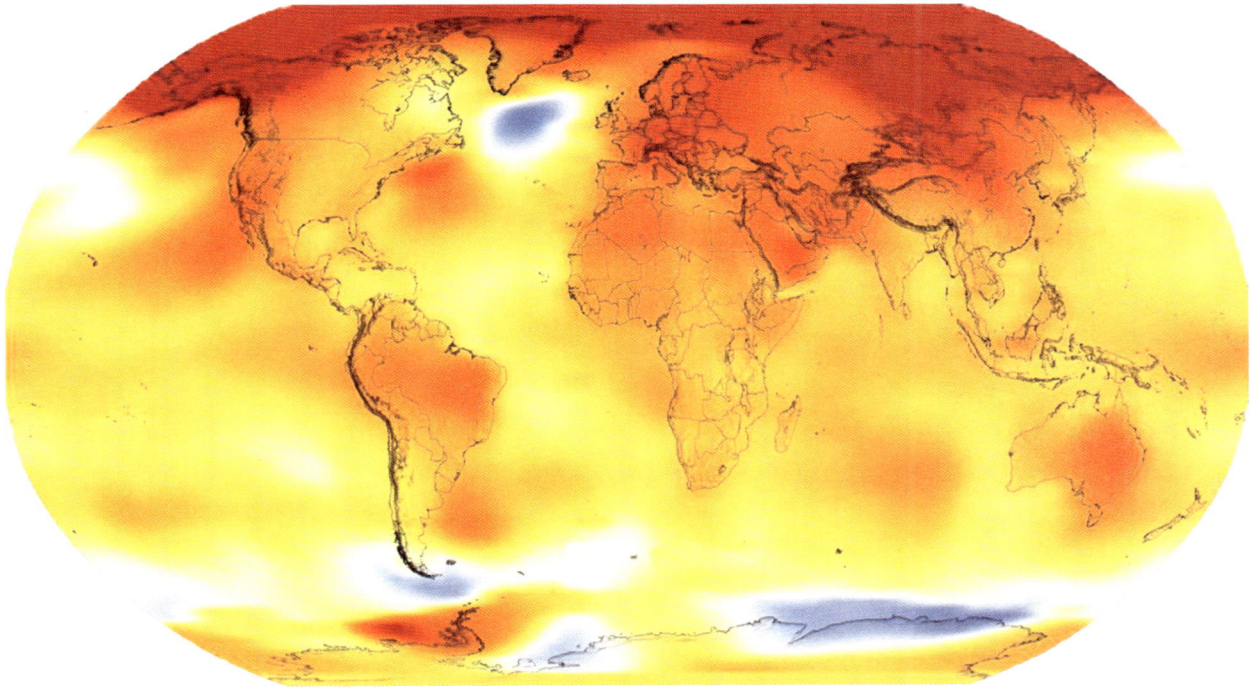

2014-2018 average vs 1951-1980 baseline

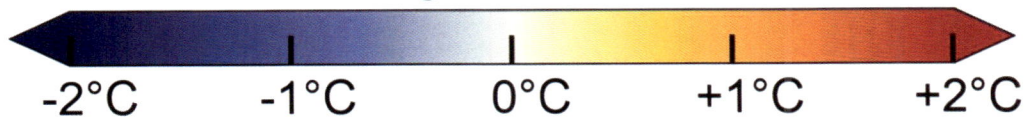

-2°C   -1°C   0°C   +1°C   +2°C

average global temperatures from 2014 to 2018, compared to a baseline average from 1951 to 1980, according to NASA's Goddard Institute for Space Studies: Temperature anomalies to date have been primarily in northern latitudes and over land masses; this map is not accurate in parts of this image.

It was one thing for Linus and his wife to smugly dismiss anything I might say about any topic—I was used to that, for decades already—but their readiness to intellectually swat aside any validity in what experts or scholars might have to say about something as complex and essential as human-driven climatic changes floored me. Worse, their need to demonize the Al Gores or (in Lucy's case) Barack Obamas of the world contradicted all that I had internalized at Sunday school about how to dance with others—not to mention their missing awareness that in any moral universe, do puny humans really have a "right" to harm, let alone destroy, Creation?

*

Our Linus, the Worker Bee

The longer I campaigned in my native Iowa for the US Senate, the more I soberly realized that I was appealing to clones of my own kin. By my math, from 1/3rd to 2/3^{rds} of the state's electorate consists of, basically, dutiful Linus—in that *his* beliefs and attitudes, *not* mine, were their norm. What characterizes their "normal"? Hard work, sustained by the assumption that through it life will get better as opportunities present themselves, "earned" by decency and loyalty to tribe. Once, during a heated conversation, Linus summarized his *raison d'être*: "I work—that's what I do; that's why I'm here." Problem was, in my campaign, I appealed to men—and women—like Linus (and Lucy) to shift focus, to see wider contexts and to initiate change: There, I lost them.

To understand my view of the archetype Linus represents, we have to go back in time:

Already in my day, Omega House boasted solar panels in the garden, which I could see from my bedroom window over the dining room, with its fancy leaded-window alcove. Only as I studied this group photo, years later, in November 2019, did I realize that the few Minnesotans in the photo were the two children and two young women (Chicky from Duluth, Laura from Faribault, r.). Otherwise, we were "foreigners" for our Minneapple neighbors: Gerry (standing left) came from Kentucky; Roy, Colorado; Gordon (seated) from Chicago; Danny from Arkansas, and moi, from Iowa. Danny's wife, photographer Eileen, came from Baltimore. Not pictured: Darlene (Manitoba), Drake (Chicago), Gina (San Francisco) or Linda (New York).

From 1986 to 1990, I lived at Omega House, a still-extant intentional inner-city commune in Minneapolis. Already then a 20-year-old project, up to nine of us urban pioneers shared a home in a massive Victorian beauty straight out of *Mary Tyler Moore*, space created, per its founders, so that "people can learn to live well together." It was the '80s, in an ascending "Mineapple," in the "Land of 10,000 Recovery Centers"—a perfect era and place for me to confront a score of personal issues, not to mention socio-cultural ones. In several of the settings I frequented (Al-Anon, individual therapy, men's groups, gay-Quaker retreats, anti-war chapters, a YMCA death-and-dying course, a Zen-Buddhist temple, the Little Earth Native-American community center and Sister Rose's Peace Center), identifying, then dissecting "family systems" served both as a core concept and a common exercise. As it made convincing sense to me that to change society one first had to confront one's family and thereby one's deeper self, I eagerly got to work. As analyzing one's family necessarily included examining one's closest kin they got thrown into it all.

In my family's case, several "systems" determined the people we had become. A primary one was how our parents interacted with each other, as well as with their shared social environment. In turn, driven by dynamics between them and influences from outside the mini-culture they had established after they left their parental homes, they treated us children in ways that mirrored all that had come before us. Then, on top of the family system from which we emerged, we participated in a nearly all-white social system that fostered its own particular set of duties, rules and rewards. To understand myself, then, I had to see that Self in relation to my generation, our parents... their parents and siblings... to the community in which we learned how to be socio-political beings. Despite being isolated, that community was in a state, that in turn was part of a nation, which interacted—and at times clashed—with other nations... which led to where we all are now, in a world intimately wired at its farthest reaches yet lonely at its core.

But, back to my family—who are stand-ins for you + your family, neighbors, lovers, boss, etc.:

Even as a boy it seemed to me that our little "Lucy" was a Doppelgänger of the "Little Debbie" of the cupcakes, brownies and Nutty Buddy fame. Gary Cooper's "Thornhill"—here stopping a truck while being attacked by a Great Plains crop duster in North by Northwest—*mirrored our region's underlying* Angst.

Lucy once quipped that had she not married straight out of high school, she might have studied psychology: What does that say about her? Her inner life continues to mystify me. I do not understand well how she ticks or why, as we see the world so markedly differently. Linus, in contrast—a typical "middle child" of one renown model—is an easier riddle to unravel. To fully grasp the "Linuses" of the American Heartland, however, we have to go back even further:

In the Iowa in which my relatives and I grew up, 99.99% of the Hawkeye State's three-million people were as lily-white as we were. In those pre-interstate-highway days, it would have taken 2-3 days to drive to the East Coast, 3-4 to the West. With its thirty or so thousand inhabitants, Mason City was the largest "city" between Des Moines and Minneapolis-St. Paul, a 3-4 hour drive to either, going south or north. Going east or west, the next true cities were Chicago (8-10 hours) and Denver (13-15). Between those four points, proportionally there was scarcely a black or brown, an Asian or Jewish person to be found; Native Americans lived almost wholly on reservations (i.e., in the Dakotas) or the tiny, self-owned Meskwaki settlement near Tama, Iowa.

Everyone we saw was white: *all* of our classmates [in my case, until the 5th grade] and friends, *every* congregant of First Methodist Church [at the time, Clear Lake's largest religious body], the *entire* membership of Lucy's Lake Ambitious Vestae[47] as well as Linus' and my Lake Ambitious Feeders [our respective, gender-segregated 4-H clubs, of which my mother had been a member and at one point both my parents had been leaders]... *every* person populating our daily world. We knew no one who wasn't visibly like us; except for occasionally on our fuzzy, black-and-white television screen, we could go days without seeing a black, brown, "red" or Asian face. In such a world, it was easy to believe that everyone on the planet was, well, like us—and Lil' Mike did.

Where my qualifying to be a member of the White-Anglo-Saxon-Protestant world ended, however, was at the line of gender politics—an invisible barrier I neither saw nor understood until after I left Ashlawn Farm in 1981 to study in England, then in Ames came out as a gay man in 1982. At that point, my clan and I separated ways—better said, our fates forever diverged.

Ashlawn Farm in the 1950s: In January 1963, my mother's parents moved into the hired hand's cottage (center right) and my parents took over the 1925 bungalow, cooled in summer by towering ash trees. My grandfather had built it, just as his father had built the barn: Our homeplace was my people's handwork. Note the 4-6 different crops being grown in just those few fields shown: Today, that same land is planted solely to either corn or soybeans; sadly, no domesticated animals enrich it with their symbiotic presence.

As a kid growing up in such a singularly insular cocoon, I was utterly naïve. It was only upon my being honest about whom I innately felt led to love, that I (to be truthful, unwillingly) forfeited the place my acculturation had prepared me to take, next to my equally WASP peers—there being no room for what a Bryan-Bryan someday would call "queer" in the realm of America's privileged white designees. Oddly only seeing it today—*after* my family's recently disowning me—do I now know how Iowa's pre-"1968 revolution"[48] social strata stacked up, top to bottom:

1. white Protestant men
2. white Catholic men
3. white Protestant women
4. white Catholic women
5. Arab Christian men
6. Arab Christian women
7. brown [i.e., Latin-American]/"red" [Native-American] Christian men
8. brown/"red" Christian women
9. "yellow" Christian Asian men
10. "yellow" Christian Asian women

11. Arab Muslim men
12. Arab Muslim women
13. Jewish men
14. Jewish women
15. "yellow" non-Christian Asian men
16. "yellow" non-Christian Asian women
17. black Christian men
18. black Muslim men
19. black Christian women
20. black Muslim women

[All the of above were presumed to have been heterosexuals, followed in terms of status and power by:]

21. known or suspected white [or even "honorary-white" Arab/Jewish] gay men of any social background

[Had they not been invisible to the above, white/Arab/Jewish lesbians' "place" might have been here.]

22. known or suspected brown/"red"/"yellow" Asian or black gay men

[Non-white lesbians might as well have not existed, for in the eyes of all of the above, they did not—as neither did bi-sexual, non-binary-gendered nor transgendering persons.][49]

The color coding assigned to a person solely by the happenstance of the skin into which they were born (and, yes, we truly *did* speak in those days—as we sent our boys to wage an ugly, senseless war in the distant jungles of Vietnam—in terms of "the yellow man") dictated to the greatest degree one's standing in the local community. And, it determined in the largest part one's chances of achievement (read: "power"). While some African Americans enduring that racist, sexist era might have chosen to straighten their hair through chemicals or hot irons, or to lighten their skin through bleaches or powders, the rest of us mostly simply accepted our fate. It was neither fair nor humane, but it was real and the pervasive birthmark of the times.

And, sexual minorities? We existed but, for the most part, self-hid. Despite that blanket, shame-driven invisibility, however, each of us knew—consciously or subconsciously—that "those sick people" were dirty, dangerous and despicable. Why would one of them ever admit their tragic flaw and their (*ah*, <u>our</u>) innate "sinfulness"? To do so would result in social if not literal death.

Happily for him, Linus was born neither dark-skinned nor non-heterosexual. I doubt he has ever meditated at length on his good fortune—an unearned bit of luck that I did not inherit, regarding the latter classification. As far as I know, as an adult Linus never had to invest energy in practicing being anything other than a WASP worker bee. The flow of his first four decades of life reflected his being globally privileged at the time of his birth, even if the decades that followed did not.

*

Laura Goes Global

During my campaign for the US Senate, I had to continually think about typical Iowa voters and our motivations—and what had influenced us. I knew that as long as one agreed to adhere to the system into which we non-minority Baby Boomers were born (doing so was almost always subconscious and reflexive), growing up in the "white America" of that era and place (the pre-1968 rural Midwest) was, to quote an apt phrase of the time, "fun and profitable." So pervasive were the dominant racial structures and accompanying social codes, it was possible for intelligent, well-intended individuals to grow up (put frankly) coddled and clueless. This was possible in large part because our personhood formed in an environment where few "Others" were present to challenge our worldview—rarely in-person and seldom on television, radio or elsewise. So homogenous was the cultural and mind-bogglingly vast the geographical landscape in which we grew up, ours was a world of its own. We never thought about walling it in; who would have ever challenged it? In that setting, we became as uniform as our endless fields.

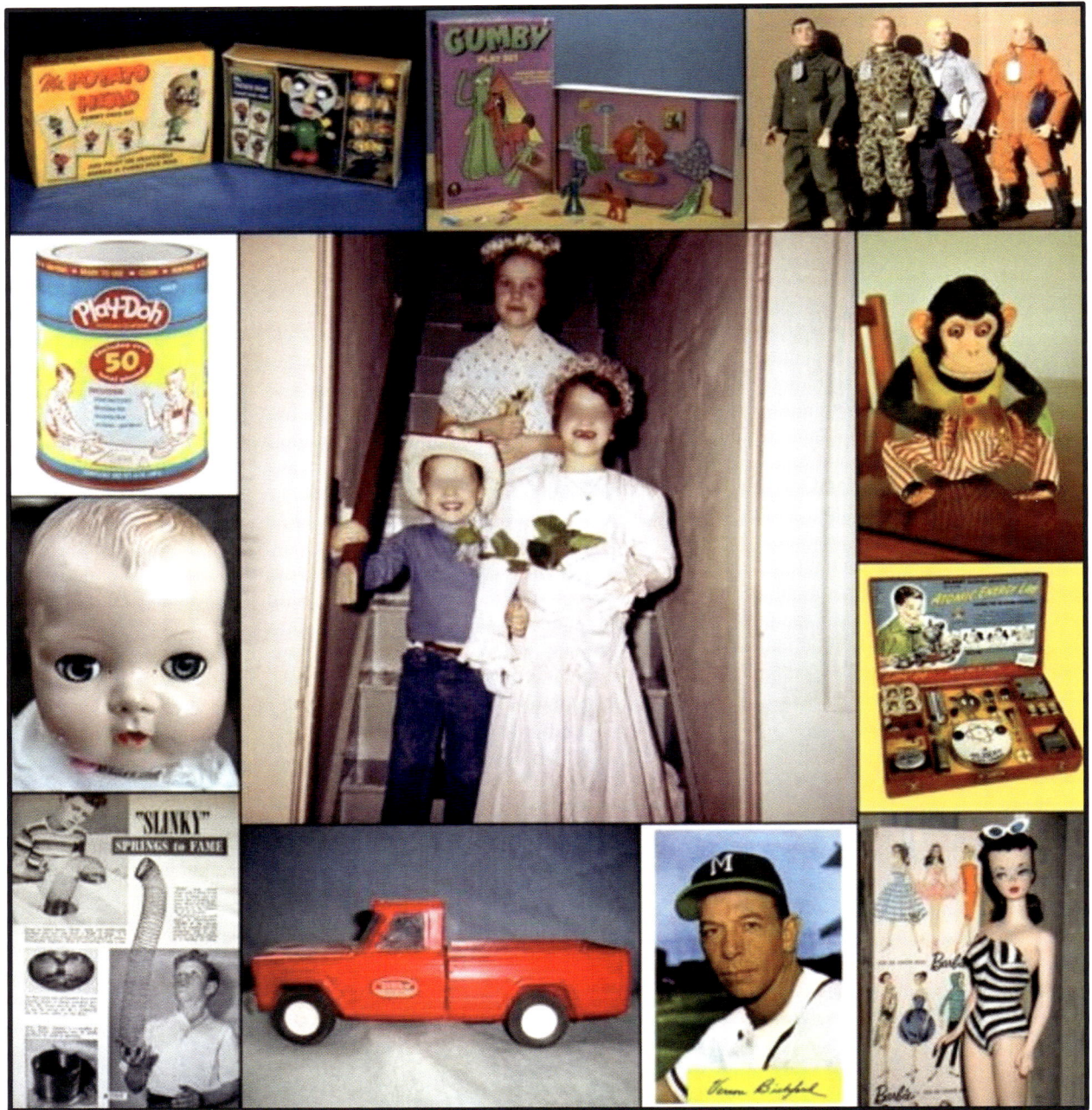

Baby-Boom cousins (Barbara Jones, top) playing dress-up, summer 1962, surrounded by toys of the era: The toys that we longed to get or our parents colluded to bestow us both spoke volumes about the times and conditioned us to internalize them. With what and how we played in our formative years ingrained what we saw as "normal" regarding gender roles, competition, [armed] conflict, "progress" and beauty.

Luckily for me, I had a renegade genetic trait—or however being homoerotically-orientated originates. Not only did I possess an innate differentness from almost everyone around me, my post-high-school biography ripped me from my roots and transplanted me in fertile foreign soil.

Remember Ian Douglas from my Ermysted's Grammar School days? Well, he was not only one of the first to deflower my political innocence with his point-of-no-return teaching about what the greenhouse effect and ensuing global warming would inescapably mean for humanity, not to mention the planet itself. In the first week of class, he also referred to Iowa in his geography lesson! Why? It seems a standard British geography textbook of the time featured Iowa as a singular example of "the most evenly distributed population density, racial homogeneity, literacy and a high-ranking rate of middle-class economic well-being in the world." Who knew? I guess, if I hadn't been mostly sleepwalking through Life up to that point, I might have. Instead, I grew up thinking my "world" was the "norm" for the entire planet; anyone who deviated from it was, well, "ab-normal" and not "what God wanted." I had somehow been lucky enough to be born as the Creator intended—a member of The Chosen: Even across the globe, "everyone" recognized it! Especially after World War II, when "we" "saved" peoples across the planet from the horrors of fascism and Japanese imperialism (my maternal uncles, Jack and Thurman, had, respectively, slugged their way across the Remagen bridge into Nazi Germany and sailed the Pacific in search of dogfights with "the Nips"), we Midwestern whites felt, truly, "on top" of the world order.

Imagine how thunderstruck I felt, then, having just arrived from the region that "Sir" was using to illustrate the demographic legacy of equitable land distribution (Thomas Jefferson's system of quarter-section farms, within townships and in turn counties, each unit meant to foster a new, democratic culture)[50] and the leveling effect it had on socio-economics. We who grew to adulthood amidst those physical demarcations crossbred with a post-WWII boom knew a general prosperity and personal public safety unknown before or since then. And, the coincidence of our ethnic origins (Northern European whites) gave the whole experience a distorting touch of cultural "predeterminism" which we enjoyed living out, even as we totally disregarded the true, deeper and wider costs of such a relatively carefree existence. We did not reflect—well, if at all, not long—on who or what (i.e., the environment) actually bore the costs of our way of life.

Oddly, that wasn't the only time that Iowa or the Upper Midwest figured into the curricula of European schools. In July 2011, during the course of a two-day on-campus interview for a teaching position at Waldorfschule-Teufelstal in exurban Stuttgart, to my amazement I took a seat in an English class, only to find that abridged versions of the Laura Ingalls Wilder's *Little House* books provided the focus of Maurice Peters' lessons. An eccentric Brit, he had trekked to the American Heartland to follow the route of Laura and her family—as I have done. Me being a rural homo of the second half of the 20th century, I have not only read her series[51] several times, but visited every place she once lived, in half of the Midwest's dozen states. Besides being well-written, loving accounts of larger-than-life adventures on America's frontier, in Laura's tales lie clues why what remains of White America voted for Trump in such disproportionate numbers:

If a person is born in the US with dark-hued skin or to Muslim parents—say—one could get the sense at times that something is innately deficient or flawed about one's Self. Healthy, strong personalities among such persons push back, lest they succumb to prejudice (a main goal of discriminatory behavior from others) and fear that *everything* about them might be "wrong" or "bad." The same could be true for white-skinned Americans, but in reverse: After centuries of subconscious, assumed entitlement, now that more of us finally are wading into discussions about racism and white supremacy, there is a potential for both our detractors and ourselves to flip into the opposite mode: Where once most of us thought we could do no wrong, now some of us seem think we can do no right—and recent "Leftist-revisionist attacks" fan such *Angst*. When cultural pillars like "our" chronicler is, in effect, blacklisted and her classics relegated to "banned-books" status, many rural whites may feel negated and retreat into a defensive mode. Instead of facilitating understanding and change, such cultural "revisionism" can result in many whites becoming deaf to the rest of the body of critique rightfully leveled against our ilk. Any group in retreat—a formerly dominating one, even more so—strikes out blindly and *en masse*.

Each subgroup in a culture has its guiding lights and representative or heroic figures—e.g., Harriet Tubman, Frederick Douglas, Sojourner Truth… right up to Martin Luther King Jr; they inspire me, too, but I suspect the first three weren't saints and I know the last one was human. For white rural Midwesterners, the experiences of the Ingalls and Wilder families mirror our own heroes— certainly, they do that for this son of pioneers who creaked out onto the prairie in swaying covered wagons, then built log or sod homes and pop-up towns amidst the buffalos. Laura's stories recount those defining experiences, including scenes that make thoughtful, honest people sadly cringe and wish history had unfolded differently—but it didn't. Do the passages in her writings that describe encounters between whites and Native Americans comprise, say, ten percent of her aggregate work? No. Is it one percent? Don't know—but it also doesn't matter, not as much as what *does* matter: Overwhelmingly, the content in her scores of chapters in nine volumes, focuses on one early Middle Border child's evolution and self-discovery; amidst the pain and the joy is much familial love, a sense of purposeful belonging and the desire to live widely.

In 1876-77, my Gramma Luick's grandfather, George Edward Moorehead (left, with sisters Mary and Jennie, r.) were "neighbors" of the Ingalls, who then lived 13 miles [21 KM] away in Burr Oak, where "Pa" and "Ma" ran the Masters Hotel. Quite literally, some of my ancestors trod upon the same ground as the future bestselling-author's family. While the Ingalls girls (l. to r.: Carrie, Mary and Laura) survived their family's respite from the recurring grasshopper plagues of the time, their only brother, Frederick, did not. Life on the frontier was marked by recurrent waves of death—as illustrated in this detailed footnote.[52]

When all that is good and enriching in Laura's writing is not only blanketly condemned but also actively erased [*vis-à-vis* the unanimous vote by the American Library Association's division for Library Service to Children to strike her name from its prestigious children's-literature award, and some school districts' removing her series from library shelves], then the sections in them that are hurtful to some contemporary sensibilities lose their value as deep-reaching teaching tools. What can touch us more than having to relativize cultural icons' light juxtaposed against their shadows; is that process not similar to doing the same with our own? Non-negotiable literary banishment seems extreme and too final to many, especially those of us who share Laura's cultural legacy. If even radical centrists like myself become defensive and angry about what is perceived by many to be the actions of "the PC police from the Left," imagine how those to my right feel in the face of such "counter-racism." Ironically, they then circle the ideological wagons that much faster and tighter, making the yawning chasms between political fronts even wider.

Just like whites have had to learn to see African Americans as fully human, to see individuality and nuance, flaws and all, those Americans who are not hetero-male WASPs should well learn to let whites be fully human, too—flaws and all. To achieve that, we will all have to relax the ideological rigidities that keep us stuck. To cite just two example of polarizing cultural battles:

I, too, abhor the racial and cultural contexts behind the hundreds of Confederate statues and memorials scattered across the South, but is it really "best" to tear them all down? Could some of them be left as examples, with didactic panels installed alongside them, making explicit what is morally wrong and culturally dangerous about not only what they represent, but why and how they got created in the first place? I suspect so. Or in a less emotionally-charged case study for Americans: Until 2016, it remained illegal for individual Germans to own or even read a copy of Hitler's *Mein Kampf*.[53] Have our cousins been too rash in their rush to remove first all Nazi-, then all communist-era memorials or realia? I would say so—for when we reflexively banish shared physical culture to oblivion, we also lose tangible reminders to reflect, to learn and to do better.

One of the things that Alex Haley's *Roots* saga did not only for Southerners but for all Americans was to give faces, names and emotional complexities to a people that whites for centuries had worked so hard to not see. A part of our nation rendered "subhuman" by whites refusing to see their fuller humanity, African Americans could be treated so abysmally because those of us on the abusing end clung to our blindness: We did not want to know the names or struggles, the pains or dreams of those we were oppressing. It was only by resisting demonizing "them" that *all* of "us" could move forward—a step that has to take place now between ideological fronts...

But, back to the story of Linus' banishment from the WASP-Heterosexual-Male Eden:

As a white-skinned, heterosexual-male Protestant, young-adult Linus "should" have had it made. Linus seemed—as did tens of millions of WASP boys like him—preordained to occupy a place in the top stratum of that social hierarchy of rural Midwestern culture into which we, the first generation to follow World War II's blood-letting, were born. All he had to do was loyally serve the system whose lottery he thought he had won. He was set for life—or so he could have expected until, that is, Life conspired elsewise; or, put more explicitly, until the American Dream spit him out of what was supposed to be an assured, ever-upward career track. Now, instead of being free to think about Life from generation to generation, Linus and his Fate mates are forced to think about how to live, paycheck to paycheck. How could he *not* feel angry about losing something "rightfully" his, let alone his life's legacy for his family? That being the case, how could he and his kind resist the hate-filled tunes of an orange-haired Pied Piper who comes along and promises to build "a big, beautiful wall" to keep out those who would take what the Linuses all across our land thought to be the prize owed all dutiful white boys—America's worker bees?

*

Betrayal from Within: Type III

Ashlawn Farm, where I grew to young adulthood, was home to a strange mix. It embodied the inheritance of my mother, Phyllis Thrams, the daughter of landowners—modest ones but owners of prime Iowa loam, all the same. The young man she hauled onto the property, "Bud" Luick, hailed from tenant farmers who moved almost yearly for some 20 years. The closet thing the Upper Midwest had to the South's pitiable sharecroppers, tenant farmers on the prairie clung to the lowest rung of middle-class or the highest of lower-class rural folk.

All three of Grandpa Elmer Thrams' siblings and he graduated from high school—he in Mason City's Class of '16. Grampa Donald Luick, in contrast, was the first in his family to do so, in '31. Later, his son—my intelligent but under-educated (for his abilities) father—longed to go to Iowa State College [by Linus' and my day, "Iowa State University"] to become a veterinarian. "*Pisssh*" hissed his father, "college is for playboys"—and, in any event, Dad lied to himself and everyone else, that Thornton High hadn't bestowed him adequate math and chemistry skills. So, instead of following his dream, he drudged about in the dirt at Ashlawn Farm for over two decades and seemed to resent every moment of it—not to mention his mother-in-law, now-widowed Erma.

So, when it came time for Linus to leave the area, he made sure he found enough funds to get a college education. Linus worked every summer in construction or lower-level engineering jobs. He had sold his 4-H calves and any other agricultural capital he might have had upon leaving high school. In short, Linus managed, with help, to be the first in his family to complete college.

After a series of ever-better-paying positions in Northern Minnesota and then the Twin Cities, Linus landed a job at Bullseye's corporate headquarters in Minneapolis, managing environmental aspects of building new stores. At one point, he directed numerous colleagues and earned well.

Then, 2008 came—and Linus went… as did most of his department, in one merciless fell swoop.

Overnight, this 50-year-old, White Anglo-Saxon Protestant male wasn't at the top of the career heap but, at least for a while, at the bottom. This is no exaggeration, and at least three realities kept him there too long. For one, his mortgage, being middle-age and the father of two college-age daughters dictated the salary he *desired*; at the same time, his training, experience and level of last position suggested the salary he "*deserved*." Second, he was only one out of literally millions of college-educated, middle-age white men then looking for professional jobs; and third, as weeks turned into months, then years of seeking "real" replacement work, his self-esteem seemed to peak, then took a battering the longer such unemployment dragged on. As it did, once-jolly and -upbeat Linus became increasingly circumspect and discouraged. It was hard for me to watch, even from across the Atlantic, during our irregular calls or few visits. I felt for Linus— and offered him my brightest ideas of possible remedies for his double-headed misery: long-term unemployment mounted atop its attendant sense of growing helplessness.

As he flailed about, attempting to find "something" to support Cherry and their girls, he chased many leads: At various times, Linus fixed vacuums, worked in a woodworking shop that kept tough teens (read: chronic court cases) off the street and did handy-man jobs. At one point, he resorted to mowing lawns in Laketon—including for Home Depot, where he applied for a sales job but was turned away as "over-qualified" given his degree in engineering and past positions. From the way he reported that Big Box' summarily declining his plea to work "as anything," if Linus had grabbed a gun at that point I would have been neither surprised nor blamed him. The banksters behind the Great Recession, who Obama and Congress didn't as much as slap on their financial wrists, went on—as a set—pursuing their pre-crash lives of luxury; their compatriots whose lives they helped ruin, in contrast, in countless cases never recovered what they lost.

From my biased and partial perspective, it seemed that Linus failed to exhaust trying to locate comrades-in-fate, men and perhaps some women of similar backgrounds and plight who might work together to create new means of living. When I suggested to him that he try joining forces with others in comparable situations, to act in concert to craft new ways of working or at to protest together the injustices they suffer, Linus quickly dismissed such talk—belying the flawless choreography of those little Ukrainian kindergartners who didn't miss a beat as they gracefully moved through time and space so many decades and worlds ago: *Oh, we prisoners of history!*

I admired, though, his determination to at least attempt to turn his lot around, despite all this:

Linus applied to a law school; it deemed his entry-test scores insufficient. He studied theology and strove to complete a Ph.D. in it, but couldn't master Greek and Aramaic, as was required. He did eke out a position at Southeastern University, a Bible college in a Twin Cities suburb where he studied; it refuses him tenure because he lacks a Ph.D. (theirs), yet shamelessly pays him second-rate wages even as it demands over-priced tuition from his many on-line students. Disillusioned by but feeling stuck in this cynical, soul-sucking "academic" environment, Linus sought pastoral-care work in several evangelical churches across the Midwest: Each arduous application yielded naught. He also interviewed as a live-in mentor for "disadvantaged" (read: disturbed and disturbing) Native youth in Alaska: Even that school's desperate staff rejected his offer to join them. Yes, he tried hundreds, zillions of times to turn his career/life around, but...

Now, Linus contents himself with driving for grain farmers in the Red River Valley of the North. His earliest task master, Bud Luick, is dead, but Linus is working now for an *Ersatzvater*, in a terrain that evokes the open prairies of northern Iowa where he once labored as a boy, yet now with fewer fencerows to interrupt his following those endless, hypnotizing rows—up and down, down and up. A couple times a year, during the two busiest seasons, he kisses Cherry a quick *adieu*, leaves her to guard their fortress back in Laketon and migrates to North Dakota. It may not pay him what check-out clerks earn today at Bullseye stores he once helped to build, but he loves watching the seasons turn—up 'round Fargo, ya know—and the Canada geese, who fly over machinery he guides as it crawls over the Plains. It is honest work and he can pretend he's his own boss—well, almost. At least he's working—which is what he does; that's why he's here.

Myself (4.5 years old), my brother and three maternal male cousins, with our Grandma and Grandpa Thrams, who was a few months from dying of cancer—on the Fourth of July, 1967.

Still, do the Linuses who thickly populate our Heartland have to go it *so* alone? As I ran for the US Senate, I grew to more deeply understand what might drive those dejected Americans my family represents in light of my campaign to reach them. Their plight *must* grow easier and more bearable, *soon*, but who will speak up for them—especially if they will not speak for themselves?

*

"The definition of insanity is doing the same thing over and over and expecting different results."

— Rita Mae Brown, *Sudden Death*

Daily-Life Madness

Want to understand why we have Trump—and why, just before he broke all ties with me, Linus said to my query about same, that he would vote for Crazy again? Well, get to know Pompeii:

Europe's answer to Egypt's pyramids at Giza or Peru's cloud-hugging Machu Picchu, Pompeii was a flourishing ancient-Roman coastal city that one day found itself buried under metric tons of volcanic ash and debris from nearby Mount Vesuvius. Just ask Google: Today, its excavated, shoulder-high ruins reveal much about early Western civilization—and our current condition.

panoramic view of Pompeii's Forum, with Vesuvius in the background; (lower row) a Roman fresco at the Villa dei Misteri and a 1993 map of Pompeii's ancient streets, with then-unexcavated regions in green[54]

Looking at an on-line map of that city's remains, imagine you were living inside its pre-eruption walls, a member of whatever profession, social class or religion your fantasies choose: Let 'em run wild! A microcosm in the vast Roman empire—the city could easily be crossed by foot in a quarter hour or less—it had trading ties that reached as far as Britannia, Scandinavia, sub-Sahara Africa, South and East Asia; it was a pinpoint on an otherwise protracted map. As a resident of that visibly-defined urban entity—either as a free citizen or an enslaved subject—you can "see" pretty clearly both the tangible and invisible political powerlines of the place.

At that time, Pompeii had eight gates. In those days, one's ultimate power depended on one's ability, one's freedom to pass through those points of entry—or not. BUT, who controlled the access? To translate into contemporary terms, what ancient equivalents of Google, Amazon, Elon Musk, Richard Branson, Uber or Airbnb controlled the flow—or lack thereof—of people and goods? What 24-hour news sources told acquiescent Pompeiians what to think or how to feel about their thoughts? To what hand-held devices did they look for instructions on how to move about in the city? What norms herded their every move; what structures defined The Possible or Allowable? From what patch of Earth did they peer upward, to their respective corners of the sky? To what degree were they willing to claim a piece of the Heavens—or forego same? In what ways were they sovereign entities—despite their class or caste—or merely subjects to be shoved around by others? How much—or how little—did each of them make out of their lives?

Inside Pompeii's walls, who held property—not just villas and hovels, but shops or market stalls, bakeries or brothels, thermal baths or temples, and the coliseum or court benches? Those with monopolies or, in cahoots with cohorts, cartels could dictate where you might—or might not—tread, trade, talk or think. Traveling back to our current day, who dictates the same in a modern "city"? Who determines what you can be or become? Who hires or fires you/r family/friends? What directs the flow of modern life? What changes might make a difference in your daily life?

But, back to Linus, his wife Cherry… and all the rest of us:

Fed from birth illusions of access to externally-bestowed privilege, Linus pursued the American Dream… until, through no doing of his own, his membership in the elite was nullified. From that day on, the man endured a veritable endless gauntlet of rejections, humiliations, dead ends, insults and ultimately despair. For over a decade, a previously unthinking pawn in an unseen system dutifully played his role—until it and he were no longer useful. Once chewed up and spit out, however, he continued to subscribe to the same systems that betrayed him: *Why?*

For the most part, our obedient little worker bee simply swallowed not only his pride, but the endless abuse of an uncaring system—one he repeatedly has refused to challenge or change. Despite his suffering in silence, however, every day, in almost every way, he has accumulated a basket full of slights, rebuffs, resentments, frustrations—and yet he quietly serves the same machinery he always has. Instead of focusing his simmering rage on those boys in their board rooms, he has wasted too much time and energy on us gay boys in our bedrooms: The Hispanics and homos, the Papists and other pagans his church has loved to kick for so long are *not* the source of his suffering. Indeed, those who have most harmed him and endangered the well-being of those he loves most have been those he has trusted most: corporate heads and church leaders, Rush and Alex, Fox and friends. It is not "wetbacks" that Linus need worry about, but the dry, cold calculations of those who pass legislation, shred regulation and dare send his son-in-law Tyler to fight useless skirmishes in the Afghani desert or in the waters off the Iranian coast.

On the home front (as Americans allow our country to be in the eighteenth year of the longest war our nation has ever waged but never declared), Linus continues to struggle to pay his bills and thus further defers the fulfillment of his dreams. Cherry does enjoy her support job in the Laketon schools but also dare not retire from it, as both of them depend on her insurance to cover Linus' and her swelling medical bills. (While I watch them scrape by, I enjoy nearly-perfect German health insurance, which is efficient, stress-free and affordable; if I need drugs, I pay no more than 5 Euros a month—about $6.) Unable to imagine that either has a cushy retirement account, I wonder how—and *why*—they so unquestioningly continue to service a system that every day squeezes out of their tired bones every ounce of possible "productivity." *Why* do they not only continue to sustain but adamantly defend a system that doesn't treat them fairly?

I know their biographies have differed greatly from mine, but did they never meet a *Tante* Herta who taught them that no system is inevitable, none lasts eternally, and all can be changed—IF people will it? How much more laborious to live must their lives become before they demand change? What imminent threats to the survival, let alone thrival of their offspring have to arise, before they disinvest their stock in hollow, bankrupt institutions that only perpetuate scarcity, cynicism and suffering? How much lower does America have to sink before we pick it back up?

In my campaign for the US Senate, I raised these same questions—and got nary a reply, from anyone, in any audience: *Why?* Perhaps, because vested self-interests strangled the message?

*

Conspiracies of Silence

Want to know a secret?

Iowa *is* the Center of the Universe.

At least, it *was* <u>a</u> geographical center of the American experience of the Third Reich. How so?

For starters, the little German-Jewish girl living in exile in the Netherlands, Anne Frank, had an American pen pal, Juanita Wagner of Danville, a small town near Burlington, Iowa. Anne's older sister, Margot, corresponded with Juanita's sister, Betty Ann. As the Frank sisters went into hiding in Amsterdam with their family, then were betrayed and shipped to Bergen-Belsen, the Wagner girls puzzled over what happened to their pen friends—only to find out the truth, later.

Who knew? TRACES Center for History and Culture board members, interns and volunteers did.

Dr. Luick-Thrams explains the contents of a panel in "Behind Barbed Wire," an exhibit shown as of April 2012 at the Deutsch-Amerikanische Institut in Tübingen and three years later at the Center for American Studies (HCA) at the Universität Heidelberg. The beige-backed and pink images are from Camp Algona.

They and TRACES' executive director (*moi*) also knew that the von Trapps of *The Sound of Music* fame came to Iowa to sing,[56] and four 1936 US-Olympic-team members came from the Hawkeye State, including Des-Moines-born Frank Wykoff, who helped runner Jessie Owens to humiliate Hitler. Cedar-Rapids-native William Shirer attended the Berlin games and reported in Midwest slang as a code what he witnessed—until he had to flee the Nazi hell, only to write his National-Book-Award-winning account of it, *The Rise and Fall of the Third Reich*. In contrast, Dubuque-born Frederick Kaltenbach had served as the Nazis' "Tokyo Rose," as he broadcast stilted radio reports from Berlin beamed at English-language listeners. And, at the war's end, Iowa soldiers helped liberate what remained of the Reich's horrific concentration camps—as documented at:

http://usgerrelations.traces.org/

While they were not death camps, German-American civilian internees from Iowa also landed in what technically constituted concentration camps—most notably Camp Crystal City, on the Texas border with Mexico. A 1945 color US Department of Justice film (viewable on YouTube) shows the camp. What the film's narrator, former camp administrator Bern Berard, fails to tell viewers, however, is that besides about 15,000 German and other Axis-born US legal residents housed there and elsewhere, thousands more came from Latin America. The US government kidnapped them in thirteen Central- or South-American countries—more than 2,200 Japanese-Peruvians alone, about a tenth of the total living there—and forcibly brought them to one of sixty or so civilian-internment centers in Texas or beyond, including in Wisconsin, North Dakota, Omaha, St. Paul, St. Louis, Chicago and Cincinnati. Washington traded hundreds of those hapless souls for American nationals held by the Axis powers in Berlin or Tokyo. Those swapped included Jews who had fled the Nazis and sought refuge in Latin America: Was that legal—or moral?[57] No.

Who knew? Critical-thinking people who wondered why Berard cited "mailroom censors who read German, Spanish and Japanese"—or why, during corresponding footage, she referred to "suits made by Peruvian tailors." *Thousands* have heard both, but *few* asked. One person who did want to know more was—wait for it—Charles Grassley. In partnership with Russ Feingold, a "liberal" Democratic US Senator from Wisconsin, the two repeatedly sponsored a bill to have Congress investigate not only German-American and other non-Japanese-American US-civilian internment during WWII, but also the kidnapping and internment of Latin Americans. Each time unnamed "political figures to reckon with" in DC torpedoed even floor discussion of their bill. At least, some of the Japanese-American internees were compensated $20,000 each in 1988 under a law signed by Ronald Reagan;[58] still, Latin-American Japanese Americans only got $5,000.[59]

But, back to our story about Iowa's playing a central role in America during the period 1933-48:

Three more sub-chapters of America's larger WWII-era experience distinguish Iowa even more from our country's other 47 states at the time. For one, of some ninety-thousand US prisoners of war held in Nazi-occupied Europe, the most came, per capita, from Iowa. The first soldiers to fight in that war (before the US officially was in it) consisted of men from Iowa's 34th Division, based then in Red Oak. "Red Bull boys" fought the longest uninterrupted stint of any American soldiers in the European theater—617 days in total. The only time Army General George Patton disobeyed orders was to interrupt his advance into almost-defeated Nazi Germany to rescue his son-in-law, who had been captured with Red Bulls at North Africa's Kasserine Pass in Tunisia.

Who knew? All professional or even hobbyist historians who have been paying attention did, as the documentation was made public decades ago and can easily be found by anyone who cares.

For another, only Iowa's two base camps, Clarinda and Algona, housed POWs from all three Axis countries. (The US' total number consisted of 375,000 Germans, some 50,000 Italians and 6-8,000 Japanese.) The camp in Algona remains alive today in the form of a large-scale, half-life-size nativity scene created by German POWs *after* the war but *before* they were sent—*not* back to Germany, in most cases—to England or France, to whom the US government gave the men as imprisoned farm laborers and miners, with some being held as late as September 1948. They were the "lucky" ones: A third of the three-million German POWs sent to Soviet gulags in Siberia after the war never returned home—and the last of those who did came back in 1956.

Who knew? It *could* have been you: TRACES staff, volunteers and I have contacted National Public Radio about this and related stories for over twenty years, with literally not one response. [A few state Public Radio affiliates—Iowa, North Dakota, Texas, etc.—did air in-state features.]

Finally, and most famously, America's largest project to assist refugees fleeing Nazi-occupied Europe was based in Iowa. Housed in a former Quaker boarding school, Scattergood Hostel brought 185 mostly Jewish but also other escapees to the American Heartland. While Robert Balderston—husband of the hostel's second director, Martha—worked in Europe to get exiles visas, tickets and travel funds, Iowa Quaker farmers and college students provided, in the words of one grateful refugee, Austrian Rudolf Schreck, a "place of peace in a world of war, a haven amidst a world of hatred." Again a school after the war, Scattergood embodies a rich legacy.

The depicted are thought to be Betty Forman (center) coaching Ewald Peissel as (from left) Adolf Beamt, staff-sister Naomi Snoop, Lisa Beamt, (from right) Angela Schuber and Gus Weiler listen, summer 1940.[60]

Who knew? I did—already in the early 1980s, standing in a lunch line at a gathering of the Iowa Yearly Meeting of Friends (Quaker), chatting with Robert Berquist, a onetime hostel staff. Then, a decade later, the Berliner *Senat* awarded me—twice—generous scholarships to fly to faraway "*Amerika*" to interview forty former Scattergood "guests" and their hosts, now almost all being deceased. But, a better question: Why didn't <u>you</u> know about this timely, inspiring history? It is, after all, eternalized as part of the Iowa Holocaust Memorial on the grounds of our Statehouse.

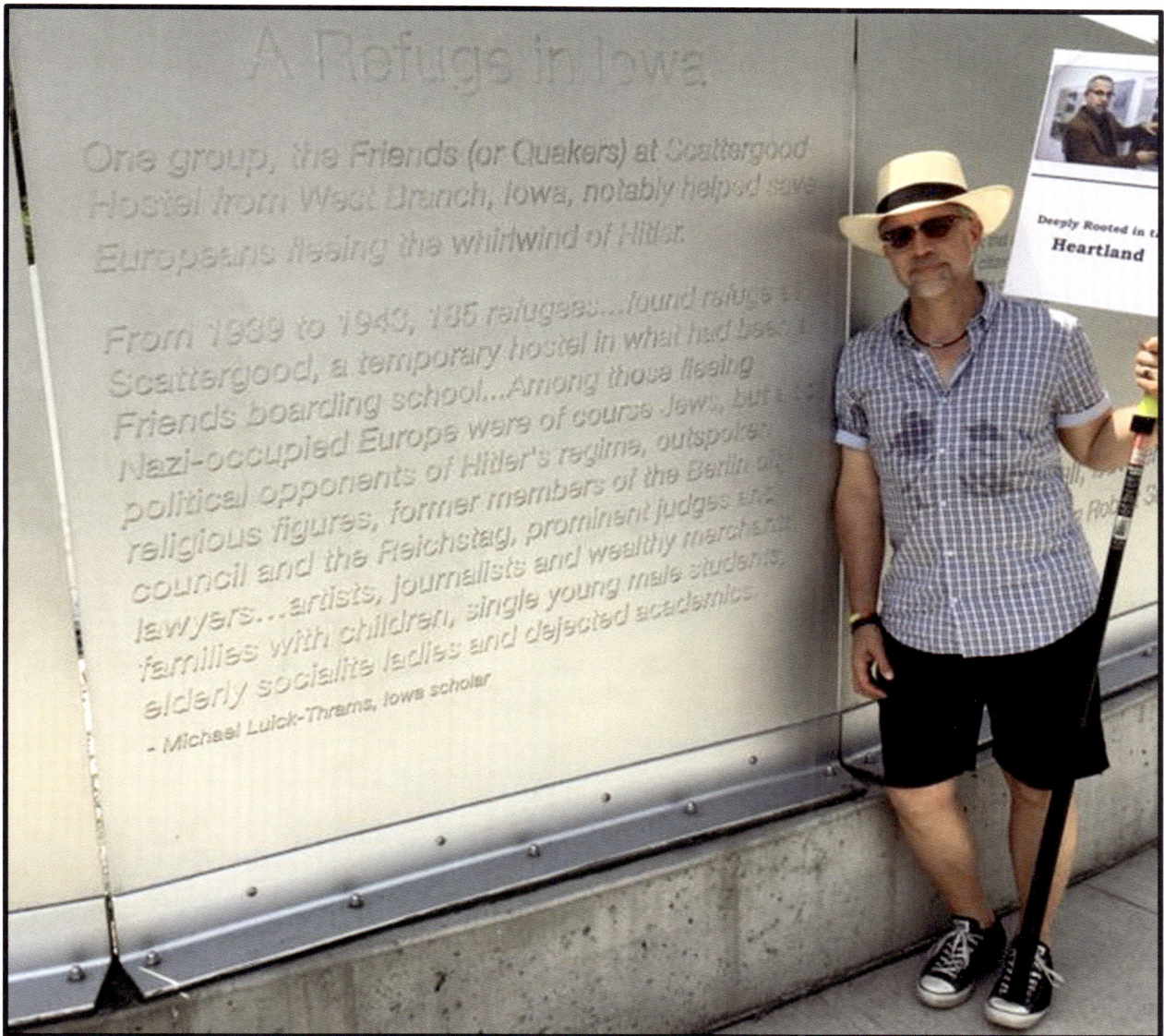

With temperatures at over 100 °F (38 °C), the author clings to shade in front of the Iowa State Capitol Grounds' Holocaust memorial on 11 June 2016, during that year's Gay Pride march in Des Moines.

In large part, you and likely those closest to you never heard of it because of the US Holocaust Museum Memorial's stubborn silence regarding the entire story. Despite being partly publicly founded and so financed, with the express assignment of preserving and popularizing among Americans the larger Holocaust saga, the USHMM has failed to tell this rare tale: *Why?* Despite venturing west of the Potomac twice to acquire documentation about Scattergood Hostel, the USHMM didn't mention it once in its current non-permanent, later traveling exhibit "Americans and the Holocaust:" *Why?* For the same reasons Iowa media sources "overlooked" covering my 2016 US-Senate campaign—for "political" considerations wedded to advancing or protecting individual careers and institutional interests. How can <u>you</u> change this? Just ask the USHMM...

I assume most Americans agree that knowing how some of us alive then responded to the Holocaust as it unfolded constitutes important civic knowledge. Similarly, would you agree that knowing why sixty percent of the candidates who qualified to run for the US Senate from Iowa in 2016 were scarcely mentioned in the state's media for many months preceding the election?

I do—as I was one of them. Just as the above-outlined stories were silenced by inattention, so was I, as a candidate.

*

> "What ya don't know, won't hurt ya."
>
> — Midwest translation of an old saying

NOT "Iowa's Newspaper"

Dad was an avid reader—of newspapers, farm journals, *Reader's Digest*… and, post-retirement, Louis L'Amour's pulp novels by the score. While still on the farm, when daily chores or seasonal distractions like calving/farrowing/foaling/lambing or plowing/planting/cultivating/harvesting didn't require his abstaining from his daily fix, my father would bury his nose amongst the newsprint during any free time he had. Over breakfast and at the end of lunch, he'd cover the kitchen table with the printed page. When Gene Tannehill or other regular callers came, Mom served the obligatory coffee and rolls or cake or pie atop piles of paper. Later, Dad would sit eternally "on the throne" reading, and thus block the rest of us from heeding nature's calls.

Keen and eager—especially in winter—I often volunteered to walk the length of our long lane to "the box" to fetch the *Des Moines Sunday Register*, as I loved the white, slick-but-sun-soaked landscape. Other than the "funnies" section, only after our father had combed through the rest of it would we dare disturb the venerable *Register*'s pages. Following his perusal, when she wasn't wintering in Arizona, Grandma Thrams awaited my relaying it to her small cottage across our second driveway. If I was late doing so, she'd call and ask if I'd forgotten—an unforgivable offense: After all, it was—as it proclaimed atop its masthead—"Iowa's newspaper." Indeed, in the days of my youth, it took pride in having regional offices throughout Iowa—and we took pride that it did, along with its often-won prizes for its journalistic excellence. It covered our Hawkeye news so vigorously, in the '30s it flew its own plane, "Good News II," around the state, spiriting reporters and photographers to cover breaking news like the "Cow War." Known then as a "liberal Republican" paper, it mirrored the essentially decent, open-minded state we mostly had.

Clears J. B. Stever in 'Cattle Deals'

Embattled Cedar County Farmers Swarm Mitchell Farm

This aerial photograph picture, taken from The Register and Tribune plane Good News II, shows the hundreds of farmers who gathered on the E. C. Mitchell farm near Tipton Saturday afternoon to protest compulsory tuberculin testing of cattle. The meeting followed ejection of Dr. Peter Malcolm from the farm Friday evening when he attempted to complete a test of the Mitchell herd. The photograph was rushed to Des Moines by The Register and Tribune plane which had carried staff newswriters to the scene of the meeting.

photo in Des Moines Sunday Register, *12 April 1931; see Robert Blomme's detailed report*[61]

"The paper Iowa depend[ed] on" originated in a log cabin near abandoned Fort Des Moines, in 1849. Still, in 1985 it succumbed to "McFluff" Gannett's insatiable appetite to acquire evermore regional papers; as of this writing, Gannett owns over a hundred dailies and more than a thousand weeklies and specialty publications throughout the United States.[62] Since it absorbed the *DMR*, that paper has been in a tailspin ever since in terms of quality, editorial independence and objectivity. In recent years, it has shrunk in readership, as well as in surface size and page count. Still, despite having closed almost all of its satellite offices around the state, the *Register* remains a tone-setting source of information and opinion. As such, as a candidate I <u>had</u> to court it—yet, without exception, I found the *DMR* to be a coy and, ultimately, unrequiting love interest.

The *DMR* with which I <u>had</u> to interact was not the paper of my youth. It mimics almost all of the few surviving big-town papers, which have (intentionally?) buried contact information under mountains of digital debris. As normally happened the hundreds of times my volunteers or I tried to contact print or electronic media, dialing a finally-found number meant navigating a gauntlet of options, hardly any of which yielded the exciting rarity of finding a real, live person. Sending a press release or a request for an interview, either by email or via voicemail, most likely was met with a defeating silence. We spent inordinate amounts of time just to locate a possible conversation partner at a paper, radio or TV outlet: Typically, they stiffly deflected us.

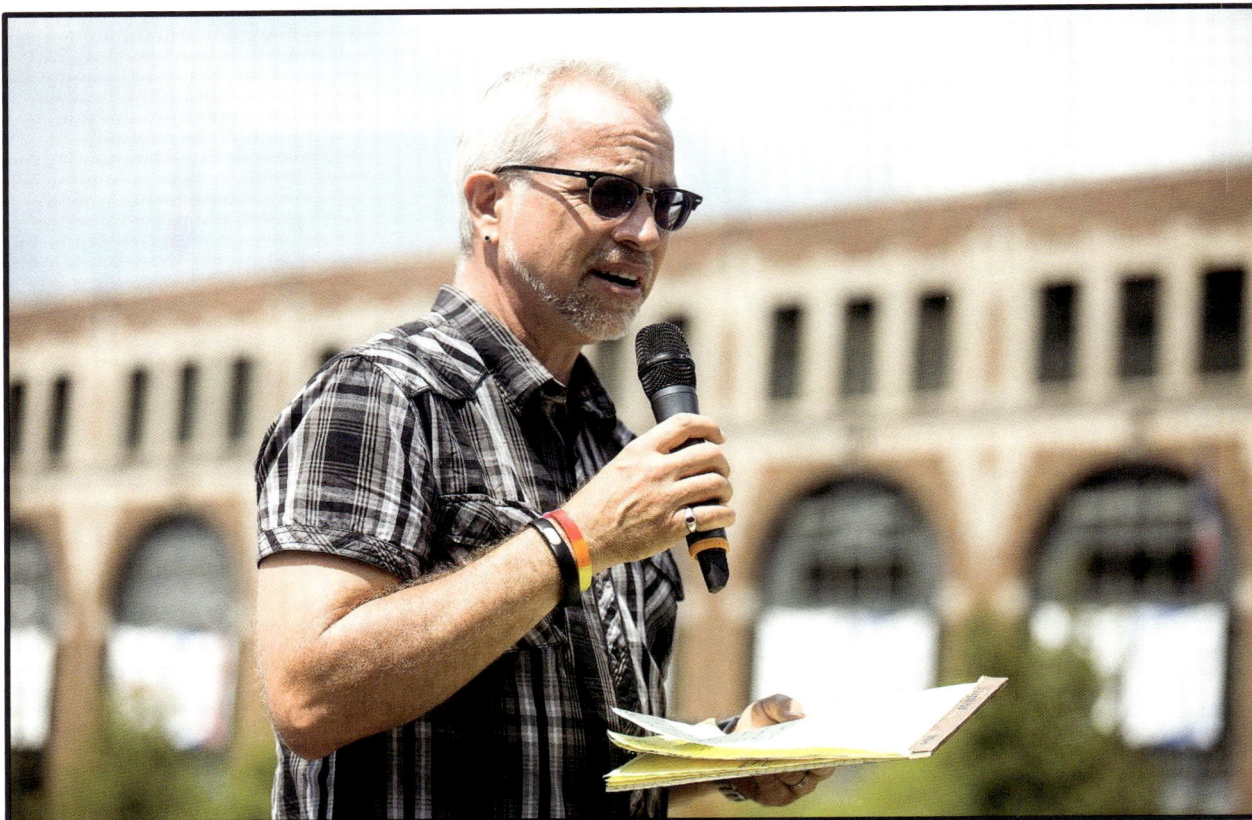

On Sunday, 14 August 2016, I attended Des Moines Valley Friends Meeting. Afterwards, as that spiritual community is wont to do, those present took hands, formed a circle and shared "joys and concerns." When it was my turn, I mentioned feeling "petrified by the prospect of speaking at [that] afternoon's Register Political Soapbox at the State Fair." A video recording of my opening documents my Angst.[63]

Once, I did sneak through the mostly impenetrable filter placed between *DMR* staff and the public. I was told "Like all the other candidates for all higher offices, [I would] be granted a few minutes at the *Register*'s Political Soapbox at the Iowa State Fair—but other than that, we won't be interviewing you or covering your campaign unless you do something worthy of it." And, in any event, for undisclosed reasons, per *DMR* policy regarding electoral coverage, Iowa's largest newspaper does not mention independent candidacies by name until after 1 August. [Kathie Obradovich's two "semi-autonomous" pieces on 31 May and 11 August 2016 citing me as an independent candidate was written despite of, not per assignment from *DMR* editorial staff. I greatly appreciated her mere mention of my candidacy, but a review of either article shows that rather than explore my perspectives or proposals, she cited me as an example for her own use.][64]

At some point, I had had enough: I simply drove to the *DMR*'s offices. Then housed in a mid-rise downtown skyscraper,[65] overlooking a chic-but-ghostlike granite-and-steel atrium, it took some waiting, but eventually an editor dispatched a younger colleague to placate me by sitting a few moments in the atrium and chatting over a quick coffee. Initially pleasant, she hailed from Wisconsin, so I liked her for being a "Cheesehead"[66]—until I grew weary of her hollow excuses, why the *Register* "could not" interview me about my US-Senate candidacy. When I pointed out that almost daily it covered Grassley's or Judge's latest moves around the state, she smiled falsely and stumbled over "That's different, they're real—I mean, mainstream—candidates."

Channeling Willy Hawk and Thom Lee, Lindsay (or was it Ashley?) explained that the *DMR* only reports on "events" and, post-primary, not on candidates *per se*. "For one" I countered, "we non-Democratic or -Republican candidates never had to go through primaries. For another, we also are registered, qualified, bona fide candidates: We three will be on the fall ballots, yet no one will have ever heard of us if media outlets like yours continue to ignore us. Do you find that fair?"

"The solution's simple" explained (was it?) Brittany, "you just have to hold an event and if enough people come and it generates enough buzz, we'll come and cover it—but to report on an event, not about a candidate." At that, she tucked her bangs behind her ear and grabbed her bag.

"But how should we throw an event that draws 'enough people' if none of the media report that such an event is about to take place? And, even if we *did* generate 'enough buzz' at a given event, how would any of you ever be on-hand to cover it, since you would not come until—?"

"Look" Emily barked, but again with a fake smile, "every candidate has campaign staff who can generate buzz on social media"—she began to take to her feet—"but that's your job, not ours."

"Oh, I understand that" I shot back, "but is it not your job to inform your readership of their full voting options, across the electoral landscape? Isn't the media charged with edifying people, so they can make enlightened choices that, in the end, affect us all—our entire political system?"

"We only have so much space" Charity retorted, standing rigidly across from me, over the table.

"But, we can buy as much of it as we wish, right?" She didn't react. "For having limited space" I pressed on, "you find ample amounts of it to cover outlandish Donald Trump. Hey, at least his daily outrages sell newspapers, don't they?" Regrettably, I glowered at her by this point. "They are a most sordid affair: Doesn't it ever repulse you to digest his ham antics on a daily basis?" Again, Chastity simply sat and stared at me, expressionless. "Ironically, the 'liberal' media can't get enough of his freak show. You all seem to vie to get exclusive interviews or at least report on his latest shocking comment seconds after it tumbles out of his big mouth. The *Register* has room to cover every imaginable aspect of The Donald, yet we here, on the ground, go begging for mere mention. While you are busy helping to get him elected, you are helping to erase us."

At that, Mandy plopped back down in her seat, her stern expression melting as she did. "We admire what you are doing—we *really* do—but we have a paper to run, and to keep afloat. Our readership wants to follow Trump's rapid rise—and we want to give them what they want."

"So, is that it? Big parties have big advertising budgets, so you bend over backwards to please them" I grilled, "but small, independent campaigns don't, so we're not sexy enough for you? In a democracy, doesn't that favor those who have big bucks and fancy machinery, over ordinary folks who don't? If so, how will the system ever change, if 'liberal' media play whores for cash?"

Peering into the bottom of her empty coffee cup for a moment, Tiffany wagged her head, then looked at her watch. "It's been good talkin' with ya" she lied as she again took to her feet, "but I have to go. Keep in touch!" she called out, as she bolted from the café and ran up the escalator.[67]

*

> "The opposite of love is not hate, it's indifference.
> The opposite of art is not ugliness, it's indifference.
> The opposite of faith is not heresy, it's indifference.
> And the opposite of life is not death, it's indifference."
>
> — Holocaust-survivor Elie Wiesel, *US News & World Report*

NOT an Exception

It would have been one thing, had the reception my volunteers' and my attempts got, as we tried to interest the *Register* in covering our campaign, been a one-off "event" (*ah-h-h*, sorry!), but it was the sad norm. (The few exceptions to our meager record of drawing media interest most notably included the *Cedar Rapids Gazette*, which not only sent newbie Mitch to cover my announcing, but checked in at points throughout the campaign, welcomed guest opinion pieces from me and, later, sat a handful of journalists down with me to dissect me and my quest.) At least the *DMR*'s editors sent a sacrificial offering to try to throw me off their elusive trail, while other media figures we approached were not so horribly "Midwest nice" to me. For example:

One day, driving through the home of what some detractors dismiss as "Maharishi Moonbeam Meditators' University" in Fairfield, I happened across a radio station at home on the town square. On a whim, I stopped, went upstairs to its crammed-full office and offered an interview. "Oh, no" the big-boned, blond-haired man gushed with exaggerated emphasis. "We aren't allowed to feature political candidates on our radio. No—we could lose our license." As he said this, I spied hanging on the wall behind this Boris-Johnson-look-alike dozens of large and small framed pictures of this same station owner posing with scores of Republican figures: Ronald Reagan, both Bush presidents, Grassley, Governor Branstad, local figures and on down the line.

"Well" I floundered verbally as I considered making a scene, "that doesn't look like the case."

"Oh, yes" prattled the 50-something man further, "we strictly protect our political neutrality."

"Oh, do you?" I mocked as I felt the veins in my neck begin to bulge and my palms sweating.

"Indeed, we always have" he concluded our brief exchange as he walked sideways towards the door. "I do wish you the best of campaigns" he said as I swore I could smell hot smoke wafting upwards from the back of my pants. Opening the door and gesturing to it, he bid "Bye, now!"

That bullshitter in Southeast Iowa was an extreme example, but at least I quickly saw what I was dealing with. More exhausting was the insidious greeting my campaign got from media staff who had no intention of granting access to the channels they so tenaciously guarded, yet led me on interminably, maintaining a *façade* of being nice while pursuing an unseen agenda. In true Midwest tradition, most of them smiled or spoke sweetly as they delivered a tart message:

"You no pay, no play."

In terms of media access, in the US, if you don't own wealth, you don't have a voice. Of course, in a literal sense, there is not "The Media" *per se*, as every media-based entity is unique. As such, they differ according to format (print vs. electronic), operating norms, financing, reach, influence.

There is the older print media, dating back to 1439 and German inventor Johannes Gutenberg (who midwifed literally "the press:" books, newspapers, magazines, newsletters), and newer electronic media (first transmitted in broadcast, now in digital forms). Except for a few religious presses or far more numerous non-profit institutional newsletters or magazines, print media mostly runs per commercial models. Electronic media—first radio and television, then cable and the internet, but now also on-line versions of "print" media such as newspapers—are predominantly for-profit, except for two exceptions: "Public Radio" and "Public Television."

Lurking around in the commercial electronic media world are power-hungry menaces like the Murdochs and the hate-spewing figures they legitimized, like Limbaugh, Jones or Hannity. Sex, shock and scandal sell, padding its peddlers' pockets. Each projects a certain persona, whether or not it's genuine; they tailor their messages to audiences they have cultivated over decades, whether or not their content is true, probing or fair. In such an environment, entrenched extreme ideology both drives and is driven. The level of public discourse it fans diminishes us all—and is possible in part following Reagan-era conservatives' shredding the FCC's "fairness doctrine."

The bias of extreme electronic media sources—whether *à la* Murdoch or Maddow—has pushed millions of Americans to "public" outlets in their search of more objective reporting. Confident that the outwardly less strident or ideologically-rabid inhabitants of the "public" realm are more trustworthy, many users of such sources don't question them. But, they should—as I found out.

During the Iraq War, Tony Blair wasn't the only lapdog of the right-wing establishment pushing that illegal, immoral ruse: National Public Radio's Scott Simon consistently gushed with enthusiasm for attacking, then later occupying a country which *never* possessed alleged "yellow cake" uranium or weapons of mass destruction. Despite his Quaker, thus presumably pacifistic leanings [Presidents Herbert Hoover and Richard Nixon were "birthright" Friends, despite the latter having been "read out of meeting"[68]], Scott was a loyal cheerleader and—after our "shock and awe" invasion—apologist for a military action that claimed some 460,000 Iraqi and just under forty-five hundred US soldiers' lives.[69] Generally, during the leadup to, then execution of that disgraceful farce, National Public Radio's reports were too uncritical—and thus abetted that war.

(In the Me-Too Era, can't we launch a parallel campaign to expose ideological inappropriateness among those in positions of power—especially in media? Just as "toxic touch" needs to be called out, so does "toxic thinking" and its lingering damage. Certainly, the misuse of power among those influencing the flow of information and opinion is as insidious and long-lasting—if less tangible—as that of their physical-abuse counterparts in, say, film [*ach*, "media" again], music, publishing or such industries. Can't we demand that public-trust violators at least acknowledge their earlier misjudgment? As far as I can discern, Scott has never publicly disowned—let alone "owned"—his keen eagerness to play pawn to the powers-that-were during that shameful war.)

One hopes (and assumes?) that state affiliates of NPR are less swayed by New York's and Washington DC's political persuasions. Still, they remain dependent—if not on advertising revenue, like their commercial counterparts—on Federal or other public grants, corporate (e.g., Wal-Mart and Target) or non-profit institutional underwriting (like from the infamous, ill-intending Koch brothers), and listener memberships. Perhaps for that reason, out of sensitivity to possibly "offending" their underwriters' political sensibilities, my supporters and I consistently found Iowa's Public Radio and Public Television to actively blacklist our campaign.

[Iowa's affiliate of the 1846-founded, not-for-profit cooperative Associated Press did the same. As I wrote later in a piece I titled *What to Expect, Should You be So Naïve as to Run as an Independent for Public Office*, "If you're not a Big Name, the Associated Press will sideline you, too, until you demand an explanation for why they haven't announced your announcement— and all you will get back is a phony, cheap, hollow, lackluster 'Well, we don't always mention every candidate for the US Senate' to which you reply 'Well, in the name of journalistic fairness wouldn't you either mention all, always, or none, ever?'." Still, 'twas one snub out of scores.]

What had been Scattergood School's Main Building became an "ark" during its incarnation as a refugee hostel. The first load of European exiles and their 22-year-old Quaker guide (below) arrived to a throng of reporters, on 15 April 1939. For more information, see the Cedar Rapids Gazette's in-depth 2019 article.[70]

The rebuff that stung the most was that of Katherine Perkins, almost two decades earlier the first major Iowa media figure to feature my telling of the Scattergood Hostel story. Then a moderator and now a producer at Iowa Public Radio, my numerous approaches to her or, later, to her leading colleagues, Michael Leland or Rob Dillard, fell on deaf ears. [As I noted in *What to Expect*, "If you're not a Big Name, IPR won't announce your announcement—not until you finally chase down its news editor and he capitulates and assigns the story ten days after the fact, issuing the most perfunctory of 'Oh, and this just in, too' brief mention-in-passing."] At one point, IPR did interview me—along with the Libertarian and a third non-aligned or non-mainstream candidate in the US-Senate race from Iowa—but I felt it did so to be able to later say it had gone through the motions of providing "equal time" rather than to seriously explore worldviews that differ from those of the partisan heavy weights. It seemed IPR had little if any heart to do more. Like the *DMR*, IPR did devote much time to covering—in largest part, via NPR—Trump's rocket ascent.

Out of my enduring respect for Katherine's excellent work, my personally liking affable Michael and my admiration of Rob's singular journalistic talents, I did not push individuals at IPR to cover my candidacy like I did slick-talkin' Justin Beaupre at Iowa Public Television. While I assumed IPR's gatekeepers' considerations to be about public image in nature and not about me, my sparring with Justin took on personal nuances. Ultimately, my challenging his (to me, faulty) rationale for *not* including 60% of the US-Senate-race candidates in IPTV's political coverage became a matter of integrity and honor: As IPTV had invited Grassley and Judge to appear on its set, but no one else listed on the same ballot, we boxed per phone or email long and hard over issues of inclusion, access and fairness. He *always* said "I see your point," yet *never* bended: "We set our roster of guests on this summer's political-race forum months ago, so *should not* alter it now."

Justin cited five criteria that "acceptable" candidates had to fulfill. The first one was to be either a Republican or a Democratic.[71] If a candidate wasn't either, s/he had to fulfill all the other four— the stiffest of which was, to have raised at least $50,000 in donations. In my piece *What to Expect*, I groaned "[I couldn't] imagine spending that much" as I found "that much invested in a single person's candidacy [like mine] wasteful, ridiculous and immoral." But, other principles were at stake here, which for me far outweighed party affiliation or monetary considerations.

As IPTV's head of programming, Justin's job was to bait his station's critics into galloping into dead-end "conversations" that were little more than proforma dismissals dressed in billowing bunting laced with Midwest Nice. When I argued that the "public" in his organization's name implied "open to" or at least "accountable to" same, he disclaimed any obligation to "universal access." When I protested that we three non-partisans were not "just anyone off the street" but rather Secretary-of-State-qualified candidates, he resumed his robot mode: "We set our roster of guests on this summer's political-race forum months ago, thus we *cannot* alter it now."

Since any plea from me on behalf of the "rights" of candidates to be presented to the public via IPTV moved Justin not in the least, I tried tapping his humanity from the opposite side of that argument: I championed the "rights" of consumers, of dues-paying members of his institution to be presented the full roster of candidates from which to choose in November. Wasn't that the public-interest-minded mission, the very duty of his non-profit body, to inform, not just entertain Iowa Public Television's ardent and loyal viewers? And besides, do the airwaves not belong to *all* of us? Sure that such reasoning would be the fulcrum I needed to win a toehold in Justin's steely heart, he dashed my hopes—and again muttered, unflappably: "We set our roster of guests on this summer's political-race forum months ago, therefore we *must not* alter it now."

When I chided him for his obstinacy and accused him of perpetuating an elitist electoral system where only those with vast war chests had the firepower needed to seize, then protect their monopoly over power, Justin offered arguments I found to be weak-kneed and patronizing, meant to wear me out rather than win me over. In louder moments, he insisted I simply abide by IPTV's policy and desist all further objections to it. His command infuriated me, as I expected "due" access to "public" discussion of and debate regarding Iowa's US-Senate race. In quieter moments, he might concede I was "right in principle" but in the next breath parrot his mantra: "As we set our roster of guests on this summer's political-race forum months ago, we *will not* alter it now." His intransigence incensed me and only spurred me to push harder to be heard.

*

> "You will seek me and find me when you seek me with all your heart."
>
> — Jeremiah 29:13, the Old Testament of the *Bible*

Blindsided by the "Conservative" Right

Just who were the bulk of Justin Beaupre's prized viewer-members—and *why* was he trying *so* inexhaustibly hard to shield them from me and my ideas? What did he smell that put him off?

Having reincarnated several times already within this lifetime, my varied biography's wake still is peppered with diverse friends from differing phases. The "liberals" among them kvetch that I am "too conservative," while the "conservative" ones claim that I'm "too liberal." In truth, I am neither—even as I am both. This stumps the hell out of my friends, as well as political pollsters.

During my US Senate run, finding that the "liberal" left mostly would not touch my non-aligned campaign, I fished among the "conservative" right for support—but they already had "touched" Iowa's political landscape far too much. This, their misnamed ilk had done my entire adult life.

First, a bit of backstory:

While my tenant-sharecropper paternal grandparents were old-school Democrats (think of the "Minnesota Democratic-Farmer-Labor [DFL] Party," which grew out of the grassfire-populist, Upper-Midwest rural tumult of the 1920s and '30s), my land-owning maternal ones, with their *bourgeois* aspirations, were staunch Republicans. Driving till daze in those pre-freeway days, Elmer and Erma Thrams trekked with Wisconsin kin to Washington to watch their beloved "Ike" be inaugurated in January 1953. Still, any fanaticism they might have felt in their deep-seated esteem for the man did not mirror a shred of extremism in him. According to Professor Pedia:

> [pacifistic-Brethren raised, in Kansas] Eisenhower adhered to a political philosophy of dynamic conservatism. A self-described "progressive conservative" who used terms like "progressive moderate" and "dynamic conservatism" to describe his approach, he continued all the major New Deal programs still in operation, especially Social Security. He expanded its programs and rolled them into a new cabinet-level agency, the Department of Health, Education and Welfare, while extending benefits to an additional ten million workers. He implemented integration in the Armed Services in two years, which had not been completed under [Democrat] Truman.[72]

Staunch Republicans, my Thrams grandparents drove with longtime friends of theirs from Wisconsin, Dick and Serena Dixon, to witness Dwight Eisenhower's 1953 inauguration: One of them captured the newly-sworn President as he passed their capital perch in an open car. Perhaps one of the reasons Elmer and Irma so "liked Ike" was that he married an Iowan, Mamie Doud—here with her new husband on the steps of San Antonio's St. Louis College in 1916, the year my grandparents graduated high school.[73]

As my family's historian, I have found little documentation that indicates my GOP-activist grandparents' political worldviews were based on or would have tolerated partisan policies or behaviors fueling hate or racism. (To the contrary, as stated earlier, their daughters had black and brown friends, as did they. In contrast, my father's grandfather had been active in the Iowa Ku Klux Klan in the 1920s.) Prominent in the Cerro Gordo Republican Party of their era, my Iowa-farmer maternal grandparents today most plausibly would be appalled by the rants and chants of the most-rabid contemporary Republicans. Certainly, having just helped overthrow Hitler, they would have not condoned imprisoning tens of thousands of anyone on the US' borders, and found child trafficking to be anathema. Paradoxically, a political party initiated, in largest part, in opposition to human bondage and servitude, has changed radically. Again per Pedia:

> The GOP was founded in 1854 by opponents of the Kansas–Nebraska Act, which allowed for the potential expansion of slavery into certain U.S. territories. The party supported classical liberalism, opposed the expansion of slavery, and supported economic reform. Abraham Lincoln was the first Republican president. Under the leadership of Lincoln and a Republican Congress, slavery was banned in the United States in 1865. [...] Following the Civil Rights Act of 1964 and the Voting Rights Act of 1965, the party's core base shifted, with Southern states becoming more reliably Republican in presidential politics. Since the 1990s, the Party's support has chiefly come from the South, the Great Plains, the Mountain States and rural and exurban areas in the Midwest.[74]

So, during my early childhood, shifts in the racial politics of the larger society surrounding tiny Ashlawn Farm would come to help set in motion some of the same Federal policies that would be my agrarian family's downfall. As mostly well-to-do white Republicans began to fret that an ascending "them" might come to take "their" wealth, GOP policies grew increasingly reactionary as blacks gained greater access to the ballot box. (That same fear has intensified today as minorities increase in raw numbers in our country's overall demographics.) Their policy became narrowly focused on an underlying goal: to protect existing privilege while combating possible threats to whites clinging to power, be those based on skin color or socio-economic class. With a swing in the party's focus, Republicans such as Charles Grassley had to shift their personal stances to match their party membership—as seen, in Chuck's case, in his continuing drift from once wrestling with the Pentagon over waste to now abetting our military's haste, from defending freedom to deafening indifference to the trampling of same. Gerrymandering enables this sham.

On the ground, in America's Heartland, conservatives "should" have fought to "conserve" the best, basic elements of the Good Life as once enjoyed by tens of millions of Elmers and Ermas across the region. Those who said they would defend the economic hallmarks of that system (living wages in towns and sufficient income on farms, allowing for parent-raised children who could grow up, healthy and in peace, attend college if they chose, then follow Big City lights to jobs in a burgeoning, prosperity-drunk America—and all the rest of that now-elusive national mythos) betrayed not only their own espoused beliefs, but *all* of us. It was also but much less Democratic than Republican policies that pushed Midwest farmers to "get big or get out" of agriculture, forsaking age-old, sustainable practices in favor of chemical-based industrialized crop and livestock production. Deadliest of all, we were coached to abandon centuries-old cooperation between us tillers of the land, done in order to prosper long-term. Instead, in order to profit short-term, we were to consider our neighbors as our "competitors." This consciously-cultivated greed, coupled with slammer waves of grain boycotts as pillars of anti-Soviet politics, led millions of farms—and thousands of small towns dependent on them—to fail, then vanish.

It was not just our physical culture (cow barns and school buses, silos and shops, houses and hardware) that disappeared at accelerating rates as of the so-called Reagan Revolution. More importantly, "conservative" policies failed to *conserve* the social culture that held our prairie world together. With diminishing on-farm or in-town income, wives felt compelled to leave home to seek a second income; young children got dumped on grandparents or, more typically and less beneficially, on veritable strangers. With US Department of Agriculture policies eagerly peddling—basically—mining the land for the sake of marketing a yield wrung out of increasingly weary soil, farming morphed from being a way of life to more a way of making a living—a job.

Ramping up production to such extremes—far beyond what our soil can naturally bear without artificial input and what our domestic market requires or can absorb—met two US government objectives: 1) It enabled the "cheap-food" policies of several administrations, and 2) over-production provided massive food exports the US also could use, at will, as a political weapon. (President Nixon's Hoosier-born Secretary of Ag, Earl Butts, admonished farm folk to "tear out the fence lines an' groves, an' plow from ditch ta ditch, 'cuz we're gonna feed the world!") Given economic incentives to do so, farmers' repertoire of crops shrank greatly. (Grandpa Thrams had raised up to sixteen different crops on Ashlawn Farm's 160 acres; his post-industrialized son-in-law, Bud Luick, grew mostly corn and soybeans, with perhaps a smattering of hay or oats if he "had a reason" to do so.) Yes, yield per acre rose, but so did the amount of Iowa loam and nitrates pouring into the Gulf of Mexico's "dead zone" southeast of the Big Easy—as I explain here:[75]

The left photo, circa 1950, documents how Elmer Thrams divided Ashlawn Farm into almost 20 parcels the year this image was taken. Doing so enriched the soil by rotating crops while fighting erosion. A 2019 view of the same land shows two essential problems with industrial monoculture agriculture: The topsoil is thinning from wind and water erosion; 120 acres of erstwhile Ashlawn Farm belong to a non-farming neighbor who rents it to a farmer who raises one crop, for years in a row—with the other 40 also the victim of monoculture, in another non-farmer's hands. So weakened, yields ever depend on inputs.

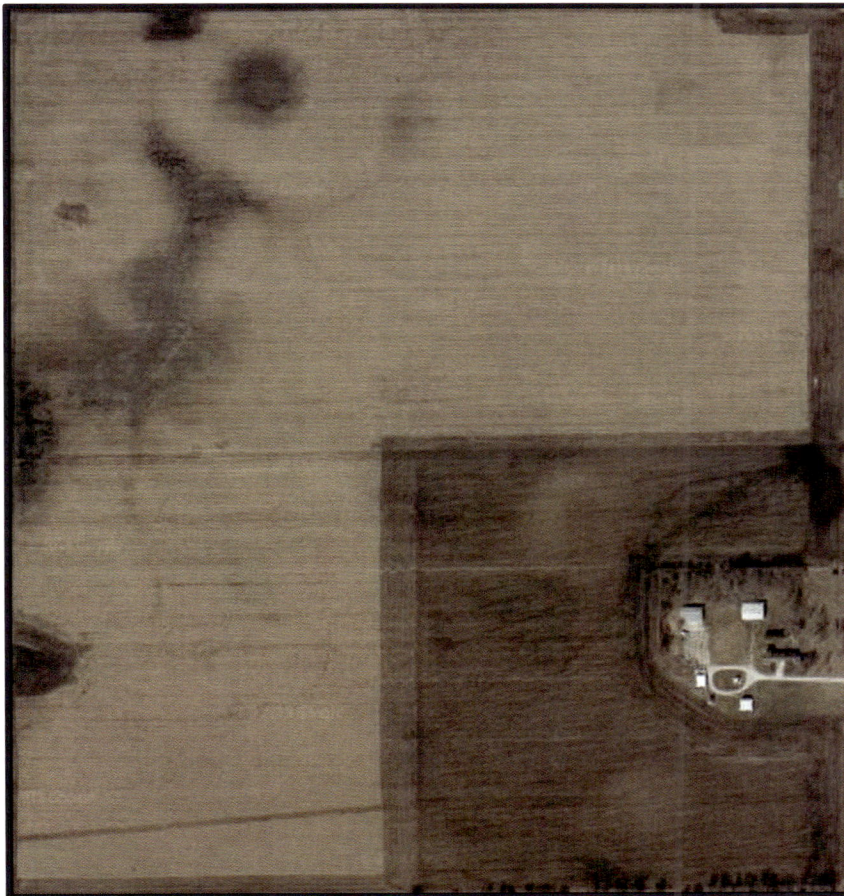

Bud Luick (on combine), an unknown helper and Grandpa, 1960;
Elmer Thrams (below) reaping wheat at Ashlawn Farm, circa 1920:
Heavy equipment compacts soil, suppressing porosity, flora and fauna.

The Great Difficulty with all this, was that ancient ways of living not just off but *with* the land faded, then mostly evaporated completely: An entire culture, passed from generation to generation, since the first wheat was cut with crude sickles ten millennia ago in today's Turkey, became forever extinct. It was this loss that was the greatest, most socially costly and least spiritually bearable—but, at least Republican-promoted gambling "islands" springing up across the state provided farmers and un[der-]employed small-town wage-laborers to soak their woes with cheap drinks as they fed their precious quarters and dimes into hungry slot machines. As Iowa's rural population aged and younger residents drifted off, schools closed, pews emptied, social clubs folded... hope for a better future withered, as did our willingness to talk about it all.

Since the '80s, a once-prosperous, once-flourishing rural Iowa has, like its Mid-American neighbors, been a place of freefall decay. Rather than renewal and expansion, it has been stuck in cycles of retrenchment and contraction. Feeling disrespected, un[der]valued, unheard and unseen by urban elites on either coast, too many of my fellow Iowans have succumbed to the calcified, regressive rule of eternal-officeholders like Charles Grassley, Terry Branstad and too many others. In such a petrified socio-political environment, getting voters to depart from the known and support an Unknown has few chances of ever succeeding. Despite my deep, abiding support for sustainable, restorative agriculture and the Main-Street merchants needed to stoke and supply it, I never had a chance to interface with Iowa's most-conservative citizens, who summarily dismissed me and my ideas as having no relevance to their plummeting prospects under the current system. How could I ever open a real dialog, with so many minds so closed? Were those minds in such an inaccessible state, perhaps, because their owners' hearts had been battered by decades of decay all around them—by shrinking populations, job loss... hope?[76]

Once upon a time, Americans actually could converse about matters of common concern: As yellowing, dog-eared newspaper accounts and staticky, fuzzy audio-videos attest, open public discourse was less confrontational, seldom snarky. With the rise of self-serving policies crafted to keep "them" at bay, however, divisive issues had to be found and fanned. Those having or dispensing an abortion, single-mother welfare "parasites," fags and, most recently, "wetbacks" became bogeymen and -women, posterchildren called to the fore upon demand by politicians lacking other, more substantive ways with which to vilify opponents as they built dirty careers. Distractions like men wearing left-lobe earrings [my sad-but-true story will come] keep us from finding left-brain remedies to our current malaise. Obsessing on personalities—for ad-selling media, a coveted zillion-dollar industry—rather than on policy minutiae, confuses us and coaxes an estimated every third American to simply turn the channel and tune out the "noise" that is inherent to the process of distilling democratic consensus. Much of that same disaffected third consistently fails to vote, assuming "Mine doesn't count." Such apathy only serves those elites working feverishly, mostly invisibly from behind the scenes, to protect "their" wealth from "us." (Our self-imposed disempowerment suits the elite jus' fine—jus' ask the stealthy Koch brothers.)

Trapped in chasms of distrust and ill will, Iowa's demise continues. Its people plagued by policy discombobulation, we are unsure of how to proceed—and thus ensnared in paralyzing fear, do too little, too late, too seldom to turn the rising tide of diminishing options. How did we become like rabbits hypnotized by approaching disaster; why don't we hop out of harm's way?

*

> "Not everything that is faced can be changed,
> but nothing can be changed until it is faced."
>
> — James Baldwin, *As Much Truth As One Can Bear*

The Last Straw

Strength in numbers, right? I hoped so 'cuz by this point I was gettin' purdy antsy. Despite all of my volunteers' and my efforts, it was obvious that we were gettin', like, zero traction. Seeing that our presumed "friends" in the "liberal" media weren't, and seeing so much indifference among the "conservative" mainstream, who simply shrugged and looked away, I conceded that I needed to change strategy. It pained me to do it, but I opted to lock shoulders with other non-mainstream candidates to fight a common battle against the seemingly impenetrable forces determined to keep all of us "independents" invisible, impotent and irrelevant.

In search of comrades, I reached out to Jim Hennager, a political-science instructor in Iowa's community-college system. Sadly, after several attempts, I concluded this multi-cycle candidate was essentially a self-serving schmuck. (I remain casually curious to hear what Jim thinks his several, class-run campaign stunts have wrought.) The third non-mainstream candidate for the US Senate from Iowa, in contrast, instantly proved responsive and cooperative. Problem was, as a Libertarian, Charles Aldrich embodied what I often disdain about independent candidates. As he was never forthcoming in answering my repeated, albeit low-level, queries into his past lives, present condition or future goals, I cannot say so conclusively, but it seemed likeable-but-aloof "Chuck" was a situational candidate: He'd recently run as a Libertarian in his native Minnesota; now, as far as I could ferret out of him, living at times on the sofa of his daughter's house in Clarion, Iowa, he'd felt inspired to run as a Libertarian in the Hawkeye State.

libertarian-anarchist Emma Goldman, 1911; the August 1860 edition of Le Libertaire, a libertarian publication printed in New York; Pierre-Joseph Proudhon, the first to declare himself an "anarchist"

Previously unreceptive to Libertarians' standard contrarian, self-involved message—and given that I actually believe in government (always better a streamlined effective one, over a bloated incompetent or corrupt one)—I held my ideological nose and offered Chuck to undertake campaigning in tandem. We would either attend organized speaking forums or, in their absence, create our own in public spaces. He could share the portable speaker and cordless mic I had purchased. We should take turns speaking, as the other handed out his flyers or held quiet, small-group parleys with passersby. If I might tag along on the invitations he got to speak at venues that overlooked, either inadvertently or purposely, offering me also to appear, in turn when I booked venues, I always asked if he might come, too—which he always could. He usually drove us to all appearances, which afforded me a chance to generate and edit press releases, update my campaign's media list, call would-be interviewers or simply stare out over the endless cornfields and plot my/our next move. Over the hundreds of miles on the odometer that we racked up, I appreciated Chuck's serving as a sounding board, as well as his obliging company.

At the same time, as he spoke, the government-so-small-you-can-drown-it-in-a-bathtub tenet that Chuck not only fed on but likewise fed to others wore on me ever again. Always sure to quietly but clearly note to folks that while we shared a bullhorn, we were spreading very different bull, I envied him that his "non-party party" yielded infinitely more name recognition than my utterly unknown one. Still, the people we reached in common seemed to understand and also appreciate the diversity we embodied. In our collectively quirky ways, Chuck and I complemented each other well. At the very least, sharing our campaign-damning invisibility made it endurable.

Our lovefest, however, had limits. Decidedly a man's man, Chuck could accept and tolerate my being gay, but not celebrate it. It seemed to be for him a "character trait" of mine, like his being fair-haired or stocky—nothing more: When I mentioned, in-context, past partners or current romantic interests, he'd switch channels. I enjoyed his dry humor, but could not look to him for belly-busters or the round-the-campfire camaraderie one might hope for in such a relationship of shared purpose. Still, we both acknowledged that we were in it "for real and the long haul." What we did not realize wading into our mutual-aid association, however, was… it might kill us.

But, before our shared journey took us that far, we had more immediate concerns. Above all, we searched for effective, publicly-acceptable ways to jump over the hurdles put in our way of being heard. Early on, over a post-appearance *Bier* (for him) and *Rotwein* (mine), we discerned that we had suffered the same series of slights: Unanswered requests for interviews or airtime, omission from election-race panel-discussion rounds, being dismissed as "jokes"—the works. How could we conquer such obstacles? "Together!" Having identified common ground and possessing complementary goals, Chuck's and my union seemed easy—until, that is, it got hard.

And that, we found, happened soon enough.

Despite both of us being veterans to media indifference to our candidacies, just before the first—and last—public, televised debate between Charles Grassley and Patty Judge (to which we were deliberately not invited), Chuck and I reached a saturation point in how much invisibility we could bear any longer. The final straw in an interminable series of slights came in the form of a poll:

One weekend, a volunteer warned "Brace yourself" as she handed me a copy of the *Des Moines Sunday Register*. When I saw that the *DMR* was asking readers, for which US-Senate candidate they likely would vote in November, yet omitted—as always—60% of the total candidates for that office, I went ballistic. "Should I call for a defibrillator for you?" the worried woman asked.

As early on Monday morning as I thought I might reach some office slave at the *DMR*, I called Mindy (or whatever her name was) and demanded "Who do you people think you are by airbrushing over half of the candidates for this fall's US-Senate race from your readership poll?"

Immediately, as soon as embarrassed Stacey stumbled for a half-plausible reply, the smell of smoke again wafted up from my seat. "We reserve the right to—" she began, but I interjected:

"Don't your readers have a right to know the complete list of candidates running for the US Senate from Iowa? Eleven percent[77] said they wouldn't vote for Grassley *or* Judge, but had you offered other choices, your readers may have chosen one of us. Doesn't that matter to you?"

"But" Tracey tried to butt in, but I would not let her.

"But, 34% percent of those who planned not to vote for Patty" I charged on, "said they'd be open to voting for a Democratic candidate if it weren't *her*. And, another 24% said they *might* be, with only 42% of 'Patty's' voters committed to supporting *only* her. If you had told them about us—"

"But we didn't" Casey blurted out. "We have the right to pose whatever questions we choose."

"Doesn't honesty or integrity have any meaning or value to you people anymore? Who have you become? The *Register* was once 'The Newspaper that Iowa Depends On' but not no more."

"You're free to send a letter of complaint to our—" Cathy began to offer, but I had had enough.

"Never mind" I snipped as I hung up on her, "see ya soon out on the sidewalk!" Turning to Chuck, I asked "Ya ready ta possibly get arrested tomorrow?"[78]

"You bet" he bid, grinning. "Let's do it!"

*

> "The proof that one truly believes is action."
>
> — African-American gay-Quaker activist
> Bayard Rustin, cited in *Brother Outsider*

Belief in Action

Months earlier, I had invested the time and expense to make an attractive, durable campaign sign out of foam core, an extendable pole and spiffy graphics to mount on it. I carried that sign on the marches I went on, held it as I addressed crowds or passersby (usually standing on a three-rung step ladder, topped with a padded curved railing) or stabbed it into the ground, like a Conquistador's royal-emblem flag planted on some distant shore, while at farmers markets or street festivals. Now preparing to take on Iowa's media behemoths, it would serve me anew.

In olden days, kings or *Kaisers* awaiting to attack sent emissaries to ask if a targeted enemy might not wish to capitulate rather than face armed conflagration. Instead, we simply distributed a press release to a hundred or so recipients on Chuck's and my shared list-serve, announcing the picketing and our reasons for it. To my knowledge, not a single news outlet printed it, which read:

Soon after sunrise on the next morning, Chuck and I parked his clunky old van on the edge of downtown, then marched to the pavement northwest of the *Register*'s tower. As I had phoned all four media outlets which we planned to picket that day, announcing our calling them out for their unwillingness to include us in their election coverage, a *DMR* security heavy was already standing behind a curtain, in a window a floor or more above the treed area we had chosen for our rush-hour stand against imposed invisibility, monitoring us. Just then, another employee appeared on the loading dock to taunt us, "Now don't you trespass, or you'll be mighty sorry." Despite his disapproving scowl, I thought he should join us, as he might be as much locked into a dead-end system as a worker for The [Media] Man as we were as candidates.

"And if we do?" I shot back, knowing already that we would not—nor need to: I had confirmed that we had a right to express our opinions on public property, including on all city sidewalks.

At that, the testy older black man disappeared inside, saying "OK, man—have it your way then."

Chuck and I soon forgot him, however, for a German man and Romanian woman—election observers sent from the OECD,[79] with whom we had met over dinner the previous evening to talk—appeared to see how political protest would be received in America's Heartland. Just as we greeted each other, two office workers paused long enough to ask what we were doing.

"We are protesting the *Register*'s refusal to cover our campaigns for the US Senate" Chuck belted out. The two young men looked blankly at him, then at each other, shrugged and walked away.

To that, I breathlessly added "But they won't even come out to cover our picketing, of their not coming out to cover our picketing." I offered the bolting worker bees my pamphlet, but in vain.

As Helmut and Sandra began to ask what the reaction had been so far to our *"Aktion"* the first of eight police vehicles arrived (one, a paddy wagon), bringing the initial wave of a total of thirteen officers dispatched to quell the reported "riot" forming in downtown Des Moines. Eying the swelling ranks of police but not our latest dining mates, I absently replied *"Ah-h-h*, I think you'll soon see the answer to that question yourselves." I could barely believe it myself, that the orderly expression of personal opinion in America could result in such an exaggerated police response.

The head officer then stomped up to us and demanded an account of what we were doing, as well as our IDs. As Chuck explained who we were and what we were doing, Helmut clucked under his breath "Dies could not verk so in da Europeen U-ni-on." Sandra's eyes were bulging.

The man at the loading dock reappeared and resumed ogling us, but as we had not tread upon private property, the officer in charge deemed we were guiltless and could continue. A thin crowd had begun to form around the small army of DMPD cops ringed around us, but soon dispersed as the excitement faded. For our parts, Chuck and I raised our signs high and chanted "We're running, too! We're—" as no one listened other than two foreigners assigned to do so.

"Tya" Helmut tsk-tsked as he offered *"Aufwiedersehen!"* and Sandra bade us "Good luck!"

"I vill include dies in mein report venn ve are back in Europa" Helmut promised, then strode off.

My heart still racing from our potentially explosive confrontation with heavily-armed police, I reminded Chuck, "Come on—it's time to head to our next three gigs: We've survived this one."

"Great" he smiled, as we struck off for his jalopy. "It's gonna be a long day—drink lotza water."

From the heart of downtown Des Moines, we moved to two broadcast studios on its periphery, one being Central Iowa's largest television channel, KCCI, the other its most venerable radio station, WHO—where a greenhorn Ronald Reagan began working as a sportscaster in the early 1930s. We took turns at knocking on their doors and asking to meet with their managers; both refused to interview or report about us. Our "hosts" responded icily and curtly, and, once again, passersby—the few on-foot or the many in zipping cars—looked at us bewilderedly. Still, Chuck and I smiled—and waved freely: We were committed to making a statement, not a scene. As we had at the *Register*, we spent not quite an hour at each stop. At the end of the second one, I sang "Now, my friend, 'tis time to visit our friend Justin Beaupre, to shame his dogged intractability."

Per Professor Pedia,[80] Ronald Wilson "Dutch" Reagan "worked as a sportscaster with WHO from 1932 to 1937. Among his duties were re-creations of Chicago Cubs baseball games [after he] received details over a teleprinter for each play[; he] would act as if he were in the stadium, reporting on a game while seeing it from the press box." A son of America's Heartland, the future US President grew up in the county seat of Dixon, Illinois, then headed west to build a career in media—first as a radio announcer in Iowa, then a B-list actor in Hollywood. His ability to fake reality served Republicans well as they took over America.

Johnston has been a Des Moines satellite for over a century. Home to the Iowa National Guard at Camp Dodge, today it is also synonymous in many Iowans' minds as the home of Iowa Public Television. Set back from the curvy suburban boulevard which winds past it, on park-like lawns lined with trees and bushes, IPTV's stolid brick building resembles a tastefully camouflaged prison or bunker. Noticeably lacking sidewalks like most suburbs, Johnston's car-catering layout dictated that we set up an awkward beachhead next to a stop sign as the site of our protest.

Once so settled in, we waited for anything to happen. But, nothing did: No cops, no honking or cat calls from passing cars, no *nothin'*—jus' happy birds chirpin' their late-mornin' joy… an' us.

"This is sortta silly, ain't it?" I finally conceded. "Justin's no more gonna show up here than the Queen of England might, so we might as well call spades what they is an' blow this joint, huh?"

"Ya" Chuck moaned under his breath—and at that we prematurely abandoned our assault on IPTV's fortress on Corporate Drive. Having been vanquished rather than having conquered, we modern swashbucklers retreated to a nearby Mexican restaurant's patio to regroup. There, over tequila reinforcements and *mucho* munching, our day's quixotic mission turned deadly serious: We downed our grub, then tore off to a potentially violent showdown in Sioux City.

*

128

To Protect and to Serve

A mid-sized city—Iowa's fourth largest—Sioux City's "Gateway to the West" supertitle belies its many characteristically Eastern touches: live-music joints and edgy eateries lining brick-paved streets, a 1918-built county courthouse the National Park Service called "one of the finest Prairie School buildings" in the country, a high-class art museum, large parks and much rolling green space, as well as several colleges. It arose as an early trading point on the Missouri River where three, almost four Upper Midwest states meet. It was long home to a flourishing Jewish community, which produced the twins Esther Pauline and Pauline Esther Friedman, later known to the world as "Dear Ann [Landers]" and "Dear Abby [Van Buren]." It also was the hometown of Harry Hopkins, an architect of the New Deal and one of Franklin Delano Roosevelt's closest advisers: As such, Hopkins helped America navigate a dangerous world from behind the scenes.

President Franklin Roosevelt and Harry Hopkins in the back of an automobile in Rochester, Minnesota, after visiting son James Roosevelt in hospital, in September 1938; Pauline (née Friedman) Phillips, in 1961

On the afternoon that Chuck and I barreled along Interstates 80 and then 29, hellbent to reach Sioux City before it literally was too late, I could have used help from the likes of Hopkins to navigate a dangerous America. That day, all around me, I sensed aggression and subterfuge.

129

As typically-silent Chuck sped on, staring forward, motionless, I sat in the other front seat of his crusty ol' tin can on wheels and processed what had happened to us a few hours earlier, on the sidewalks of downtown Des Moines. "Ya know" I told my partner in non-crime, wagging my head in disbelief, "all of that excessive force called out to intimidate us was simply *not* OK."

"*Um-m-m*" he grunted, checking the side mirror to see who might be overtaking us—or not.

"Ya know" I peered at my hands and adjusted my rings, "we can't jus' let that go unchallenged."

"*Uh-h-h*, *huh-h-h*" he barely audibly agreed, from his end of our old-married-couple exchange.

"So, I won't!" I declared as I fished my cellphone out of my ever-overflowing shoulder bag.

After much trawling, I finally got the Des Moines Police Department's number and dialed it.

"Sargent [something or other], DMPD" the voice on the other end answered, gruffly.

"Sorry, I missed that—what'd ya say your name is?" I asked timidly, already feeling intimidated.

He responded merely with "Whaddaya want?"

"*Ah-h-h*, I'm calling to file a complaint, but I'm not sure who my conversation partner is."

"What's the complaint?" he commanded, his voice broadcasting a monotone barking cadence.

I thought the officer had asked about the nature of my complaint to know to whom to relay the call. "I'm calling to file a civil-rights violation" I replied meekly, as I looked at motionless Chuck.

"What civil rights violation?" he demanded. In the background, I could hear paper rustling, punctuated by a door nearby that kept banging shut with a dull *THUD!*—then only dull silence.

"Oh" I punted, "are you the person I need to talk to?" even as I prayed he would transfer me.

"What civil rights violation?" he demanded again, sternly, as the ambient silence grew louder.

"Well, this morning a colleague and I were demonstrating in downtown Des Moines and—"

"Your civil rights weren't violated" Sargent Something interrupted.

"Sorry—" I swallowed hard, "—but were you there?"

"No, but I heard about it."

"Well, we were there and were intimidated by an incommensurate response to our protest."

"Your civil rights weren't violated" the man asserted again, louder and increasingly aggressive.

"But you weren't there—how could you know that? We were and we felt they were—and, in any case, we have a right to file a complaint" I argued, "so that the matter can be investigated."

"Look, your civil rights weren't violated. [Pause.] There. Was. No. Violation. You understand?"

"Pardon, but we—" I pleaded into what was now a roaring silence pouring through the phone.

"Are you listening to me?" he shouted. "There! Was! No! Violation! Do you understand me?"

I had not understood his name when this man had answered, but I did hear him say "-elli" or "-ella" at the end of whatever name he rifled off. *Hum-m-m*, I thought, *jus' like in the movies*.

"We counted seven squad cars and a paddy wagon on-hand" I informed him, expectantly.

"So?"

"And thirteen officers were present!"

"And? So what's the problem?"

"The problem is" I stammered, "we felt intimidated and thus hindered in the exercise of our right to speak freely." Silence. "We are candidates registered with the Iowa Secretary of State" I noted, although it was clear that this big beluga would not be impressed one iota by that detail. Still more silence. "OECD representatives were there" I squeaked, "an' they'll file a report."

"You were lucky to have so many a' my buddies there to protect ya."

"'Protect' us?" I echoed him, faintly.

"Ya—an' serve."

"'Protect' us from whom?" I challenged, as a parallel conversation taking place in my head went along the lines of *"-elli" is Italian. Figures* I groused to myself, *those people invented fascism!*

"Look, yer civil rights weren't violated, so you can jus' give it up."

"You weren't there" I countered, "and besides, you aren't a judge—"

"How you know that?" he interrupted. "You think ya know ev'ything or sompthin'?"

"Are you tryin' ta intimidate me now?"

"I'm tellin' ya, there was no violation. Anything else ya wanna say? 'Cuz, I got reports ta write."

Stunned, I shook my head and breathed into the phone, unsure how to respond to this travesty.

"No, not now" I finally mustered, then hung up. Turning to Chuck I sighed "We're screwed."

"What was *that*?" he wondered without tearing his blank eyes from the empty highway ahead.

"No idea" I shrugged, slumping into the seat. Feeling like I had just sparred with Lucifer's son, a general sense of creepiness crept over me. I looked out the window at the passing prairie. *Where am I?* I asked myself. *Who are these people—and what is going on here?* I felt truly ill.

"We'll be in Sioux City soon" Chuck bid as reached over to turn on a country-western station.

*

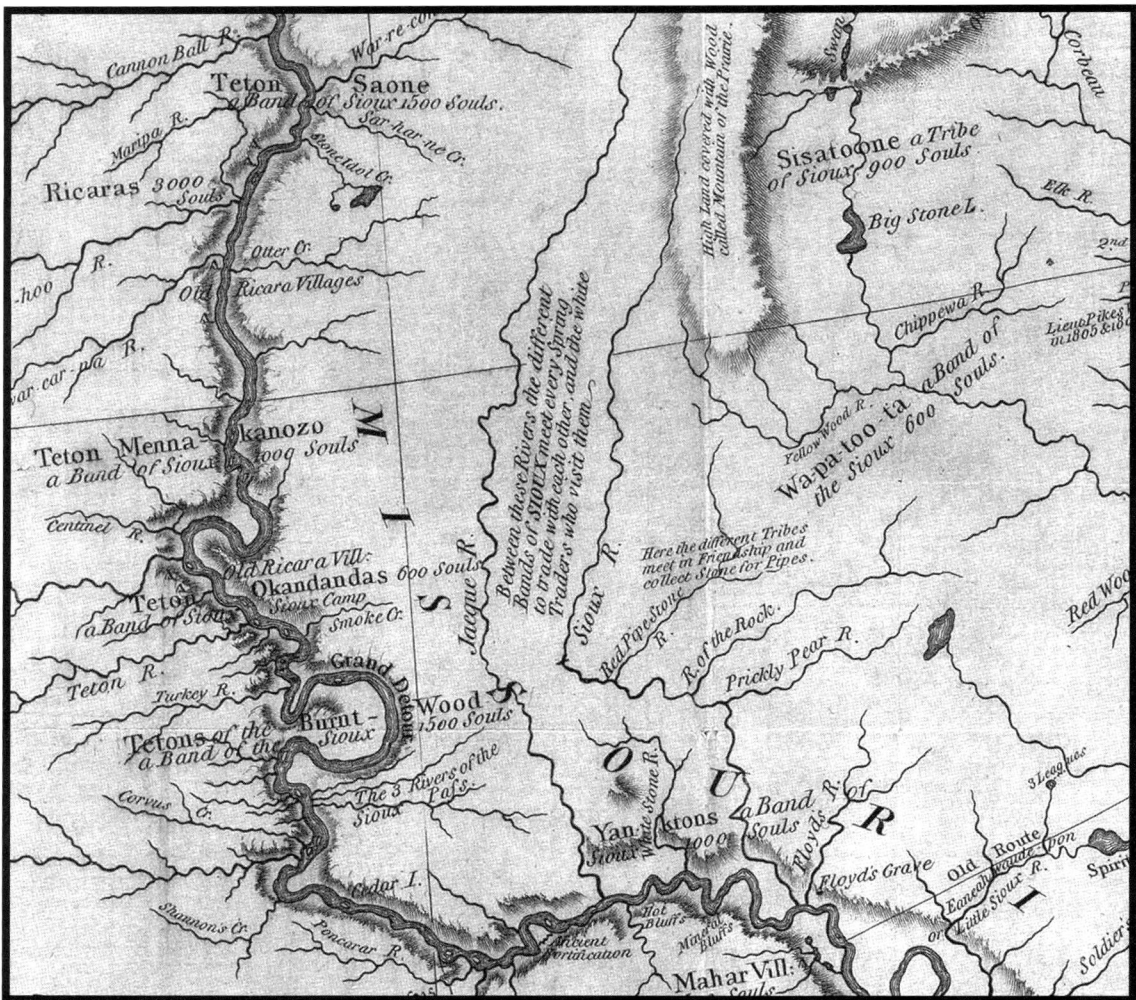

This excerpt of a Lewis and Clark 1814 map, posted to Wikipedia commons, shows rivers in what is now known as northwestern Iowa and eastern South Dakota. The map and written account of the expedition changed American mapping of the northwest by giving the first accurate depiction of the relationship of sources of the Missouri and the Columbia, and the Rocky Mountains. The map was copied by Samuel Lewis from William Clark's original drawing, engraved by Samuel Harrison.

"I live my life in widening circles
that reach out across the world.
I may not complete this last one
but I will give myself to it.

I circle around God, around the primordial tower.
I've been circling for thousands of years
and I still don't know: Am I a falcon,
a storm, or a great song?"

— Rainer Maria Rilke, *Das Stundenbuch*
[*"The Book cf Hours"*]

The Primordial Tower

By now headed north, following the broad, meandering Missouri River on the left and Iowa's Loess Hills on the right, I fell into myself and soon got stuck in sticky thoughts. Among other reasons, we passed blighted Awano, behind which I could make out tiny Milan, where half a decade earlier I'd encountered several Princes of Darkness, with equally unsettling effect. It had been in Milan where I had tried to facilitate positive social change through organic gardening and alternative energy at the TRACES-sponsored Burr Oak Center. Ironically, a parallel objective of that ideal-driven project was to revive rural communities, but it was the one immediately surrounding us that, in the end, led to Burr Oak's demise and premature closing. With such shadowy images dancing through my mind, I meditated on deflating unanswerables, like *Why is it that such forces can continue to exist in the world?* Before those thoughts completely ground my soul into powder, however, I spied Floyd Monument atop a nearby bluff: We were "there."

The Loess Hills are one of the Midwest's most scenic landscapes—as captured by Kenneth G. West, 2011.

As soon as we entered the outskirts of the closest thing Iowa has to a Cowtown, Chuck asked if I was hungry. "After all that's happened so far today?" I cringed. "No way! I'd lose my stomach."

"OK, then" he queried, "where next, what first? It's your show now. I'm jus' along for the ride."

He surprised me, as we had plotted this *Aktion* together and agreed to undertake it in tandem. That Chuck seemed to be relinquishing its co-directorship gave me pause—but also a free hand.

We had two have-to-do tasks we had to do before we could set into motion the plan for protest that had brought Chuck and me to Sioux City to begin with. One was to drive to the city's north side to the home of Richard Steinbach, a Briar Cliff University music professor and a masterful pianist who often housed homeless me. I wanted to retrieve a suitcase I had left there the last time I had flopped at his cozy Arts-and-Crafts gem: I was going to go out in a suit, if I had to go out at all that day in a momentous instant. The other was to pay a tetchy visit to KITV, the sponsor-broadcaster of that night's live debate between Chuck Grassley and Patty Judge, from which we had been blacklisted: "We're not going to succumb to obscurity silently!" I had vowed.

As Chuck navigated Sioux City's chopped-up street grid, following the vague hand gestures that I gave from the passenger's seat, I observed first my feet and legs, then my fingers and arms grow heavy. My breathing was slowing as my lungs grew wooden, my heart sluggish. I literally could feel my body shutting down. Life seemed to be seeping out of my soul's flesh envelope. It was all I could do to drop my leaden head back to the side and watch tree-lined streets flash by.

On a non- or even metaphysical level, I felt my Self caving into myself, sinking ever more deeply and becoming ever-less retrievable. My cohort and I well knew, that our pulling the emergency brake at that evening's event entailed the likelihood of at least ejection from the audience, if not arrest, and the possibility of physical violence—or worse. The security heavies would be heavily armed and, this being America, would shoot first and, perhaps, ask later: We'd be **dead**!

Was it the potentially violent encounter with Des Moines cops that morning—or the frightening one with Sargent Something of the DMPD on the phone earlier that afternoon? Was it the cruel irony of Chuck's and my persistent invisibility, even as we publicly protested that invisibility? Was it driving by that still-stinging reminder of my squandered efforts at Awano and Milan to castrate the beast that is eating away at the heart of America? Was it the intensity of all these things, squared with the insufferable banality of every thing? What was it that was killing me?

My rarely-faulty intuition has served me well all of my life. It must have, for Life has given me an exceptionally rich, planet-roaming biography that few Iowa farmboys could ever imagine having—and I embraced this unique life intuitively, always going to where I was led, taking the next step based not on what my brain coached, but what my heart coaxed me to take. Having been entrusted with much of great value, I had long intuited that much was required of me, that

Life demanded me not just to live differently, but to live to make a difference. For four decades, I had pursued the paths Life whispered were correct for me—and the ensuing journey had been singular. Now, though, this ("last"?) act entailed a sense of finality. Was the ride over?

Just as my mind sank to the lowest level my thoughts could sink at that point, Chuck screeched his van to a juddering stop and, smiling for once, called out "Our first stop, Steinbach Station!"

I did not smile back: I could not move. Then:

To this day unaware of from where the energy burst for it came, my inert body began to thaw out of its inertia enough to pry the door open, drop my deadweight legs to the curb and make my way up the interminably long concrete steps from the sidewalk to Richard's screened porch door. After I found a housekey he had hidden for me, I fumbled with the lock until it gave way.

The task of fetching my wheeled suitcase was easy, the matter of a few moments, but the "trip" from the door to the upstairs guestroom and back seemed to take an eternity. As I stumbled through his well-appointed living room, I remembered the many conversations we had shared here, including about Richard's growing up on a hardscrabble homestead in western Nebraska's dryland-farming region. Striding past his sleek, shiny-black baby grand, his tales of touring— repeatedly—in Europe, Asia and Latin America on concert-piano performances came to mind.

Why does Richard have it all so easy? I heard that irritating voice in my head taunt me. *Why do others get to play and flirt their way around the world, but I have to schlep school supplies to kids in Nicaragua or scrub floors at Mother Theresa's musty mission? Why can't I be content* I wondered, *throwing cool patio parties instead of landing in the heat of heavily-armed demos?* As I turned up the stairs and headed past the door to Richard's bedroom, I kvetched *Why do others get to have stellar partnerships with above-average mates, but I go begging for touch?*

Having at last grabbed my bag, turned and began descending those short steps, my suffocating sense of self-pity swelled even more: *Why can't I jus' relax, coast a bit and let Life carry me? Why do I always have to be on some damnable, endless mission to do well while doing good? I am tired and lonely! How much longer do I have to do all this? When will it ever end—tonight, maybe?*

Chuck, sitting in the van like a lump of lifeless matter, turned his head at a sloth's pace to ask "Is everything all right?" as I opened the van door, then slowly slid onto the seat. I merely sighed.

"We're off to see the wizard" I hummed with noticeable indifference, "the most wonderfully excluding wizard there ever was." Taking a breath, I turned to Chuck. "Drive ahead, turn right."

*

Storming the Castle

After too many stomach-churning curves atop Sioux City's stretch of Loess-Hills ridges, we arrived at the bottom of Airwave Hill Drive. Chuck cried out "Next stop, Suppression Station!"

I did not react to that. I would not, as instead:

My eyes were busy following the paved path that snaked up Airwave Hill to the KITV building, which resembled a '70s version of a squat Medieval castle. It seemed so brooding, so menacing and impenetrable. I expected to hear a haunting wolf's cry or see black bats doing big swoops. A chill coursed down my spine and my skull shook from its base, I so dreaded doing this deed.

Still, somehow, I harkened Chuck with "Let's do it!," sprang out the van and stormed the door.

Thankfully, my sidekick suddenly assumed center stage and did a flawless job of explaining first to the guard, then to a manager and finally to the owner who we were and why we were there. As if suspended in a sea of lava-lamp sludge, I simply watched this confrontation unfold—most of the time through a milky-glass partition between myself, seated in the lobby, and the rest, standing in a swelling huddle in the narrow central corridor of that busy fortress. Monitoring their motions and filtering out stray words from a crescendoing buzz, I continued to inhale the out-of-body air that had punctuated the myriad events of the entire day. I felt drunk and testy.

At some point, after the station owner had been summoned, I sensed an impasse in Chuck's handling of our mission. So, I intervened. Striding up to the cluster of staff that had formed around my fellow candidate as he volleyed accusations with the gloss-polished manager, I said "I'm Michael." Stunned by my appearance, she stared at me. "Ya know, here it is, in short form: We're on the ballot, so why weren't we invited to tonight's debate? We're here to say, loud and clear, that we will *not* abide with being sidelined and that we *will* be heard. We *insist* on it."

"When we set up this debate in July" Ms Wellheeled squirmed, her eyes not blinking once the whole time she or we spoke, "we didn't know who the unaffiliated candidates would be—"

"You *well* knew" I persisted, "as in *every* election cycle, that non-mainstream candidates *would* be approved, *after* the two big parties' primaries, but only *as of* August 1st, so *why* didn't you reserve space on your stage for *us*? You *knew* we'd be coming, even if you didn't have *names*."

At the point that she insisted that—contrary to my fiery claims—she and her husband were not "cowing to the elite" or "perpetuating a system that assures big-budget bucks for media outlets like [theirs]," I repeated that we weren't leaving without being heard. Stumped, she froze for a pensive moment, then suddenly jolted to life, turned to a minion named John and ordered him to "Call the studio and tell 'em to interview these two gentlemen—*pronto.*" I nearly fainted.

As moments later the station's confused news anchor conducted an impromptu interview with Chuck—dressed, as usual, in jeans and a faded plaid shirt—I waited outside the swinging door to the studio and tried to call up pieces of my elevator pitch. Both tired yet wired, my mind balked at this, so I busied myself with flicking lint off my dull-blue suit and adjusting my snazzy tie. It seemed like half a day dragged by, but in short order Chuck appeared and producers herded me to the seat he had left sweaty. Lights flashed on, cameras rolled, I stuttered something—done!

In the van, as we drove to the debate's venue, Morningside College, we reviewed the spoils of the skirmish we had just waged and weighed whatever gems that remained. We both marveled over, then regretted that each of us had been bought off with a cheap, 90-second cameo. *Crap!*

Then, as we pulled into Morningside's lot, Chuck announced "Last stop, Hangman Station!"

I did not laugh at that—but I did almost cry.

*

AMERICANS.....
DON'T PATRONIZE REDS !!!!

YOU CAN DRIVE THE REDS OUT OF TELEVISION, RADIO AND HOLLYWOOD.....
THIS TRACT WILL TELL YOU HOW.

WHY WE MUST DRIVE THEM OUT:

1) The REDS have made our Screen, Radio and TV Moscow's most effective Fifth Column in America . . . 2) The REDS of Hollywood and Broadway have always been the chief financial support of Communist propaganda in America . . . 3) OUR OWN FILMS, made by RED Producers, Directors, Writers and STARS,are being used by Moscow in ASIA, Africa, the Balkans and throughout Europe to create hatred of America . . . 4) RIGHT NOW films are being made to craftily glorify MARXISM, UNESCO and ONE-WORLDISM . . . and via your TV Set they are being piped into your Living Room—and are poisoning the minds of your children under your very eyes ! ! !

So REMEMBER — If you patronize a Film made by RED Producers, Writers, Stars and STUDIOS you are aiding and abetting COMMUNISM . . . every time you permit REDS to come into your Living Room VIA YOUR TV SET you are helping MOSCOW and the INTERNATIONALISTS to destroy America ! ! !

Televison-related Wikimedia Commons images from the 1950s include typical anti-communist literature of the era, specifically demanding the entertainment industry to "drive the Reds out."

"Courage is more exhilarating than fear and in the long run easier. We do not have to become heroes overnight, just a step at a time, meeting each thing as it comes up, seeing it is not as dreadful as it appears, discovering we have the strength to stare it down."

— US First Lady (1933-45) Eleanor Roosevelt, *You Learn by Living*

Flirting with Death

The westernmost of Iowa's some half-dozen Methodist-founded colleges, Morningside first entered my life in the late 1970s, when one summer a troupe of kids from the Clear Lake Methodist Camp trekked "out West" to Sioux City as part of our focus on social justice. With past or present congregants as diverse as George W. Bush and Hillary Clinton, few non-members are aware of how activism not only spawned but historically defined Methodism, named for its "methodical" renewal and ordering of society, one redeemed member at a time. A movement arising in England and its colonies during the initial displacement caused by the young industrial revolution, it took root among first Britain's laboring classes, then among aspiring professionals. It emphasized temperance—both individually (in my mother's staunch upbringing, "good" Methodists did not drink, dance or play cards) and socially (public campaigns against Demon Rum and the ruin it did rack among especially the poor). In the spirit of its official "social principles" that two centuries after its founding, Methodism still swept up Iowa farm and small-town kids, and carried us to places we otherwise likely never would have tread. Such was this case.

a postcard of Sioux City's Morningside College in the 1910s: Both buildings still exist today.

That hot, steaming summer in the bad-hair '70s, some ten to fifteen of us endured a four-hour sweltering van trip from Clear Lake to Sioux City. Encouraged by two veterans of Vietnam—no, not men who had fought *in* but rather *against* that then-recent war—we came to Cowtown to interview Native Americans and African Americans. As Iowa's Governor Ray—a noble old-school Republican—had not yet dared bring the first "boat people" to our state from Southeast Asia,[81] and Mexican-American laborers at that time mostly sojourned on the edge of towns as seasonal workers, those "Indians" and blacks were the main, albeit tiny, minorities then in Iowa.

As Chuck and I, almost forty years later, pulled into Morningside's lot, I recalled with fondness and gratitude the efforts of Jim Dale[82] and Del Dawes, as those two pastors gently yet persistently exposed us [then, mostly uncomprehending] youth to whole worlds that coursed orbits other than the one from where we hailed. Even I—then a budding Republican, who on an ice-covered day in winter 1979-80 braved the freezing cold to go to Mason City's airport to hear Ronald Reagan (dressed in even-then-garish red-plaid slacks) address dedicated Northcentral Iowa admirers—was moved by the "Other" we met in Sioux City. Even if it did not consciously do so at the time, later that experience proved a formative one in my awakening.

In 2016, Chuck and I ironically found ourselves stalking a man who I first met as an adoring Young Republican in winter 1978-79. Already then precocious and recognized for emerging-yet-clear potential, my Clear Lake High School counselor, Don Kacer, had secured for me a scholarship to attend the Hugh O'Brian Youth Leadership Foundation's Outstanding Sophomore Seminar in Des Moines. Soon after I arrived, I met Beth Shadlow, a mousy but moxie-driven poor girl from New Hartford, Iowa. We became fast friends—and later fiancés… but that is a different story—while attending lectures and workshops at Des Monies' then-faded-lady Hotel Savery. While there, a fellow New Hartfordian of Beth's, then-US-representative Charles Grassley, addressed us kids, who predated the "talented and gifted" tag. At the time, this ex-factoryworker was waging his first US-Senate campaign. Fast forward four decades: Getting ready to interrupt his only 2016 campaign debate, I remembered almost nothing of what then-young Chuck had said. But, I did recall that (perhaps due to ill-operated lighting?) the man appeared to have dull-glowing, faintly green-tinted skin, the shade of the then-popular E.T. about whom every kid alive was aware.

Now, about to see him again, as two adult men and fellow candidates for the post he had held by 2016 for far too long, I expected to see not glowing-green but pasty-white, wrinkled skin. Having visited Grassley's Washington Senate office several times—usually in conjunction with protesting nuclear arms or intervention in Central America, demonstrating for gay rights or, most recently, retrieving much-appreciated cups of hot cocoa while attending Barack Obama's icy inauguration in January 2009—I had watched the man age over the course of all of my adult life. An unwanted yardstick against which to judge my own curriculum vitae, "Uncle Chuck" had been half of Iowa's Senate presence in our nation's capital since I was 17 years old. Now, I wanted to deprive him of serving a seventh term in that position—but *how*? I was not sure: In his case, term limits were too late to fit a train already out the station. Going forward, as I did before and after it, during my campaign I advocated strict term limits for all elected officials, who under my plan could serve in any *one* office, at *any* level, for up to twelve years. People could still make [even a lifelong] career in politics, but *never* again would a Grassley so grossly dominate a given post.

What was clear, was that the man still commanded deep, rabid support from his supporters. As "my" Chuck and I walked to Eppley Auditorium, we first heard, then saw rows of rapturous campus Republicans (would a Democratic equivalent dare raise its head at Morningside, deep in Steve King country?) line the sidewalk down which their messiah soon would have to pass upon arriving for the debate. That I did not see a single Judge poster or even identifiable followers struck me as odd—a portent to her 549,460 votes verses Grassley's 926,007. [I netted 4,441.][83]

Approaching the large, eager crowd, which had decked the area with Grassley signs (in violation of at least a pretense of maintaining visible non-partisanship?) I noted the large number of SCPD police officers reinforcing the hefty campus-security presence. As I did, I wondered which one(s) of them would be the first to lunge at me when I stood up, as planned, to interrupt the debate at the end of its first third, as well as who among them would deck libertine Chuck once he did the same as the last third commenced. Who would knock me down or punch me in the gut or face; which of them would kick or strangle me as he swore obscenities? Which man whom I could see and study closely might panic and pull a fatal trigger? For whom could I one day be a stinging memory of a rash second, an in-the-line-of-duty casualty cum ghost to haunt his and his family's lives forever? Or, was I to be a forgotten suspected assassin, relegated to oblivion?

As I surveyed the larger landscape around me—the armed sentries, the debate moderator, the lighting and film crews, the animated audience members taking their seats—I felt intensely mindful of my Self, of my own presence in this lively sea of excitement, of energy and verve. My mind also pondered if these were, indeed, to be my last moments on Earth, and my last breaths taken into lungs that soon would be lifeless and cold. Would my exhilarating, improbable biography now flash to a bloody end? Would Cowtown be the anticlimactic end of a long road? I despaired, as it all felt so void of glory or fanfare. Who would mourn me? Would my death for The Cause be worth a few seconds of Statement, a loud but flickering interruption of Iowans' late-summer-evening telly watching? Would I die a fool's death, rather than a hero-martyr's?

Sitting there in that steamy auditorium, it did not escape me that I was thinking end-of-Life thoughts one second, then entertaining deadening thoughts in the next: *Have both candidates arrived? Is the debate about to begin? Will soon all the cameras roll and folks at home settle in for routine rounds of mundane questions an' even more tepid answers? What a thing, that all of this will be broadcast across the state, carried by lotza lil' stations. That'll line Ms Wellheeled's deep pockets even more.* Then, catching myself, I realized what I was doing. *How odd, yet how fitting* I mused, *that my last Earthly concerns should be so ordinary an' dull*. I could hardly bear this banal but basic contradiction: *My human existence is about ta be snuffed out like a candle flame, yet the setting surrounding that flame assumes larger-than-life dimensions*. Still, I had no choice: Meditating on my likely demise had a context—even if a stupid, sad, pedestrian one. If I wanted to focus on that motif or not, the film I now found myself in was already well in motion: *How can I stop it—but do I even wanna? Do I know, how trustworthy is this "knowing" I sense?*

US Senator Chuck Grassley stands with the Democratic candidate for the US Senate, former Iowa Lt. Governor Patty Judge, after the debate at Morningside College on Wednesday evening, 19 October 2016. Was it just me or did the stage that night lack anything resembling vitality or passion? Here's a clue:[84]

Paralyzed for a few moments that took on the weight of a few hours' wait, I soon rallied: After Uncle Chuck did arrive (we had not noticed Patty's appearance), my Libertarian co-conspirator and I took positions about ten rows back from the stage, spread some twenty or so seats apart. Having already practiced the rant we would both chant ("We're on the ballot, so we should be on the stage!") during our respective acts of defiance, we felt as prepared as we could, given the unforeseeable circumstances of a fluid situation. Then, as the two appointed candidates took positions on a mostly-empty stage, I meditated on my imminent political, if not physical suicide.

*

Backing Away from the Abyss

I did not hate Charles E. Grassley—but neither did I love him. Now, mindful of the looming moment that would stick out in the ultimate chronicle of his interminable public-office service, I pondered the career, moreover the Life of the man who embodies so much of what I disdain.

Although convinced that my quixotic campaign was not primarily fueled with private vitriol tied to his person, I was aware of several points in my list of resentments of him that *did* involve me:

Besides my general objections to the man's eternal domination of half of Iowa's presence in the US Senate [as outlined early in this tome, in the section titled "Our National Tragedy"], I usually did not share the rationale behind most of his positions—then the most recent display of such reactionism being not letting "his" judiciary committee consider President Obama's nominee to a hung US Supreme Court. His purely partisan stance deprived the nation of needed movement: I begrudged him his lynchpin role in our nation's political division and DC deadlock. (Later, I would scorn his histrionic behavior while chairing Brett Kavanaugh's farce as Supreme Court material.)

I had not, however, always disliked Chuck's positions. One of his early, most visible ones had been his challenging military-spending largesse—for one, his much-celebrated questioning the Pentagon's paying $436 for hammers and a sweet $640 for toilet seats.[85] We characteristically thrifty Hawkeyes cheered his daring, rare dissent in what is now called "The Swamp." Still, as the man grew confident that he could win what became a string of terms, it seemed his need for grandstanding stunts diminished, as Chuck's tenacious scrutiny of wasteful spending waned.

Tied less with political stands and more with personal style, I have increasingly grown weary of the "aw-shucks" persona Grassley cultivates. As both of us are North Iowans, the man's bumkin speech has always perplexed me: I personally know no one else in our shared region who speaks with such a hick accent. (Wouldn't more than four decades in The District have softened what he must think others expect Iowans to sound like?) I also find his manners crude, demeaning and embarrassing. On top of which—as painfully seen in his clunky, self-involved responses to the Merrick Garland but also Brett Kavanaugh Supreme Court nominations—Iowa's senior US senator lacks the gravitas, the polish commensurate to such a long career, not to mention his several top positions on key Congressional committees. His advanced age is not only a problem *per se*, but his seeming to embody Old School from his nose to his toes keeps many younger Iowans from perceiving his office as one that reflects their own lives and values: So, we drift off...

Merrick Garland with Barack Obama at his Supreme Court nomination, 2016: President Donald J. Trump looked on as retired Associate Justice, Anthony M. Kennedy, swore in Brett Kavanaugh to be the Supreme Court's 114th justice in October 2018. He was joined by wife Ashley, and daughters Liza and Margaret.

Apparently no longer worried about acting in ways that might appeal to the growing diversity of his constituency, Charles Grassley also appears to feel less compelled to respond to its wishes or needs. Until my dyed-in-the-wool Democrat father finally convinced her of Republican excess and hubris during the George Bush Jr. administration, my Iowa-farm-wife mother had been a life-long believer in the GOP. As Dad's health began to diminish and his faulty heart threatened to (and later did) take his life, for the first time my Mom turned activist: She wrote and even called Grassley's office, desperate to secure adequate Medicare funds to cover her ailing mate's needs. Getting neither assurance of full healthcare coverage nor even a response from Chuck's staff, my mother recounted with shock and raw anger how, in the middle of a heart operation, the surgeon walked out to the waiting room for her to choose: Would he install a stent *or* conduct an angioplasty—because Medicare would *not* pay for both. Beside herself with agony, she chose— and a half-year later Dad dropped dead one evening as they sat in bed, talking. She never forgave Grassley's failure to respond to their dire need—nor have I. But then again, by now unassailable in holding office until his ultimate demise, why "should" he have bothered?

Despite being well shy of the chronological point where I should have had to contemplate my own demise, sitting there watching Charles Grassley go through the motions of defending his ironclad hold on his impregnable perch in Congress against lightweight Patty Judge, my mind ticker-taped through my Life's timeline. I had been blessed, from early on, in uncountable ways, but now, as a middle-aged expat, single and denied my family's good graces, running against a heavyweight career politician not so much as to make policy but to make history, I sensed a spiritual paucity and a scarcity of time left; in my head hung a long list of things not done, sorely underscored by an unsatiated desire to linger longer on the planet. At the same time, I knew we all have to let loose our grip on Life at some point—*What better way ta go out*, I reasoned, *than ta do so in the name of nudging humanity in a new direction, away from systems that no longer serve but rather enslave us?* I looked around the packed auditorium: *If I stand an' pierce the* façade *of democracy in action, won't that be a lasting legacy? How else ta slay this beast?*

Noticing the hands on my watch ticking furiously, mercilessly forward, I soberly noted that "my moment" was approaching—that the time to take a stand, possibly a last yet lasting stand, was nigh. Would I do it—*could* I do it? My heartbeat was accelerating, my knees slightly shaking, my nerve evaporating. *Come on*, I ordered my resisting Self, *make a decision! Ya gonna do this thing—or not?* I peered for a second to the right, down a long row, past an endless wall of stoic Iowans' faces, to Chuck Aldrich, who returned my searching glance with a questioning one: A sense of guilt, of disappointing him if I did not proceed as we had rehearsed, spread over me. Unable to bear Chuck's knitted brows and panicked eyes, I again looked forward, to the stage.

At that moment, two disarming thoughts came to me and robbed me of a planned martyrdom:

As a Quaker, I long have held that there is something sacred, something of the Spirit in each of us, regardless of an individual's origins, present condition, personality, practices, preferences or fate. Staring at Charles Grassley rambling on in response to Patty Judge's own hollow verbiage, I could hear their dueling voices yet not distinguish their flood of words. Instead, I became mesmerized by Chuck's moving lips, by his eye movements—or lack of them. I watched him shift his weight from one leg to the other, adjust his collar, then cover a cough with a stiff fist. I heard his lungs take in a deep breath and swore I could feel his heart beat—or was it mine? At that moment, the distance between my opponent—between The Other and me—was... totally gone.

That being the case, I felt compassion for him. His policy positions might still leave me cold, but I suddenly felt a warmth, a glowing appreciation for what he must have been feeling in that exact same instant. Yes, his ego-driven refusal to release the reins of power still pissed me off, but I also felt compelled to acknowledge the decades of tireless service he had given our people. A wealthy, certainly well-connected man, I never sensed him to be an evil one—which I could not say about other figures in power. Surely, Uncle Chuck felt he was faithful to his office and the folks back home, per his understanding of both. Always aware of both, he had devoted half of his time on this planet to serve—right up to this present moment... to HIS moment, no?

As much as his intransigence infuriated me, as much as I disdain his positions on life-and-death issues (waging war, detaining would-be immigrants and all the rest), I could not deny that this man had spent all of my adult life—and half of his—working his way to Now. Could I steal this moment, now, in the name of wanting to make it my own? Did my Statement warrant dissing his long career built on *his* chosen Statements? Was my conviction in the justness of my cause more pressing and worthier than letting this man—and Patty as well—have their say to Iowans?

Among those Iowans watching them spar and banter was my 80-something mother, in Mason City. As puerile and kitschy as it might seem, I then meditated on Mom, sitting in her quiet living room, watching this wingless debate drag on—until, that is, I might jump to my feet and denounce the entire rigged gig, in my effort to bring the whole thing down. How would she react to seeing her "baby" throw such a spectacle? *She'll die a thousand deaths* I fretted to myself. *How would she ever be able to face her friends, let alone our family? This'll* <u>*kill*</u> *Mom…*

More than my own possible death, that—either literal or, more likely, figurative—of my viewing mother kept me anchored to my seat. While part of me wanted to rise up and overthrow our oppressors, a larger part wanted to bend down and throw my sheltering arms around my *Madre*. I had come so far, enduring so many injuries to reach this moment, only to have it fade in the face of larger truths—like those of Charles E. Grassley and Phyllis Ann Luick [née Thrams].

*

US Senate candidate Michael Luick-Thrams in Central Iowa, summer 2016

Book Two: How We Rise Up Faster

> "What we call the beginning is often the end.
> And to make an end is to make a beginning.
> The end is where we start from."
>
> — T. S. Eliot, "Little Gidding" from *Four Quartets*

The Roots of It All

Sioux City proved to be my Waterloo—an' I *don't* mean that ol' tractor town in Eastern Iowa.

Having looked Death in the eye, then walked away to live Life another day, I began anew my campaign to chip away at America's current systems, even as I proposed different ones. Having forfeited my shot at taking on the systematic silencing of any candidates who do not subscribe to the current, rigged structures by aiming at the US-Senate-seat incumbent and his anointed Democratic "challenger," I once again focused on the electorate, rather than other candidates.

First, I had to take on the so-called "Left," which almost without exception actually consisted of Center-Right or Near-Left adherents—in any case, folks mostly to my right despite my being a Radical Centrist. I had long confronted and even called out such people: the Willys and Thoms, the "liberal media" figures in "public" radio and television, the "fake liberals" at the *Des Moines Register* and, most recently, the Ms Wellheeleds of the world. The last in this list had seemed genuinely injured when I accused her and her slick anchor husband of "cowing to the elite" and "perpetuating a system that assures big-budget bucks for media outlets like yours." Even as she blew smoke up our tired backsides, placating us with 90-second cameos wedged in between car-chase and hog-belly-futures reports, she lied glibly to us "We're really *very* inclusive here."

By this stage, I knew that dynamic too well. In fact, I had become rather inured to this ever-repeated refrain, to the point that I hardly took it personally anymore. What hit me harder and sat deeper were not rebuffs from Iowa's minority liberal set—those at the top hailing largely from our modest state's managerial and professional classes, those at the bottom being the few remaining old-school labor unionists, radical farmers or other bodily toilers—but from the majority conservative crowd: people of my own blood and flesh. Their lack of affection for my positions or interest in my proposals pained me the most, because we once had been one. That deepest ache was inseparably connected to my having long been ostracized for something primal, innate and intimate, something that I could not change yet others could not overlook. My personal experience reflected part of America's great divide, an "irreconcilable difference."

My falling out with the Lucys and Linuses who peopled the world from which I came had come early on and hit hard: Almost as soon as I had left Ashlawn Farm, my childhood blinders fell away as I had to face worlds from which I had been sheltered for all of my life up until that point. As T.S. Eliot once said, "My easy god [was] dead" so I had to learn to dance with peoples very different from my own. I had no choice but to deal with nuances where earlier there had been only white and black; I had to grow comfortable with ambiguity and possibility; I had to embrace diversity, if I was to allow my own hunger to live widely and deeply to be fed.

Since the late '70s, then, I have been trying to come to terms with how my relatives and I could turn out so diametrically different despite having come from the same ancestral households, shared the same genes and teachers, been weaned on the same cultural and religious diet, and gone on some of the same trips. For decades, chasing evasive answers to that riddle seemed a personal puzzle, specific to me. As a candidate in 2016, though, and now as an American trying to unravel why a third of my compatriots supports the policies of a man I find abhorrent, my quest for answers to old questions has taken on current relevance and urgency. While labels are growing increasingly inadequate to the task of identifying ever-more complex humans, ideologies and political bodies, kernels of truth reside in most clichés. The blanket dismissal by coastal critics of "Midwest conservatism" does reflect real people's real reactions to our world:

*

The Right's Unhealed Achilles' Heel

I say I want to love a man; my family tells me I openly do so to show hate for or to hurt them.

I press on because my heart leads me to do so: I cannot be anything other than what I feel I am.

I say I am a gay man, but others inform me that I am not a "real" man. I am used to being told who I "am," as I follow Jesus' tenets yet my own kin inform me that I am not a "real Christian."

I soldier on, because my sense of an autonomous Self, sanity and survival depend on it.

I choose to wear an earring; my parents say it brings shame onto them and our family: "STOP!"

I march on, as to war, determined to persevere. My father and I do not speak for eight years.

A young gay man living in the city, I call my mother back on the farm, to ask if I should stop by when I drive past on the freeway; she declines, saying "I have to ask your dad" but never does.

I call again and again, because I want my mother's love.

A young gay man taking a U of MN-YMCA death-and-dying course, I call my mother and ask "If I had a deadly disease, would you take care of me as I was dying?" Her answer? "I'm not sure."

I live on, because I can do no other—but I have never felt so small and alone in this big world...

Fast forward: The world's oceans are rising, landslides falling, forests burning; Parliament and Congress are flatlining as "evil empires" entrench and expand. Still, all hopped up by zealots over straw-man issues that should have been settled eons ago, my now-elderly mother denies her adult baby, living across the planet, a rare visit—just because I wear a sole earring—and all involved waste precious energy and fleeting time that could be invested in saving humanity.

This elderly woman, widowed for most of a decade, finds a beautiful love in her waning years. Her older children, afraid of what others might say, talk her out of living with him "in sin."

A friend gets pregnant but cannot support a child or, perhaps, was raped or, based on family history, fears complications; third parties (her neighbors, some church's congregants, Senators in DC or even my own family) tell her she cannot terminate that fetus' being carried to birth. They do not offer to help her support that child but are willing to pay to imprison it as an adult.

A single, working mother turns to public assistance to help buy food or pay rent; my relatives would tell her *they* will have to underwrite her raising her children, rather than tell Walmart or McDonalds—or any other of the corporate fiefdoms they support—to pay her a living wage.

A Central American mother fears for her teenage children's safety: Scared Lucy wants to build a wall to protect us from "them" harming us or taking our property; our unlucky Linus wants to stem competition for low-paying jobs (i.e., mowing lawn at Home Depot) from Rosa's family.

Thousands of Latin-American children languish in camps along a hot, dusty border, too often left to huddle at night under foil "blankets" and drink out of unattended toilets.[86] A scene out of neither Ellis Island nor Bethlehem, it is a modern travesty that we tolerate and thus condone, even as millions of "them" do the grunt jobs that WASPS refuse to take. Still, thousands gather in half-filled stadiums to roar against these modern slaves, those who we use upon demand.

An African-American man drives with his girlfriend through a Minnesota suburb. A Hispanic cop pulls them over: In the course of checking the man's ID, he shoots the driver as he sits in his car.[87] I attend Philando Castile's funeral in Saint Paul's cold, packed cathedral and wonder what is so deeply rotten in our nation's soul that we continue to assassinate darker-skinned citizens. I also go to the bittersweet reception at the school where "Phil" had supervised the cafeteria; I hear and see how beloved he was by fellow staff but most of all the children. My heart weeps.[88]

I took the top photo as I watched Philando Castile's funeral procession cross Saint Paul's Cathedral Hill, in July 2016. The inset shows a memorial at the shooting site in Falcon Heights. Diamond Reynolds—who, seated next to him, watched her boyfriend being killed—spoke at a rally in his memory on the day after Castile's death. Mourning the shooting, community members marched from the Minnesota Governor's mansion to the J.J. Hill Montessori School where "Phil" worked, then back to the Governor's mansion

An African-born cop in Minneapolis shoots a white Australian woman from within his squad car.[89] For this, he is sentenced to twelve years in prison. Meanwhile, a white cop in New York continues to work five years after having choked African American Eric Garner—prone on a Staten Island sidewalk—who eleven times said he could not breathe.[90] Aching for justice, I wonder why my country's Justice Department refuses to get involved in the matter—and mourn our apathy.

A child somewhere enters his school and begins shooting wildly in all directions, wounding scores and killing some. How did he get a gun? It was easy: They are lying about, everywhere.

Despite authorities having never identified a plausible motive, a white-collar WASP man knocks out 32nd-floor hotel windows and shoots 480 of his fellow Americans—58 fatally.[91] Still, millions of my compatriots insist on their "right" to buy assault weapons designed to use on battlefields, so they can feel "more safe" barricaded in their suburban fortresses. More Americans have died from gunfire since 1968 than those killed during all US wars since the Revolution, yet the madness continues because "I" have a "right" to arm "my" nation to the teeth.

And so it goes…

Fear—of "fags" or foreigners, of losing property or one's standing at church or in one's wider community; fear of feeling used or useless, of isolation or the insanity wrought by it. All of us, but it seems particularly those inhabiting the right-of-center regions on my General Political-Rainbow Graph, too often let unconscious or unconfronted ANXIETY drive us. The problem is, where FEAR dominates, HATE can reign but LOVE *never* can—and therein lies Our BIG Problem:

> We're too individualistic, too welded to our own rigid ideas of how we think things should be, too unwilling to listen to others without feeling offended by differing opinions. We are too busy doing our own, isolated thing to accomplish much anymore of real greatness as a group. We fail to generate enough citizens capable of acting effectively as a whole, in concert, to reach shared goals. All the while, out of mental laziness, we habitually reduce those who do not share our beliefs as stupid or "evil;" we reflexively assume that what others think or value, what they do or say ultimately affects us—so we try to "protect" ourselves from them: If need be, we will belittle, shame, beat or even kill them so that we might "survive." Ironically, those who reach and prevail at the top are usually the most-wicked, least-deserving of us. This *must* change! It can, however, *only* if we are willing to surrender shared, calcified systems of living, of thinking and acting—including how we hate or try to love—that fail to serve us at present. First, we must see that no system is inevitable, none lasts eternally, and all can be changed—IF people will it. But, our willful blindness keeps us from demanding systemic change, which is possible and long overdue. Fearing change, we refrain from making better lives than the ones we have now, for ourselves and those who will follow. We must cease our self-imprisonment if we're to restore a world reeling from our abusing it, let alone save ourselves. We must, in short, recast our souls.

Our nation's psychological makeup fuels our shared strengths even as it casts deadly ideological straightjackets that keep us from re-evaluating our **values**, updating our **beliefs** and altering our **behavior**. Why do we so often fail at this in terms of how we move through "the city" when:

- Each year, we renovate millions of old houses with latest-technology insulation, building materials and furnishings to make them more comfortable, more efficient and more pleasing. Why is it so hard for so many, then, to renovate old **values** that also cost us much?

- Companies update brands, even packaging all the time to reflect innovations in design, efficiency and appeal. Why is it so hard for so many of us, then, to update our **beliefs**?
- A young man goes out, woos women (or men) and wanders from bed to bed. At some point, he meets The One and settles down. Does he continue to act like an untethered bachelor? He could, but he likely would pay for those "little freedoms" with his new Big Love. So, he updates his behavior. Why is it so hard for so many of us, then, to adapt our **behaviors** to new situations, to what we know now that may not have applied earlier?

The Amish are a fascinating, often admirable people, but they also quit schooling after the 8th grade. Try working with them: Many are unable to cope with the daily intricacies of living in the modern world.[92] If YOU had frozen your intellectual development at its 8th-grade level, how well could *you* navigate insurance policies or tax forms, master new apps or try other cultures at the end of a jet-propelled flight? Imagine, then, YOUR Self in the ancient world, where only the elite (the king/emperor, administrators, priests) were allowed to read and write. If Moses or Jesus, Mohammed, the Buddha or Confucius had come to you at your level of understanding then and expounded complex ideas today found in zillions of self-help books, could you have fathomed the seemingly strange concepts they instead conveyed in simple fables, parables and snippets? Why, then, do so many of us base our lives on ancient tales, sealed in the oldest of books, and rather than follow the spirit of their messages instead get lost in the letter of the "law" in which their wisdom was locked? Are Jesus' words true because they are in the Bible, or are they in the Bible because they are true? Do you follow fluid wisdom or sit on stone tablets? Which is it?

Have YOU noticed that the narratives that have driven the world for half of eternity no longer apply? We have refrigerators and pigs are vaccinated, so pork is no longer potentially deadly; mixing meat with milk no longer has to lead to food poisoning. Women today dare to show or cut their hair, without men around them jumping to rape them. We do not stone "adulterers" anymore, because if we did 2/3[rds] of the workforce would not show up for work—neither do we summarily sever the hands of suspected thieves nor do many other of the millions of things proscribed humans by our mostly un[der]educated, superstition-guided ancestors. Why, then, do we humiliate or at least boss around each other, based on outdated, often lethal ideas? Why do we continue to serve and sustain a social order that is anti-social and strangling Life itself?

The task before us cannot be accomplished only by those who abhor the current order: To succeed, we also must recruit at least some of those who adore the way things are—but how?

*

Chick Comes Home to Roost

It was one thing to face the world and seek recruits among its masses as a single, white, privileged gay man. It would prove another, to face it no longer as a "DNA dead end" but rather as a parent whose genes will live beyond my life to experience whatever will come next. Little did I imagine before it happened, but something most unexpected yet revealed in a peaceful moment would deepen the divide between my family and me. And, it would make all the difference to me, as this event would force me to re-evaluate my values, update my beliefs and alter my behavior.

It happened something like this:

On a frozen Friday morning last January, I pried myself out of *Bett*, plopped down at the keyboard and summoned my email. My sleepy, half-shut eyes soon popped open, however, as I scanned one message in particular. Hearing my *Haus*mate, Jörg, stirring in his bedroom down the hall, I called out *"Du, komm schnell!"* As he raced into my room, I explained "Look—some lady in Iowa thinks I'm her daddy!" And thus began the beginning of a climax in a forty-year feud with my family—ostensibly due to a sperm donation I had made way back in 1984: Who'd have thought?

At first skeptical, as I read the young woman's earnest communiqué, my reticence soon melted. As my condensed, paraphrased account of those initial events that swiftly brought my daughter and me together suggests, her deduction was plausible; knowing what I knew, it was probable:

> Some donor-conceived offspring seek their biological fathers for months, more typically years. From the time of the arrival of the results of her DNA test until Nicole hesitantly drafted a query to the man whom all data indicated was her father, then I responded, eleven hours passed—a breathtakingly short time, perhaps a world record in such searches. The information her now-deceased mother had given her about the donor ("a student at Iowa State") squared with my participation over two years in McFarland Clinic's AI program. Still, she expected a rebuff—thus my immediate, receptive response surprised her, as countless other donor-conceived seekers had reported in their on-line support messages on fathers who summarily rejected any contact, some even via letters from their lawyers demanding they "cease and desist." I was different.

My first reaction to all this, shock, soon gave way to a second: longing. Here was a young mother, likely truly my daughter, who had cleverly located me on the other side of the planet from Iowa, and wanted a relationship with her long-lost father. I immediately was willing, called in what was the middle of the night in Central Standard Time to tell her that, and felt overjoyed.

In an essay she soon penned, to announce to all who cared what had happened, Nicole wrote:

Many years ago, when I was a girl of eight or nine, I discovered a secret I am sure was never meant for me to know. I learned that the man who was my "father" was, in fact, not. I lived in disbelief for a few years until I mustered the courage to confront my mother about it. She reluctantly confirmed that it was true, and that after many years of her and my "father" trying to conceive, she had sought assistance from an anonymous sperm donor at a clinic in Ames.

For years, this was a topic of confusion I carried around, wondering who my biological father may be—daydreaming of what he must look like or if he was an astronaut, or a farmer, or maybe he was a zookeeper. It also gave me a clearer perspective of what was really happening around me: I had felt, for as long as I could remember, that I didn't fit in anywhere [and] just didn't know why. But, after learning the truth, I saw it all very clearly: I knew then why my "father's" family always seemed to have a disconnect with me, why my "grandparents" seemed to always favor their other grandchildren. The disgusted and discounted looks I had felt weren't in my imagination: They were because of my genes. I also never felt that I fit in my mother's family. She herself was the black sheep, which made me a second-generation black sheep.

In fifth grade, when assigned to write about our ancestry and where we came from, I chose instead to lie and make up a story, to just tell the teacher "This assignment is bullshit!" When I was 15 or so, I went to my mother asking for any information that the clinic may have given her. She informed me that the donor was an ISU college student[.] Through the rest of my teens and into my early adulthood, as I became a mother myself, the meaning of genetics and ancestry meant a lot to me because there was an entire section of medical history I had to leave blank every time I visited a doctor. In 2003, when my [firstborn son, then three] had been diagnosed with leukemia and was fighting for his life, I was robbed of an opportunity to find him a bone marrow match because I didn't know where an entire side of my genetics came from. For decades, I agonized over where I came from, always feeling like I didn't belong anywhere. The giant void I felt became more painful in 2012 when my mother—who had given me the only unconditional love I had ever felt—took her last breath and left me alone in this world[.]

On Christmas 2018, as I laid in my bed while the rest of the world celebrated the holiday with beloved family, I stumbled upon an ad for AncestryDNA. Anyone who knows me, knows I am strictly a clearance-thrift-store-buying kind of person. But, my boys and [partner] insisted I buy one, so that maybe I could find some of my siblings. Me being the pessimistic person I am, I didn't want to "waste" the $100. They won… and I ordered it: A few days later the kit arrived; I did the thing and sent it back. Still, I told myself I'd essentially wasted $100—and quietly made a list of all the reasons it was dumb. I wasn't going to find siblings, or the donor, and there is so much involved with genealogy that I didn't even know the first thing about it and so on[.]

On Wednesday, January 29th, while at work, I got results and my closest match was a cousin on my mom's side—two 2nd cousins and lots of 3rd up to 8th cousins. I felt disappointed: I was hoping to find a sibling. After work, I sought help from a very knowledgeable [friend,] who was optimistic that anything could be discovered in any match. She had a plethora of experience with making family trees and genealogy and helped sort my matches, from maternal to paternal: She guided me in the right direction of starting a tree by figuring where my matches fit in... and a few hours later I messaged a lady who was a 2nd paternal cousin's mother. Thankfully, I was blessed with another angel who messaged me [the donor's uncle's daughter-in-law]—who by the grace of god had experience in this department. With her help, I saw how my DNA matches were lining up, and then I got it narrowed down to 5 guys!!!!!

I was in shock. Between my helpers' input, I was able to exclude some of the men based on their locations at the time, marital status—oh, yeah: She was willing to discount her husband, as they were stationed in another state at the time and, besides, he was my second cousin's father!

And so, then, there was one!

"Shocked" is an understatement: I googled him like it was my job—and the man I found was completely extraordinary and I was in disbelief that this could be my biological father! This man had run for senate; he has written books and traveled the world, he has the word "doctor" in front of his name... and what was most profound, was when I looked at his picture: For the first time in my life I saw *my* face, *my* nose, *my* eyes: I saw the man who made me!!! Tears flowed...

So, I sent an email, carefully prepared and edited for hours, thinking I had come this far and I deserved to be acknowledged—and that at the very least I needed him to know I am a person and I exist! I didn't expect a response... and I didn't really know if at that point I cared.

The next morning, I woke up with 2 missed calls from Germany [where] he currently lives. And, he left a voicemail... I had never been so nervous in my life! I heard the first few words come out of his mouth and they were soft and kind and not what I expected!

Super-long story, short: We spent hours on the phone over the next two days, talking about everything and nothing, and shedding a few tears! God took me on this journey and led me somewhere to fill a void that I have been sickened by for years—and I found the most beautiful piece of myself that was always inside of me but missing my whole life...

So world, meet my father....

Dr. Michael Luick-Thrams.

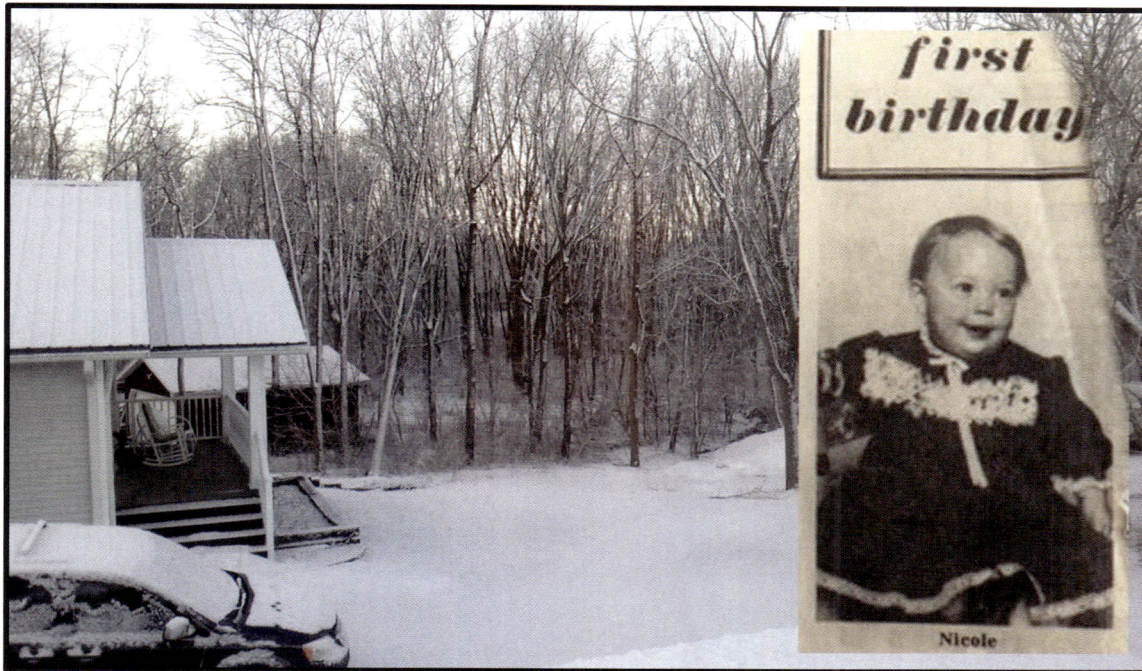

Nicole's first birthday made the local news! On the morning after we met, an unexpected snow had fallen in the night, as if to cover the world in cleansing white, and cold, crisp air punctuated the weekend. I took this picture from the cozy couch where she and I had sat fixed for hours, strangers talking about "family."

Drunk with the euphoria of no longer feeling family-less in a large, cold cosmos, I wrote the following, then emailed it to "my peeps"—and Nicole, upon my request, posted it on Facebook:

> Life'll surprise ya! (Or, as my Iowa-farmwife-philosopher mother puts it: "Life's what happens when you're expectin' somptin' else".) It all began with an innocent Christmas present—the nudge from a young son to his mother in Southcentral Iowa to take a DNA test. It has led to:
>
> ### "World — I have a daughter!"
>
> As a student in the '80s, I contributed to a donor bank[.] Now, 34 years later, *one of my children has found me!* For her and her four sons (ages 9-16), it makes all the difference—for me, too!
>
> Unexpectedly, that "gift" I gave has come back, expanded and enriched countless times over—among other things, six people have been on this planet who wouldn't be. (Nicole has since lost her first son and mother; she has no extended kin.) For me, however—amidst the smoke still arising from such a searing shock—loom two immediate realizations:
>
> For one, my heart rate has literally dropped. At first, I had a feeling as if the floor beneath my feet began falling away, but that's been replaced by a deep sense of peaceful wholeness. For the first time in my adult life, I don't feel so unmoored and sentenced to a life of familial solitude. It feels as if some unconscious, evolutionary requisite has been fulfilled: "Now, I'm eternal."

And, while I've been an activist for decades, championing the well-being of abstract millions, for the first time I'm wondering "How will those four young boys cope with rising temperatures and shrinking resources; where and how will they find love and work and Life's satisfactions; will they make decisions out of compassion and magnanimity, or fear and pettiness?"

More than my reactions to this unsettling news, the reactions of others have surprised and perplexed me: I get hearty "congratulations" from folks I've never experienced to be empathetic in the past—as if I'd done "a great thing" yet 'twas actually a simple thing. OK, ya: Without me, there'd be no Nicole nor her boys, but their biographies have consciously included me only for a mere couple days now: What role have I played in molding their personalities or characters? *Zip!*

For another, since learning I have a daughter, my biography has come under a microscope, and the findings are neither insignificant nor without stinging realizations. There is a [hi-]story here:

When I came out at age 19, in September 1982, as a man who sought the love of another man, 'twas a different era, another world. It's hard to imagine such things in today's social climate, but being a pioneer did not come without losses. One of a handful of openly gay men in Iowa, I paid a price for my daring: I lost jobs and an apartment mate; I could feel strangers' freezing stares and got shoved a couple times in public by people unable to deal with differentness.

Most devastating of all, except for a 20-minute confrontation in the middle of it, my father and I did not speak for eight years; during that time, my mother declared "Your coming out has forced me to choose between my husband and my son—and I <u>had</u> to choose my husband."

And, I went to war with my relatives. Although we were raised mainstream Methodists, in that era of fundamentalist revival, [those closest to me] became what for me seemed religious fanatics. [...] Today unsure how (or if) they remember those events, I remember [one] telling me I was "full of Satan"—with [the other] concluding that I am "sexually addicted." The devout-Catholic father of my first partner, one-time-priesthood-candidate Tim, equated our "lifestyle" with "abortion, euthanasia and bestiality". For me, such blind religiosity *was* The Enemy.

By now, much grave, lingering damage has been done, which I'm unsure can be reversed. Among others, I've been shut out of my [wider family members' lives, some of whom] reported [when young] that I "scared" them—but I assumed the tension in the air they felt was fed by their parents'—and church's—pervasive homophobia and fear of all things different or unbound. Having missed not only my [relatives'] lives, it seems I soon will step into the midst of a ready-made family that doesn't share this fractured, tragic past, and wants me in their lives. I celebrate this unexpected turn of events: What fortune!

Nicole reports feeling as if riding a "whirlwind" but what do *I* feel? Humbled; grateful; cautious even while optimistic; hopeful. As a historian, I also feel the weight of decades, of centuries of "twisted ladders," of microscopic DNA strands of Life reaching across myriad generations, across time and space, across millennia and continents, always with the same question: "How can Life on Earth not only survive, but thrive?"   ***Michael, who is part of the answer—as are YOU!***

My proclamation ended with references to noble ideals, implied crescendoing theme music and endless credits. Like Nicole's testimonial, mine plucked heartstrings without trying: The content spoke for itself; we need not embellish. Even my signature entailed a grand image—an inspiring one, indeed. Sadly, though, it soon proved to be a flawed fantasy: I had forgotten my known kin.

*

> "Do not conform to this world,
> but be transformed by
> the renewal of your mind."
>
> — Romans 12:2, the New Testament of the *Bible*

It is ALL About Survival!

In the course of hundreds of subsequent phone calls, emails and WhatsApp exchanges, my quintessentially Millennial daughter quizzed me, uncountable times, "Why do you bother with your relatives?" Pretty and smart (albeit not well-educated), articulate, sociable yet ever wary and full of pluck, Nicole nonetheless often lacks full wisdom—at 34, still a forgivable deficit, no?

Despite repeated attempts to make my case plausible to her, however, she remained steadfast in her disinclination to meet my Lucy and Linus, which I then regretted. After my admittedly biased recounting of only a fraction of their and my respective frustrations, Nicole wrote off her closer relatives—and, among them, most likely many cousins, peers she said she seeks as friends.

Why is it not self-evident to the Nicoles everywhere that in this country—yea, in this world—that we have today, we genuinely and literally *need* each other, for at least three reasons?

1) On a spiritual level, our current estrangement from each other increasingly eats away at our modernity-stressed souls. Human beings spent hundreds of thousands of years evolving in small bands, first hunting and later gathering together the means to survive. It is in our genes: We *need* close, safe, sustaining contact with other human beings. Living in isolation makes not only prisoners but all of us mentally if not also physically ill. To counter spiraling rates of depression and suicide, we *must* refuse to live in silos.

2) In so-called liberal democracies like in the US or Western Europe, we can overcome our current political paralysis only by refusing to be further divided by our inner demons and by outer influences: We must recognize documented facts, that forces such as Russia's megalomaniac leader actively fund movements among us—for example, the likes of France's *Front national* fanatics, Italy's Five Star darlings, Britain's Brexiteers, the US' Breitbart crowd and Brazil's snake-eyed Jair Messias Bolsonaro—and acknowledge that while Hitler could not overtake us from

without, Putin is laying us lame from within. If we prize and wish to preserve our individual, let alone collective freedoms, we *must* expose and counter such malignant cells. First when we remember that we not only *need* but actually *like* one another, will we again act as <u>one</u>.

3) More pressing than anything else, however, is the unavoidable, immutable truth that no one faction, in any land, can counter global climate change alone: Either *all* of us *must* do our share, or <u>all</u> of us will go down. We will persevere and, ultimately, survive—as individuals, but moreover as a species—only to the extent that we can overcome our divisions, distrust and adopted disinclination to give our all to this overriding issue.

Nicole and I grew into our current personhoods in different eras, under differing circumstances. I was 19 when I came out: At just under 20, I needed a family but in my Iowa of then, there was no visible, viable gay community. So, reasonably, I felt that the only "family" available to me was my biological one. Thus, for my own survival, I tried again and again—uncountable times—to please them, to win their favor... but now, at just under 60, I see that ain't no longer so. Meeting one of my many offspring shifted my worldview, forever: I no longer will beg or bend to be loved.

Temples at Khajuraho, in India's Chhatarpur district near Madhya Pradesh, are known for their architecture and erotic sculpting. These sculptures depict then-contemporary stories about sexuality. According to Wikimedia, this sculpture can be seen on the exterior of Kandariya Mahadeva temple.

historical experiences of being "gay:" lovers Zephyrus and Hyacinthus, portrayed on a Roman cup from Tarquinia, 480 BC; the burning at the stake of the knight Richard Puller von Hohenburg and his squire, Anton Mätzler, in Zürich, 1482; a Victorian meaning of the word "gay" as used in Punch magazine, 1857; "Annual Reminder" activists picketing Philadelphia's Independence Hall, 4 July 1966; Barack Obama signs into law the 2010 Don't Ask, Don't Tell Repeal Act, with Nancy Pelosi behind him, Joe Biden 2nd on left[93]

In ways she may not understand, Nicole helped me free myself from the tyranny of no choice. She helped free me from my known past even as I helped free her from her unknown one. But, now what? This planet is sagging under *our* weight—but we cannot bolster it by ourselves. We <u>need</u> the Lucys and the Linuses of our world, who *must* hold up their end of the sky, too, if, together, we are to save this world from... us. To save the world from us, though, do we not have to transform what we are? We painted ourselves into this corner: Can we get out, clinging to our blindness? Is not finding compassion for The Other any longer an option? I believe not.[94]

*

Wiping Slates Clean

I cannot say that my relatives are bad people. I also cannot say that they are good people, for I have not seen much of their goodness. Or, if they thought they were showing me love, I did not recognize it as such. What I can say, however, is that they remain important to me—at least in theory. I wish they were important to me in practice, but at present they do not grant me any. Still, as stand-ins for the third of my nation that not only tolerates but continues to support a man—specifically his behavior and policies—that I believe are poisoning our country, this world and also my life, to unlock our deadlock I "have" to try to crawl inside their brains and hearts.

As they exist for me now only in absentia, any healing or making of peace between us also will have to take place in their absence. Thus, as much as I am loathe to do so, I must speak for them—or at least weave suppositions about what I guess they would do or say, were they here.[95]

 The voracity of their anger about and feeling hurt by an email I broadcast announcing Nicole's existence makes me think that they, too, carry singed baggage from our crash-and-burn relationship. Part of the accrual of real or perceived trespasses likely has to do with their having felt disrespected, unvalued, unheard or unseen by me. As I take ownership of my half of our history, I wonder what I know—or think I do—about my past or present roles in their feeling

- disrespected: Ever since the '80s, I have held what I considered extreme religiosity in contempt. I have blamed it—and them—for much everyday suffering not only of gays and lesbians, but of single mothers, people of color, immigrants, non-Christians or even non-"born-again" Christians. I have wanted nothing to do with their church services or their theologies, Bible readings or study groups; I avoided their sons' "Christian wrestling" matches and "Christian rock" concerts; I also challenged the motivation and effects of their missionary activities in foreign countries: I have told and shown them all of this, repeatedly. I have informed them of what I see as the dangers of ideologies unbalanced by exposure to other perspectives or others' experiences; thus, I championed their or their children studying or at least traveling abroad—mostly in vain.

- un[der]valued: Because I could not tolerate what I saw as their intolerance, I have looked down at my paternal relations as being—in my mind—racist and sexist, elitist and reactionist. I could not fully value their skills, accomplishments, careers, interests or values to the degree that they did or might have liked me to have done. Less so Linus—who has possessed and actually used a passport—but more Lucy has been the object of my cloaked scorn for her lack of travel as well as lack of interest in it. I have never forgiven her (for example) for telling me to eschew non-Christians as friends, for failing to find not only Germany but also India or China on an ISU-era test map with borders but no names, for guessing as late as 2016 that Muslims worship "Buddha or sompthin'"—worse still, for not knowing the truth and not caring that she does not know it.

- unheard: Especially Lucy has always enjoyed telling me what to do and what I do "wrong." Already as a boy still yoked under her watchful eye, I tried to tune out most of her commands and much of her "chatter." As an adult, I have not taken everything she has said to me or others in my presence fully seriously; I too often refuted it, also in her absence. More than not, I have discounted her advice and rebuke, and failed to engage either of them but especially Lucy about their views on current issues or religious matters as I feared conversations about same would not end well. Not liking or wanting their expected message, I have long reflexively censored the messenger out-of-hand. More recently, I did poll some relatives regarding their thoughts about my deceased father: Only with great effort could I hear their answers with any real receptivity.

- unseen: Even if at points I desperately sought my relatives' approval or at least attention, as late as January 2019 I failed to "[fore]see" them or their possible reactions as I drafted a text I sent to them, as well as to other family and friends or acquaintances of mine: I was surprised when they took it as a personal reproach, rather than being primarily about me and my newly-found daughter. I often see them as a monolith, not as individuals; I regularly dismiss my closest kin's or their children's socio-political values as being "right-wing," their religious values as those of "fanatics:" While I would not put them in "baskets of deplorables" I often relegate them to simplified archetypes. As such, I long ago wrote them off as being more "The Problem" than part of any of the practical solutions now so sorely needed not only in our country but in our world.

One of my oldest (almost forty years and counting), most cherished friends, Bug, came to dinner recently. As I cleared the dishes, this former member of my 2016 campaign committee answered my query, that she wanted this account of my crusade to be "a roadmap and a teddy bear." She, too, sees the process of reconciliation between our country's frozen fronts as being unavoidable, yet grasps for ideas how to thaw the domestic cold war in which we now find ourselves. My "hottest" idea is what I have just modeled: We—*all* of us—*must* own who we are and what we have done, even as we ask others to do the same. Perhaps then, finally feeling respected, valued, heard and seen, we might all move on, together, to tirelessly tackle the greatest threat, ever, to humanity's survival: our own abuse of our only home—this weary planet Earth.

In that spirit of mutual disclosure and joint reckoning, were my family "here" I would expect them to ponder how I perceive them as having facilitated *my* feeling

- disrespected: Lucy continues to call me "Mike" even though since 5th grade I have asked her and all others to call me by my chosen name, "Michael." Much more grievously, despite my telling her for almost four decades that a person is *born* gay (or hetero-, bi- or whatever) and that the only "choice" s/he makes is to be honest and open about one's deepest leadings about bodily pleasure and romantic love, she insists—even in a recent communique to me—on referring to my "choice to live a homosexual lifestyle." Even if she thinks so in her head, I ask her to not insult me with words I find disrespectful and denying of *my* perceived truth about *my* deepest

Self. And I have never felt truly loved by Linus: His occasional mouthing of those words leave me feeling snowed and teased, because his actions magnify what was always missing between us.

- un[der]valued: In 2016, every time I declared to either Lucy or Linus that I would not be voting for Hillary Clinton that fall [I voted for Green-candidate Jill Stein], I felt they doubted my word—that I was "a closet Clintonite;" at least one of them referred to her as "your [meaning 'my'] candidate." Similarly, since I fled The Church—not because I disdained Jesus but because of the hypocrites who claimed to be his friends—did my family ever consider it possible that I might be more "Christian" than many of the self-proclaimed ones they know by the score? By now, I am weary of their assuming that Quakerism is a cult and Quakers "godless;" their indifference to reality appalls me. In contrast to the detailed outlines I wrote about Linus' career misery and both their moves, kids, etc., I doubt either knows enough about my adult life to fill a page.

- unheard: When I was in high school, I told college-boy Linus (and likely young-mother Lucy) about the inappropriate sexual scene into which I inadvertently walked in on one morning on the farm—one that had involved neither of them. Years later, feigning unfamiliarity with that experience, Linus let me recount the entire, prolonged moment from start to finish. When he admitted that he had, indeed, heard me relive the same details before, he confessed "I let ya do it to see if you were lying." Most recently, Lucy charged in a heated email that I "should" have been "adult enough to [...] have a private conversation" with my family, although I *did* suggest exactly that—repeatedly, over the eight months of my US-Senate campaign and again during my October 2018 speaking tour. Why am I being beaten up for "not" doing something I *tried* to do? Why did my invitations to meet for a parley fail to register on her (and his?) end?

- unseen: While I was on the 2016 campaign, Lucy and Linus cleaned out my parents' last home, to ready my mother for moving into assisted living. One day, as I stopped by Mason City *en route* to an appearance, I found in the near-empty house a "to-dump" pile containing mementoes I had brought my folks or, later, widowed mother from around the world. Now, photos of Lucy's clan hang throughout Mom's unit; mine always disappear. Speaking of homes, I think I have been in every one they both have occupied since they left high school: Except for Linus visiting me in Czechoslovakia and both of them having come for Easter dinner at Omega House in 1988, neither has been in any of my many addresses. And, they have *never* inquired about my life abroad: Despite my constant queries about their careers or kids, they *never* asked me about <u>me</u>.

One does not rehash such stories for the "fun" of it, but rather to illustrate that both sides of divided fronts: a) carry grievances; b) feel those are legitimate; and c) want to "bare rather than wear them," to finally be able to unload heavy old baggage, then move on to present-day living.

One of the things that keeps supposed ideological opposites at each other's throats (figuratively or, gulp, literally), is that both want to be respected, valued, heard and seen, but at least one of those two parties "isn't feelin' it." The challenge, in a thoroughly narcissistic culture, is to coax <u>both</u> sides of a Great Divide into actually listening to The Other, rather than to their own echo. Who takes the decisive step, then, in doing that hardest work, to wade into the deepest truth? And, from where do we find not just the courage but the clarity to do so? What happens, if the other side does not respond as we would wish—if they insist on being who they have always been? If they revert to the very behavior we originally found unacceptable—where from there?

*

Symbolically, this former Iowa farmboy sits atop a bronze bison,
but one tucked away in a corner of Berlin's vast Tiergarten park.
"What are these two prairie natives doing in faraway Prussia?"

> "Your life is a sum of all the choices
> you've made along the way."
>
> — an elderly woman quoted by
> June Kjome in *Justice: Not Just Us*

Clearing the Deck

I chart the flow of my Life along lines embedded in a few core narratives—as do most mortals.

For one:

I live much of the year in a country that for at least a dozen years committed acts of joint evil. Having earned a Ph.D. in, essentially, Nazi-German history, I remain today mindful of dynamics that can lead a people—any people—to mass hysteria, typically followed by mass crimes in response to a hysterical urgency the majority of a given population feels at one time, be they Cambodians, Serbs or their neighbors, Hutu or Tutsi, Mideasterners or too many myriad others.

The Hitler-led regime in many ways was a textbook dictatorship: A small band with vast dreams of power identified a smaller, largely indefensible group to blame for the collective's problems, real or perceived, historical or recently hyped. In this specific case, the Lutheran church mostly coalesced with the Nazi program; to some degree, segments of the Catholic one resisted it—in part, a continuation of the *Kulturkampf* ("cultural struggle") taking place since Bismarck's *Reich*.

With Catholics by default seeming suspect and "needing" to be kept in-check, the hierarchy of powerlines both ruling and ruining Nazi-German society looked more or less like this:

—

[My codification of these groups is listed with those the Nazis typically favored most at the top and those they most despised and indiscriminately persecuted or tried to exterminate at the bottom.]

1. Protestant "Aryan" men
2. Catholic "Aryan" men
3. Protestant "Aryan" women
4. Catholic "Aryan" women
5. Latin, Arab or Asian men [e.g., resident scholars/researchers, merchants, doctors, diplomats]
6. Latin, Arab or Asian women [most of whom, usually with their menfolk, drifted off by the outbreak of war]
7. *"freikirchliche"* [i.e., Methodist, Baptist, Quaker, Mormon, Jehovah Witness] "Aryan" men
8. *"freikirchliche"* "Aryan" women
9. brown [i.e., "mulatto" babies born after World War I; by this point mostly young, often castrated] men

10. brown women [in some cases "only" sterilized, but allowed to live "freely" in wider society]
11. [All the of above were presumed heterosexual, followed in terms of toleration or persecution by:] known or suspected non-Jewish gay men and lesbians of any racial or social background
12. the mentally or physically disabled (i.e., who were typically sterilized or murdered)
13. Jewish men
14. Jewish women
15. Jewish children
16. "gypsy" [Sinti or Roma] men, women and children

—

Although we Luick children—like almost all of our peers at the time—were raised to believe that the riots then taking place in New York, Chicago and even Minneapolis[96] resulted from the racism so visible in and synonymous with Dixie, in truth, forty years earlier, great-grandfather George Michael Luick marched with the Northcentral Iowa Klan down Mason City's Federal Avenue. With hardly any African Americans living in the rural Upper Midwest then, our Yankee "better Klan" was more rabidly anti-Catholic and anti-immigrant than it was anti-black. The KKK hierarchy of our local social order pitted whites against whites, rather than against black or brown residents.

My relatives resent my making public our family's buried legacy, but I feel compelled to air it. By owning, then renouncing that strand—one out of endless strands that existed before we arrived on the scene, yet got woven into the warp and weave of who we have become—we rob the toxic waste brewed up by our lesser ancestors a chance to further pollute us or our initial impulses.

Keenly sensitized to even a hint of such ranking of human worth based on alleged ideological or "racial" differences, I call out what I presume to be my "born-again" relatives' working hierarchy, which places them atop all the rest. Much like racism divides people, as do ideological extremes like Nazism or Klanism, unbridled "Born-Again"-ism places more value on even the most wayward among them than on even the most virtuous non-"born-again" peoples. Although it might pain them to recognize it, "fundamentalists" of all stripes share horrific, reptilian reflexes: The ISIS scourge, for one, persecutes and murders more non-"born-again" Muslims than it does non-Muslims, while zealous Burmese Buddhists—improbably—murder Muslims. Nationalist Hindus strive to make "democratic" India a "Hindu state" while radicalized Jews push Israel to become a "Jewish" one. As a scholar of the Nazi disaster and a resident of a country still contaminated by the Third Reich's legacy, my obligation to warn of the dangers of racism arises from my core: I am committed to avoiding repeating past collective disasters by becoming better people, ASAP.

*

167

"Love is all we have, the only way that each can help the other."

— the ancient-Greek tragedian Euripides, *Orestes*

Fifteen Feasible Strategies

My conviction that we must change led me to run for public office—but, I had *no* concrete ideas. Still, back in March 2016, when I boarded that KLM flight back in *Flughafen* Berlin-Tegel, bound for the Upper Midwest, I felt certain that I "had" to do this: I felt compelled to run for the US Senate from my beloved-if-benighted Iowa if I were to contribute to bringing down the "thing" which I saw as enslaving us to outdated, even lethal systems of "moving through the city." Possessing not a single plausible strategy in my campaign quiver, I simply started shooting stray arrows, then chasing after them to see where they might have landed. There, I found Life.

Today, if we are to recast our collective souls radically enough, quickly enough, do we not need to grasp whatever, even remotely-plausible ideas we might muster for how to fulcrum change? From the beginning, as I drafted this tome my dozen or so proofreaders expected, begged, *demanded* that I provide "The Answers" to the problematic questions posed or at least implied in these texts. It seemed they were awaiting grand, complex schemes when, all along, some of the most effective strategies for building bridges to span chasms of deadlock are some of the easiest, most ecological available—including things we (or our grand-/parents) used to do "automatically." As a culture we may have forgotten them, but we *need* to recycle them—<u>now</u>!

To change the world, fast:

1) reach out to "The Other."
2) host autonomous local-action parties.
3) heal primary relationships.
4) practice real kindness.
5) speak your truth.
6) be neither "victim" nor "perpetrator."
7) renounce all forms of violence.
8) reject systemic injustices.
9) confront others' wounds or wounding.
10) confront endemic apathy and resignation.
11) "fall in love"—then listen.
12) instigate transformative change.
13) think outside boxes.
14) learn to "dance" together—again.
15) celebrate being human.

So, here begin some of my best recipes for real and lasting change, the first of them being:

1) reach out to "The Other."

Bake Kindness Cookies—but make (*not* buy!) your <u>finest</u>. Take a plate of them not only to each person or family who moves into your neighborhood, but also to each new colleague that joins your staff or to folks who become members of your spiritual community, etc., as a sign of welcome. Given the suspicious age in which we live, you might take and immediately nibble a random sample in front of those receiving your gift, but present a plate of them to new Love Objects nonetheless. If they are open to it, they might invite you to stay long enough to share a few more—over *Kaffee*, *horchata* or Arab-style mint tea, Indian *chai* or whatever. If they do and you both feel well about whatever connection may arise between you, invite them to a "diverse dinner," perhaps along a model currently being developed by African Americans in Milwaukee: https://www.4diversedining.com/[97]

Another "culinary tip" for cooking up social change consists of building upon those "cookies:"

2) host autonomous local-action parties.

No matter how or even if you name it, if your new friend(s) and you are enriched by sharing food then ask them to co-**host a weekly dinner** (or even just drinks) in a home or other quiet setting (a community hall, church basement, youth or senior center), with the expectation that of those invited, they who agree to come are willing to commit to attending for four weeks. As those pioneers in Wisconsin do, be sure to scatter couples or cliques of friends, so that those who already know each other do *not* sit next to one other; the mixing of Unknowns *is* the point. In your welcome, avoid issuing rules but do verbalize goals such as sidestepping partisan issues in favor of sharing personal tales—for now. Emphasize the event's social, not political potential: We gather to rediscover what we like about each other, *not* what we cannot abide in another.

Based on how that month-long series of sharing food and/or drink goes, consider extending and expanding the weekly meetings to three months, during which socializing, not politicizing is both motive and goal. But, IF you, with your neighbors, colleagues, co-congregants or whoever thrive in this circle, go to www.HeartlandParties.US for ideas on how to ease such a "meeting" into a longer-term, more comprehensive vehicle for getting to know and, where it naturally arises, like each other. Once genuine trust has been sown, begin to consider together how <u>together</u> you might effectively address local needs: getting the playground updated to be more enjoyable even while making it safer; planting flood-resisting trees along a local stream, ideally after having thrown a public "cleaning party" to comb it for and free it from debris; start a citizens' initiative to help your town/city council to review the energy efficiency of all of its buildings (strive to use less fossil and instead more on-site solar or small-wind-generated fuel), grounds (less mowing, more pollinator patches) and services (less paper/carbon, more digital/recycling); create a tight group to visit your town's shut-in, differently-abled or senior citizens—and so on, *ad infinitum*. In the ideal scenario, cells focused on local needs relevant to all—regardless of background or current worldview—might prove strong and long-lived enough to consider regional needs; if they mature past that challenge, perhaps they might tackle state, national or global issues, too.

I suggest such circles not without empirical knowledge that they *can* work: What was the "local need" being addressed? The lack of alcohol-free, non-pick-up places to meet. In early 2003, before I moved to Des Moines with my eager assistant, Rayf, he and I issued a public invitation for "Folks Like Us" to Central-Iowa gays, lesbians and our allies to meet Friday evenings in the basement of the Des Moines Valley Friends meetinghouse. Each was to bring a dish or drink to share; after relaxed potluck socializing, we would remove ourselves upstairs to watch [typically foreign] gay- or lesbian-themed films. As long as the interest of those present afforded it, we would stay after the credits to discuss what we had watched or share our related experiences. I called "FLU" into being, as I could not bear Iowa's capital city's sole "public" social settings to be bars or "worse," environments that seemed to require our leaning on alcohol or drugs rather than on each other to find company, connection or perhaps love. FLU still meets to this day.

Speaking of Quakers and our meeting places:

When I moved in June 2013 to Dresden—the Saxon capital where I lived for four years—it wore on my soul to have no contact with other Friendly-minded folks. So, I somehow got ahold of a list of local Quakers who had not met since just before the fall of the Berlin Wall yet still lived in the area; I called each one for whom I could find a number. We soon met in my home for meeting for worship, followed by a potluck and—*voila!*—the group continues to meet monthly, now in an ecumenical center in the *Altstadt*. More than "just" spiritual and culinary communion, the tight-knit circle fills important social needs. For a time, individuals from the group worked with Spuren to host guest speakers, exhibits or film showings; German Quakers continue to contribute to support Spuren's programs to—for example—integrate refugees, increase social tolerance and keep Quaker-related social history alive. Since the group's revival, it has met a couple times a year at Jahnishausen, an intentional community between Dresden and Leipzig, near the Elbe—a main draw for the pilgrimage there each spring being to savor woods carpeted with wild garlic.

Want a third, more diverse and fluid example, more representative of society at large?

Before World War I, the most English-speaking expats living in Europe resided in Paris; after that, Dresden: The "Florence on the Elbe" catered to them with a score of English-language newspapers, bookshops, cafés, social clubs, gravestones—including even an Anglican, a (Scottish) Presbyterian and an "American" church. Sadly, three-quarters of a century of war, dictatorship and an Iron Curtain killed Anglo-American culture in first Nazi, then communist eastern Germany.

Now, in Thüringen, however, we're changing that. Since New Year's Eve 2017, a group of native speakers of English and our allies has met each month [other than during school breaks, as many of us teach] to build an even better life here through potlucks, exchange, programs... community.

Fifteen expats attended Anahita's presentation "The 17th-Century Safavid Diplomatic Envoy to Siam" in January 2020. They included (back row, from left): Tim (Texas), Jeremy (Ontario), David (Ireland), Lelah (Ontario), Anahita (Iran and the Netherlands), Carolina (Spain), Sabine (Erfurt) and Shelley (California and New York); and (front row): John (Yorkshire), Barbara (Missouri), Stefan (South Africa), Marianna (Romania and Britain) and Michael (Iowa). As a group, we have lived in myriad countries, in addition to those listed: Turkey, South Korea, [then-extant] Czechoslovakia, France, Bangladesh, Brazil, Ecuador, etc. To see what other topics have riveted Global Salon attendees in other months: http://roots.traces.org/

Of the three cited examples, the Global Salon resembles most closely the dynamic intended by the "Heartland Parties" model. First meeting over food, then for conversation, the group (no monolith, despite our many commonalities) has evolved to not only offer cultural programming we all appreciate and grow from. Some of us have also—for example—lobbied for city funding for Erfurt's cultural co-op, the "*KulturQuartier*," applied for grants to fund immigrant-integration projects (patterned after our Global Salon) and passed petitions between us. We regularly share tips ranging from culinary to visa-related ones via a shared WhatsApp page; through our on-line forum, revolving numbers of us might go to the cinema or opera, for bicycle tours along the Gera or swims—or any number of activities. We have met for Robert Burns Night (celebrating the Scottish poet and Renaissance man), Thanksgiving banquets at Cajun-themed "Louisiana Café" and to care for members who are ailing. As Barbara from Saint Louis has said, "Sharing is caring."

The success and survivability of such bodies depend on core **social norms**, among the most essential being <u>consistency</u> (a core group initiates and for the project's initial phases shepherds the practical execution of meeting: As far as I know, FLU has met *every* Friday night for over fifteen years, no matter what other local events might conflict or distract from attending—and that record despite Iowa's often erratic, unwelcoming weather); <u>transparency</u> (I think it accurate to say that Global Salon members have not felt subjected to covert political or religious agendas by others; any "community issues" have been aired and shared openly, with no compulsion to respond or act); <u>openness</u> to *all*; <u>no affiliation</u> to existing parties or institutions; the expectation, collection or payment of <u>no dues</u>—other than say a donation basket to fund coffee filters, rent space, etc.—as practiced not only by the Dresden Quakers but also the "alternative" gay group in Des Moines. (The second-to-last stipulation preempts a group from being co-opted by existing bodies or special interests. The last one avoids [also future] tussles over bookkeeping or possible graft, and opens doors to all to attend, both those "hard up agin' it" and those able to carry costs.)

Beyond core social norms—applicable to infinite numbers of community groups—a handful of core **political norms** can help self-initiated and -directed social-political bodies survive, thrive and succeed. In contrast to America's current political culture, these proposed norms depart radically from business-as-usual partisanship. I build them on ideas articulated by a Quaker activist-educator, Parker Palmer, author of the celebrated *Let Your Life Speak: Listening for the Voice of Vocation*. In a talk he gave about his newest book, *Healing the Heart of Democracy: The Courage to Create a Politics Worthy of the Human Spirit*, Palmer reflects on a set of norms that can heal our current social discord and unlock political deadlock.[98] I adapt his suggestions as follows:

1) All that takes place (in this case, after a shared meal/drinks or whatever vehicle for shared social time) be undertaken with two queries in mind: Is a topic or source <u>local</u> and <u>personal</u> in nature?

Palmer warns us deadlocked Americans against talking when in public groups about "them"— those in Washington… or London, Paris, Berlin, Moscow, Ankara… or wherever non-local, non-direct power rules… or hides. He instead invites us, literally, to talk about "us"—the people *in* a given space, *at* a given time. This context, he says, was the genesis *and* the genius of American democracy out of which "they" arose. To restore, to reclaim democratic power, we *must* return to dealing with the most important issues in *our* lives, locally, with others who also are affected.

As Palmer points out, "We the people are foundational to American democracy […] but how much attention do we pay to the strength of this foundation?" To illustrate this, he bids:

> Listen to ourselves talk about politics[,] on our own political discourse. Listen the next time you get together with friends or the next time you're at a meeting of a voluntary association or any kind of citizen gathering where ostensibly the topic is American politics. Almost all of it […] is about 'them,' those powerholders in distant places, at whom we love to throw brickbats or bouquets, depending on which side of the aisle we sit on; 'them,' those people who are largely

172

beyond our reach; 'them,' those people who make decisions behind closed doors. The net result of this is a political discourse among we the people which is inherently disempowering. [...] Our political discourse almost always is about people who aren't in the room. When was the last time talking about people who aren't in the room fixed anything?

My idea to form citizen-initiated groups is not new; countless have been begun—and failed. The most reoccurring reasons? Individuals or cliques arise, inadequately challenged by others or held in check by protocol, who then dominate not only a group's process, but its goals and projects. Seeing little chance for influence, less-vocal members drift off—until hemorrhaging attendance and engagement assure a group's demise. How to preempt that from happening?

2) *No one person* may speak for more than five minutes at a time, unless a 2-3rds consensus agrees (upon being polled after three minutes) on granting an individual more, specified speaking time. Exceptions might be *local* figures invited to address a specific matter, agreed upon *beforehand* by 2-3rds consensus as being of direct interest to the majority of those ongoingly *in* the group.

[Someone in the group, during post-socializing discussions, should be an official "timekeeper."]

Granted, some individuals choose not to speak publicly—or are reticent to speak publicly until late in the process of a given meeting. What a group can do to avoid a tyranny of the severely introverted or shy is to ask, at key points, if anyone might wish to speak who has not yet had a word: If no one steps forward to speak, then those who already have spoken might speak again.

It is key that:

3) *No* topic be discussed as a group that is not *personally* relevant to at least one person present.

To clarify through hypothetical examples:

Rather than perpetuate deadlock by once again trying to convince our fellow Americans to take a particular stand on, say, abortion or school prayer or gay rights, leave those issues for each to hammer out in her or his own conscience and then live accordingly—unless, say, Pat's teenage daughter has become pregnant and wants to keep the child, but cannot afford to do so alone; instead of her feeling forced to have an abortion, might the group launch a community-based fund to help her raise a healthy child, in material dignity? Or: Ms. Smith wants to instigate prayer each morning in her 5th-grade class at Meadows Elementary, whereas down the hall Mr. Brown is dead against it: How might the parents *in the room* with children attending *that* school respond—and how might the non-parents present support them in clarifying their responses? Lastly: Joe and his partner José have just announced that they are going to be married, but their landlord—now realizing that they are a couple, not "just friends" as she earlier thought—has found a ruse of a reason to evict them: The men ask others in the group for swift, practical help.

Generally, though, "issues of conscience" are better left for individuals to confront and solve alone or in other settings. Is not the most pressing matter facing community-based groups how to solve tangible "issues of survival:" safe water, clean air, shared carbon-locking projects? We *cannot* solve environmental challenges alone; we *must* look to others for ideas and help.

Palmer has looked to others for help in distilling his "radical" ideas. For one, Bill Moyer has influenced Palmer's worldview, fundamentally by Moyer's maxim that "The only antidote to the power of organized money is the power of organized people." Just that core concept, that ultimate power ultimately lies in the hands of *each* of us, not—as we have long thought—in those of "powerful" people one rarely encounters and basically never sees "in the room." The antidote, then? To return not only "to the city" (the "*polis*" in "politics") but to our various shared "rooms."

Coming together as a self-initiated, mutually-beneficial group, given its longevity FLU obviously has stilled real, ongoing needs even as it has filled a niche not addressed before in the same way, on the same deep-reaching level. On the surface, these weekly get-togethers might have seemed casual, even superficial, yet at their core they have touched participants profoundly. In this busy, distracting world, it seems we moderns hunger for profundity, as otherwise we are starving on a steady diet of the superficial served to us too much of the time, in too many settings.

At the same time, if we successfully shower strangers with Kindness Cookies or host regular social gatherings that then evolve into longer-lived, wider-scale forums for change, yet earlier, established relationships go neglected or remain broken, our achievements on a social-political level will pale if we cannot bring our most intimate connections into harmonious equilibrium. That private "work" is often harder than what we undertake in public, as it is by nature deeper.

*

Do "Deep Work"

Do *not* be deluded, friends:

Baking Kindness Cookies, then tossing them about your immediate realms as you frolic your way down a shared path to environmental Armageddon, is not enough to save a weary globe. It might—nay, *will*—feel good, but 'tis only a beginning. It is one viable, effective way to come into contact with others in search of common ground—regardless of background or current worldview—but it does not go far or deep enough to recast our collective soul. So, what will?

We must become the people we have been waiting for—or as the popular motto admonishes, "Be the change you wish to see in the world." Problem is, happy thoughts or cheery gestures—while needed and usefully motivating—can get us out of our cozy chair, but not into the driver's seat on the road to real and lasting change. For that, we need to also undertake "deep work."

As Quakers long have known—and early Friend George Fox put it in the now-stilted language of his time—"I saw that there was an ocean of darkness and death, but an infinite ocean of light and love, which flowed over the ocean of darkness." Modern translation? There *is* "darkness" in the world, figuratively as well as literally: Blackholes and "dark energy"[99] exist in the cosmos— but *why*, to what "purpose?" According to Professor Pedia "In physical cosmology and astronomy, dark energy is an unknown form of energy which is hypothesized to permeate all of space, tending to accelerate the expansion of the universe." There *is* more that is of the light in our universe than is of the dark, yet rather than light, darkness "accelerates expansion." Can we conclude that the human world "needs" spiritual-emotional darkness, too, in order to accentuate the light? Do we need disharmony to heighten the harmony, or hate to highlight love?

While a diet of increasing Love and Light would help us all, spreading such sustaining spiritual nourishment will be hampered by a heavy darkness that has accompanied humanity our entire journey, from once swinging in trees to where we are now. Dark energy can be transformed only by infusing Light into it; it <u>must</u> be confronted before it can be converted to a new form: It must be aired so it no longer has to be borne. Where to start? Well, with those closest to you, which brings us to my next idea:

3) heal primary relationships.

My most poignant personal example of healing primary relationships that are broken? I alluded to it in this tome's first paragraph:

> Today, my torn family is at war with itself. At the same time, our divided country is, too. Inadvertently, I ignited the spark that unleashed my family's current ugly, tragic warfare. Unexpectedly, the flaying of our own flesh has given me insight into America's deadlock.

In October 2019, as I was finishing this book's last five sections, my mother began to end her sojourn on this planet. Her dying, slowly, over a couple months, led me to cut some thirty pages from this book—pages which explored in-depth the germ of my relatives' and my estrangement, yet now seemed unfitting to publicize at such a raw time. Thus, dear reader, please trust that what divides me—and so many millions of other Americans—from family members, colleagues, neighbors, fellow shoppers and baseball spectators at our kids' games, is essentially *idea*-ology, our respective *ideas* about how people "should" live… or not. Such deep discord cannot exist, however, one-sidedly: In every relationship, there are at least two parties—so to heal a broken one, at least one side has to grow to the point of taking responsibility for her or his role in our becoming broken. One of the things that got cut amongst the thirty pages was this admission:

> To my family:
>
> I regret that over decades you have found some of my words or actions hurtful, as that was not my conscious intention. I really am sorry that the differences between us seem to have become irreconcilable; that even for the sake of my mother, we seem unable to find ways to heal our conflicts enough to shield her from feeling in the middle of them. I dread that even to up until the day we lower her into her grave, we might fail to reconcile—an ultimate, eternal injury to her. I wish I knew how to restore and strengthen true, lasting trust between us, but at present I do not. I truly am trying to understand you more fully in your palette of values and experiences, your fears and dreams, as doing so might help you finally feel respected, valued, heard and seen by me. I sorely long for the bad feelings between us to dissipate and be replaced by better ones: Please tell and show me your ideas, so that we might make that happen, together and soon. We have felt hurt by and disappointed in each other for a long time, but one thing's never changed for me: What I want—what I *need*—is your love and acceptance, which I can then return.
>
> *Michael*

No doubt my relatives, too, have suffered from our endless impasse, from the toxic sea of hurt and deep distrust swirling between us. Our deadlock, however, resembles on the microlevel what others feel on macrolevels. If we can crack the code of our culture's widely-spread ill will, we also can heal enough to be able to face a tumultuous, uncertain future, together and better.

I have not written at length in this treatise about my never-ending struggles with my family for "fun and profit" but rather because they have been grist for my spiritual mill, kernels of sand in my heart's hard-shelled "oyster" that may yet yield a pearl. Even without knowing it, they have challenged my faith, called me to examine my own brokenness and offered me paths to much growth. As bitter as the medicine has been at times, their constant rebuke and repeated rebuffs have been gifts which have enriched my Life even as they strained it to its core. Nicole may not (yet) understand, but we "need" such fencing partners, people who, for whatever reason, with whatever motive, are willing—yea, are called—to spar with us. It is this exercise which stresses not just our physical but our emotional muscles enough that they can grow. At times stand-ins for our own inner demons can be pains in the *Arsch* who piss us off, but without them—be they siblings, cousins or grand-/parents, friends, old classmates, [also former] lovers, bosses—inertia.

It is, however, an art and hardly a science to find a healthy, sustainable balance between going after "them" and going after what is broken in one's Self. There is no healing, no movement or progress, no new strength or wisdom without engaging in such taxing work—but let us at least become more skilled at it, more efficient, that it might be concluded well and sooner than later, so that we might then turn to the pressing, vital work of confronting <u>our own</u> impact on the Earth.

Want a few practical tips that might help you, too, on your journey along the path of healing stuck spots with people close to you? In the section "Wiping Slates Clean," although I did so in Lucy's and Linus' absence (their choice), I allotted ten lines each to pondering my past or present roles in their feeling disrespected, un[der]valued, unheard or unseen by me. Although daunting and subjective, I made this inventory as concise, brutally honest and comprehensive as I could. Had either one been on-hand for the process, I would have asked her or him to take an inventory, equally as concise, honest and wide-ranging.

Whether you undergo this process with your "partner" absent or present, give yourself the *same* amount of time and space [the ten lines I allotted each side were arbitrary; that length seems do-able and adequate, but use your best judgment, fit your own needs] to take the *same* inventory. What remains paramount is a real and built-in balance, along with The Other being represented in some way. A tricky part of the process, in either scenario, is that we have no control over The Other or her/his/their "truth." Still, undertaking such honest, deep-reaching inventories can be part of the process of revisiting formative experiences, at key moments, that got us to "here"—and keep us stuck in a "there" where we do not wish to stay longer, squandering our attention and energy needed right here, right now, to confront the essential tasks facing our species.

Going beyond the surface of things, wading into the heart of our existence is challenging to humans everywhere—and likely always was. As an American, however, who has spent half of his life outside of the United States—and who thinks he has a reasonably realistic sense of what it is like *not* to be an American—it has been my observation that many of my co-nationals share my struggle to not take Life and the world at face value; it often challenges me to sink deeper. If we are to successfully accomplish Deep Work we cannot do that casually, merely by baking cookies or hosting "fun" neighborhood parties. The world we have now is not the one we WASPS reigned over half a century or so ago: The insular, insulated existence we cultivated after World War II was illusionary—just like the feeling, growing up in the rural Midwest, that we lived in a "white America" where "everyone [was] jus' like us." Now, *seeing* and <u>knowing</u> that certainly is not true today, we need to part with our rose-colored glasses and self-induced disrealities: The world can no longer afford such self-serving, environmentally-costly lies.[100]

*

back row, l. to r.: Bud Luick, holding Debbie; Jack and Eleanor [Thrams] Hunt, Bernice [Reid] and Willard Thrams; the author's mother, Phyllis [Thrams] Luick; Irene [Thrams] and Thurman Floyd; Elmer Thrams. front row: Marcia & Terry Hunt; Stephan & Cindy Floyd. Ashlawn Farm near Mason City, Iowa; circa 1955

"Good Midwesterners," we were publicly almost always polite but privately, not so much—a passive-aggressive behavior that reflected the Scandinavians among us squared with postwar pretensions. It now seems like the most important, substantial things were brushed aside; banalities ruled the day.

Practice Real Kindness

Something else the world no longer can afford is the soul-devouring lack of real kindness. So,

4) practice real kindness.

Oh, don't worry: There are scads of examples of fake "kindness" all around. How many times have you, too, groaned with glazed-over eyes as you endured the hollow refrain of "Hi, my name's Brittany and I'll be your server tonight. If there's anything at all that I can do fer ya guys…" It is only one of myriad examples of "kindly" behavior, words, appearances that, at their core, aren't. While it may seem obvious that what Brittany wants most is to massage loose a generous tip, in that moment when we are enjoying the motions of someone focusing on us, of seeming to take our wishes into account, we *do* enjoy it—but just as quickly forget that "fun" isn't "joy." False kindness not only pollutes our planet, but it occupies space where genuine joy might reside.

If you wish to break the deadlock presently paralyzing most developed countries, take a fourth step to change our world: Call unkindness what it is and, instead, **practice real kindness**.

There are so many sorts and instances of unkindness in our everyday lives now that new, fused *portmanteaus* have arisen to distinguish them: "snarky" for "snide remark," or "refudiate," first used by Sarah Palin when she misspoke, conflating the words refute and repudiate.[101] Turn on any American current-events, "news" or talk show: Pejorative, hypercritical words have become so common, so "normal" we do not even notice their real toxicity as we hear or, worse, repeat them. They are dipped in such emotional poison that unkind words spread a polarizing taint all of their own: The subject or recipient of verbal aggression hears unmistakably the speaker's implied disdain and dismissal. Once exposed to it, it's like a plague that jumps from one to another. Feeling so little regard for others' thoughts and feelings gives us permission to ignore their humanness—the very delicate, sacred parts of them that distinguish each of us in the cosmos. In the process, not only do targets of our unkind words suffer emotional and social devastation, but we, too, are left feeling—consciously or not—remorse; our loneliness and displeasure grow.

Why do we so easily succumb to this snowballing social sickness? How do we stop or at least mitigate it? The Dalai Lama, for one, recognizes that kindness lies at the center of well-being:

[Our] very survival depends even today upon the acts and kindness of so many people. Right from the moment of our birth, we are under the care and kindness of our parents; later in life, when facing the sufferings of disease and old age, we are again dependent on the kindness of others. If at the beginning and end of our lives we depend upon others' kindness, why then in the middle, when we have the opportunity, should we not act kindly towards others?

As he went on to say in his preface to Piero Ferrucci's 2006 masterpiece, *Forza della gentilezza* [*The Power of Kindness*], the Dalai Lama went on to note:

Kindness and compassion are among the principal things that make our lives meaningful. They are a source of lasting happiness and joy. They are the foundation of a good heart, the heart of one who acts out of a desire to help others. [...] Consideration for others is worthwhile because our happiness is inextricably bound up with the happiness of others. Similarly, if society suffers, we ourselves suffer. On the other hand, the more our hearts and minds are afflicted with ill will, the more miserable we become.

When I watch Congressional—or, monitoring the Brexit disaster, Parliamentary—proceedings, the nasty, negative, unloving and utterly unkind hues woven throughout leave me cold. That emotional chill is the same I experience when I observe my compatriots crossing verbal swords over Trumpian themes or, on a personal level, when I think of Lucy's and Linus' refusing contact with me. The Dalia Lama has noticed this coldness of heart, too—and offers us an antidote:

[K]indness creates a sense of warmth and openness that allows us to communicate much more easily with other people. We discover that all human beings are just like us, so we are able to relate to them more easily. That generates a spirit of friendship in which there is less need to hide what we feel or what we are doing. As a result, feelings of fear, self-doubt, and insecurity are automatically dispelled, while at the same time other people find it easier to trust us, too.

On one hand, I lament that it seems most of humanity needs to see benefits to one's Self in order to practice greater kindness towards others; on the other, such self-serving behavior exists and hardly can be erased. My ears, too, perk up when I hear of the purported perks of new habits.

Likely knowing this, the Dalai Lama goes on to cite "increasing evidence that cultivating positive mental states like kindness and compassion definitely leads to better psychological health and happiness." As Abraham Lincoln is said to have quipped, "Most folks are as happy as they make up their minds to be"—a favorite saying of my mother's—yet aren't momentary states of mind but building blocks for a larger, long-lasting structure of an entire life? As the Dalai Lama says:

We were not born for the purpose of causing trouble and harming others. For our life to be of value [...], we need to foster and nurture such basic good human qualities as warmth, kindness, and compassion. If we can do that, our lives will become meaningful, happier, and more peaceful; we will make a positive contribution to the world around us.[102]

That's the good news.

The bad news is, Ferrucci warned already in his 2006 classic of an "Ice Age of the heart" that he more than a decade ago had concluded now grips our species. He holds that we are in

> ...the midst of a "global cooling." Human relations are becoming colder. Communications are becoming more hurried and impersonal. Values such as profit and efficiency are taking on greater importance at the expense of human warmth and genuine presence. Family affections and friendships suffer and are less lasting. Signs of this decline are everywhere, visible especially when they touch us in the small catastrophes of everyday life.

Is this not obvious? In my adopted homeland, German teens drop "cool" as frequently as their English-native-speaker counterparts Stateside. Like teens likely always have, most of them are sure to let the world know that their parents are "embarrassing" and "*abgefuckt*" (an English-German *portmanteau*)—but what's new, is that many seem to have written off *all* adults, and too often also "*kleine* Kids" and, well, almost *everyone*. Many also—like Peruvian and Nepali, Bahamian and so many other youth, worldwide these days—wear buttless pants and knitted caps, squat at the knees as they squawk into invisible mics held in pulsing, index-finger+pinky-stretched hands as they bob their heads back and forth atop stiff necks. It seems everywhere on the planet it is "cool" to be cold, to show few, even "better" no emotions, to project a reflexive indifference and aloofness in any way possible. I take away as an ultimate message at the core of this posturing—laced inseparably as it is from nihilistic-yet-angry lyrics—"Leave me alone! Do not come near me with your needs and wishes, your own view of things and stupid sentimentality."

Real kindness, however, isn't real if it cannot focus on The Other's needs, wishes and emotions. At present, it is hip to affect not caring, yet in my students, my young neighbors and my daughter I sense a disavowed, pervasive longing for the opposite of what our youth emit—for connection and conviction. Publicly, modern culture is signing off and shutting down, but privately millions of young people literally are dying for lack of closeness, warmth... of *so* many "uncool" things.

As a socially-aware father, Ferrucci says "the Ice Age we are passing through is worrisome, and I am not surprised that it goes hand in hand with the epidemic of depression and panic attacks, probably the two psychological disturbances most linked to lack of warmth and of a reassuring and protecting community, and to a weakened sense of belonging." As a holistic psychologist, he seeks clues to our present malaise in its past roots. Thus, he sees it as having arisen with

> the Industrial Revolution and [it] continues on our post-industrial age [and he says the causes are many:] new living conditions and forms of work, the establishing of new technologies, the decline of the extended family, the great migrations in which people are uprooted from their birthplace, the weakening of values, the fragmentation and superficiality of the contemporary world, the accelerating pace of life.

As a social historian, I can echo Ferrucci's observations—in civic contexts, indicated by the ever greater shrillness used by ideologues of all political stripes, generally; specifically, also by the acerbic tongues and ugly tone of partisan exchanges. Recently, I had the edifying opportunity literally to *see* proof of this, when I had occasion to review political-affairs-program footage on Minnesota and Iowa television channels in the 1960s and '70s. Observe how our grand-/parents discussed matters of polity in decades past: The contrast is sobering and humbling to witness!

Indeed, during my US-Senate campaign, it repeatedly took my breath how quickly my fellow Iowans could tune me out, then turn against not only my politics, but my person. Why do too many Americans insist on demonizing those who do not agree with everything one might say? Not only was it not always so, but there are places in the world today where it is still not the norm. In Germany, for one, there are multiple parties in the Bundestag, the nation's parliament in Berlin. The larger parties have long supported provisos that the state give special subsidies to support the fortunes and growth of small opposition parties; with that country's dictatorial past still a stain on the soul of its people, most agree on the need to encourage loyal opposition.

On a personal level, in Iowa my mother trained me to "not discuss religion or politics in public." (Sex was *so* taboo, it was a taboo to even mention that it was taboo in "polite society.") In Germany, in contrast, one is expected to be able to articulately and cogently explain one's personal views. If you can't, then one loses one's standing—but if one can, rarely is personal offense taken and, well, expect to be invited out for a *Bier* afterwards. In my experience, most Germans actually respect a person more, not less, for being able to rationally and calmly discuss political matters. To not to be able to do so is considered being poorly-reared and -educated. To often interrupt one's opponent, to resort to screaming or swearing is considered a sign of a low level of personal maturation and development; doing so alienates others and self-sabotages.

But, I am not a German—nor did I run for office there. It was in Iowa that I experienced personally, repeatedly, how difficult it was to find folks who could discuss the affairs of "the *polis*" (again, how we share power in "the city") without, early on, growing testy or, later, rude or insulting. I saw in the Hawkeye State, on local levels, the civic ill-will that typifies our nation. It saddens me.

Many of us older social observers have witnessed the rise of such dynamics, as well as their democracy-strangling effects—including Parker Palmer. In a video about his book *Healing the Heart of Democracy*, he reflects on causes of our current social discord and political deadlock—and the vital role "civic kindness" plays in restoring, then strengthening democracy. He decries

> ...what's happening to "we the people." What's happened to our sense of civic community? What's happened to our capacity to hold our differences with some kind of hospitality rather than hostility? I'm not against differences: I think democracy's about negotiating our differences and hammering out solutions that we wouldn't come to if we didn't see things differently. I've always been impressed with the fact that American democracy did not start with "those people"

in Washington, D.C., far away with all the power and money, dictating something. It started with "we the people" calling this democracy into being. And my sense is, that it's we the people who need to call it back, to its deepest purposes and its most significant goals. We're not going to be able to do that if we don't learn to talk to each other with respect and civility, and so [...] I'm very interested in how it is that we develop it in our local lives, [in] all of those settings where we have an opportunity to interact with each other as citizens, and reweave and restore the civic community on which democracy depends. [...] This book is an appeal to remember that politics, American democracy, isn't just what happens out there in Washington DC or in the state capitol, but it's also about what happens [author points to his chest with his hand] in here. We need to take responsibility for both the inner and the outer dimensions of the dilemmas of democracy. We need, in order to be good citizens in a democracy, chutzpah and humility: The chutzpah to say what it is we care about, to make a claim on our society and on each other; and the humility to know that we have to listen because none of us has the whole answer.

How should we ever overcome political deadlock, if we cannot [re-]learn to care about the feelings of others, to pay their thoughts and wishes at least a minimum of seriousness and due respect, to show real kindness, even while disagreeing? As optimist Ferrucci (below) maintains:

[We] are living in an extraordinary epoch. If we wish to cultivate solidarity, kindness, care for others, we have more knowledge, instruments, and possibilities than ever before. [...] It is up to us. It is a choice in the life of each of us—to take the road of selfishness and abuse, or the way of solidarity and kindness. In this exciting but dangerous moment of human history, kindness is not a luxury, it is a necessity. Maybe if we treat each other, and our planet, a little better, we can survive, even thrive. And by becoming kinder, we might end up discovering that we have given ourselves the best, the most intelligently selfish gift.

*

"Be patterns, be examples in all countries, places, islands, nations, wherever you come; that your carriage and life may preach among all sorts of people, and to them. Then you will come to walk cheerfully over the world, answering that of God in everyone."

— early Quaker George Fox (1624-1691),
in a letter from Fox to ministers in 1656[103]

Speak Your Truth to "Power"

It is *always* good to be kind. At present, however, many Western democracies are drowning in waves of public nastiness. For those of us trying to grope our ways out of that darkness, being kind remains crucial, yet it alone will not leverage the breakthrough in deadlock that we need if all of us are to move forward. For that, even kindly citizens must share something substantial, worthwhile and powerful, even as we do so with the utmost care to our actions and impact. So:

5) speak your truth.

But, practice how to **speak "Truth to Power"** *after* you have a sense of what real "power" is. Ex.:

A year after the collapse of *Apartheid*, I trekked to the "New South Africa" for a month to see what might have changed—or not. Traversing the breadth of that stirring land, I learned much.

To cut costs, moreover to meet people and see places through local perspectives I otherwise would not, I mostly stayed with L/GHEI and Quaker hosts in those pre-Couchsurfing days.[104] Iowa State University Press sponsored my tour, during which I spoke about recently-published *Out of Hitler's Reach* at Friends' meetings in Cape Town, Pietermaritzburg and Johannesburg. Thus, I had the pleasure of meeting many big-hearted, sharp-minded South Africans. Although my white hosts/new friends ordered me *not* to do so (or, me being me, *because* they did), I haughtily took the "black train" from "J'burg" to Pretoria. (Whites of all stripes, Anglo or Afrikaans or others, also advised me to *not* venture into intimidating SOWETO—the dreaded, downtrodden suburb South Western Townships, into which the white regime had crammed thousands of black and "colored" Africans—so, *of course*, I toured it, too.) Full of my cocky self right up until the conductor blew a shrill whistle and the railcars' doors thudded to a dull close, as the packed commuter line creaked its way out of downtown Johannesburg I quickly had second thoughts.

Endless lines of mostly scruffily-dressed, abjectly poor black South Africans filed past me with disbelieving eyes: Almost all stared at me, as a white man (not to say a white woman) likely had not ridden that line in years. Sitting there now humbled and even whiter with raw fear, I looked out the window and forced myself to meditate on something other than my own being robbed or getting killed. (Spoiler Alert: Neither happened.) Deeply touched by the fortnight I already had spent in that geographically-stunning country, filled with lovely, endlessly-kind people of all colors or backgrounds, I sifted through multitudes of mental images of my sojourn there so far.

Sitting in that dusty, dilapidated train, rumbling across spectacular scenery even while seeing some of the saddest specimens of white privilege's victims silently parade before my pained eyes, I experienced several epiphanies. For one, knowing now inarguably that I have directly benefitted my entire life from having been born on the coddled side of the global color line, I sought to understand the essence of the power I still wield, no matter if or how I might use it.

"White [Male] Privilege," anyone? The author visited Wisconsin's Taliesin (left) in 1998 and Lima in 2018. If I were a Native-American or African-American historian-activist, could I have so easily led such a life? I have asked myself this question for decades—already as a "[school] boy" at Ermysted's: One morning, after having been chosen to speak at devotions, I was walking out of the assembly hall in step with the then-headmaster, ever-solemn John Woolmore—his black knee-length robe at times brushing against my navy-blue blazer. My talk seemed to have been well-received, as many of my schoolmates cheered at the end when I challenged the school's, moreover the society's status quo. Having caused a stir even as I had made a strong impression, without looking at me Woolmore whispered as he admonished "You know, Master Luick: 'To whom much has been given, much will be required.'" I knew that then; I know it now.

In South Africa under *Apartheid*, "whitie" told "darkie" where to live (or not), what to learn (or not, as studying beyond a basic education was out of the question for most non-whites), who to become in the workforce (or not, as professions were almost exclusively the realm of whites), whom to marry or even share sexual closeness with (or not)—and so on. Whites assumed the unassailable power to determine how all non-whites might live as well as literally die, as solely whites exercised power—but I *had* to ponder that loaded, key word: It meant… <u>what</u>, exactly?

That day, as an Iowa farmboy most improbably sitting in an all-black train snaking its way from Southern Africa's largest city to its nearby capital, I distilled for myself a working definition of:

POWER is the ability to facilitate or, conversely, to hinder the realization of potential.

In an era passing before me, on the other side of a smudged, hairline-cracked window, whites had told non-whites what they "may" (or not) make of their potential: where their lives might take place or lead, how much they were allowed to develop their minds through education, what they might make of themselves or as a wage—right down to whom they "may" kiss or fall in love with. The unbearable unfairness of such an abusive exercise of power based on skin color grew from white privilege being taken to its most immoral extreme. While not a white South African, I felt ashamed of my co-complexioned humans' susceptibility to gladly wearing poisoned crowns.

I could not wag a finger at them, however, coming as I do from a country once, in too large a part, built by and on *Apartheid* Light. In the US, the color line proved to be more permeable: A sympathizing white person—to cite two historical examples—might grant a specific black one the scholarship needed to attend college, *vis-à-vis* Alex Haley or Grandma Thrams' podiatrist's father. Still, the power to so change the entire course of another human being's life laid in white hands, not the darker ones of the person so longing for a leg up in Life. At the same time, historical records document that before the Civil War, some African as well as Native Americans kept blacks as property, in human bondage, despite their own exclusion by the white elite. Even Southern Quakers and nuns kept enslaved persons, though internal pressures ended its practice by 1800.[105]

We do not, however, have to time-travel back a couple centuries to find instructive examples of the exercise of power—or the need to call out the flawed use of it. Here, for one, is a true gem:

Maundy Thursday, April 4th, 1985—spring in Iowa's capital city.

As I recall it, five Iowa State students had been selected to attend the 24th annual Governor's Prayer Breakfast—with 2020 being its 59th year.[106] As it was sold to us, post-secondary students from all over Iowa would gather and have a chance to speak with Terry Branstad, the polarizing governor then presiding over the worst farm crisis to hit the Hawkeye State since the Great Depression. Told by cogs in ISU's *nomenklatura* that we were among our university's "best and brightest," thus charged with representing "all Cyclones" to Iowa's *apparatchiks* in Des Moines, I agreed to go but remained lukewarm, as I saw the gig as an Iowa version of Soviet suck-up.

As the ISU van barreled from Ames to Des Moines that morning, we diverse delegates looked at each other, then the African-American honors student from Cedar Rapids clowned "They've invited us to feign diversity at Moo U by sending a Jew, a fag, a Spic, a nigger an' a cripple!" The curly-haired co-ed in the wheelchair squealed with delight, but Barry Cohn from Clive grinned uneasily. Jose' seemed unsure how to react to the allusion to him, while I only rolled my eyes.

"Jus' messin' wit' ya" the Eastern-Iowa brain teased us before she cleared her throat as well as the affected accent, then dropped her voice and warned earnestly "If we don't want to play the fool, we need to agree on a roster of issues we wish to address during our turn to grill Terry."

In surprisingly short order, we soon agreed on three:

1) How did the governor propose Iowa's students fund our education yet avoid vast debt?
2) Once we graduated, how might the State help us remain in Iowa, not have to leave it?
3) What did he propose to alleviate the worst effects of the farm crisis devastating Iowa?

Feeling as if we were the coolest cats to attend that day, we entered the catered dining hall full of conceit—abruptly shattered when we spied handfuls of equally, if not visibly cooler students.

"Oh, jus' look at those Grinnell snobs over there" Barry snarled, trying not to cast his eyes in their direction as his head threw muted nods their way. "They think they're so damned hot!"

"Well" The Brain chipped in, "those Luther students seem pretty pious—an' gitta loada those Coe an' Cornhill kids" she scoffed. "They think Cedar Rapids students 'should' stay in-area. *Geez*!"

Not interested to stooping to such petty inter-collegiate rivalries but rather keen to press Terry against the wall and demand answers to our pressing queries, I called out "There's our table!" and made my way to our seats faster than any ISU quarterback bound for beckoning goalposts.

While the others fell upon the breakfast soon served us as if starving strays, I shook my finger in the direction of the lectern and wondered "So, when will today's speakers start regaling us?"

The guest speaker, Nebraska-native William Lester Armstrong, had just been sworn into a second term as a Colorado US Senator, having served first in Colorado's House and Senate, then the US House before beating astronaut Jack Swigert in the GOP primary race for the US Senate. The onetime radio-station owner would go on to preside over Colorado Christian University for a decade and serve on the Board of Directors for Campus Crusade for Christ. He also became known for his catchphrase "Jesus, Jesus, Jesus!" Indeed, he fit right in at Branstad's breakfast—but not at all into the separation-of-church-and-state tenet that we five Iowa Staters embraced.

Senator William Lester Armstrong, circa 1980

Before Armstrong could impress us with his many accomplishments and make us love him for some surely wonderful qualities which I immediately forgot, our callow governor strode to the mic to open the morning's program. Expecting the promised time for a deliberate dialog with the most powerful politician in our state, our hopes were dashed when, instead of meditating on or even acknowledging the issues that drove us to trek to Des Moines in the first place. Terry wasted no time in closing his eyes, lifting an open palm heavenward and thanking "God, that [his] son Marcus was been born on Right-to-Life Sunday." Ironically, Terry's demi-god hero, the Gipper, had designated 22 January 1984 as "National Sanctity of Human Life Day," noting as he issued his presidential proclamation that it would be the 11th anniversary of Roe v. Wade, in which the Supreme Court had issued a ruling that guaranteed women access to abortion.

At that, I glanced at the other Cyclones, all of whom looked at least ill if not in the first stages of insanity. The Brain rolled her big head between clenching shoulders, while Barry tsk-tsked. As a chandelier transfixed Jose' and our paraplegic colleague clicked a knob with a crooked thumb, I contemplated feasible escape scenarios: *Could I hitchhike back ta Ames—or maybe jus' walk?*

*

"The truth is rarely pure, and never simple."

— Oscar Wilde,
The Importance of Being Earnest

Serve Your "Truth" More Palatably

Being a student at Iowa State University afforded sensual pleasures, such as savoring that huge campus' natural splendor, which gracefully glided across each new season, always offering real beauty. As a land-grant college emphasizing agriculture in the middle of one the world's most fertile farming regions, a series of inspired administrators as well as grateful alum bestowed ISU several stunning architectural gems, which only accentuated the campus' natural gorgeousness.

Three of the four sides of the 1925-built, limestone-clad Parks Library contain names with much renown—plus on the east *façade* the quote "AND YE SHALL KNOW THE TRUTH AND THE TRUTH SHALL MAKE YOU FREE."[107] Almost each time I passed that passage I pondered *But, what is "The Truth?"* My mind chewed on that riddle until I had distilled a working definition for me:

TRUTH is what simply happens, free of interpretation or assessment of value.

We can exercise this perspective on "truth" by revisiting the previous section, rife as it is with contradictions—ones we can disentangle simply by summarizing the "truth" of what happened, without interpretation or assigning the event neither "positive" nor "negative" values. Thus:

- For decades, South Africa found itself ostracized by most other countries in the world, which said they objected to the system of *Apartheid*. At the same time, South Africa scores higher on the Human Development Index than 45 other African countries:[108] Workers in neighboring Southern African states were willing to live and work there, if possible, despite *Apartheid*.
- Before the Civil War, some African as well as Native Americans owned black slaves. Seven of the eight orders of Catholic nuns in the US owned enslaved persons by the 1820s; the Jesuit priests who founded and ran Georgetown University were among Maryland's largest slaveholders.[109] Other slaveholders included some Quakers, all of whom ceased practicing slavery by 1800.[110] Each of these groupings of slaveholding Americans contradicts modern preconceptions of what sort of people owned other human beings, whom they forced to work for them or their clients.

Easy—right? Might appear that way, especially about events from long ago that might seem to have little direct connection to one's own life. In fact, distilling historical events down to their essence—like a dutiful reporter would—can be an enjoyable pastime. It can, that is, 'til at least one of two things happens: 1) You feel called to present your findings to another human being, biased by her or his own filter, agenda, etc., or 2) you seek to "truthfully" relate an event with close connections to you or people [or perhaps even pets, possessions or places] you love.

Trickier, huh?

Ok, then, dear reader, as you were not there, try "truthfully" recapping my quick trip to Des Moines with other Iowa State "show pieces" to attend the 1985 Governor's Prayer Breakfast.

Ready? Set—go!

[Time passes while you try…]

So, how'd ya do? Sortta tough, no? Imagine you were trying to "report" one of your *own* tales!

Here's how I did:

> Five Iowa State students attended the 24th annual Governor's Prayer Breakfast, having been told they would have a chance to speak with Terry Branstad, which they desired. As they rode to the event, the diverse group agreed on three questions to pose to the governor, regarding: funding student education, finding post-graduation positions in Iowa and addressing the "Farm Crisis."
>
> After noting other student groups in attendance, they took seats at a table assigned to them and waited for the guest speaker's address. Before that took place, the governor began the event by sharing a familial anecdote about the date of a son's birth. The ISU students reacted strongly.

How'd I do? How well does my summary avoid interpreting or assessing value to those events? In any case, now our assignment gets even trickier: Let's envision we want to "do something" with this text—like, relay it to someone else, say to Terry Branstad… indeed, let's speak our "truth" to *two* historically-powerful Terry Branstads. First, to the greenhorn governor of 1985:

> Governor, five of us Iowa State students came here today to pose three questions we consider to be of vital importance to our lives and others'. As we feel you are in a unique position to either take action that addresses our concerns or relay them to others who you know in relevant leadership positions, who might initiate policies or programs to mitigate these problems. As our highest elected representative, we ask you to seriously reflect on our concerns and act on them.

Now, to the Terry of today:

> Ambassador, almost 35 years ago, I heard you speak at the Iowa Governor's Prayer Breakfast. I and four other Iowa State University students sought to pose to you three questions we agreed were vital to our well-being as young Iowans, preparing for our adult lives. Now, as the US's most visible representative to one of the most powerful countries on a planet reeling from climate change, I ask you to seriously reflect on how you might influence the Chinese to…

If you think "speaking truth" to (I've never been granted an opportunity to talk "with") Terry in a measured, dispassionate manner is natural for or comes easy to me—guess again. In my long activist career, I've resented, despised, even demonized the man; I've felt *so* angry by positions he's taken or policies he's pushed through the Iowa Statehouse that I could have spit nails—and likely still could if I meditated long enough on the effects of *his* political career. But, now, I *need* him; we <u>all</u> do. We *need* the Terry Branstads of this world to hear us, to see us, to respect our concerns and value how we came to hold them. We *need* the Lucys and Linuses; we need *all* of "them" now like we've *never* needed anyone before—because without them, <u>we</u> are *all* lost.

As I write this, I can hear the Young-Campus-Activist Me kvetch "Why waste time on tryin' ta reach smug Terry? He's in the pocket of Big Ag anyway. Ya don't stand a chance ta move 'im!"

Ya know who else we *need* right now? Our Best Selves! It's one thing for you or me to rehearse speaking coolly and collectedly to "distant" figures who populate and still dominate our world; it is quite another to reach out to those closest to us—to family, friends, colleagues, lovers—yet we must not only practice but actually **engage in** this tough assignment. If we can't share our "truth" effectively with those nearest to us, how do we hope to move those farthest from us? The Great Divide currently keeping America, most of Europe, Turkey and too many other lands trapped in immobilizing deadlock can be bridged only by "real" individuals, doing "real" Deep Work. Each of us possesses at least one stone to contribute to the foundations of new conduits to close the chasms between citizens and neighbors alike, locally and across our battered globe.

You know why we, why *all* of us *must* do Deep Work now? Because we have solely two choices today: Either 1) we try to dispassionately show those who do not agree with us how our shared dangers will affect <u>them</u> and theirs, or 2) we continue to do too little, too late and we all perish.

In the past—a time and a non-physical "place" now gone forever—we could afford indignance, self-righteousness, outrage, even hate, but we can't any longer. In that now-extinct "then" we still had the luxury to fret or fight over banalities like men wearing right-lobe earrings, prayer in school, teens "just [saying] 'no'," single-parent households or any number of other, now-non-essential concerns. We felt entitled to ignore deeper truths occurring around us; apathy was ours. Today, the margins of our main job description have shrunk: We are left at the core, in the heart of our existence on Earth. Either we recast our souls, or there'll hardly be any left to fret about.

With only so much time and finite energies, why "invest" in massaging loose calcified hearts like those of the Terrys and Chucks who continue to hold disproportionate abilities to facilitate or, conversely, to hinder the realization of our collective potential to save ourselves? On practical levels, for one, Terry knows China's head, Xi Jinping, who most recently visited Iowa in February 2012, when he met first with President Obama at the White House, then with his erstwhile host family in their farmhouse near Muscatine,[111] whom he met during a 1985 tour of the Hawkeye State as a still-obscure provincial official. And Chuck? He remains the gatekeeper of several US Senate committees—most infamously, having served as the space holder for Bret Kavanaugh by refusing for months to let the Judicial Committee he oversees consider Obama's nominee to the

Supreme Court, Terry Branstad's second cousin, Merrick Garland. ('Tis a shrinkin' world, no? An', like I confided earlier, "Iowa *is* the Center of the Universe.") Still, how do we recruit either of the men?

Terry Branstad has *never* had to contemplate, for himself, to abort a fetus. I cannot imagine he has ever considered applying for food stamps or carrying baby Marcus, Eric or Allison across a treacherous river in the hope of escaping gangs, chronic unemployment or hunger. I assume the same of Charles Grassley or Patty Judge or... but I do *know* this, without a doubt: *Every* Iowan needs clear air to breathe, pure water to drink and temperatures conducive to living, *not* deadly to same. Terry now lives in Beijing; like me, he has breathed the lethal air there: Can he deny that air quality in China is hazardous to human and other life? He and Chris, his wife of 47 years, have eight grandchildren: Do they not worry about *their* survival, just as Lucy and Linus must fret about that of theirs? Do we not *all* share such common concerns?

Then-Iowa Governor Terry Branstad toasted Xi Jinping in 2012, when Xi was China's vice president and Donald Trump had not yet appointed Branstad to be the US Ambassador to China—which he is still.

Yet, what can I, moreover what can <u>we</u> do? I can't whisper into Xi's ear reminders of our global interconnectedness, our shared humanity, the pressing need to curb China's especially coal but other carbon emissions—but, Terry *can*. I can't pick US Supreme Court justices who, going forward, will overturn the singularly anti-Democratic Citizens United[112] decision—but Chuck *can*. I can't do a *lot* of things—but I *can* ask probing questions (as now-retired Jim Dale recently confirmed I did already as a know-next-to-nothing confirmation-camper) and learn ostensibly obscure yet crucial facts (like Xi's Iowa links—or Terry's familial ones). And, in addition to all the other useful abilities I now can, nay <u>must</u>, tap for our common good, I *can W R I T E* ! I also can continue to go deep into my soul, inspect and repair its health, then return to share its wealth.

So… what can <u>you</u> do?

Once you feel you have more fully understood how individuals, groups, nations have exercised power over others in different eras, in various places, in diverse ways, then reflect on this: How can *you* take the findings of *your* inquiries, distill them to their most dispassionate core, then frame your "truth" of what matters most to *you* in ways that others can hear and see them? Practice sharing essential yet often uncomfortable messages kindly, with steadfast compassion, so that others might more easily respect and value not only your message, but its messenger.

Once you feel you have mastered all of that, examine how power plays out in your life, in your immediate environments—and your roles in either facilitating or hindering potential. Then, begin to share what you think you see with others, as clearly, concisely and respectfully as you can. (Be sure to make your words sweet, as who knows: You may end up eating them!) Watch for indications of how your naming the power dynamics you perceive in the lives and actions of those around you affects others; try to refine your own exercise of power, as it matters—greatly.

And, watch how your new relationship with "truth" changes <u>you</u>, for as M. Scott Peck promised,

> By their openness, people dedicated to the truth live in the open, and through the exercise of their courage to live in the open, they become free from fear.[113]

At the same time, Peck—who readers will encounter in-depth, later in this work—also warned:

> A life of total dedication to the truth also means a life of willingness to be personally challenged.

*

"A Native American elder once described his own inner struggles in this manner:
'Inside me there are two dogs. One of the dogs is mean and evil,
the other dog is good. The mean dog fights the good dog all the time.'
When asked which dog wins, he reflected for a moment and replied,
'The one I feed the most.'"

— George Bernard Shaw,
from a Cherokee legend
"The Tale of Two Wolves"[114]

Be Neither Victim nor Executioner

When I observe parties with contradicting viewpoints engaged in animated discussion, I soon see both sides feeling not listened to or seen—in short, feeling victimized by opponents who they consider perpetrators on some level of the great wrongs that both sides claim the other is committing. Once "discussion" devolves to a level of arguing who has been more victimized by whom, typically no one can truly hear the other; communication, like trust, has broken down. How can we back out of such exchanges—or, better yet, avoid reaching such stalemates at all?

Another idea:

6) be neither "victim" nor "perpetrator."

To do this, truly **reconsider how you see "victims" versus "perpetrators"** in Life and the world.

For me, the month I spent in South Africa forced me to reconsider my attitudes toward both. As an undergraduate at ISU, I had read French philosopher-author Albert Camus' discouragingly dense but stimulating essays in *Ni Victimes, ni bourreaux* [*Neither Victims nor Executioners*], which forever altered my understanding of both ends of the victimization process. And once again, given my unusual, niche-academic interests, I viewed the "South African problem" through various lenses, including that of the North European one under Hitler's Nazis:

The Berlin regime knew it lacked the manpower to execute each job necessary to rule every person in Eastern Europe, including in the Jewish ghettos. Cynically, it offered "power" to select Jews who either had played leadership roles before the Nazis invaded or, in the new political landscape, were willing to assume "helper" roles for their occupiers. Both found themselves in disconsolate situations but, in the latter case, the "*Kapos*" (arm-banded, club-wielding Jewish "police" who kept order, even during deportations or liquidations) through their collusion with their captors did little more than buy a bit more time before they, too, would be murdered—as well as a little physical comfort until they were. Why did either group accept this Faustian deal? Many in the first group genuinely believed their representing the dejected Jews through a *Judenrat*, a Jewish council, might alleviate their co-congregants' suffering, as well as delay their

194

community's almost certain annihilation. The *Kapo*s, however, rarely took their wretched posts out of altruism; instead, in most cases naked (albeit doomed) self-interest motivated their new "careers" under the Nazis. Sadly ironic, both groups had little ability to facilitate or hinder the realization of potential inside the ghettos: The Germans had veto power over the *Judenrat*—and burst any illusion of power on the part of the *Kapo*s by periodically executing them all before their "power" might encourage rebellion—and before the next wave of slaves took their posts.

Jewish children at Scattergood Hostel: The boy is Louis Lichtenstein, the girl with a kitten his sister Edith; the girl to the left is Annette Keller, the girl to the right is thought to be Monique Schumacher. The man was a Kapo leader at the Salaspils concentration camp in Latvia; he wore a Judenstern ("Star of David") identifying patch and a Lagerpolizist ("camp policeman") armband. Still alive as of this writing, Edith has given oral and written interviews, both of which can be accessed via leading Midwest media outlets.[115]

[A telling historical footnote: Distilled to their essence, the story of the Scattergood Hostel for European refugees (1939-43) contains several contradictions, embodying how lines between being "victims" and "perpetrators" can blur. Well-intentioned Quaker farmers "on the ground" in Iowa, for example, had reached out to Jewish communities in Iowa City, Cedar Rapids and Des Moines in order to prepare the soil in which to plant their idea of providing a safe haven to those fleeing Nazi madness; East-Coast Quakers at the American Friends Service Committee, however, rapped their proverbial knuckles, warning to not "come off as coddling the Jews." This ambivalence towards rescuing Jews was not unique: Even American, especially German-descended Jews were reticent to "rock the boat" of underlying anti-Semitism in this country. They feared bringing thousands of particularly Eastern-European Jews would unleash a backlash all later would bear. Once at West Branch, the "Prussian" Jews from Berlin typically disdained the "frivolous" Viennese *Walzer*," while both sorts of Germanic Jews spurned their Slavic cousins: Pathetically, even among Europe's equally-rejected Jews some felt more "equal" than others.]

In the case of black and mixed-race South Africans, what motivated the vast majority to submit to and duly accommodate their oppressors? The answer is easy: physical survival. Whites—and the few blacks or "coloreds" they co-opted enough to trust—held the power, in particular the armaments needed to erect *Apartheid* after the Second World War, then sustain it for almost five decades. There was resistance, by individuals and by whole groups, yet the system ground on, year in and year out, as both "victims" and "perpetrators" played their roles.[116] Without a critical mass of those in either camp playing their roles, *Apartheid* could not have existed. Yes, whites had usurped all ability to facilitate or hinder the realization of non-whites' potential. In general terms (with noble, inspiring exceptions: Nelson Mandela, Steve Biko, etc.), the majority of non-white South Africans accepted the beastly order imposed on them from above: With too few (yet ultimately successful) exceptions, most accepted whites stifling their vast potential.[117]

Today's equivalent of *Apartheid*-era non-white South Africans or Nazi-era European Jews? Well, that'd be just about <u>all</u> of us: Whether or not we choose to think about it or even believe it, our Earth's ability to survive *us* is making *our* survival questionable. What do we want? Like South African laborers or ghetto councilors and *Kapos*, we want to survive. What did I want as a young gay man? I wanted a family, where I might find the emotional means to survive. What did I get? In some ways, to some degrees, what others stuck in unconscionable situations get: Just enough to (if barely) survive, but not enough to thrive. This, we *must* change—especially now that **all** of us, *without exception*, face the real prospect of being the last of our "race."

Climatic "events" are decimating crop and animal production, worldwide. Millions of climate refugees are bolting devastated or doomed regions, heading to areas less impacted. Yet, some regimes attempt to steer their populations' perceptions of the rate or degree of danger and of damage due to climate change. In turn, too many so duped blame "them," those fleeing. In the tussles to come over resources, it'll be easy to kick The Other. In truth, *none* of us are guiltless in how our planet got into the jam it is in; *all* of us will endure the consequences caused by the blindness of our ancestors and ourselves: There are no "pure" victims or perpetrators in the drama of environmental degradation. Forming fonts is senseless, for as in ghettos the Nazis administered in large part through "victims'" coalescence, there are no winners here, only...

We can feast on turkey at Thanksgiving and wag fingers or shout at each other about abortion or school prayer or gun control—and lob "victim" or "perpetrator" labels freely round the room—but in terms of environmental degradation, such distinctions serve no purpose. In fact, they distract us from the Deep Work at hand: owning our roles in our current, shared quandary. One of the reasons we got into this pickle, into social deadlock stretching broad swaths across much of the world at present, is because self-righteous radical politicos like me did not care to listen to "truths" felt by radical religionists like my closest relatives—a disinclination presumably shared by "liberal" Muslims sitting at holiday feasts with their ISIS-admiring cousins, "reformed" Jews visiting orthodox cousins, moderate Hindu teachers enduring rabidly-nationalist students. It is true that even our best, thoroughly dispassionate, seemingly rationally irrefutable theses might fall on barren soil—but seeds sown often lie dormant in drought-chiseled cracks, only to be awakened by rains that surely do come, in their own time, and wash the cracks whole again.

Still, what we *can* shift is the rate of receptivity to our "truth" and the percentage of those who subscribe to the narratives that arise out of it. The Linuses and Cherrys among us might continue to tread upon glaciers and erroneously conclude, then report that the accelerating rate of ice melt around the globe to be "naturally-occurring cycles." Their audiences, though, need not let such unfounded, damaging statements go unchallenged. "Why bother" the Nicoles might ask, "why waste energy trying to convince the willfully ignorant?" Yet, have we a choice?

Based on my experience with Lucy and Linus, one *can* "move" them, even if—at least initially—it may not be in the direction one might wish. How? Like their man Trump, who consistently protests "I'm *not* a racist/sexist" but goes on encouraging his base to bellow "Lock her up!" or "Send her back!" (Ever notice, it is never a male subject, always a female one, and increasingly [Congress-]women of color?) It "hurts their feelings" for racists/sexists to be exposed. In the case of my family, the email I wrote announcing Nicole's arrival in my life contained *not one* statement that was not true; problem was, I stated my experience of their past behaviors <u>publicly</u>. *That* is what has prompted them to cut all contact with me: Not that I lied, but I aired their dirty linen publicly, and they were incensed. They do not speak to me now, but that might change—or not.

When we, when <u>you</u> speak your truth to others in the name of swaying minds even while opening hearts, in what ways do <u>you</u> perpetuate dichotomies by lining up false fronts, of environmental "perpetrators" verses climate-change "victims?" How easily and often do you succumb to the smugness that soiled many of my earlier efforts, back in the day when activists "luxuriated" by fighting over what we now can see were trivialities in comparison to our species' extinction?

*

Do NOT Push the River!

Sometimes, when I think "too long" about the world's woes, I grow angry. Especially when I meditate on images of what I perceive as clear injustices (access to clean water, food, medicine, adequate housing, education denied to the disenfranchised—in an age when there is more than enough of everything to meet everyone's needs on the planet), I almost glow with rage. At that point, I also become susceptible to flipping to physical force as a means of expediting "enough" change, fast enough. But—*whoa!* After more than half a century on the planet, I know from personal experience (let alone ideological conviction) that force = violence, and violence = destruction + death. Thus, I come humbly to my next suggestion for overcoming deadlock:

7) renounce all forms of violence.

But, **renounce violence** *after* you have a fuller sense of how that dynamic diminishes us all.

Different perspectives on violence exist—above all, a dominant one focusing on physical force. Some subscribe to that view of it, but wrestle to see it on deeper, more nuanced levels. Palmer Parker, for one, puts an emotional twist on it when he says "Violence is what happens when we don't know what else to do with our suffering." We see manifestations of that daily, by the hour: "I can't find a job—then you come and take one I didn't get. YOU are to blame for MY pain—so take this!" While I don't find dominant definitions "wrong," I do find them incomplete.

Sojourning in post-*Apartheid* South Africa expanded my views on violence. Although my understanding of that ageless, all-present scourge of human existence today remains rooted in historical experiences of it, in South Africa I could no longer overlook tangible expressions of it. It was in that clanking, clunky commuter train full of bedraggled day laborers and bored maids that I saw in their resigned eyes what both low- as well as overt-level violence can do to human beings. I became convinced that their tragic stories deserved, for me, a profounder definition:

VIOLENCE is a physical or non-physical attempt to force changes in behavior or of property.

In the tortured country in which these people had come into being and formed as they had, they were used to the few whites among them forcing them—at gunpoint but more often by pointed fingers—to comply. They felt helpless in the face of whites' demands to change their property (e.g., non-white citizens often awoke to find bulldozers leveling their shacks, destroyed to make way for white housing, shopping, industrial or agricultural developments) or behavior (e.g., non-white rural men typically abandoned their families for weeks, often months in order to migrate to where menial jobs might be had in mines or factories, on farms or grand estates.) Both occurrences became protracted practices of the *Apartheid* system, yet who is to apologize for the endless, generations-long damage it did not only to non-whites, but <u>everyone</u> involved?

Sadly, *Apartheid*'s cruel abuse of most of South Africa's people was nothing new. Throughout history, a forced change of property or behavior through physical or intangible means has been the rule, not an exception. Recent Western history is peppered with that dynamic—explicitly in America's wars. Violence erupts periodically as it feeds on imbalance: It is forced change on the part of one group, to the supposed benefit of another. Every day, in every society, injustices take place but, during times of war, systems of imbalance become exaggerated, thus clearer: Divisions between "winners" and "losers" become sharper, with stakes higher than during times of relative "peace," as property or personhood gets pushed about like so many pawns. War and its attendant violence highlight injustice—as the following mini-histories illustrate in painful detail:

When the Puritans came to the sandy, scrubby shores of New England, they needed to eat; the natives gave them food—including part of what became the celebrated first Thanksgiving. Later, English gratitude gave way to greed for more land and trade: Ongoing raids provided an excuse to pass native-held lands into colonists' hands. When some tribes resisted, armed conflict erupted—blamed on the "savages." At the end of the Pequot War in 1638 (one of its leaders was an ancestor of mine, Robert Jennison), some 700 braves were killed or sent to toil under the tropical sun on faraway Bermuda: Most soon perished. Pequot women and children who did not vanish into the woods were enslaved as domestics, in the manner of the South American native slave Tituba, who played a key role in the Salem Witch Hunt of 1692-93, when the warring settlers' offspring used accusations of being possessed by demons to settle old scores over property contests or to gain neighbors' land. Thus, in a way, that war lasted over half a century.

In 1619, a year before the Pilgrims arrived on Cape Cod, the first [Dutch] boatload of Spanish-captured Africans arrived in Jamestown, Virginia. Those detained previously had lived and labored for themselves. Desperate for workers on their burgeoning tobacco plantations, English colonists showed little compunction to forcing the "chattel" they "indentured" to change from working freely in their native regions of ancient Africa to toiling involuntarily, under a constant threat of physical punishment, in the fields of the New World. The forced surrender of their sovereignty meant that for the next several centuries, their offspring would have next to no say over how—or even if—they might live. Whites reserved power over life and death for themselves, rationalized by bogus claims of racial "superiority" and "God-given rights" to do so. As "war" can be waged as either a "hot" or "cold" conflict, America's ongoing racial "war" drags on as we continue to struggle to redress injustices committed long ago yet still festering. Our task might be easier, were both slavery's roots and its lingering effects not so all-pervasive:

The swelling population of what were first British colonies, then the young United States, fueled the new republic's appetite for ever more land—especially in the South, specifically on which to grow cotton, corn, rice and indigo, along with the earliest North American cash crop, tobacco. Southerners coveted the future fertile fields they envisioned on the plains of East Texas—a challenge being that they were held first by Spain, then newly-declared Mexico. Willing to force a change not only of landownership but from a non-slave to a slave-based economy, Anglo Americans eventually constructed a narrative of abuse and oppression to rationalize seizing Texas from Mexico exactly two centuries after New Englanders had grabbed Pequot lands—and a decade before other concocted claims provided the rationale for the United States not only to declare war against Mexico, but to seize over half (!) of that country's territory, mostly north of the Río Bravo del Norte, which to this day the United States calls the "Rio Grande." One of the first impasses of agreeing what to do with newly-won land involved whether to admit future states as slave-holding or "free" ones. The Compromise of 1850 only delayed a larger fight.

Willard Drake Johnson showing a buffalo wallow on the treeless plains of Haskell County, Kansas, 1897

In those pre-irrigation days, north and west of East Texas much of the newly-acquired territory consisted of what Americans "back East" named the "Great American Desert." Thus, other than elite plantation owners, relatively few whites' hunger for land was quenched by this booty of war. Some fifteen years later, the growing nation's appetite for what Nazi Germany later called "*Lebensraum*" or "room for living" had expanded exponentially. Quasi separately from the societal fracturing caused by America's first experience of forced conscription during the Civil

War, already extant social pressures boiled over in the form of race riots in New York in 1863. In response, a desperate President Lincoln turned to the Homestead Act of a year earlier to speed the distribution of "free land," a western valve for releasing especially East-Coast civil unrest.

The American Civil War, like *every* war *ever* waged in human history, was undertaken by two sides convinced they had the capacity to force a change of behavior on the part of The Other. As also in the case of every war ever waged, that conflagration caused countless unforeseen consequences and indelible wounds which still beg to be healed. Some Southerners insist on misleadingly deeming that struggle as one over "states' rights"—and do so refusing to acknowledge that any germane "rights" breakaway states then claimed were asunder centered around preserving human bondage and servitude. The erroneous nature of such Southern narratives—eternalized across defeated Dixie in the form of hundreds of defiant statues erected decades after the war—does not negate exaggerated Northern narratives of the war having been "to abolish slavery." Many Yankees—including Lincoln and some Abolitionists—held deep, unbending reservations about African Americans' ability to integrate successfully into "white" America, let alone "govern themselves," to the point that many who supported manumission also favored shipping freed slaves "back" to Africa.[118] At the heart of the war itself laid Northern elites' motivations for forcing Confederate states back into what had been a mostly united Federation: Industrialists south to expand in a market of "free" waged labor, not slave labor.

Finally, leap-frogging a century and a half over the Korean and Vietnam Wars, etc., at some point, the US elite no longer had use for our former, government-backed "friend" in Iraq, the infamous killer Saddam Hussein. (Our supporting that sadist was not a historical anomaly: A man worthy of the sordid ranks of the Shah of Iran, the Philippines' Ferdinand Marcos, and too many Latin-American thugs to list here, President Roosevelt said Nicaraguan dictator Anastasio Somoza García "may be a son of a bitch, but he's *our* son of a bitch!"—and do not forget, FDR "allied" America with the bloodthirsty, Josef Stalin, in a pragmatic yet distasteful pact to defeat an equally vicious Nazi despot.) Wanting to force a change of the ownership of "our" oil fields inconveniently lying under "their" territory, hiding under a cloak of Neo-conservatism, oilman and puppet George W. Bush pushed our nation to war against Iraq under cooked claims of Saddam possessing "weapons of mass destruction." As phony yet as effective a call to war as the one a century earlier to "remember the [sunken US ship] *Maine*" (which netted an imperialist bonanza, the annexation of Cuba, Puerto Rico, the Philippine Islands and Guam; around the same time, "American" Samoa and other entities around the globe were declared US territories) the "yellow cake" assertion Colin Powell knowingly dishonestly peddled at the United Nations brought about unending misery, including the birth of ISIS and other scourges, for which we are paying until today.[119]

A beloved—yet usually misattributed—cliché holds that "History is written by the victors." As evident in the above examples and entire sections before that, there have been few "pure" victims or "pure" perpetrators in the annals of history. As just illustrated, great crimes are committed—and great fortunes amassed—during war. To secure the opposite of war—real and lasting peace—we must eradicate injustice. How? By building systems of balance, so that those who toil can live, so that everyone has enough, yet no one in excess—realizing what Gandhi admonished, that "The world has enough for everyone's need, but not for everyone's greed."

*

studio photograph of Mohandas Karamchand Gandhi; London, 1931

Reject a "Colorblind" *Apartheid* System

There are different kinds of "poverty"—the classical kind being lack of adequate material wealth to assure health and contentment. But, there is also "spiritual poverty"—loneliness, lack of passion, chronic boredom, lack of ideas how to "better" or simply change one's life—as well as "intellectual poverty," "social poverty"… right down the line. Ironically, great material wealth does not assure happiness; in fact, I have seen endless examples of people possessing vast tangible wealth who were spiritually, emotionally, socially or otherwise impoverished—e.g. Michael Jackson or Robin Williams, perhaps? As most conflicts arise out of some deficit, if we wish to reduce future or, even better, overcome current conflicts, we need to take another step:

8) reject systemic injustices.

If we are to break up deadlock, we must **reject injustice**—both insidious or overt, institutionalized as well as "random," wanton individual expressions of it. You will succeed, however, only *after* you have honed your abilities to see and stem all types of injustice. Once you do, take consistent yet measured stands against injustice wherever you encounter it—but be prepared for resistance: Entire populations condone injustice simply by tolerating it. When we, as individuals, also tolerate injustice, doing so depletes our motivation to work for change; complacency robs us of the sense of urgency needed to drive us to dismantle injustice or build bridges: Our implicitly condoning the status quo allows social and political deadlock to persist.

Wars characteristically are built upon (and often purposely waged to distract from) injustices. And, they beget further ones. As the six above-summarized "wars" the US waged against domestic or foreign foes illustrate, physical or intangible attempts to force changes of property or behavior does not, in the long run, play out as any of the original players intended. With few exceptions, war only exacerbates and perpetuates injustice; it does not mitigate or conclude it. "War" does not play out only between nation-states but on the streets of any town, anywhere.

INJUSTICE takes place when there is no system of balance.

All around us, we see injustice in the form of everyday violence. If justice is a system of balance, injustice occurs when there is no balance between individual sovereignty and collective needs or wishes, when unfairness recurs habitually and usually without effective forms of redress. To counter injustice, then, we must reduce the occurrence of unfairness and increase forms of addressing it that are proactive, not punitive. And, we must address basic human needs:

> All of us require clean air, healthy drinking water and nourishing food. We must be able to retreat to safe and comfortable shelter, from which we can seek and secure healthcare adequate to sustain physical wellbeing, and education that is empowering as well as enlightening. When any of those basic human needs are not met, when they are not fairly meted out to all, then the ensuing injustice leads to conflict. At the lowest, least explosive levels people whose needs are not being met still feel disrespected, undervalued, unheard or unseen. At the most extreme level, they are prone to take what they feel is being denied them, by force.

In the world to come, to replace the systems now in place that have midwifed the mess that may yet be our downfall, we must find ways to take what resources remain available and share them equally, "justly," so that no one has nothing while a few have everything. We must end poverty, even while recognized that poverty is not just a material deficit, but also can be a moral, spiritual, an intellectual or cultural deficiency. Where poverty reigns, peace cannot take root and grow.

To sow and sustain peace, we must assure justice; to do that, we must counter poverty, as it renders true and lasting justice impossible. Justice can be established and maintained only through constant vigilance; injustice must not be allowed to become embedded or systematized. What we see at present, however, with—for example—the three wealthiest Americans hoarding more than the lower half of the population, is embedded injustice. That must be challenged and transformed, as the entire nation needs access to the means to securing basic needs of all, not to mention the means to redress our mounting environmental disaster. What we increasingly have, not only in the US but worldwide, is an economic *Apartheid* not based solely on race, but on economic class. This, we literally cannot afford, for leaving that imbalance intact will prevent us from restoring the natural order. We cannot correct that imbalance, however, without confronting those who prefer and perpetuate it, either consciously or unconsciously, for their own benefit or those whom they represent.

*

Confront Those Who "'Live' Backwards"

All three branches of Western monotheism—Judaism, Christianity and Islam—have spent much time and energy contemplating injustice and its even more sinister cousin, "evil" or "sin." I, too, have racked my brain for decades over the possible natures and probable legacies of evil (e.g., my doctoral studies into Nazi Germany) and the existence (or not) of sin. I am cautious to throw the label "evil" around, however, for I have come to see it as relative and subjective, so I use the word hardly at all. I never talk about "sin" as I find it an even more problematic, utterly unhelpful concept: As a self-accepting gay man, I know too well the historical abuse—and sheer subjectivity—of the accusation of being "full of" that moral taint. Still, I am not blind: There *is* Darkness in the world—just as there most assuredly is Light. How are we to dispel the Darkness unless we name it? How are we to expand the realm of Light if we do not make space for it? I…

9) confront others' wounds or wounding.

Happily, I am not the only one who grapples with such forces. While I was never uncritical of her experiences or interpretations of same, I was for a time, in the 1980s, interested in Shirley MacLaine's accounts of her Life. Living at Omega House in the late '80s, I burrowed back into our commune's couch like a snug bunny in a cozy warren as we Omegans all watched together the TV-mini-series based on MacLaine's book, *Out on a Limb*. As I earlier had read her book by that title, I nodded agreeingly when she declared "To be 'evil' is to 'live' backwards." *Yes,* I thought, but even as that recognition struck me, I realized there are different levels or degrees of impact from "living backwards," from immediate-impact personal ones to delayed-impact political ones.

Shirley MacLaine (left) attended the Deauville American Film Festival in Normandy, France, in 1987. Alice Miller's theories on children created a sensation, as she repositioned the family as a locus of dysfunction with her theory that parental power and punishment lay at the root of nearly all human problems.

Around that same time, another figure admired in that era's New-Age circles was Alice Miller. Born "Alicija Englard" to a Polish-Jewish family in Lviv, Ukraine, almost exactly a decade before Austrian Adolf Hitler came to power in Germany (where her family lived by that time), she later built a career in Switzerland as a psychologist, psychoanalyst and philosopher. She became noted for her books on parental child abuse and its lingering impact on "adult children." Miller's most acclaimed studies focused on the psycho-biographies of Adolf Hitler and Jürgen Bartsch, a German serial killer who murdered four boys and attempted to kill a fifth. While dissecting the childhoods of Hitler and Bartsch, she concluded—according to one source's summary—that:

> …worldwide violence has its roots in the fact that children are beaten all over the world, especially during their first years of life, when their brains become structured. [The] damage caused by this practice is devastating, but unfortunately hardly noticed by society [thus] children are forbidden to defend themselves against the violence inflicted on them, they must suppress the natural reactions like rage and fear, and they discharge these strong emotions later as adults against their own children or whole peoples: "Child abuse like beating and humiliating not only produces unhappy and confused children, not only destructive teenagers and abusive parents, but thus also a confused, irrationally functioning society."[120]

Alice Miller advocated that only through becoming aware of this dynamic can individuals as well as the larger culture break this chain of violence, which impacts individuals on personal levels and groups of people on political ones. Thus is my ninth challenge to **confront everyday "evil"** on <u>both</u> levels—*after* you distill your own definition of that nebulous force among us. For me:

IF MacLaine's take on "evil" is correct—that those who commit the most and most heinous "evil" acts "live backwards"—then Miller's case studies seem to confirm that view. We social historians know that recurring themes and patterns emerge in "modern-monster" biographies such as those of Hitler, Stalin, Idi Amin, Pol Pot, Saddam Hussein and too many others. As Miller saw it, the Hitlers and Stalins of the world inflict their childhood traumas on millions. It seems plausible that such individuals try to "recast," to transfer violent abuse to [millions of] others—each victim not just paying for the unconscious emotional chaos of their perpetrator but that of their perpetrator's perpetrators. In each case, the "evil monster" appears unable to release his [rarely are we speaking of women as mass murderers] internalized distress, so tries—as an unconscious outlet for what seems consciously unbearable—to "overcome" it by acting [it] out.

Using Miller's model, historically and now, mass-scale perpetrators "re-live" their broken pasts[121] unconsciously, by again and again creating scenarios in today's adult world in ways comparable with their having felt injured or helpless in now-vanished childhood worlds. The main difference being, this time, the wounded "child" is now an adult who can abuse, not be abused. Though seemingly present, vital parts of abusers stay stuck in a haunted past. Using MacLaine's unusual terminology, acts or results that seem to be "evil" are the consequence of those who commit or create them, who appear to make choices based on today's situations yet, in reality, are "living backwards" rather than living forward into *this* day or an alluring future. It is past curses more than present blessings which pitilessly drive such people; each day, they relive yesterday more than they are focused on what the morrow might bring: They remain booby-trapped hostages.

In any political system that claims to be democratic, such dynamics—self-evident and, by now, accepted canon of most psychological schools of thought—"should" serve as ongoing warnings to self-ruling citizens. We must know, at least in broad strokes, our leaders' backgrounds in order to better anticipate likely present and future trajectories: Despite acknowledging this in theory, in practice we shy away from translating this awareness into concrete forms. We allow the world to be "a dangerous place, not because of those who do evil, but" as Einstein warned us, "because of those who look on and do nothing." The opposite of doing nothing is to do *something*—not just "anything" but to take actions that are strategic and targeted, like calling out those whose own shadows cast darkness over all of us. In a "democracy" worthy of the term, the citizenry must *constantly* monitor those allowed to lead. First, though, we must see how this dynamic functions, how it informs those with power in how they use—or abuse—it.

Like going regularly to a gym to exercise our physical muscles, we must regularly exercise our mental and civic muscles; we must stimulate our minds in ways that build our abilities to *see*. Today, for more and more people, Miller's case studies of Hitler and Stalin seem increasingly remote; too many moderns know few facts about either man. Miller compellingly illustrated in her exacting tomes that not just parents of such persons left lasting, overwhelmingly damaging influences, but their wider family also played central, often negative roles in their formation. A summary of more-recent-figure Saddam Hussein's early life humanizes those classic dynamics:

> Before he was born, cancer killed both Saddam's father and brother. These deaths so depressed Saddam's mother (Sabha) that she attempted to abort her pregnancy and commit suicide. When her son was born, Sabha "would have nothing to do with him," and Saddam was taken in by an uncle. His mother remarried, and Saddam gained three half-brothers through this marriage. His stepfather, Ibrahim al-Hassan, treated Saddam harshly after his return. At about age 10, Saddam fled the family and returned to live in Baghdad with his uncle Kharaillah Talfah, who became a father figure to Saddam. Talfah, the father of Saddam's future wife, was a devout Sunni Muslim and a veteran of the 1941 Anglo-Iraqi War between Iraqi nationalists and the United Kingdom [and] later became the mayor of Baghdad during Saddam's time in power.[122]

Peering into the biographical baggage of world, national or even local leaders is not voyeuristic but rather practical. When we marry, even if we think we know future in-laws well but want to mate with their offspring "anyway," we often realize too late that we "married an entire family" rather than just one person. So it is with leaders: We might think we voted (or had foisted upon us) a self-contained, sovereign soul, yet in truth s/he always brings an entire lineage with them.

A more socially-contemporary example: Increasing numbers of millennials—especially some of the hundreds of thousands worldwide bestowed life through donor conception—want to climb about their family trees in search of genetic flaws or simply medical history, preventively. My own daughter did, having lost her three-year-old son to leukemia, as she was unable to secure matching bone morrow, not knowing his genetic inheritance—truly a matter of life and death.

Just as it is "sensible shopping" to get to know a potential partner's or donor's family before committing to spending much of the rest of one's life with someone… you know. In the tragic case of Saddam Hussein, after he no longer suited America's elite and they turned against him, the ensuing two wars the US fought against him in the Mideast claimed millions of casualties and at least hundreds of thousands of dead. Especially the second war unleased the scourge of ISIS (in part because of the inept way the US "decommissioned" suddenly-unwanted weapons), which fanned regional unrest… which threatened to topple Bashar al-Assad but failed, sending millions of Syrians packing… and all the rest. So, was Iraq's leader's pedigree "relevant" to us all in as far as it impacted world events and the lives of millions? Historical events suggest it strongly was.

How about the biographical baggage of a world leader more current than sad Saddam Hussein?

Saddam in his youth, in 1956; Donald Trump, pictured in the 1964 New York Military Academy yearbook

While we hope that Donald Trump's daily acting out never results in untold deaths,[123] he seems driven by things unseen or not understood—neither by much of the public nor, apparently, by himself. Still, an observant citizen might ask "What role did his five years deposited in the New York Military Academy boarding school play in his development?" Before that, how did his Scottish-immigrant mother's heritage color his worldview, given that Scottish-Quaker activist Alastair McIntosh has documented that all four lines of Mary Anne [MacLeod] Trump's family had been forcibly cleared from their land on the Isle of Lewis in the 19th century: Poverty drove thousands from the Highlands, scattering those economic refugees from Canada and the US to Australia; Mary Anne came to New York in 1930 at age 18.[124] How might her own "resocialization" process—necessary for integrating into a culture not one's own—have influenced her parenting? (As an American who has lived decades abroad, I can attest: Living long-term in a foreign culture exacts a hefty, if imperceptible, toll.) Does Trump's preference for immigrant wives—and his ambivalence towards "economic" or other kinds of migrants—stem from his mother's own trauma over her family's marginalization? In contrast, what values or "tricks" did he learn at home from his money-driven father? In short, what—or "who"—happened to Donald Trump during his formative years, to have formed him into the injured and injurious figure he became?

Whatever influences determined Donald Trump's current inner repertoire of reflex reactions, to what extent does he embody Shirley MacLaine's definition of "evil"—or M. Scott Peck's, about whom we will learn more in this tome's ensuing section? While hers involves how one "lives backwards," his rests upon the question of to what degree a person "loves backwards:"

> Evil people hate the light because it reveals themselves to themselves. They hate goodness because it reveals their badness; they hate love because it reveals their laziness. They will destroy the light, the goodness, the love in order to avoid the pain of such self-awareness. [Evil] is laziness carried to its ultimate, extraordinary extreme. As I have defined it, love is the antithesis of laziness. Ordinary laziness is a passive failure to love. Some ordinarily lazy people may not lift a finger to extend themselves unless they are compelled to do so. Their being is a manifestation of nonlove; still, they are not evil. Truly evil people, on the other hand, actively rather than passively avoid extending themselves. They will take any action in their power to protect their own laziness, to preserve the integrity of their sick self. Rather than nurturing others, they will actually destroy others in this cause. If necessary, they will even kill to escape the pain of their own spiritual growth. As the integrity of their sick self is threatened by the spiritual health of those around them, they will seek by all manner of means to crush and demolish the spiritual health that may exist near them. I define evil, then, as the exercise of political power—that is, the imposition of one's will upon others by overt or covert coercion—in order to avoid extending one's self for the purpose of nurturing spiritual growth. Ordinary laziness is nonlove; evil is antilove.[125]

Had the electorate known more about Donald Trump's fuller Sick Self in October 2016, would he have become president? The man may not be a Hitler (despite authorizing camps on the US-Mexican border that concentrate humans according to their ethnic origins or legal status), yet he does yield enormous influence. How do we, who find the man's behavior unacceptable and wish it to change, call out ways our current president is driven by his (apparently unconscious) past, in ways that might help him avoid his typical extremes—or at least mitigate their effects? Since most of us have no direct access to him, who in his circle might we convince to so act?

These considerations are not rhetorical, but requisite to overcoming deadlock and enabling movement, on *all* levels. On immediate "personal" levels, where family members, neighbors, colleagues or co-congregants cling to values or views that initially seem in opposition or even irreconcilable, what to do? On the surface, the drawn fronts seem clear: Either global warming is a threat to human survival, or it is not; either Americans condone separating families on our southern border and confining adults as well as children in camps, or we do not; either voters support single-payer health insurance for all, or they do not. How do we move beyond deadlock on issues of such great import? Part of the process *has* to include seeing and hearing The Other, but that is only a start—and even then, such tactics are not enough to midwife lasting progress: "Reasoning" or requesting sweetly have been tried—and failed. Have we any choice but to call out those on opposing sides? How do we do so, effectively, without causing further stalemate?

There are values and behaviors that have produced the world we currently have that are *not* working, that *must* change—somewhere, on someone's part—for movement to be possible. We *have* been here before: In the 19th century, men actively persecuted suffragettes, arguing that "the weaker sex" was prone to vote based on "hysteria;" women's conventions were frequently attacked, at times their meeting halls torched. US law long counted African Americans as "3-5ths a man:" Families, church congregations and states split over the question of slavery, with some abolitionists championed sending them "back" to Africa, as "unfit" to live in a "white" country. Deemed unworthy of "deserving" it earlier, Native Americans were denied US citizenship until 1924: As recently as the 1990s, my Aunt Sheranne snarked "The only good Injun's a dead one."

My family's and my deadlock is a microcosm: Linus and Cherry tread on rapidly melting glaciers yet refuse to acknowledge that the rate of their demise is accelerating "unnaturally," while Lucy insists on seeing a "homosexual lifestyle" as a "choice" and Muslims as "worshippers of "Buddha," thus perpetuating cultural ignorance that sustains sexual and racial injustice or ignites violence. In a less charged era, such attitudes might be endured, but in an era like ours "global-warming denial" *literally* is lethal. Fossil-fuel energy companies' investing millions in misleading, false information about the matter is well documented: Those cynical campaigns helped coax Congress to kick the legislative can down an increasingly dire road for decades—and politicians like Pennsylvania's former US Senator Rick Santorum to badmouth tree planting as an antidote to increased carbon levels, because he deemed doing so to be "useless." When we consider how much critical time cynical posturing has squandered, it seems criminal.[126] (As I wrote earlier: English schools taught about global warming as early as 1981, as I experienced at Ermysted's; when I breeched the topic in Linus' and my chat in circa 1983, my mention of it evoked in him hardly a shrug—despite his holding a degree in environmental engineering. Ill-motivated corporate and Congressional collusion cultivates such indifference.) Since World War II most of the world has come to condemn—and many countries made punishable by law—"Holocaust denial," so why can't we hold individuals and organizations legally liable for denying climatic truth? It is not a "nice idea" or "luxury" to call out those who endanger our world; it has become imperative. We cannot afford false comfort that lulls us into inaction or, worse, downright denial of our plight. Just as yelling "fire" in a theater can claim many lives, lying about climatic facts can, too: Denial isn't a personal "right" when it affects millions, globally.

It is not only the physical environment that is crumbling at present, but in key ways the social. We cannot shore up global ecosystems yet let our cultural ecology collapse: What sort of living hell would we have to endure then? In the US, those increasingly-frequent occurrences of mass shootings are symptoms, not causes per se of collective social demise. It's one thing to confront the relatively harmless Lucys and Linuses among us, but what about those who we do not know personally, yet given the chance would harm us or people we love? How do we intercept them?

In extreme cases, how can we preemptively "see" or "hear" the most wounded among us (i.e., potential mass shooters), that they disavow dark, "evil" acts and contribute to con-structing a better world, rather than de-structing things we hold most dear—like our children in (ideally, violence-free) schools, innocent shoppers at a mall, students working in university chemistry labs... all of which have been settings of US mass shootings in recent years. How can we also confront those souls "living backwards" and help them "live forwards" so that all might live better, safely? We must ask, what went wrong in the rearing of young, white men who commit most mass shootings? Were they so neglected that they think, consciously or unconsciously, the best way to "finally" get attention, to be seen and heard, is to drag dozens with them into death? Am I oversimplifying the matter? If so, it's because I have no other better explanation.

a "Welcome to Fabulous Las Vegas" sign adorned with flowers on 9 October 2017, a week after the Mandalay Bay Hotel shooting; a historical representation of Quaker meeting for worship, circa 1800

Such considerations have spiritual implications. Unprogrammed Quakers, for one, do not have churches or "holy places" as we believe the Spirit is everywhere, in *all* places. While we typically meet on Sundays, we can meet just as happily on other days as we hold that the Spirit is equally accessible every day, in every hour. Most importantly, we maintain that "something sacred" is in *every* person—even in those many would deem "evil." (Apparently some Amish and African-American communities do, too, as some of both have, in recent years, publicly and *personally* "forgiven" the perpetrators of mass shootings among them—indeed, a radical act of healing.)

To be honest, even as I assume there is something sacred in the heart of Donald Trump, I often have a hard time seeing it for all of the harsh, histrionic camouflage with which he seems to cloak his Inner Light. (I must confess: I usually enjoy my hero Stephen Colbert's wicked fun at Trump's expense.) To help myself see past wounded Donald's *façade* of uncaring *bravado*, at those points

I recall the Little Hitler in me—and the Little Stalin, the Little Ivan the Terrible... and the Little Bud Luick. (Happily, I also believe there is the likes of a Little Mother Teresa in me—at least I hope so, as that led me to volunteer in about 1994 to mop floors in her Calcutta mission.)

I *must* be able to recognize the Spirit in the face of each "Other" because if I cannot, how can I recognize it in my Self? On a social-political level, if I cannot continually remain mindful of the Inner Light in *each* person I encounter, with whom I might discuss or even spar over issues each of us cares about, how can I expect to ultimately value what s/he has to say and show them—as my "karmic partner" in any given moment—that I see, hear and try to respect them? Doing so is a spiritual practice, to cultivate genuine compassion (from the Latin *compati*, or "to suffer with" someone)—a precursor to experiencing empathy and, in turn, vital to practicing real kindness.

At the same time, how can I confront ways in which others might "live backwards" if I cannot confront my own lapses of reliving old angers, longings, disenchantments or resentments, rather than living in *this* moment, mindful of what's possible *now*? As a "wounded healer"[127] I often find it difficult to reach a sustained balance. As an educator for whom the discipline of understanding humans in our historical contexts constitutes a near-religion for me, where is the line between confronting past experiences "enough" to be able to name, own, work through and then move beyond them, and being free enough of old baggage to travel unburdened into what awaits?

It helps me immeasurably to practice compassion for those I otherwise might dismiss or at least disdain. In my best moments, when I meditate on Donald Trump I feel sorry for him, that he seems unable to *ever* get "enough" attention or affirmation—as sometimes I also am. I feel outraged when he speaks of women like pieces of flesh, but condemn him less loudly when I think of the scores of men with whom I have scored. I cringe when he speaks of other countries as "shitholes"—but then I remember my own prejudices regarding some lands and cultures. I am appalled that when our non-friends, the Saudis, chop up critics in their embassies abroad, instead of condemning such wicked acts Trump speaks of weapons contracts—at which point I must examine my own self-serving hypocrisy and selective moral blindness. I cannot stand Donald Trump sometimes—but sometimes I cannot stand my Self, either. Finding compassion for him and his weaknesses helps me grant my Self the same. More often than not, it works.

I did not always possess this ability. When I was much younger, I used to hate my father. With practice, my loathing his mean slaps, constant belittling, volatility and disloyalty cooled into milder disappointment that he—and I—seemed unable to do better. By the time I confronted him about skewed dynamics that marred the Luick generation preceding mine, I pulled up to the end of the stud barn where he was painting, fearing a physical assault for my daring to broach the topic. Instead, my gently, non-accusingly wading into it with "I" statements evoked the opposite: Instead of flying fists and kicking feet, I got flat affect as Dad continued to brush ox-blood-red paint onto the gable atop the ladder. I felt compelled to call out my father about his nuclear family's crossing lines because, a decade or so after having walked in on it, that experience would *not* let me go: I continued to dream nightmares about it. Ironically, thinking that my calling him out would liberate *me*, it seems, in the end, it freed us *both*.

If the main question of this book is "How to overcome deadlock?" then the part of my answer that includes "Confront Those Who 'Live' Backwards" also has to include this caveat: While we consider calling out each other for "living backwards," one also has to continually ask oneself "When does a past event still 'need' to be confronted?" or "Are we now ready to move on?"

The question of whom, how, how often, how rigorously and until when to confront those "living backwards" is central to getting from where we are now, to where we want to be. Again, there are different levels or degrees of impact from "living backwards"—from immediate-impact personal ones to delayed-impact political ones. On a personal level, I still regret that I failed to ever call out my school director—who I liked very much, a New York Jewess whose Berlin-born parents had survived the Holocaust, then served with the US State Department in occupied West Germany—in an American school in Hessen, who used to slap my ass in the photocopier room. I weighed confronting her, but yielded to others' reasons *not* to do so. In contrast, when I had a chance to face him directly, a couple years later, I confronted a Quaker man from North Carolina who assaulted me one night while I was sleeping in our shared dorm at a conference. His violation of my personhood was on a vastly different, more grievous plane than that of the school director, yet I've been able to let go of his trespass, which I confronted, more than her unchallenged one.

On a political level, I have long wondered what foul things happened in their childhoods to men like Rupert Murdoch, Rush Limbaugh, Bill O'Reilly, Sean Hannity or their angry ilk, that they are so driven to influence, manipulate, agitate and foment hate in millions. Until now, I had no access to them, no chance to call them out directly. I did, however, challenge Iowa's mini-Rush, Jan Mickelson of Des Moines-based WHO—once the Hawkeye State's most infamous radio hate-baiter. As of the late 1990s, Mickelson featured me on his morning talk show when it served his purposes.[128] One time, in fall 2015, I was in Iowa on a speaking tour and he agreed to talk with me on-air about the 1.5 million refugees who had walked from the Mideast to Germany, seeking a safe haven. By that point I had lived in Germany, on and off, since 1993, had earned a Ph.D. at Berlin's oldest university and spoke fluent German. During our "interview" he scarcely gave me a chance to speak; instead, he went on interminably about his encounters with guards in the German capital during a layover *en route* to Prague. Piqued that he peddled his own, to-me-anecdotal and exceptionally subjective perspectives over my insider-outsider views, I asked him on-air "So, Jan, *how long* were you in Berlin?" His gall, to assume that his fleeting impressions might bear more insight into contemporary German politics and society than my couple decades of empirical observations, floored me. More importantly, the incendiary tone and acidic disdain in his every utterance about refugees fueled hate and violence. Such hate-laced hubris is sad.[129]

(Media figures on the left can be equally ego-blinded. I cannot watch MSNBC's "Morning Joe," for one, as Joe Scarborough constantly interrupts not only his co-host wife Mika Brzezinski, but too often their in-studio guests—typically in order to strut along his own parade of inner impulses. Do guests—let alone his wife—ever call him out on this irksome, self-absorbed habit? On Iowa's mediascape, Jan Mickelson's ideological opposite, radio host Ed Fallon, once spent some ten minutes of one of our interviews talking about having locked himself in his toilet that morning. Why did his personal "trauma" outweigh exploring that of thousands fleeing war?)

There are also other, more influential individuals' biographies to mine for explanations for their (often clandestine) political machinations. The Koch brothers, for example, have poured endless vast funds into steering not only popular perceptions but public policies. *Why?* What in their biographies not just motivated, but apparently *drove* them not only to grasp such power but to strive to warp America's social fabric in ways they too often succeeded in doing—thus resulting in most statehouses now being under one-party dominion, not to mention Congress' deadlock.

A few societal references as mental exercise: Some visitors to Monticello's exhibit on Thomas Jefferson's "concubine" Sally Hemings[130] (to use her son Madison's term for her status) and their descendants have complained to guides "Enough about how bad white people are—you should be focusing on the garden." Such people are not alone, as the swelling numbers of projects considering white privilege are increasingly meeting with backlash, with some whites not only rejecting the message, but resisting even considering the matter. What is it in some people's biographies that lead them to reflexively reject questioning social power lines? Why do they feel a need to make "true" what cannot rationally be (e.g., Australian Ken Ham's Creationist exhibits in Kentucky that maintain dinosaurs were on Noah's ark)[131] or deny what is clearly fact (humans have been on Earth longer than some six-thousand years, as biblical stories seem to suggest).

"Is it time to 'move on'?" regarding social issues like slavery's toxic legacy? As long as African Americans continue to be racially profiled, suffer disproportionate rates of incarceration or being shot by police; as long as African Americans continue to earn significantly less than whites of comparable training or experience, to benefit less from commensurate capital and die younger than whites, then "It is *not* time" to leave the matter, as it continues to diminish us *all*.

At the same time, as Earth's regurgitating humans' abuse grows more lethal and humanity's survival more precarious, many currently "pressing" matters will surely decrease in urgency. We who want change will have to consider more often and intensely, which "evils" might warrant confronting and which "greater evils" trump lesser, current concerns. What is key in any event, is the manner in which we confront others' living in a fading past—and doing all they can to sustain what surely is doomed to not last in its present forms—and, instead, insist that social inequities, moral outrages, personal injuries (physical or emotional) be addressed swiftly and effectively, so that all of us might return to the most pressing matter of our day—survival.

Stay the Course

In order to persist long enough, single-mindedly enough to make real and lasting change,

10) confront endemic apathy and resignation.

It helps to identify role models—in an earlier age known as "heroes." But, where are they now?

As I write this, just hours ago the 16-year-old Swedish climate activist, Greta Thunberg, again made global news, but this time not by calling for her fellow pupils, worldwide, to demonstrate every Friday or by sailing for a fortnight, carbon-free, over the Atlantic to attend the United Nations General Assembly. This time—with tears swelling in her eyes, pained anger contorting her face—the petite girl with plaited hair shamed world leaders for their cynical inaction, while:

> People are suffering. People are dying. Entire ecosystems are collapsing. We are in the beginning of a mass extinction, and all you can talk about is money and fairy tales of eternal economic growth. How dare you! For more than 30 years, the science has been crystal clear. How dare you continue to look away and come here saying that you're doing enough, when the politics and solutions needed are still nowhere in sight. You say you hear us and that you understand the urgency. But no matter how sad and angry I am, I do not want to believe that. Because if you really understood the situation and still kept on failing to act, then you would be evil.[132]

Greta decried in clearest, most poignant terms, that despite occasionally mouthing sympathetic soundbites, too many of those holding power around the globe consistently go on acting as if "business as usual" would someday, "somehow" save us. How otherwise might she have spent her few allotted minutes addressing the world's largest governing body to greater effect? Still, some commentators reacted disparagingly on Thunberg's Facebook page with—paraphrased— the likes of "Can't roll my eyes enough on-line" or "When I was 16, I spent my free time playing soccer: Just go out and play!" Low-level negativity can be set down, but harder to deflect is the sting of widely-cast, lightning-fast public lashings: The *Daily Wire*'s Michael Knowles referred to the teenage activist as a "mentally ill Swedish child" until commentator Christopher Hahn called him out for being "a grown man [...] attacking a child. Shame on you[.] Have some couth."[133]

In April 2019, Greta Thunberg closed the European Parliament's Environment Committee, as shown here.

As an Iowa State undergrad I, too, incurred public censure for unpopular stances I took in my frequent *ISU Daily* pieces or my outdoor speaking appearances on central campus. Actively and openly opposed to Ronald Reagan's Central-America and nuclear-arms policies, I could expect critical, opposing letters-to-the-editor a few issues later or, more rarely, personal on-campus confrontations. What was *not* possible in those pre-digital days was the instant, widespread, even global humiliation—or, worse, threats to one's personal safety, let alone integrity—that today is standard fare. It was one thing to nurse a bruised ego at home, paging through day-old newspaper rebukes; it is quite another to tap one's cell phone and watch "live" as one's person is being figuratively torn apart in sickening ways—always with a latent fear that one might be physically taken apart in some horrific armed ambush. Is the constant, gnawing dread of an ugly fate "sometime" not expressly demotivating and singularly disempowering all the time? Is not such public reproach exactly meant by those dishing it out to silence and immobilize The Other?

In such a toxic climate, how do mortals sustain the motivation needed to express our deepest, most passionate convictions in the most effective ways? I have strategies that work for me, but my tenth challenge for you is to **confront apathy and resignation** in the world—*after* you have confronted your own. Understanding those intertwined moral failings is not easy, but vital: An attitude of "How—and *why*—'should' I engage those who I find disagreeable?" assures doom.

Like depression or aggression, apathy remains a complex, often not-well-understood human reaction to one's external environment. Look at toddlers: How many truly show extended bouts of depression, aggression or apathy? It is *not* natural to human nature to so behave, long-term and from our core. By nature, like other primates—indeed, other mammals—humans are inquisitive, sociable and prone to bursts of joy. What sets us apart from other animals, is our capacity to possess convictions—which the Oxford dictionary's "Lexico" series defines as:[134]

- "A firmly held belief or opinion" or
- "The quality of showing that one is firmly convinced of what one believes or says."

While those definitions seem accurate to me, I am dissatisfied with Lexico's take on "apathy:"

- "A lack of interest, enthusiasm, or concern."

What is missing for me in that definition is a "lack of... conviction." Apathy is not just the lack of curiosity about the world or its contents; it is not simply the absence of an eagerness to be fully alive in each new moment; it is not merely a dearth of caring for one's Self or for others. When I feel apathetic, my beliefs seem questionable, ill-chosen or hollow, my opinions small or stupid. When my convictions have fallen dormant (from the Latin *dormire*, "to sleep") I have, at least temporarily, lost touch with my soul's deepest stirrings: I have forgotten what I believe—and why I believe it. This, for me, is infinitely more dangerous than "not caring"—a sad state but one that has always proven fleeting and, per my experience, more remediable than being separated from one's Self. Let me come close to others, I will care (again); but divide me from my heart, I will wither and die—at least emotionally, socially and spiritually, if not physically. My apathy swells or fades to the degree I lose faith in my beliefs or abilities to move on them.

Is our becoming divorced from the most intimate parts of our Selves not a greater threat today than blips of boredom, declining keenness or waning worry about the morrow? To lose one's conviction is to forfeit one's very belief in one's existence and about one's place in the world. *This* modern spiritual poverty is what we must battle, if we are to overcome ecological decline. To return to Greta Thunberg: It is one thing to have to deflect doubt from others; it is a fully different chore to deflate one's doubt in one's Self. How does one soldier on, when so many mock and naysay us or what our hearts call us to do? To overcome apathy, we have to steel our belief in the soundness of our cause(s)—and *that* can be excruciatingly difficult, for the process of confronting our own shortcomings, real or imagined, can drag us into daunting existential drama. Even more exhausting, this minute work must be done *every* day, in *every* hour, in *all* that one does. The task is enormous, yet crucial and urgent. Only after we have confronted our own apathy can we help others surmount theirs. As long as apathy reigns, demise accelerates.

The specter of accelerating atrophy—environmental, social, political and otherwise—brings with it its morose offspring, resignation. The main ingredient in the sure recipe for disastrous failure is resignation—that inner capitulation that is so facile but so fatal. In order to stay the course, we cannot succumb to doubting the rightness of the course. Resignation is the kiss of death to being effective, to bridging gaps between others and ourselves, to moving beyond deadlock and thereby unlocking the key to further life on Earth. Many become defeated by the magnitude of the mission of saving an entire planet and ourselves. But, is there any other choice?

We each must confront apathy and resignation—both our own and others'—if we are to have any hope of rescuing a world in freefall. Restoring the Earth's natural order constitutes both a practical but also philosophical challenge: To restore it, we have to plant a new Eden, recycle or repurpose the usable bits of our disintegrating "liberal" industrial culture, recalibrate our usage of resources, then steward the regenerated, sustainable final mix; to maintain that restoration, we have to see anew our place in the natural order—along with it our obligation to preserve it.

The Garden of Paradise, *by an Upper Rhenish master; circa 1400-1425*

On a moral level, even if we were not facing the extinction of thousands of species on this planet that we share with the rest of creation—not to mention the demise of humanity itself—we have long been called to serve others as one expression of spiritual practice. As Marian Wright Edelman wrote in *The Measure of Our Success: A Letter to My Children and Yours*, "Service to others is the rent we pay for living." What good would it be, to find a Magic Cure for our environmental woes but to perish morally? None of us alive today created this world; we inherited it from an endless parade of generations of our human as well as non-human ancestors: What right has our generation, to destroy the results of millions of years of evolution? Stepping back from the brink would be the highest act of service we could offer.

*

"Come together... in the wisdom, love and fellowship of god, in gravity, patience, meekness and unity and concord, submitting one to another in lowliness of heart and in the holy spirit of truth and righteousness... hearing and determining every matter... in love, coolness, gentleness and dear unity."

— English Quaker Edward Burrough in 1662,
cited in *Testimony,* in "Letters of Early Friends"

"Fall in Love"—then Listen

It is easy to dislike, disdain, even hate one's opposites. But, that doesn't help. What would is to:

11) "fall in love"—then listen.

The struggle to love rather than hate is as old as humanity itself. And it's tied to so many things:

It began innocently enough—the idea, the belief, that Arctic-native languages possess more words for snow than does English—a simple concept that led to and fed academics' complex, decades-long debates over a linguistic-relativity hypothesis: a language's structure (e.g., sound, vocabulary, grammar) shapes its speakers' view of the world. At first, in 1911, German-born American anthropologist Franz Boas reflected on how some languages' structures allow more variety in how word roots can be modified to form single words—with much of the ensuing controversy involving how a given observer defines "word" or even "word root." In short: How many separate words—thereby concepts—might a given culture possess for related things?

Later commentators on this thesis heaped loads more onto Boas' earlier observations. Related studies in the 1940s, '70s and '80s kept inflating what the "Father of American Anthropology" was said to have said, so at first "Eskimos" supposedly had 50, then suddenly 100 words for what in English is merely "snow." While the "strong version" of the initial hypothesis by now has become largely discredited, a 2011 study did support the basic notion that Arctic-native languages *do* have more root words for "snow" than English has; according to Professor Pedia:[135]

> Studies of the Sami languages of Norway, Sweden and Finland, conclude that the languages have anywhere from 180 snow- and ice-related words and as many as 300 different words for types of snow, tracks in snow, and conditions of the use of snow.

Why does this matter? Because words *do* influence individuals' perceptions of "reality"—which in turn dictates actions. In an era when ideology, when **ideas** of how a thing "is" or "should" be can lay entire, established democracies lame (*vis-à-vis* Britain under the Brexit bruhaha) and can divide houses, rendering families torn and their governments deadlocked, words—moreover the concepts they represent—must be parsed for deeper meaning and possible impact. To overcome deadlock, to build bridges with those we might initially see as opponents, do we not need to approach them less out of a cauldron of hate and more out of a kind of love?

While "snow" might seem to be a value-free, emotionally-uncharged concept, "love" isn't. Just as educated, well-willed academics for decades could not agree on how humans refer to the frozen, white form of water, one person's "love" is another's… what? As with "snow," English seems deficient in how native speakers of this lingually-rich language refer to positive feelings between humans, and by default fetters them to one term. The ancient Greeks, in contrast, coined eight words with which to distinguish various kinds or gradations of emotional bonds:

1) *agape* = selfless love

2) *eros* = erotic love

3) *ludus* = playful love

4) *mania* = obsessive love

5) *philautia* = self-love

6) *philia* = affectionate love

7) *pragma* = enduring love

8) *storge* = familial love

"Interesting," right—but, "What do such lingual nuances have to do with overcoming stubborn social stalemate?" Based on experience, I recommend an eleventh tactic: **practice "going low,"** in the sense that 17th-century Quakers meant with "lowliness of heart." Their use of language might seem archaic to us moderns but, according to Merriam-Webster's definition, "lowliness" fits perfectly as an antidote to our current social malaise, as a ground-breaking state of being:[136]

1 : humble in manner or spirit; free from self-assertive pride. 2 : not lofty or sublime; prosaic. […]

Per one empirical case study?

For decades, my family and I have disagreed, vehemently, over matters ranging from "not fraternizing with heathens" to causes behind glacier melt. In the course of fervent discord, both sides felt slighted by words or actions from the other, a feud which reached an apex in February 2019: Thereafter, Lucy and Linus disavowed all contact with me—a sad state that shifted only when my mother began to steadily decline in October 2019. Then, at one point, as Lucy and I were about to bring a telephone update about Phyllis' condition to a close, I said quietly "Ya know, you continue to be important to me an' in my life"—in a rather unemotional contrast to the slobbery, effusive "Oh, I *love* you!" that Hollywood might have suggested.

Why did I shy from letting the L-word pass over my lips? It was neither because of recent events nor a lack of liking for her (which, perhaps surprisingly, I do have), but rather my ongoing, inconclusive pondering what "**love**" actually is—not only what I feel for the Lucys of this world, but for lovers, parents… pets, passions… causes… my nation. If I am going to "love" my "enemy" (let us speak rather of "opponents," those who hold opposing views or values than ours), what does that <u>mean</u>; how does that <u>look</u> like in tangible form; what does it <u>entail</u>—and will it <u>hurt</u>?

Morgan Scott Peck; the former Guthrie Theater, next to Minneapolis' Walker Art Center, in 1980

Already as a young communard with a mullet, living at Omega House in the mid-'80s, I searched for a working definition of that most elusive of hyperbolic emotions. To my great pleasure, then-"in" M. Scott Peck came to Minneapolis to speak at the Guthrie Theater. I was ecstatic! In that period, M. Scott Peck's bestseller, *The Road Less Traveled* (1978), scratched an itch many Baby Boomers had not realized plagued us. In circles I traveled, Peck enjoyed guru status; we Friends savored the fact that like several bright lights in American history (Thomas Paine, Daniel Boone, Whitman, Grant Wood, Joan Baez and Bonnie Raitt), he had at least one Quaker parent—and he had graduated from Friends Seminary in New York.[137] We spoke of Peck as "one of ours."

His definition of love spoke to me then—and still does—on several levels:

> Love is the will to extend one's self for the purpose of nurturing one's own or another's spiritual growth[…] Love is as love does. Love is an act of will—namely, both an intention and an action. Will also implies choice. We do not have to love. We choose to love.[138]

Now, decades later, as I search for solutions to our world's current catastrophe, Peck's words take on new relevance—and urgency. When I think of that third or so of my compatriots who—as of this writing—continue to unwaveringly support a man whose acts I find increasingly reprehensible, I feel overwhelmed. Even the thought of trying to decode what for me is the enigma of why they continue to defend "their" Donald J. Trump—despite all that has happened and all that has been revealed over the past three years—makes not only my head but my heart ache: I feel immobilized—literally, as if I could not move—when trying to respond to this stupefying mystery. Still, if I stop meditating on an abstract, faceless "third of my compatriots" and instead start calling up images of Lucy and Linus, conjuring up loving responses to *them* is not only easier than doing so for amorphous "someones" but conceivable at all. I fail, miserably, when trying to "love" abstractions; I can only "fall in love" with concrete, "real" humans—and learn to "fall in love" we *must*, if we are to move beyond failing to reach out to our opponents.

Again, Peck's wisdom can guide us. A trained psychiatrist, he labeled "falling in love" by the clinical term "cathexis," which he defined as "being attracted to, invested in, and committed to an object outside ourselves."[139] Yes, he acknowledged that when we "cathect" someone, that showering of affectionate attention almost always proves to be fleeting; but, when we practice "falling in love" with those whom we otherwise summarily would dismiss and, likely, disdain, the act of investing even a few moments and at least a drop of genuine care or compassion, we *all* win. Few opponents will look to us for a deep, sustained love relationship, yet all will recognize and be touched by sincere attempts to show them respect, and truly see or hear them, in-person.

Out of a convenience fettered to the limits of (in this case, the English) language, I talk here of "falling in love," but I speak not of *Eros* (romantic love) but rather of *Philia*, affectionate love. (William Penn—founder of America's only Quaker colony—loosely translated the latter kind of love when he named its capital "Philadelphia," a "City of Brotherly [or Fraternal] Love.") With echoes of Piero Ferrucci's call to be kind to one another still reverberating in these pages, I am calling people of good faith and all political stripes to practice cultivating affection for even those who, at first encounter, do not naturally awaken it in us. Though necessary, it is not always easy.

I recall sitting in the Guthrie Theater on a wintery day, mesmerized by "our Scott," and noting:

> Love is the willingness to extend *or* expand one's Self on the behalf of another.

I find it natural to focus on those whom I already know and love, and relatively easy to **extend** my attention and care to a few of those who are only briefly passing through my Life's journey. To **expand** my Self on yet others' behalf, however—to enlarge my capacity to be kinder, longer, with more souls whom I encounter along my way through the world—at first seems daunting. It requires of me even more energy (which Peck foresaw, as for "an extension of oneself, vast amounts of energy are required"), discipline and maturity. I'm not complaining, rather warning. It is good for me to exercise my heart muscle, but first I must—as the Germans say—overcome my "*innerer Schweinehund*," my "inner hog dog," or internalized propensity to procrastinate. To succeed in following my own suggestion to others, I must grow—but growth is scary "work."

an artistic representation of "Mein innerer Schweinehund" displayed in Bonn by the Danish sculptor Jens Galschiøt, 1993; a medieval artistic portrayal of a "Schweinehund" on the door of Quedlinburg Cathedral

What also does not come to me easily but only through effort is to wade into "lowliness," to "submit" to others' personalities, moods, realities, needs, wishes, etc. Of course, others may also find it "unnatural" to consider my (or your) needs, wishes and so on. Most Americans now alive grew up in prosperity [relative to global conditions], in a country exercising more power in the world than any other ever has; children of the Reformation and the Enlightenment, our cultural training has been to focus on the Self: What do we know of submitting to others, of the humility needed to recognize that we are not always the "best" and also not the only? Does the US' current social stalemate not reflect hubris accumulated over decades, if not centuries, of self-touted "exceptionalism"? Our national experience has pampered us—and as a result, how intimately do we know modesty or moderation, critical self-reflection or our fallibility? How are we to bypass impasse if we cannot temper unrestraint? How should a "democracy" function let alone survive if the people inhabiting it are not willing to consider the will of others even as we try to push through our own? Mechanically, that cannot work—yet is that not where we are today, stuck in deadlock so long as no one is willing to rein in her or his unending willfulness?

Might we better circumnavigate much of others' willful bluster, were we able to "hear behind the words," to listen not so much to the words others utter but to the content and intent *behind* them? When Lucy—for one—crowed, on July 4th 2016, about Trump building a wall between "us" and Mexico were he elected, what was the core of her intent? As soon as she had mouthed the words, I stopped thinking about her and started focusing on me, on how repulsive a racist I perceived her to be at that moment. What if, instead, I had thought it possible that rather than her feeling superior to those with darker skin or from a different culture (a "preference" I cannot easily address), she feared for her husband's seasonal job driving grain trucks or her long-term un[der-]employed brother's ability to find lawn-mowing gigs? I could have spoken to that [to me, exaggerated and unreasoned] *Angst*. Stuck as I was in my head, there was no hope that I might find an entrée into hers: So, once again, we both fell down, like countless other times, and fled our latest tangle feeling bad about each other, as well as our Selves. I failed not only to <u>extend</u> to Lucy the benefit of a doubt—let alone my full ear and my clearest, deep-reaching mind—but to <u>expand</u> my own ability to live deeper than just below the surface. I chose to cling to my fear of again being my family's odd-man-out and to myriad resentments, rather than to push Lucy's— and my own—growth; I chose to revert to dead dynamics rather than to live out love.

*

> "All that is necessary for the force of evil to triumph
> is for good people to do nothing."
>
> — Edmund Burke, distilled from
> a letter to Thomas Mercer

The Left's Unhealed Achilles' Heel

Tuesday, 21 September 1982—I make a BIG splash:

Freshly returned from a life-changing year studying in England, traveling across Europe, I want to make a difference. I organize Iowa State University's First Annual UN International Day of Peace Observance. I book dozens of speakers to talk all day about peace, at the ISU Campanile.

The *Ames Tribune* and the campus radio station bill the event, where I first encounter native-American, African-American, Jewish, labor and other activists—and for the first time meet an openly gay man, Mark Dupont. I set out to change the world, but find my own altered forever.

Me being an exception, all my Mennonite Student Center housemates are Anabaptists—some the grandchildren of Old Order Amish: Their activism mirrors their simple, solid origins. Their pastor, Keith Schrag, inspires me to plant a "peace tree" in civil disobedience at a SAC base.[140]

Most days I wear overalls, collarless shirts, straw hats and clogs, and ride a Puch bike to class. I also come out as gay—which "my" otherwise "progressive" Mennonites stoically reject. I move out but soldier on, because my sense of an autonomous Self, sanity and survival depend on it.

Iowa State Daily editors print my long, lively opinion pieces almost weekly. So emboldened, I accompany an American Lutheran Church[141] delegation to tour war-torn Nicaragua, for which Iowa Quaker farm women pack suitcases full of medical and school supplies to send with me.

With Tim, my first partner, I garden and join a food co-op; we make our own yogurt and jams, granola and wholegrain breads. On warm days, dancer Tim does yoga on our lawn and spins wool on our stoop. Weekends find us folk-dancing by night, attending Friends meeting Sundays.

We sleep on the tacky floor of a school bus *en route* to DC to be at the 20th anniversary of MLK's March on Washington.[142] At a vigil against US military actions in Grenada and Honduras, a man in a gigantic, cherry-red pickup almost drives over me. Still, I march on, determined to persevere.

"Portrait of the activist as a young man," 1983; Tim (blue cap) and me (Amish hat) at a 20th anniversary March on Washington, with David (sunglasses), who we later heard died of AIDS in California

A friend starts to get mysterious skin lesions: The so-called "gay cancer" arrives in Ames, Iowa. When I came out no one I knew had ever heard of the word "AIDS," but soon scores are dying. I decide to donate sperm at McFarland Clinic, unsure if my DNA will live beyond me if I do not.

I fall to my knees to hug Ashlawn Farm's snow-covered ground on a December night as Mom confides that the previous June Dad and she were served foreclosure notice—at a quarter to midnight! More than being gay, being a farmer's son spurs my most intense campus activism:

I write an independent-study paper, *Rural Iowa: Its Past and Some Proposals for Its Future*, which the *Des Moines Register* features. It's 1984: I advocate retooling the state to wind-, solar- and methane-generated energy, phasing out ag-chemicals and revitalizing rural communities.[143]

Tim and I split up. I move into my own place, where I host Helen Caldicott's husband, William, who speaks at ISU in her stead. He sleeps on my '50s hand-me-down couch, as the anti-nuclear student group I head lacks the funds for a hotel. We go on long walks, for even longer talks.

I also host German Green politicians, who tour Central Iowa to speak about the US' placing of Cruise and Pershing II missiles on West-German soil. During the frequent, midday outdoor "sermons" I give on central-campus, I advocate Green values with all of the zeal of a convert.

My status as a campus "radical activist" solidifies. My reputation spreads; it draws supporters. I find myself in the center of a fluid clique of left-leaning, would-be change agents. Slowly, I grow uncomfortable with recurring dynamics: I question where I "belong" ideologically and socially.

The Campus Democrats invite me to join them—me, who had campaigned for Ronald Reagan. I decline, not finding my prairie-farmboy worldview among sophisticated kids from Des Moines, suburban Chicago and cool Denver. Still, interactions with the Campus Republicans leave me cold.

Despite unsettling doubts and feeling like a partisan orphan, I press on because my heart leads me to do so. I cannot be anything other than what I feel I am: young and curious, passionate and largely uninhibited; I am *alive*! I seek ways to translate that vitality into civic engagement.

There is a deadly nuclear arms race not only going on but accelerating. Reagan's saber rattling seems real—and threatening: A US invasion of Central American countries appears imminent. We young campus idealists want to live, so band together. We commiserate over boxed wine.

Repeated meetings take place in my pristine pad or upstairs at Amelie Hillary Smythe's[144] sloppy attic loft, solely so she can continue chain-smoking cigs that leave beige spots on her index- and middle-finger joints. A half- to full dozen of us plot possible acts to pierce deep student apathy.

Like patrician-WASP Amelie, dark-haired Linda del Pinocchio hails from Des Moines—also from money. While we all deliberate, she bakes endless rounds of brownies, bars and cookies for us. Oddly, as surly and darkly cynical as Amelie is, is her sunshiny pal Linda sweet and optimistic.

Literally bleary-eyed (from a congenital affliction), self-described "straight-but-not-narrow boy" Larry Horey, from Chicago, blows into our crowded, excitable cadre—but always out again. He lingers once to reveal that he wants to bed me "Because [his] brother had a gay experience…"

Grasping for splashy statements against "nuclear madness," prissy "professional fag" gay- activist Zane Napier and former cheerleader Renee Oberholtzer tell us about the Shadow Project that is "all the rage in urban centers." We agree to replicate it one night on the central campus.

Amelie advises "sexy-black dress" for us and Linda bakes cookies "to carry in our pockets for any emergencies." While Larry eyes me, beefy, blond art-student Ben from Denver promises to check for possible ISU-policy pitfalls. Me? I pilfer a 50-pound bag of barn lime from Dad's feed shed.

On the appointed night, Amelie "can't come because [she] broke a nail" and Ben admits he forgot to check the legality of our laying on the ground in contorted poses while others etch our silhouettes with soluble barn lime. Being inept, we swiftly get apprehended by campus security.

Threatened with charges of "vandalism" or "disturbing the peace" and expulsion, we half-dozen who had not suffered broken nails and were caught suffer through administrators' humiliating scolds. As we retreat to Amelie's smoke chamber, Linda offers to bake brownies. I fume inside.

I live on, because I can do no other—but I have never felt so small and alone in this big world. I despair over the human condition; I feel disgusted by "broken nails," absentmindedness and "students who jus' wanna drink an' fuck—but don't give one 'bout truly makin' a diff'rence."

At some point, thinking such impotence to go beyond much posturing and pointless politicking reflects "pampered college kiddies who wear a cloak of activism like some passing fashion," I trek to Saint Paul to attend a national Green-Party organizing conference at Macalester College.

At the registration desk, I sense these cats' seriousness: The sign-in list includes well-known Anglo activists from BosWash, peppered with disproportionate numbers[145] of "Goldfarbs," "Silversteins" and "Perls." Nina Rothschild and husband Eric Utne tout their hot new *Reader*.

As the conference opens, it is clear that most of those assembled represent a residual "Spiritual Left" from the '60s Cultural Revolution. I feel hopeful that if anyone can, such seasoned sages can plant Germany's Green Dream on American soil, where it might take root and fully bloom.

As the conference unfolds, I feel exhilarated to sit among intellectual giants. I revel in the depth of thought and breadth of experience. I still believe, yet wait for concrete proposals for action. Some are debated, but none are adopted. Many present quibble over "ideological impurities."

As the conference drags on, it alarms me how quickly it bogs down in ego-driven squabbles: "How should 'The Movement' be called—and those who shepherd it?" Some Boston Brahmin and Grayline WASPS push for "Committees of Correspondence," but several Jews balk at this.

As the conference ends, I feel defeated to see that even adult veteran activists do little better than Amelie & Crew back in Ames—to where I return with my ideological tail between my legs. I live on, because I can do no other—but I continue to feel so small and alone in this big world…

Fast forward: The world's oceans are rising, landslides falling, forests burning; Parliament and Congress are flatlining as "evil empires" entrench and expand. Still, all hopped up by both big-bucks and social media, populations around the globe are bitterly split along intractable ideals.

Around the globe, as of this writing (November 2019) demonstrations are taking or in the past month have taken place in: Algeria, Bolivia, Catalan, Chile, Ecuador, England, Ethiopia, Haiti, Hong

Kong, Indian Kashmir, Iraq, Iran, Lebanon, Nicaragua, Venezuela—where next? The planet's people are on the march, but to where? The marchers are loud, but sing discordant refrains.[146]

A 16-year-old Swedish schoolgirl chides world leaders and spurs people's consciences, yet little changes—and what does is too late, undertaken by too few. Paralyzed by political deadlock, the world's two oldest modern democracies sink into myopic miseries, inspiring and leading *no one.*

And so it goes… but, humanity has been here before:

Most postwar Americans default into the comfortable-but-simplistic stanch that "all Germans were Nazis," but 'twas *not* so. In the 1920s, Communists and their ideological Leftist cousins, the Socialists, enjoyed nationally about as much support as the *Nationalsozialisten*, or "Nazis." Unlike Hitler's ability to recruit rabid Brown Shirts to solidify his power, however, the Left was forever frayed by tussles over "ideological impurities:" Thus immobilized, it could not successfully offer Germans a comparably compelling narrative—and so hold sexy-but-toxic Nazi madness in check.

While on a vastly different scale, the impotence of left-leaning Iowa State politicos in the early '80s mirrored dynamics too common throughout history and across the globe. We, too, failed to offer a compelling alternative narrative and tap our convictions enough to muster arousing, sustained public engagement—*à la* our one-off Shadow Project fiasco. As we dithered, debating what "sexy-black" garb to don or whether Linda should next bake brownies or bars, the Campus Republicans pulled off well-attended, boisterous rallies in support of Reaganomics and military actions around the world. Amelie's "broken nail" and Ben's lack of disciplined perseverance assured that our hollow actions would end pathetically, *sans* meaning. Yes, our going through minimal motions afforded a stage where our *de facto* leader, Ms A. H. Smythe, could strike cool poses—smoldering cigs in-hand—and Larry might prove his manliness to his older-bro hero, but other than that what did our lively *tête-à-têtes* and all of our group meetings yield? Maybe we felt better, at least about our lost little selves—I surely did—but other than that… *anything*?

On a scale larger than a covey of college kids wistfully dreaming of each one's "15 minutes of fame," I now shudder to think of the mass squandering of human, let alone natural resources that crash-and-burn Green-party "launch" in 1984 entailed. Ironically, our vain efforts violated the very values that purportedly brought us together: We likely were not 100 but at least 50, maybe 75 attendees; collectively, our respective travels (mostly from either coast) to far-off Minnesota generated *tons* of carbon, truckloads of unrecycled consumer waste (road-food containers, hotel-bathroom and automotive supplies), extra Macalester College air-conditioning and lighting, etc. Our "investment" in social change (ultimately, an ecological extravagance) only added to the environmental emergency we now are facing. Yes, our going through many motions (which, without exception, failed to pass) afforded a stage where we could parade our personal political prowess and prove our possessing anointed Truths, but other than that what did our sideline *tête-à-têtes* and all of those threshing sessions yield? Maybe we felt better, at least about our lost little selves—I partly did—but other than that... *anything*? It seems... *not*.

A more recent and international textbook example of "the Left's Unhealed Achilles Heel?"

demonstrators at the Women's March on Washington, held in the nation's capital on 21 January 2017

On Saturday, 21 January 2017, the Women's March on Washington snaked its way through the streets of the US capital, the epicenter of global actions organized in protest of Donald Trump's election. Channeling Ms Smythe's "sexy-black" campaign, one of the more eye-catching aspects of the march consisted of the Pussyhat Project, with hundreds of thousands of pink caps ["hat" here a misnomer] being specially made.[147] (As far as I know, the marchers set off without Linda del Pinocchio's cookies, bars or brownies.) According to a Wikipedia entry (presumably written by supporters), "After the marches, organizers reported that around 673 marches took place worldwide, on all seven continents, 29 in Canada, 20 in Mexico, and 1 in Antarctica." Whoever compiled the Wiki accounts of the 2017 marches took great effort to highlight that some of the marchers carried big names, not just sassy signs or pink caps:

Alec Baldwin, Drew Barrymore, Cory Booker, Simone Campbell, Cher, Angela Davis, Robert De Niro, Tammy Duckworth, Jane Fonda, James Franco, Al Franken, Whoopi Goldberg, Jake and Maggie Gyllenhaal, Kamala Harris, Felicity Huffman, Jesse Jackson, Scarlett Johansson, Van Jones, John Kerry, John Lewis, Madonna, Michael Moore, Yoko Ono, Ellen Page, Katy Perry, Cecile Richards, Tim Robbins, Julia Roberts, Gloria Steinem and Elizabeth Warren[148]

For having been "the largest single-day protest in US history," why is it, this show of displeasure caused barely more than a media blip the day and years after? Perhaps, its failure was built-in:

> The goal of the annual marches is to advocate legislation and policies regarding human rights and other issues, including women's rights, immigration reform, healthcare reform, reproductive rights, the environment, LGBTQ rights, racial equality, freedom of religion, workers' rights and tolerance. According to organizers, the goal was to "send a bold message to our new administration on their first day in office, and to the world that women's rights are human rights."

How to wrap one's mind around all of <u>that</u>? A sidebar elaborated the march's "Goals" as being:

> "Protection of our rights, our safety, our health, and our families – recognizing that our vibrant and diverse communities are the strength of our country" [followed by a list, including:] women's right, LGBTQ rights, gender equality, racial equality, worker rights, disability rights, immigration reform, health care reform, freedom of religion, environmental protection

Those are noble, worthy aims—but perhaps a few too many? Just as a person has only so many hours in a day and thus can accomplish only so much, so fast, a body of people—an organization, a community, a nation—also has only so much time and energy. Doesn't trying to address almost "everything" almost always result in changing almost nothing? Our chic ISU clique wanted to wear sexy-black camouflage and carry still-warm cookies in our pockets for sustenance, but I pleaded beforehand that we assign a designated watch, one of us to signal the rest with a pre-agreed sound or motion that campus security was nigh. My protests had not prevailed, but we *did* look *very* dashing and certainly *would* have savored those yummy cookies, *had* our throats not been so swollen-dry by the chilling prospect of being summarily expelled from university. Perhaps, had we focused on the essentials of using art to awaken, we might have succeeded in our efforts, not squandered them. Obsessed with the trivial, we overlooked the fundamental.

While rash readers might conclude that I am flogging past co-activists in absentia, my goal here is not to expose individuals' character flaws but rather collective cultural ones: What did my ISU cohorts all have in common? We were all European-descended Americans who had grown up in postwar prosperity. Although in those pre-*Oprah Winfrey Show* days we rarely thought about it and spoke of it even less, we brought with us deep, unconscious socialization that indelibly cast our being. Our shallow, short-attention-span urges rendered us unable to work as an effective whole to impact our university in ways we never could as frail fragments in a vast universe.

In a similar vein:

Why did hundreds of thousands of women, worldwide, take to the streets in January 2017—the greatest number of whom apparently did so as a one-off "girls-day-out" jaunt. Clearly, they were displeased with Trump's unexpected rise to power—but, then, once stirred, why did the majority come out just once? Was it a "statement," a passing mini-outrage that quickly cooled and lost importance amidst other possible pastimes? Could energy showered on precious props like pink caps or glitzy gimmicks like Hollywood stars flown in to assure bigger, bolder headlines be more effectively invested in other things? What other, more sustainable tactics might grab an otherwise skeptical, distracted public—not to mention cynical, foot-dragging politicians?

Not to insult the main or sub-marches' organizers (who I presume to be committed individuals with staying power—at least, enough to successfully fill the streets with sisters), but I assume a large part of those who found enough motivation to join that march came from the "superficial" or "center-left" categories of my General Political-Rainbow Graph. That in itself is no shame, but it also is not enough to leverage real, lasting change—especially not in relation to the crisis we now face. What if those same women's [great-]Aunt Rosies had taken up rivet guns or their [great-]grandfathers ones for combat "jus' for kicks," to "make a statement" and feel good about their lost, little Selves? They never would have defeated the Nazis: We'd *all* be goose-stepping today. And do not underestimate: The threat of ecological calamity trumps the threat from Nazis.

Besides the problematic of women, of men, of anyone being politically active for primarily one's own sake over that of the whole, there is a larger dilemma: Non-committal, one-off and loose-cannon "activism" cannot sustain, over time and space, the impetus necessary to make real and lasting change. If the Suffragettes had been so easily discouraged from the daunting task of overcoming men's efforts to keep them disfranchised and marginalized, if they had lacked the depth of conviction to maintain their campaign over what became decades, then the women who marched in DC and elsewhere in 2017 would never have had a right to vote to exercise. The same is true of the American Civil Rights movement of the mid-20th century: Fickle or thin "commitment" would never have overturned the insidious legacy of slavery and racism; black and white activists succeeded as a group, not as lone wolves—for as a popular saying has it,

If you want to go fast, go alone; if you want to go far, go together.[149]

Change-sabotaging behaviors, however, are neither limited to female marchers nor just about staying power, but rather also the magnanimity needed to bear non-fatal power plays or lesser lapses in ideological "purity." Those who do not possess greatness of heart easily succumb to eternal internal organizational bickering and partisan division; those who have or find it prevail. Why is it, the Right's foot soldiers seem to be more genetically predisposed to possessing this ability, while those of the Left have proven, across time and geography, to so often lack it? Yes, the Left *does* reach some of its goals, but seemingly only after great effort and too much delay.

Central to successful engagement, of course, remains convincing and competent leadership. The deadly divisions over ideology—*à la* the German Left of the 1920s and '30s or the pathetic performance of the would-be American Greens—that otherwise might render any movement lame often can be overcome by effective leaders. The Suffragettes had, in Britain, their daring Emmeline Pankhurst and, in the US, towering figures such as Susan B. Anthony and Lucretia Mott (both Quakers), Elisabeth Cady Stanton, Sojourner Truth and others, while their later comrades in spirit, the Civil Rights activists, followed the calls of inspiring Martin Luther King, Jr. Such activist ancestors were not saints and they certainly endured their share of ideological spats, but they clearly overcame *all* divisions successfully enough to leave the legacy they did. The same cannot be said of contemporary activists among the women marchers or US Greens.

As I did cursory, rushed research for this section, in tracing the evolution of today's miniscule Green "movement" in the United States, I found it took some seven years after that fruitless gathering at Macalester College for another effort to bear anything resembling real results. As with our first attempt, following ones often fractured over form (names) and content (goals). In 1991, the Greens/Green Party USA (G/GPUSA) arose during a gathering in West Virginia—again per Professor Pedia—by "restructuring the Green Committees of Correspondence with the idea that the Green movement and Green Party would operate as part of a single organization."[150] So, it seems the WASPS at Macalester—or at least their labels—triumphed in the end, after all. *Oh!*

the longstanding German Green Party sunflower symbol (left) and logo of the short-lived East German "Grüne Partei," founded November 1989 and fused with West German Greens in October 1990

German Greens (now a central, ascending presence in Germany's parliament) have long united around "Four Pillars" (social justice, ecological wisdom, grassroots democracy and nonviolence). Apparently having learned too little from recent historical experience, the American Greens—reflexively reflecting our larger culture—chase ten diffuse, mostly amorphous "Key Values:"

1) grassroots democracy
2) social justice and equal opportunity
3) ecological wisdom
4) nonviolence
5) decentralization
6) community-based economics
7) feminism and gender equality
8) respect for diversity
9) personal and global responsibility
10) future focus and sustainability

Again, all worthy goals, but as our national, nay *global* house burns up, which of those "extra" Key Values do we wish to pursue *instead of* focusing on top-priority, life-essential projects?

While America's Greens (for whose 2016 presidential candidate I voted, unable to flout my own conscience—let alone my ardent pleas to Iowa's electorate—and vote for a woman I still hold in searing contempt) haggle over ideological purity, down the street America's Right continues to rule the day. And the future marches envisioned by the 2017 organizing committee? There were marches in 2018 and '19, but only shadows of '17's Mother of All Marches: Each ensuing year saw increasing fragmentation over charges of organizers tolerating anti-Semitism, homo- and transphobia.[151] In both cases—that of America's Greens and of Women Marchers—internal fighting caused each movement much more deadly harm than external attacks by opponents.[152]

Why is it, actually, that the Left across eras and regions has struggled to draw followers even as it has called for and fed public debate, yet the Right calls most of the shots, day-in, day-out? Perhaps, because human beings see their own perceived needs first, only *then* others'? If so:

Let us consider some primary forces behind the traditional Right (in Western culture, generally "conservatives" or, in the US, "Republicans") and traditional Left ("liberals" or "Democrats"). Again, according to Professor Pedia:

> Right-wing political thinking holds that certain social orders and hierarchies are inevitable, natural, normal or desirable, typically supporting this position on the basis of natural law, economics or tradition. Hierarchy and inequality may be viewed as natural results of traditional social differences or competition in market economies.[153] [In contrast:] Left-wing politics supports social equality and egalitarianism, often in opposition to social hierarchy. It typically

involves a concern for those in society whom its adherents perceive as disadvantaged relative to others as well as a belief that there are unjustified inequalities that need to be reduced or abolished.[154]

Translated and simplified? The Right wants to "conserve" the existing social order—including letting the current system's benefiters retain their privileges—while the Left seeks to "liberate" people from past limitations or injustices (including those disadvantaged by inequality), in order to create a new system. [Note: "Liberal" comes from *libre*, the Latin root for a "free [person]" or, now archaic, "free from restraints."] If that is too abstract, consider concrete examples:

In the US' current political landscape, the Right consists largely of Christian Fundamentalists or more moderate evangelicals. They and other American conservatives tend to be past-oriented: "Let us return to, or at least conserve, what once was" (read: "WASP America.") As I experience my relatives' and their offspring's values and behavior, their change-resistant worldviews rest a great deal upon judging the [real as well as erroneously or at least only-partially imagined] past.

Concerning the past: Conservatives often claim to defend traditional and "right" values, yet the policies their leaders push, and the rank-and-file mostly blindly support, actually weaken existing institutions. As I cited earlier, decades of Republican-driven legislation in—for one—Iowa has forced women into the workforce (leaving children isolated and dependent on paid, non-family figures), farmers from their land and educated young people to seek careers out-of-state. While Democratic administrations also have pushed farmers to expand and over-produce, above all Republican ones have relentlessly pursued soil-diminishing, community-demolishing ag policies. They did so in large part to repay political favors and monetary donations from ag businesses.

On the other hand, liberals claim to know how to realize a "better" future—and nanny people accordingly. In fact, their professed guiding lights often are outshone by their fascination with... their Selves: Ms Smythe most focused on our group when it most focused on her; Larry lingered in my place after the others had left not in pursuit of setting up collective action but scoring some solo action with me; even sweet Linda could scarcely see the issues for her obsession with icing. Somehow, others smell this Self-absorption and, appropriately, suspect many Leftists' motives, thereby impeding the formation of trust—more an intuitive knowing rather than a rational one. [So chide me as they will, my Hillary-loving East Coast lesbian friends can *not* disabuse me of my visceral distrust for that woman. Why? Because I sense she is all about the Clinton brand and its dynasty—thus I will *always* welcome her Chelsea to serve in charity but *never* in public office.]

Concerning the present: Hardcore conservatives tend to be punitive, rather than preventative: If someone commits a crime "PUNISH" (!) her or him, regardless of that person's pre-offense circumstances; an archetypal liberal tries to tailor "PENANCE" (typically done in a "penitentiary;" today, "restitution" or "restorative justice" are preferred) to each individual case. Scores of more in-depth studies have done far superior jobs of presenting such vast, complicated matters than I am now, but to superficially summarize one of them: In some ways American conservatives resemble stern, strict parents, while liberals play the more permissive, ever-forgiving one. Each one's particular psychological makeup predetermines much of how each of us dresses down The Other: As my relatives perceive their all-vengeful-or-all-loving god, so they also see "right" and "wrong," punishment and reward—and they expect "their" public servants to do the same.

Or, to use another analogy: The Left happily plays Good Cop to the Right's Bad one. Problem is, this behavior entails dichotomies—always way too much or too little. In her or his own way, the Good Cop as well as the Bad Cop are playing roles rather than acting sincerely and honestly, in each moment as new stimuli arises. Better than "Good" or "Bad" would be "Fair" or "Just" cops, of which a political equivalent would be neither "too far" Right nor Left, but rather up-front.

Concerning the future: Conservatives tend to shy from anything truly new, instead reactively clinging to the old, to the perceived "known;" Liberals tend to suspect old ways, and embrace ones seen as "new." Which, then, will fare better in a future of shrinking natural resources and spreading social misery? The Right's allergy to change and innovation, but also compromise, damns the Republicans to remain the "Party of 'No.'" If the Right too quickly nixes proposals from anyone not of their ranks, the Left too quickly says "Sure, why not?" to too many. With notable exceptions (e.g., Eisenhower's completing US Army desegregation or Nixon's creation of the Environmental Protection Agency), the Right rarely introduces truly socially-beneficial reform—a public good over which the American Left continues to enjoy a solid monopoly. Still, the Left struggles—not just in the US but in most countries—to win public trust and support to a degree needed to implement, then cultivate reforms until they become a durable success.

One reason that conservatives so often thrive while liberals scramble to win support in a series of self-defacing apologies, is that what the Right peddles *now* is more easily visible (in part, as it already "is"). In contrast, what the Left would have the public buy is mostly only imaginable for, in large part, it does not now exist. Thus, the Right and Left are in constant, loud competition to earn the trust of the Near Left and Near Right, those swayable "undecideds" or supposedly "independents" that every election campaign exhausts itself to win over. It was this "middle-third" that the nutty Nazis succeeded in luring away from Germany's Communists and Socialists in the 1920s and '30s; the same ilk of "centrists" (of whom many truly weren't) voted for Trump after having approved Obama—or in 2016 signed onto Brexit, or in the '80s enabled Thatcher or Reagan to supplant, respectively, Labour and "liberal" Jimmy Carter. Those in the middle third exactly vote based on perceived self-interests—even if, ironically, they are duped into voting exactly for those who would sell out those interests in a flash. In short: Trust is a commodity, but often consists of cheap imitations, bought and sold in deals with the devil.

Do not underestimate the sway of [perceived] self-interest over Joe or Josephine Public on voting day, no matter how informed or uninformed they might be. The most conservative pull the levers that punch the names of those candidates who will "protect" the Publics' property and privacy. Less fear-driven segments of the electorate, however, might take a breath, then take a risk on some newcomer who seems to have the common good in mind, though advocates a change of course. Idealism might pull voters behind the curtain, but egotism mostly pulls the levers. The Right understands this: Just as the Left appeals to amorphous idealism, peddling a palette of identity-driven causes, the Right appeals to concrete egotism, pandering to self-protective instincts and fear of The Other, of would-be competitors from "the other side of the wall."

Voting solely based on perceived self-interest, however, is not enough—it is enough neither to create a decent, worthwhile society nor to make an individual happy, someone who gets her or his own needs met, but does little or nothing to touch the lives of others. Humans are not built to live in vacuums or silos; we always were and continue to be social animals, despite whatever gadgets an Industrial and later Technological Revolution might have showered upon us. With one hand, the Nazis did a good job, handing out apartments and houses, *Autobahnen* and Volkswagens, jobs and subsidized vacations for loyal citizens, but with the other switching the rails that took cattle cars full of Jews to the ovens. Stalin, too, knew that to keep power he had to push through one miraculous Five-Year Plan after the other—but all those massive dams and factories, endless fields and towering apartment blocks depended on slaves worked to death in gulags. Yes, "self-interest" and getting basic needs met are crucial, but so is being able to live with one's Self in a society in which one wants to partake, to dwell in "a house [on] a tolerable planet." Maybe the people we were, on the planet we then had, could "afford" to chase self-indulgent interests, but the Earth has changed—and we have changed, having changed Earth. To lead us into new territory, we need new leadership, with new visions and new abilities. We need a politic that is comprehensive yet deep-reaching, speedy yet effective and honest. It cannot be too Far Left or Far Right; it must be up-front as it also pulls up the rear.

Perhaps it is liberals' general, seemingly continual state of being diffused in focus and confused about strategy that leads them to be—after all sums have been reckoned—ineffectual, at least in proportion to the raw amount of their efforts and in comparison to results born of the same amount of efforts undertaken by conservatives. Looking at American history, the Progressives *did* achieve much, but did it not take the knock-us-on-our-asses Great Depression to enable the New Deal to accomplish much more reform, faster? It was only the widespread desperation of the times, Americans' realization that their solo efforts could not move the crisis at-hand, that the electorate showed the Republicans the door and thus made space for both Democrats and those to their left to try to untangle the nation's mess. Now, though, such a scale of decisive action seems only a dream. With no Hitler kicking at Western democracies' doors… But, wait!

In the not-so-recent past, the Right in America had only to pick low-hanging fruit to find patsies to push their agendas. In the Olden Days, mostly-white neighborhoods could be incited to fight to "keep darkies out" but, as our environmental disaster becomes ever-more-difficult to wish or talk away, neighbors will become more motivated to keep floodwaters out. Single-issue cultural campaigns like prayer in school provided clever cover for other Republican objectives in years past, but soon keeping single-use plastics out of schools will trump prayer. Mounting ecological crises will overturn decades, if not centuries of political norms and alliances—opening new opportunities for civil engagement and political organizing. Question remains: Who will prevail?

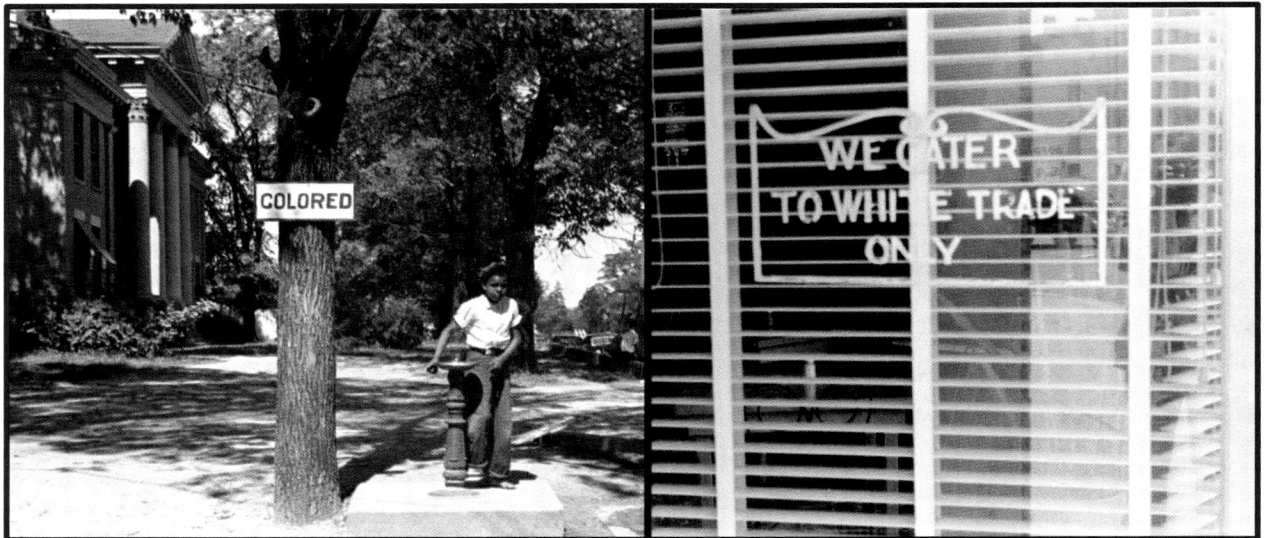

an African-American child at a segregated drinking fountain in front of the Halifax County Courthouse in Halifax, North Carolina; sign in a restaurant window in Lancaster, Ohio: Both photos were taken in 1938, the same year as in Nazi-Germany Hitler increased persecution of the Jews—culminating in the brutal "Kristallnacht" ["Night of Broken Glass" or also called the "November Pogrom"] of 9-10 November.

At present, on international and national levels, the Left is not universally inspiring. In the midst of Brexit madness, for one, Labour's Jeremy Corbin repeatedly proves to be one of the weakest, least inspiring "opposition" leaders of any democratic country. Across the Atlantic, only after three years of Trump's outrageous behaviors and illegal, Constitution-shredding dealing did Aunt Nancy and Uncle Chuck finally acquiesce to rightful calls for impeachment. More indicative of the state of American "democracy," however, is the sad absence of women in pink caps—those who on *the day after* The Donald's inauguration *so* loudly promised to "keep after him" yet since almost the day thereafter have been so silently absent from the political stage: <u>Why</u>?

Based on past performances, more often than not Left movements, leaders and projects have proven one-off or at least short-lived, scattered in direction and strategy, prone to fracturing over in-house ideological rifts, distrusted if not disdained by those not inhabiting the same echo chambers—in short, painfully ineffective. While the Right (sometimes surprisingly) learns and adapts, the Left too often succumbs to its own self-satisfaction. What are the Left's responses to extremely brilliant PR products like "Brexit" (the name itself speaks loudly) or "Get It Done" in Britain? In the States, "Make America Great Again" is an ugly hoax—yet it worked beautifully in sweeping a hustler into the White House, supported feverishly by otherwise "godly" people.

Will today's campus activists, Green proponents and marching women learn enough, fast enough, to depart from the Left's past failures and arrive at a new relationship with those multi-job Americans whose lives have no space for cozy *tête-à-têtes* and endless debates over ideological purity? Will the Left finally confront and then overcome its arrogant paternalism? Will it be able to compete with a Right that does not hesitate not only to lie, but to steal—as in the case of France's Front National, which now has as its tandem focus environmentalism next to anti-immigration?[155] As the FN makes "the greening of France" quicken throughout the land, most notably in small- and mid-size communities, will the Left in Europe as well as in the US reclaim the rural ideal from those who would wed it with xenophobia and hyper-provincialism?

For those of us not of The Right, we must, in short, recast our souls. We must stop being who we have been and doing what we have been doing; we must go inside ourselves and alter what has proven inadequate to move the world in a direction we want. To renew society, we first must renew our Selves, for if we think we are going to remake the world without remaking ourselves, we are gravely mistaken.

*

"People say, what is the sense of our small effort?
They can not see that we must lay one brick
at a time, take one step at a time."

— Dorothy Day, *Love and Fishes*

Be Your Own Teddy Bear

In order to

12) instigate transformative change,

study examples of how to provide your Self the inner stamina and fortitude needed to endure, despite hurdles to effectively reaching The Other. Some obstacles are external, others internal:

At first glance, my ol' friend Bug and Lucy would seem to be diametric opposites of each other. Where Bug personifies a "knee-jerk liberal," Lucy is reflexively arch-conservative. Bug is well-read and -traveled; Lucy is neither. Except for about ten months, Lucy has been faithfully married for over four decades, while as far as I know Bug has never even gone on a date. The two women, however, have at least two things in common: Both Iowa residents, they have been fixtures of my life—Lucy, for as long as I have been on this planet; Bug, since we met as undergraduate students in the early '80s. On top of that, even as both consider themselves to hold passionate convictions, from my perspective, for each woman's lack of enough courage to fully encounter The Other, their inner fire often fails to find full expression in our world—as I conclude from this:

About my age—close enough to 60 to see the *finale* of middle-age approaching swiftly—Bug lives with her sister, Pony, on a smallholding in a wooded coulee in Northeast Iowa. There, they keep a variety of practical as well as decorative breeds of chickens, an assortment of dogs (five, at last count) and two Norwegian Fjord horses, which Pony happily hitches up to a two-wheeled trap and takes out for endless drives down nearby lanes and across quiet meadows. Opposite gardening and canning, cloud- and birdwatching, the peaceable sisters religiously comb the daily news and watch nightly political views *à la* Rachel Maddow. Both dutifully attend local political events, sit on boards of non-profit, social-change-oriented organizations (including my 2016 senate campaign, on which Bug served as secretary), donate to "liberal" causes… in short, they engage in every "PC" project conceivable, right down to rinsing and reusing Ziploc bags.

At the same time, there seems to be a key element missing in this otherwise bucolic scene. For example: In search of a muse-inducing setting, from last May through July I rented a restored log cabin. Built in 1851 by Norwegian pioneers, this paradise mercifully lacked the temptations of internet or even a cellphone; ultimately, I wrote some 150 pages of this tome. Periodically, I invited to "working dinners" some of the two-dozen editor-critics who I had asked to assess my drafts. Along with others, Bug and Pony came. Amid multiple bowls of chard soup and Widge's oatmeal cookies, reviewers exchanged thoughtful reactions to what they recently had read. As she has our entire relationship, Bug earnestly encouraged me in my efforts, expressing genuine gratitude for "doing what [she] 'should' and want[s] to do, but jus' *can't*." The rest concurred.

As these evenings morphed unnoticed into midnights, those gathered wrestled with the mental gymnastics of how to defeat deadlock yet still prevail, to advance "our" causes and worldviews. In the end, we always agreed that doing so could be achieved *only* by making peace with "even the most ardent Trumpites," by being open and empathetic—which is exactly when we lost Bug.

"I dunno, ya guys" she would object, then roll her eyes and raise her arms. "I've tried so many, *so* uncountably many times to engage Trumpies, but each time I'm left feeling traumatized and hopeless. I *truly* tried—but I jus' *can't* face havin' my heart chopped up into mincemeat again."

On such evenings, as the beeswax candles I had placed round the rustic wood table began to burn themselves out and the fireflies' shimmering dance just outside the door was fading for the night, my chatty guests reiterated their expectations—as they began to take leave—that I "deliver concrete, specific strategies on how to bridge the chasm between opposing fronts." Each time, before going, Bug begged "If nothing else, at least provide me with a Teddy bear!" Each time, I shifted uncomfortably in my seat, unsure if or how to share with my friends, above all with Bug, what I *really* thought. If I had, my confession would have gone something like this:

"Look, Sis, we've known each other for decades. All that time, I've watched you be consistently empathetic with others, even as you just as steadily remain laser-focused on the bigger picture an' deeper dynamics underlying hot issues. For years, you've singularly inspired me by your tireless involvement with county zoning commissions to stop hog-confinement projects; with the food coop, the farmers market and organic bakeries, in order to support regional growers; with local Democrats and independent candidates—an' all the rest of your endless efforts."

In my mind, all the time I would be saying this, Bug would tighten her lips slightly and cock her head a bit atop her chin as it sank towards one shoulder. Her squinting eyes would betray her poorly-cloaked dislike of being taken to task and dressed down even by a loyal, longtime friend.

"Still" I would push on, "I also know that you're consistently an emotional sissy, a Confrontation Coward who at all costs resists taking on individuals or disagreeable audiences for the sake of instigating changes of heart, if not mind. I saw this when you feigned being 'secretary' of my '16 campaign an' I hear it *every* time we talk about the need to go out an' interact with 'them.'"

At that point, Bug's lips surely would stiffen some more and her eyes burn through me as I challenged Her Majesty, the Queen of Bleeding Hearts—the Left's She, Who *Must* Be Obeyed. The woman is better-read than anyone else in my circle of friends, yet she refuses to put that knowledge in forms and convey it on levels that might move someone other than fellow Lefties. She could make *such* a difference in educating vast swaths of the public that remain ill-informed, yet she shies from face-to-face contact with the essential conflict dividing opposing worldviews.

"You think the rest of us enjoy wadin' into lions dens or steppin' into political doggie-doo? You think facin' foes is particularly jolly or motivating? Well lemme tell ya, we don't do it 'cuz we *wanna* it do; we do it 'cuz we *gotta*! The time left before all hell breaks irrevocably loose is short an' our soldiers already weary from battlin' uphill, but that's *exactly* why we need YOU to stop bein' an emotional baby. Ya need to put on yer Big Girl pants an' march out alongside the rest o' us an' take on what ya call 'Trumpies,' 'cuz if you—if *we*—don't, nuttin's gonna change!"

Then, I would shake my head and end this solid scolding with a deep, resounding "*Harrumph!*"

Ironically, this morning (11 November 2019), as I sat down to continue this section, I received a rare email from Bug, dated the previous day. It perfectly illustrates my above thesis, as it reads:

> I'm writing this while sitting in a campaign office trying to do my share for getting out the caucus vote. I refuse to do cold-calling and I refuse to do door-knocking but I do tote things around in the pick-up truck and sweep up after the sweet but flighty young campaign workers. I think Putin and Mitch McConnell's trolls are focused on those few hundred thousand voters that will make the difference yet again in the general election. They reach low-info voters through those bizarre social-media advertisements and conspiracy-theory websites that incite such paranoia and fear.

It is *so* typical: *Such* a brilliant brain[156] quietly sitting around, willing to clean up others' messes but not willing to messy her hands by pressing flesh out beyond the campaign-office door. Almost daily—she has told me—Pony and she read the headlines, watch the news, then turn to each other and sigh "We're toast!" yet she refuses to wade very far into the fire. She is comforted by her own Self-image as an informed activist, yet her "informed" actions mostly deal with <u>things</u>, *not* people: She will move a broom but not work a room full of people; she will sweep up after others but not keep up with others' stream-of-consciousness thoughts that might differ from her own. Of course, we cannot all be leaders; yes, we need those ready to clean up, but we almost *must* have people able to shake up the public. Why does Bug think the world can afford the cool distance from the steamy masses that she maintains? Why does she assume she is more deserving of staying above the fray than the rest of us mere mortals? Is it arrogance? She has argued that it is fear—"raw, immobilizing *Angst*"—that keeps her from facing those who at least at first may not agree with her. So, self-isolating and socially isolated from two-thirds of the folks around her, Bug bides her time, waiting for her—for <u>our</u>—world to become "toast."

I present and dissect my friend Bug's behavior as a poster child for my twelfth suggestion how to confront and resolve deadlock—which is to **muster transformative courage** in order to <u>act</u>, in the spirit of Elena Aguilar's [composite] call to "**cultivate, facilitate, instigate**."[157] But, do not think I am taking aim only at some liberals' weak heels: Too many conservatives also shy from engaging The Other for lack of the courage to face their Self—staunchly conventional Lucy being one of them. (Though, to be honest, I am too often little better than she at finding the inner courage needed to do what it takes to dismantle deadlock.)

Before I offer a most-recent example of how diffusing stalemate can work, let me note one more thing that differentiates Bug and Lucy: I *imagined* the above "leveling" with Bug but never felt emotionally secure enough to tell it to her; the following partial transcript is what I recall of a rarely-frank phone conversation with Lucy that *actually* just took place. But first, its backstory:

Outraged by how I alluded to them in my announcement of having been found by a daughter to whom I had granted Life through artificial insemination in the 1980s, in February 2019 my closest kin cut all contact with me. Despite several attempts by me, they refused to confront the matter which had divided us anew. As shown in graph form and illustrated by the accompanying "colliding trains" example in my introduction to this tome, the ensuing deadlock between us occurred because each held an expectation of The Other—and awaited a "concession" to be offered by his or her opposite. When none came, no movement at all was possible between us.

Already as a babe I was "reaching out"—here with my parents and sibs at Ashlawn Farm, summer 1963.

243

In late July, just before heading back to Germany after five months of guest-teaching in Iowa at Cornhill College and a few, short speaking tours, I again reached out to Lucy and Linus: I pleaded that, if for no reason other than my mother's sake, we reconcile our current strife. How tragic it would be, I argued, if, as we lowered her into her grave, we could not raise our heads and look each other in the eye. When this appeal also failed to move either of them to respond, I desisted.

Then, in early October 2019, Phyllis fell ill—so ill that after she forfeited her place in an assisted-living facility because she could not independently go to meals, she was placed in a nursing home, but under hospice care. While Linus stubbornly maintained his boycott of yours truly, by that point Lucy initiated renewed contact enough to report on my mother's deteriorating condition. For several days, we expected her to pass soon—until she rallied, even through as of this writing.

The reality of Mom's imminent demise prompted Lucy to engage with me—by coincidence just as I received a cancer diagnosis and a date in December 2019 for two, maybe three operations. With the Grim Reaper's sickle blade hanging over all our heads, we agreed to parley via phone. A chance to resolve longstanding differences heartened me, but I feared we might revert to old fronts, err our way down dead-end tracks and thus once again watch as our hopes derailed.

Pondering before our phone date how to most effectively cultivate transformative tactics that might facilitate new results, I knew trying old strategies most likely would produce nothing new. I decided, then, to instigate a new approach: Instead of waiting for concessions from a woman whose life had hardly resembled mine after we each left our childhood home half a century ago—and thus shares too little of the same language let alone premises to easily find common ground—I would extend to her signs of compassion to show that I see, heard and respect her.

Perhaps I reasoned, *if she feels I care about her, she might care enough to listen to and respect me, too.* To have those signs come from the heart, however, I knew I would have to expand my capacity to value her as she is, despite myriad affronts that have separated us for decades.

And, I would have to expand my ability to overcome my base instincts to chase what I thought my Self wanted most: Instead of thinking about what I could get, I had to meditate on what I could give—a much more exacting, and at least at first exhausting, exercise. In terms of that opening diagram a friend had helped me lay out, I would have to REVERSE DIRECTION, to point the arrows indicating flow of movement from desired concessions *to* me, to point from my Self as I extended care and concern *from* me *into* specified acts of compassion. To tailor my attempts to show genuine compassion, I would have to expand that germ of initial *"agape"* to fit the intended receiver: Instead of flinging "any ol' nicety" someone's direction, in order to realize—literally, "to make real"—in the world what I was trying to achieve, by definition I would have to handcraft *each* act of compassion to reflect The Other whom I was placing before my Self. [For those whom it would assist to "see" what I mean, the revised paradigm would look like this:]

How deadlock can be broken:

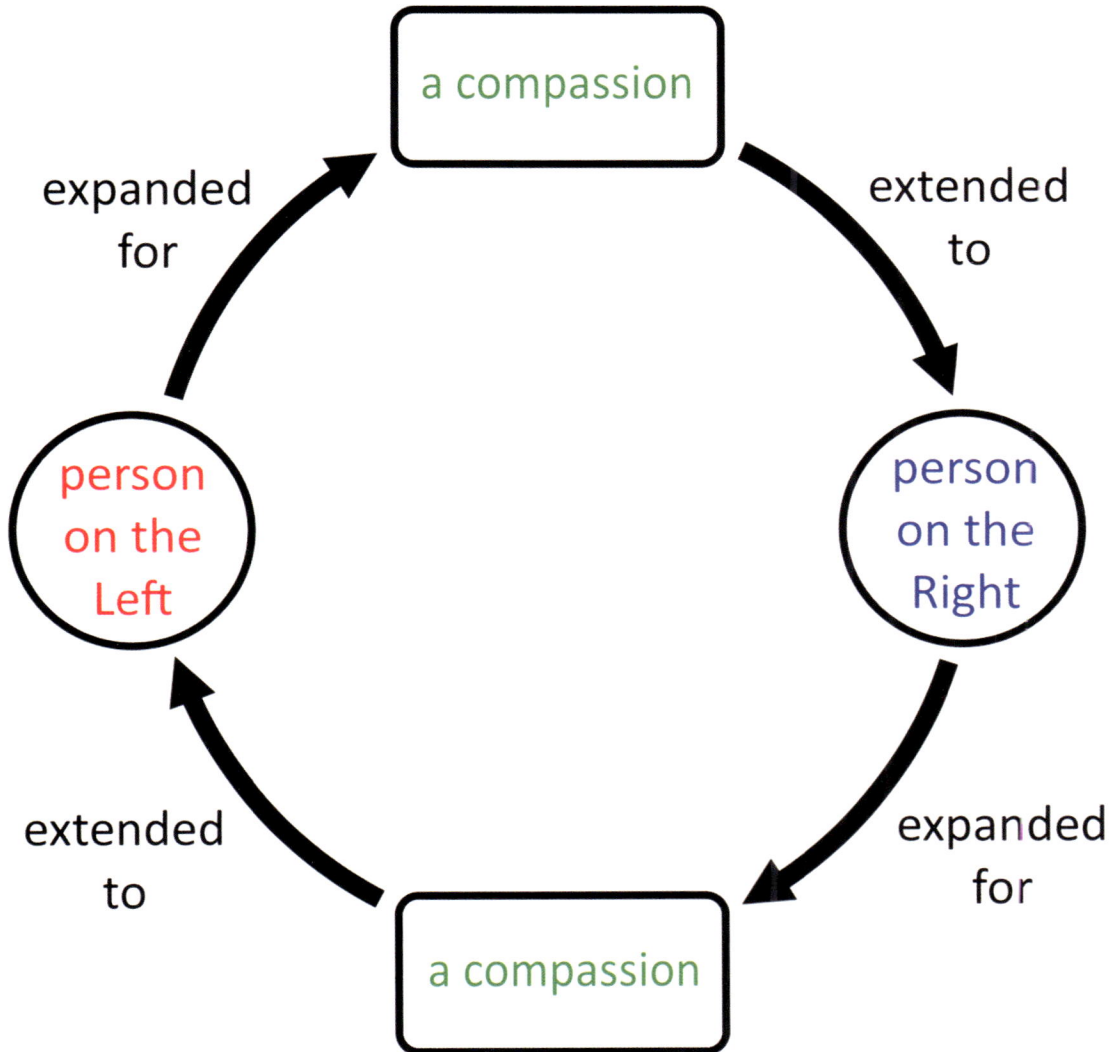

As for Lucy and me unlocking deadlock, it looked like this:

When our appointed time to talk came, I felt as if I was venturing into a Terra Nova of the heart. I eased us into conversation by expressing gratitude that we could "talk about things that have gone unsaid for many years, yet continue to separate us, one from another." After asking Lucy if she wished to air lingering issues first, I swallowed hard, took a deep breath, then waded in:

"Look, we've been estranged for decades. All that time, there have been some things that I never felt emotionally safe enough to share with you, yet which have led me not only ta avoid you, but also to judge ya severely. Now, I must come clean with you or we will *never* reconcile."

Taking the silence on the line as Lucy's willingness to listen, I forged on. "When you an' Linus were freshly off the farm and out on your own, you two told us of your having been 'born again'—despite our family havin' not raised us that way." I paused for a reaction.

Then, slowly, one came: "Yes-s-s" Lucy haltingly responded, softly and breathily, "and?"

"That was you two's choice, but when each of ya came ta me, separately, an' said that my parents were not 'real Christians' I was not only floored, but appalled." As I felt my pulse spike and my palms began to sweat, I noted "Even as I speak about this, years later, I feel *so* deeply angry, utterly outraged that you two would say such a thing about other Christians—an' that about their own flesh and blood!" Silence. "For me" I pushed on, "that is *such* an offensive thing to say, let alone even think. You were young, barely off into the world: How could *you* so judge *them*?"

"I do *not* recall havin' ever said that" Lucy replied dryly. "I jus' don't, Mike." She sighed, peeved.

Never have I known Lucy—or Linus—to lie, neither as kids nor now. But then, I cannot remember having ever lied to them, either. So, when Lucy said she could not recall this trespass which I had found so grievous, for so long, I believed her. What she likely didn't realize, however, was the very things in my announcement about Nicole's appearance that had so upset my closest relatives—reminisces of mine I referenced about their and my troubled relationship—were "true," but events they apparently could not remember. If they did, perhaps it was not that I had lied that had offended them, but that I had called them out publicly for real, historical offenses.

"I believe ya" I conceded, "but that doesn't change that I remember it too well, as it shook me ta my core. For you it seemed 'normal' to pass such judgment—at least for the person ya were then—but for me you both crossed a line after which I felt I could not trust either one of ya. I mean, Mom taught Sunday school for years an' Dad ushered at church after they quit farmin', so for ya ta decide that they weren't worthy of the label 'Christian'—well, I *never* forgave you."

"I see" was all that Lucy responded. More than that she did not say—so I conceded more:

"I'm sure there were many things I did in the past that seemed 'normal' for me, but irked or insulted you two, too, but I likely have long forgotten as havin' seemed so trivial an' everyday."

Remarkably, Lucy remained calm, repeating that she could not remember any of this. Her serenity allowed a great weight—after so many decades—to lightly lift from me and float away. I appreciated her ability to so react, yet had not expected it; I felt gratified that we had both grown. It had been my conviction for years that we were not able to hold such a conversation: That kept me a "stalled train," determined to move forward on my own steam, yet unable to.

Why'd we wait so long ta do this I puzzled, *cuz it mighta helped her, too, ta work through this.* Still in the midst of massive sorting, I felt a need to return to our conversation, to own also this:

"If ya were so willing ta condemn our parents, then I was sure you'd damn me, too—not only about not being 'born again' but, later, for bein' gay. For me, you dividing not only the world but even Christendom between 'good' an' 'bad' people seemed like a kind of ideological *Apartheid*, an elitist attitude. That's jus' *not* the way I see things or a world I wanna live in. If ya think there's only 'born-agains' an' everyone else, those not as worthy—well, *no* thanks."

"We are *all* sinners, Mike—we *all* sin" Lucy repeated, earnestly. Here, I sniffed smoke from previous crash-and-burn attempts to resolve that which had kept us separated for so long. Then, she noted "My religion is precious to me, so I don't want anybody tryin' ta tear it apart."

"I can understand that" I conceded, "I get it. Quakerism's important to me, too." As I thought I could sense her discomfort with what she earlier had dismissed as "pagan," I added "We both value spirituality," even as I quickly sought a less-loaded translation for a New-Age-esque word.

"We *all* fall down in God's eyes" Lucy repeated, "we *all* sin." I did not value Lucy's wording, yet I could accept that worldview as her belief—and move on, having stated my emotional distrust.

One, down I thought, nervously, *jus' another zillion ta go!* Feeling the way open, I proceeded.

"Ya know, there's sompthin' else I need ta get off my chest." Again, silence. "Like with my not trusting you to accept my choices for myself—I mean, you an' Linus both said 'Quakers are a cult' when I became one—so I felt I could not trust you to embrace my friends or people I love."

"We *always* welcomed your friends or people you brought to—"

"That's *not* true" I interrupted. "Do you not remember telling me in your living room in Charles City, when I was in high school, that I shouldn't be friends with Cong Cam Li?" I demanded.

"I don't even know who that is" Lucy tsk-tsked. "How can you be upset over someone I don't—"

"That 'someone' was the Laotian-refugee boy I befriended, along with his uprooted family."

"I don't know what you're talkin' about" she insisted. "What does this have to do with—"

What's most important here I grilled myself, *that she concede she was unfair to Cong—an' ta me—or ta tell her what her words meant to me an' our relationship?* Deciding quickly, I spoke:

"It has to do with you warning me that someone close to me was a 'heathen' so would 'never be able to enter the kingdom of god,' that someone I deeply cared about was of lesser value—"

"Well" Lucy protested, "if that really happened, it was years ago, so—"

"—so for *years* I have not trusted you to accept my friends, nor me, for who and what we are. I can't even answer simple questions at family get-togethers without ya pouncin' on me."

"Whatever are ya talkin' about?" Lucy asked, genuinely perplexed. "Whaddaya mean, Mike?"

"You may not remember, but ya made a comment a couple years ago that showed there are important things about our world you don't know—fair enough, we can't all know everything—but it's difficult for me to accept, that you seem not ta even care that ya don't know such things."

"Like *what*?" she quizzed.

"Well, as I recall" I stalled, "at the July Fourth picnic at your house the summer I ran for Senate, Jared asked while we all ate what I'd been doin' in Germany." I waited: No response. Even as I continued, I marveled that we were having this conversation. "When I replied 'Workin' mostly with refugees' you winced an' asked 'With Muslims?'—but I could tell you were *not* pleased."

"Ok" Lucy prompted when I hesitated before pushing on leveling a rough shared past, "so-o-o?"

"When I answered 'Yes, with people who share the same god as Jews an' Christians' you spit back 'That's *not* true—they worship a different god! Who is it, again—Buddha or sompthin'?' I didn't say anything, but I could *not* believe ya didn't know this basic Western religious history."

"*Ah-h-h*" Lucy punted, "everybody knows that—but" her voice grew louder and bolder, her words faster as she blurted out "Muslims wanna convert us, by force if necessary—an' if they can't succeed, they're ready ta kill us!" I stared at the receiver blankly. "That's the truth, Mike. It is!"

Should I really challenge her on this? I wrestled with my own judgment. Not wanting to skid off track, I merely noted gently and shyly "The statistical, verifiable truth is, the majority of victims of ISIS or the Taliban are their fellow Muslims—but that's *not* the point." Desperate to sustain our open, peaceable exchange, I didn't verbalize wondering *Do you even know a single Muslim?*

"Well, then" Lucy sputtered, unaware I had just avoided our derailment, "what *is* the point?"

"I have felt for decades that there was no room in your world for me to simply be who I am. The world I move in, every day, is a totally different one from yours. I not only don't fear that world, I actually *like* it an' feel energized by it. I can't imagine living among only people like myself."

Just as Bug mostly succeeds in keeping her daily realm tight enough to avoid encountering the Trumpites of the world, Lucy—sewn from a totally different cloth—does the same as my ol' friend, but avoiding those who abhor a man who she has adored enough to pitch to all.

Aware that Lucy was struggling to imagine feeling not fearful of difference but rather enriched by it, I extended to her a chance to shift focus from what she is or not able to do comfortably, to "I'm here, in all my color an' complexity. All I want now is to live out who I feel I am."

When the line went cold, I knew we had reached the limit of my phone partner's ability to expand her Self—at least for the moment. As I waited Lucy said not a word but neither did she hang up. Perhaps sensing the unusual care with which I was approaching this conversation, she held on.

"Ya there?" I quietly queried, some anxious moments later.

A few seconds passed, then she echoed serenely "Ya, I'm here."

"Go-good" I stuttered, "as there's more."

"Oh" I vaguely heard Lucy whisper faintly to herself, "even more."

"Earlier this year you referred to my 'choosing a homosexual lifestyle' but I wanna tell ya once an' forever, no one *chooses* to be gay—did you ever 'choose' to be hetero?—but a person *does* choose to be honest or not about being gay. It is who we *are*, not something we have decided."

Silence.

"An' this has been one of the biggest barriers between us, for eons. I can't understand why, even if you don't approve, you refuse to simply believe me when I tell you what *my* experience is, but instead tell *me* what it has been—what *I* have thought or felt. It is, after all, *my* life, so—"

"*I* know that" Lucy snapped.

"—if you can't celebrate it, at least let it simply be, without negating *it*—'cuz when you do, you negate *me*." Having a pregnant moment, I thought back to say "Your attitude about my being gay has hurt me deeply, for years. Do you remember having warned Jared that I'd seduce him?"

As I feared our trains were about to collide, she replied "What?! I *never* did no such thing—"

"You *did*" I retorted, "jus' ask 'im—I did, in March in the Cities, when we met for lunch at the Swedish Institute. He recalls it clearly, as do I." With her consent, I recounted the ugly incident:

When Lucy's oldest son was studying at the University of Iowa to become a social-studies teacher and coach, she called Jared one day to warn "I heard Mike's comin' ta Iowa City tomorrow ta have lunch. Ya better be careful, 'cuz he'll try ta seduce you!" The next day, when he confided that to me, I felt **sad** and **bad**—but nothing like how **mad** I felt when I realized the double standard: What if Lucy's then-living husband, Gerry, planned to call upon one of his two nieces—Linus' daughters, Dena or Paige—for lunch between their college classes?

"What would've been the chances" I asked Lucy at that point, "that Cherry might've called either girl an' warned them 'Be careful—'cuz your Uncle Gerry's gonna try ta seduce ya!' Zero, I'd guess—even though in my case there was absolutely *no* indication that I had *ever* or would ever instigate inappropriate physical contact with your sons—each of whom who I truly treasured."

Again, silence—but this time the pained awkwardness between us seemed to have become palpable. Lucy's breath turned heavy and hollow, while mine accelerated and grew shallow.

"Don't you remember, that any time I visited you, an' Jared, Ian or Jamin invited me into their rooms ta show me a new game or have me read a book to them, you'd always come, check on us, then leave the door purposely blocked open? How do you think that made me feel?" Silence.

Finally, Lucy spoke: "Of course I'd protect the most important things in my life—that's what a mother *does*. I will never let *any* one or thing hurt my family, if I could help it. You were having sex with men, Mike—so of course I'd shield my sons from you! Wouldn't *every* mother?"

We've never, EVER spoken about sex! Strange, but I don't feel the earth shaking beneath me!

"That's all fine" I adlibbed, "but don't ya see, in your eyes I was always guilty until never proven innocent—not just a second-class citizen, but a third-class person? I'd done *nothing* wrong, yet I was eternally convicted despite having *never* committed a crime; I was a convict *never* capable of penance or rehabilitation. Because of what you judged ta be my sinful, 'unrepentant' nature, for you I was forever a menace at large. *Your* big problem, with *my* sexuality, hurt *me* unfairly."

I liked little of what Lucy had said, but at least she had said it. For almost forty years she had avoided this conversation, although I had sought it repeatedly. *Why is she willing to go here now?* I wondered, then shrugged *but better late than never, huh?* On a roll, Lucy then added:

"Look, the past is passed—it's over. It's time ta jus' move on an' deal with what's in front of us."

"As a historian" I murmured, "I see things a bit differently." Still, I felt relieved when Lucy bid:

"Going forward, can we let the past go? You've made your choices an' I've made mine. Can we agree on that?" The offer of the peaceful co-existence I that had sought for years left me stunned.

In the silence that ensued, I realized that by this point Lucy and I both knew we weren't going to change the other. At the same time, at least our mostly pacific conversation proved that we, who come from opposing worldviews, don't have to "hate" each other; instead, we can agree to disagree *and* be civil about it. Before this, I had not hated her, but I also had felt little love. Now, though, with so much that is dark cleared from between us, I felt as if real love might grow. That gave me hope that our decades-old stalemate might be surmountable. As such, for the first time in a long time, I felt encouraged and excited about our chances of future shared harmony— including at the graveside, as we soon put Phyllis Ann (née Thrams) Luick to her eternal rest.

Suddenly, Lucy pierced my faraway contemplation and asked on the phone "Ya still there?"

Realizing that her overture had not been rhetorical but actual—and she was awaiting an answer—I stammered "Su-sure, great—agreed." We had at long-last reached a resolution, but only after an exhausting emotional dance, so the rebuilding would have to start another day.

me (left) on my father's lap at Christmas 1965, with my siblings, on Ashlawn Farm

By now depleted, I wondered *Who needs a Teddy bear most, tired me or sorely-tried her?*

*

"Everyone can do *something*, and if not, we can do something together
—and if we aren't together, then we need to find ways to come together."

— former community-college English instructor
and proofreader of this tome Gerry Schwarz,
during a working-breakfast critique in a
Decorah, Iowa, café on 18 July 2019

Think Outside Boxes

So much of our daily life, of our existence hour-to-hour, we don't even see them anymore, but in fact our world has become clogged with boxes. To break free from them and move forward,

13) think outside boxes.

How? Well, begin to see "boxes" in totally new ways. For starters:

Ever notice that there are *no* straight lines in nature? This truth might seem banal, but it is *not*…

The closest exception to this would be the creations of bees and spiders, but the structure comprising honeycomb is neither perfectly straight nor exactly uniform, and spiderwebs form straight lines if tautly stretched between two points—and then only briefly.

Solely the domesticated animal *homo sapien*s creates and lives within plane or "perfectly"-round lines—*why*?[158] (But then, "Why *not*?") Whatever the explanation, this phenomenon is pivotal.

It has been humans' ability to demarcate Earth along lines that has allowed us to create new and different—albeit "*un*-natural"—worlds: fields and farms, cities, ships, factories, prisons… anything we could imagine, from piano keys to scalpels, salad bars to computer screens… and everything needed to execute self-contained or self-generating projects, from railroad lines for crossing continents to rocket launchers for shooting for the stars. Still, we are not "*so*" special:

> First of all, humans are not the first species ever to transform the planet into a polluted hellhole. That honor belongs to cyanobacteria, blue green algae that evolved about 3.5 billion years ago and promptly began to fill the methane-based atmosphere with oxygen […] a byproduct of a new energy-making system that cyano had developed. We call it photosynthesis—it's the way all plants today make energy out of light and water. At the time, however, all the life forms on the planet had evolved to live in a methane-rich environment. As the cyano filled Earth's atmosphere with oxygen, their nasty byproduct attenuated the methane, killing off pretty much all the other life forms around them. We may love our nicely oxygenated air today, but at the time it was an apocalypse. It's also evidence that humans aren't the only species ever to change the atmosphere with a new form of energy production.

While other animals—as author Annalee Newitz points out[159]—might also use tools (e.g., chimps, crows, dolphins, sea otters) or alter their environments (beavers, ants), only we alone make tools capable of making *new* tools, or can decide to stop changing the environment in fatal ways.

On the plus side, we are the only animals to have created written languages.[160] And, being the sole layers of straight lines in our known galaxy has had both positive and negative consequences, for as Buddhist friends remind us, "a great strength is concurrently also a great weakness." Lines enable us to build increasingly complex boxes, which has liberated humankind from some scourges: plagues, hunger, ignorance, isolation. At the same time, the learned ability to construct—mathematically speaking—"perfect" boxes marked a leap in human evolution. With it, we sprang from living predominantly in re-action *to*, to increasingly taking action *over* Creation. Meanwhile, to some degrees, our boxes have enslaved us—to "diseases of affluence," debt, mental myopia and new kinds of isolation, e.g. internet addiction. Furthermore, this ability has revolutionized both how we create physical environments and how we destroy climatic ones.

Before mechanization, for hundreds of thousands of years *every* tangible thing created by humans was made by hand—almost always in single or at least small batches. Just before the dawn of industrialization, a couple hundred years ago, each glass bottle was blown individually, each shoe cobbled from scratch; each piece of clothing or furniture left its makers' hands as what Germans call a "*Unikat,*" a thing that is singular—in vernacular English "a one of a kind." While human manufacturing[161] took much longer than it does today, much of what was produced could count in our contemporary world as "art"—or at least "artful." Visit a museum displaying pre-industrial examples of those cited items and see that also handcrafted plates, toys, books, carriages and many more "everyday" objects can still delight the modern eye. Often, it is their "imperfection" that so impresses or endears us. In sobering contrast, trek to GAP, IKEA or an Apple computer-outlet store and try to find wares that truly warm the heart or calm the mind like woven wool or a piece, worn wood or weathered metal.

Again mindful of Buddhist wisdom, just as mass production allowed humans to increase the speed and output of generating "stuff," it also changed our relationship to that being generated. Clothes lost their specialness when instead of fitting a measured body fully comfortably and per the wearer's own desired design, they morphed into mass-produced ready-to-wear wares from some sweatshop. Not only do they often not sit well on one's particular curves or bodily terrains, they don't sit well on an aware person's conscience, knowing that purchasing such products supports and perpetuates unfair wages and, too often, unhealthy working conditions. But, our bodies have not only been shoehorned into having to wear box-generated clothes,[162] sold in big-box stores; our bodies are moved through space and time also in boxes. Trains are nothing more than boxes bolted onto wheeled platforms, elevators mirrored boxes lifted by cables, cars windowed boxes on rubber tires, airplanes round tin boxes catapulted through the air by explosions captured in boxed-in engines... And, our bodies are stuffed full of "food" produced in boxes—tragically, today typically without windows or sunshine: massive hog-confinement buildings and torture-chamber chicken plants. Our "fresh" vegetables and even fruit are grown not in soil but in water-filled boxes, then shipped zillions of kilometers around the globe in chilled boxes, at great cost and devouring much energy.

Such systems of production generate goods at rates and prices mostly agreeable to producers and consumers alike—but at an unsustainably high level of environmental impact. There is one cost of modern systems by which humans organize our current ways of living that is often less visible, yet deadly. In 2018, I spent two months in Peru: During my sojourn there, I had several occasions to fly over much of South America between São Paulo and Bogotá.

On one flight, as a rowdy Brazilian soccer team noisily celebrated a recent victory, I quietly looked out the window over southwest Brazil, Paraguay and Bolivia, and studied the endless jungle below. Until, that is, it abruptly ended. Even from up at some ten-thousand meters, I could see strange distant clearings, each a vast rectangle separated by a thin strip of intact jungle. A swath cut through the length of them, whereby vehicles pass from one enormous patch to the next. On the periphery of each glade stood a cluster of closed-box buildings, each seeming to be the size of a soccer field. A former Iowa farmboy, I knew immediately what all of this was: bulldozed jungles converted to soybean or corn fields, with their yields going directly to feed zillions of cattle, pigs, chickens, turkeys, etc. in batteries of dusty meat factories. Some of this converted protein might find its way to Latin American markets, but most of it goes to China.

True to our human "nature," we are clearing primal, oxygen-generating jungles to erect angular wastelands-waiting-to-happen. For a few years, the land being cleared will produce crops, but which then can only be sustained by artificial, petroleum-based inputs—fertilizer, herbicides and pesticides—not to mention seas of diesel and gas to fuel the equipment that keeps such facilities running. Again, we humans are doing what we've been doing for the last couple hundred years on a vast scale: We destroy a lineless environment, impose upon it lineated ideas of "civilization," then poorly manage it until the project turns into a nightmare of destruction on grand scales.

Self-sabotaging folly is not the sole domain of eager capitalists: The Soviet Union and its Eastern-European allies were manic masters of environmental degradation—to the point of even reversing the flow of rivers. (We Americans can't wag fingers: The Chicago River flows into the Mississippi today, not into Lake Michigan, as it once did.) Ever heard of the Aral Sea? It is now a dessert, reduced to ten percent of its 1960s size, when it was the world's fourth largest lake. It was sucked dry to irrigate endless cotton fields—for a few years, anyway. Now they, too, are barren and useless. Still, despite such glaring failures to "improve upon nature," such gigantic mistakes in how humans try to force the Earth to yield what it otherwise would not surrender on its own continue to be made. They are examples of "violence" as I defined it earlier in this work.

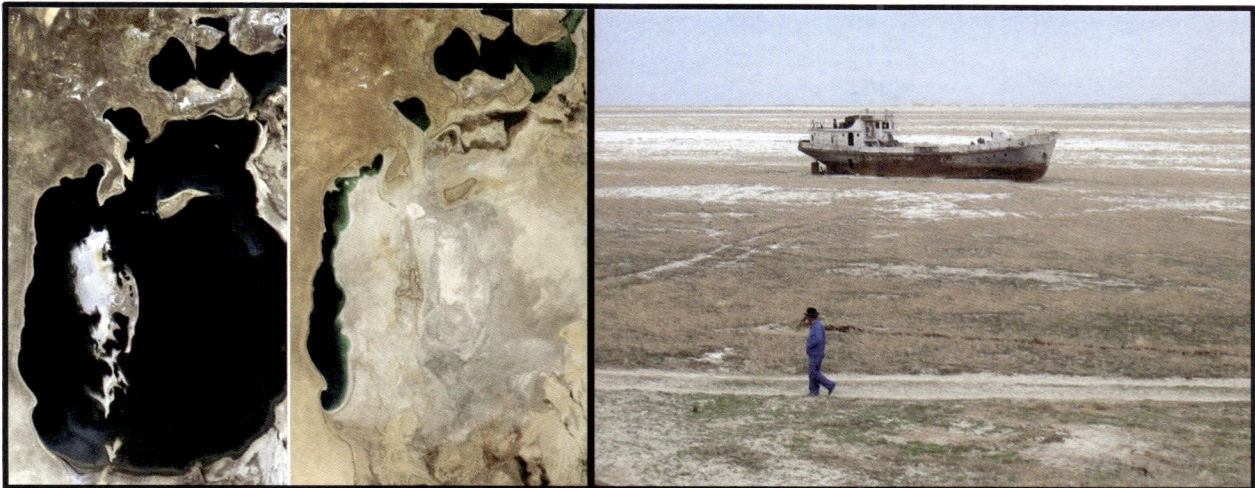

a comparison of the Aral Sea in 1989 (left) and 2014; a ship on the former Aral Sea in Kazakhstan, 2003

This "box mentality"—thinking in terms of right angles in a world where none occur naturally—is destroying not only the physical but also our socio-political world. It is sabotaging our relationships not only with mother Earth, but with our earthly mothers... with our siblings... and neighbors, colleagues, classmates... with *everybody*. Let me explain, as this dynamic is core to my thirteenth strategy for ending our current social stalemate, by learning to **think new thoughts in order to create new solutions**: Human existence as been evolving along certain trajectories for at least ten-thousand years, since we first learned to domesticate plants. If, having at long-last realized the deadly consequences of industrialization, we do not stop <u>now</u> doing what we have "always" done, we not only will always get what we always got, but we will stop doing anything at all. Over time, our clever, unique abilities to alter our environment have altered us: We cannot reverse our environmental emergency now, without radically altering our essential Selves again, but this time consciously. For individuals to change, however, we must also change society: We have to reinvent social bonds, and evolve beyond chronic social stalemate and political deadlock.

To understand the scope of this project, we have to grasp how deep inside us the problems lie. And, we have to take a long view of animal evolution—as Annelee Newitz has so adeptly done:

> Just as agriculture and a sedentary life have changed the genomes of dogs, cows, sheep and chickens, they have also changed ours. [...] But what else would we be? Are we exempt from the same forces that have changed our fellow animals on farms and in cities? Does a sedentary, domestic life behind walls exert evolutionary pressures on sheep and pigs, but not on humans? If you accept the precepts of evolutionary theory, where environmental pressures drive natural selection, obviously not. Environments are environments, regardless of whether we built them or not.

An "environment," though, does not consist only of what grows in jungles or on prairies, but what happens in schools or churches: Our social environment changes and evolves over time, just as our physical one does. And, both kinds of environments are forever altered by the things we create squared with the actions we take. Just as we, in all our hubristic stupidity and arrogant blindness, have tried to level mountains and sprinkle water over deserts and reverse rivers' flow, we also have tried to engineer social environments. We have tried to force black Americans into the backs of buses, where they never wanted to go, young Iraqi men to confess information about "yellow cake" that never was, and Uyghurs into being good Han Chinese, which they never can become. For even longer, we have abused, even burned women as "witches" to stem a sorcery which never is; we have hooked gay men up to machines and sent shocks through their brains, trying to make them desire women's bodies—which *never* works. We have tried to silence and warp our fellow humans; we have tortured and killed, trying to force our own kind to become or to do something not in their natures. Were we to abuse dogs or horses in the same way, in this social-media age the outcry would be instantaneous and ferocious—yet the US' torturing thousands of Muslims around the world during the Iraq War scarcely drew a word. We Americans spend some $30 billion annually on pet food[163] but how much do we give to feed starving people?

All along, this current, debilitating deadlock that leaves entire countries lame is also un-*natural*, for human beings are, by *nature*, social animals. We not only long for but *need* each other: The longer we allow our present, pervasive alienation from each other to continue, the sicker we will become—becoming, at some point, incurable? A social collapse is as deadly as an ecological one!

Values and behavior often drive each other: Humans behave a certain way in pursuit of what we think we value; we value what we do in large part due to behaviors absorbed by us from those inhabiting our social environment. As humans discovered how to make more things, faster, things began to overtake people as the focus of our lives: Becoming ever more self-reliant by utilizing things, we grew increasingly independent of relying on fellow humans to meet basic needs, even as we became indelibly dependent on material solutions to fulfill existential requisites.

Lured by the allure of objects, we also seem to have become ever less smitten with their makers or stewards. Today, then, we might wander into an antique shop, pick up a handcrafted jewelry box and marvel at its unique beauty, yet fail to recognize the inner gems hidden and—to our hungry, restless eyes—apparently dormant in the person behind the counter who handed us that preindustrial treasure to explore. We demand instant service as customers, yet so rarely really *see* those sent to satiate our whims; they become mere means to ends, rather than whole and sovereign people in their own rights. We can easily do this—but just as easily be invisible, too.

Especially (but not only) under capitalism, we have learned to value property and profits over people when, in reality, to survive we must return to the opposite, to earlier relationship models: We cannot eat gold coins, but we *can* help each other to grow abundant crops, to the benefit of all. To remember how to work together to achieve shared goals, however, we will have to un-learn core, deeply ingrained reflexes that erode our social landscape—interaction by minute, seemingly banal interaction. Behaviors that we adopted as we evolved in response to changing environments have come to seem "natural," but now we must leave them—and the systems that both shaped and depended on them; we must repurpose the people who we have been till now.

Do we moderns now see the whole world mostly in terms of "new" or "better?" If so, few things—and few people—have lasting, intrinsic value. Cell phones, for one, evolve rapidly over time, but just as quickly last year's model is discarded and forgotten, in ways that a handmade dress or handblown vase are not. IKEA's box-borne furniture, for another, might seem chic this season, but by the next season do we not already covetously thumb through its glossy catalog and dream of running our fingers over the next generation of furniture spewed from distant factories?

In such a transitory material environment, we can hardly help but to start seeing other human beings (not to mention fellow animals such as caged chickens, confinement-raised hogs, feedlot cattle) also as transitory, as "interchangeable."[164] Added to the fleeting relationship we have to our clothes, furniture, "food" and other pillars of physical culture, we modern humans are further, even more subtly conditioned by changes in the digital environments we create anew, daily. Whether on Facebook or Grindr, we begin to flip through faces and body parts as if they were wares in an online catalog—with even the logo of the latter being a featureless mask. In such a social environment, people lose their humanity, even as they gain in their ability to seemingly get in our way, to slow us down, to complicate our lives with their particularities and problems. (It is no coincidence that most men on Grindr seem hesitant to know their prey's name.) Even others' values seem to be an added burden: When we quickly realize—with the same rapidity that we have perfected as we search online, to eliminate "wares" even faster than we can think—that a given person seems not to share our exact same social or political values, we reflexively lapse into defense mode. Our genetically derived impulse to connect gets trumped by our contemporary reflex to "delete." This, we must resist, then replace with new social reflexes. We must rise above the ideological lines we have drawn and stop putting perceived "opponents" in boxes, from which they scarcely can emerge. In short, we have to embrace The Other, even as we embrace our deeper, timeless Selves:

> We have to tap our souls more, our cell phone screens or computer keys less.

*

Learn to "Dance" Together—Again

Socially, there are myriad peculiarities in all societies that distinguish each one from all others on the planet: In short, at first glance, there is so much of learned human behavior that divides us.

Culturally, there are a handful of universal core phenomena in human existence which unite us. *Every* culture—there have been hundreds of thousands over the millennia—has had some form of: language, familial patterns, social hierarchies, hygiene, a cuisine, religion, music and dance.[165]

9,000-year-old paintings of dancers in India; Greek bronze statuette of a dancer, 3rd–2nd century BCE

Given its indelible importance not only in a human but also social life, I include it here as strategy

14) learn to "dance" together—again.

What exactly is "dance"—and what is so significant about it as an expression of being human? How can various dance forms connect us to or, conversely, isolate us from one another, socially?

According to Professor Pedia,

Dance is a performing art form consisting of **purposefully selected sequences of human movement** [*emphasis added*]. This movement has aesthetic and symbolic value, and is acknowledged as dance by performers and observers within a particular culture.

For eons, across continents and cultures, there have been five main "uses" of dance—as a means:

- for releasing tension in the body and thereby experiencing greater relaxation or pleasure
- for expressing individual or purportedly collective longings, fears, fantasies, life phases
- to come into closer contact with other human beings, often with an eye to sex or mating
- to mark cultural events, rituals or values: hunting, harvesting, warfare, piety, birth, death
- to put in physical form intangible social hierarchies, lines of power, norms or expectations

You don't need to be Professor Pedia, however, to recognize the importance of movin' your bod to the rhythm, alone or—even better—in tandem with other human beings! Just be aware that *with whom* you dance is as or even more important than *how* you dance. Let me explain:

For thousands of years, human beings danced primarily as duos or as a group; outside of seductive, usually private dancing (e.g., veil or belly), individuals dancing solo in public existed but was rare. In the rural Midwest, our earliest pioneers held barn, square, line and other group dances—for which the likes of my great-great-grandfather Louis Luick often fiddled. As of the cultural revolution of the 1960s, however, that changed—abruptly and radically: Only Iowa's last three generations have danced primarily "freestyle," *not* in tandem with one partner or in a preplanned group formation as is the norm in polkas, waltzes, the Charleston, swing, jitterbug...

Felt Boot Orchestra members, playing under a canvas; a felt-boot patent drawing, showing the footwear component for which Louis Lee Luick (center)—for whatever reason—named his by-the-bootstraps band

In pre-iPod, pre-radio, pre-gramophone days, not only did human beings make their own music, but they generated themselves forms of dance to express physically, with their bodies, what they did not find as easy to express verbally. As pre-industrial peoples were much more dependent on others for survival than post-industrial *homo sapiens*, most forms of dance reflected this earlier, inescapable interdependence: Most dance moves not only involved but *required* an Other.[166] In any case, such dance forms were primarily *about* the Other—to show one's attractiveness or availability; to seek a date, a mate or a marriageable fortune; to sow the seeds of a romance or simply one's oats. Like with modern art, however, modern dancing departed from adapting to existing norms and forms; instead, it became all about expressing one's projected, marketable Self. Forget working with others for everyone's pleasure or advancement: "Forget the whole!" Visual art as well as most public dancing became a solitary, at times lonely venture: "Damn the collective!" How well, then, can we moderns move in tandem with others when most of us do not know how to dance hand-in-hand or arm-in-arm with other human beings? We hardly can. If Professor Pedia is right, that "dance [is] purposefully selected sequences of human movements," then it seems many moderns are no longer able to purposely select social moves very effectively.

Now near the end of this tome, I think again of those Ukrainian kindergartners who so impressed me with their coordinated dancing back in the now-disappeared world that was the Soviet Union. I did not mean to glorify them, their beaming teacher or the system that created their obedient behavior, but I did take with me back to the West that summer of 1985 proof that a given system is neither inevitable nor the only one possible. We all now know what became of that precarious Soviet-style communist experiment—and how its ungraceful collapse mere years later left in its wake a couple generations of Eastern Europeans too often unable to thrive freely as individuals.

Take my Czech college students, 1991-93, as one example:

Working in small groups or per duo they produced mostly excellent results. When, however, I insisted the university-level students work alone, they quickly grew anxious, lost, then frustrated. Now, teaching in the former East Germany, even my current crop of university students exhibits some of the worst aspects of their grand-/parents' subservient socialization under Stalinism or the cynical nonsense that followed it. The "children" of communism can work much better with each other than my peers and I back on the prairie can, but alone they flounder and often fail.

At the same time, just as the worst of Soviet communism led to unsustainable extremes and fatal flaws, the worst of American capitalism has its own. While plenty under the Soviet system stank of spiritual gangrene, profit and property had little meaning for most citizens; relations between people were paramount—if nothing else, to survive day-to-day. Under America's current social-Darwinist system, we mine people for all they're worth in the pursuit of profit and amassing property. (Ever notice that the things Americans <u>need</u> most—healthy food, housing, medical care, transport, post-secondary education... basics down to hearing aids and razor blades—have been turned into industries dolling out overpriced products, while "non-essentials" in the United States are cheap and endless?) How might we invert our dominant cultural values, so that instead of predominantly loving things and using people, we might come to use things and love people?

At present, America's turbo capitalism feeds upon the most vulnerable among us, weakening our social bonds and eroding our humanness. Loving things and using people has shredded our social fabric and pulverized our moral fiber. Living in a country that acts more like a self-contained world, most of its inhabitants seem oblivious to the spreading social inequity and alienation among us; we largely seem blind to what such a merciless, rigged, dog-eat-dog system is doing to us, how it is warping our very souls. Other countries are not spared these destructive dynamics but they run rampant here, with little to mitigate their crassness. If the market will bear it, our entrepreneurs and legislators will swear by it. Especially in the fields of technology, media, music, films and pop culture, it seems anything goes. In German, one can "*lernen*" something, but one can also "*verlernen*" (to "unlearn") something one once knew: It seems to me that many of us in the West—above all our youth—have "unlearned" how to "dance" well with others. Many of us are ruthless in pursuing what we think we want—even as our whims shift like breezes. Woe to anyone who gets in our way—and by the way, it's *our* way or the highway! So programmed, we quickly become unwilling or even no longer able to compromise, to concede something to the Other. In social settings, be they in a group or in 1-on-1 relationships, we often flounder and fail.

Take my daughter, for example:

Nicole—who a month ago turned 35—sought me out as she was seeking her roots. Being a child of donor-conception, genetics played a central role in her search. On one level, the tangible (genes, cells, faces) trumped the intangible aspects of "family"—bonds that arise from intimate contact, an abiding tolerance for differences or "flaws," borne out of a sense of belonging… love. Reduced to being "related" due to biological rather than emotional ties, our coming together was fatally challenged before we ever met: Ultimately, we both failed to fully embrace the "Other."

For her part, it appears Nicole went looking for roots, but without really knowing how to connect once one is found or even how to successfully create a relationship. She seemed frenetic in her searching, yet in her finding her drive disappeared when her focus faded: Her earlier conviction cooled into caution. For my part, I found it odd that early on—perhaps the first or second day of daily phone calls, email or WhatsApp exchanges—Nicole offered me a disclaimer, unprompted and out of context. After what to me seemed sincere, open and welcoming exchanges, she noted:

"Michael, don't take it personally, but if we meet in Iowa in March as we're talkin' about doin' an' find we're not 'it,' I have no problem jus' walkin' away. I won't resent you or anything like that, but I'm capable of jus' walkin' away if it doesn't 'click' between us. I want ya ta know that."

Stunned by this left-fielder, when I finally found words I queried "*Ah-h-h*, why do you say that?"

"I'm jus' sayin' now, before we ever meet, that I have *no* expectations—an' that you're under *no* obligation ta stick this out—if we get the sense that a longer connection jus' isn't happ'nin'."

"Oka*y-y-y*" I sighed, "I'm hearing you say this—but that scenario hasn't crossed my mind—"

Yet, obviously, it had hers, for ten weeks later Nicole boarded a plane in Chicago bound for a ten-day father-daughter road trip from North Carolina to Washington, DC and back that... never happened. The seat next to her on that Delta flight was either empty or occupied by a stranger—per Nicole's choice. Of course, there are backstories here—one and a half lifetimes of them!

I experienced my daughter to be a devoted mother: She told me several times she literally would die for her sons—and I believed her unequivocally. They are, truly, what gives her life meaning. Still, as I remember her telling of her biography, Nicole gave birth to her first baby when she was a child of sixteen. My five grandsons came from four different fathers; other non-siring boyfriends came and went. Her current partner is ten years younger than she—eight years older than her oldest living son. Nicole has had a series of surnames; when she mentioned once taking mine I counseled her to be judicious, to "try this relationship on for a while" before taking such a step.

I am not casting stones here, for my daughter's glass house resembles my own too closely for me to easily do that. I am, however, illustrating that just as before we ever met she expressed a clear, unmistakable readiness to "hit the road," it seems her *curriculum vitae* has been full of walking out. On several occasions, she lamented to me having but one friend—and having been alienated from her for several years. It broke my heart to hear my own flesh-and-blood recite a list of woes: feeling lonely, depressed, adrift; not being eager to live once her sons grow up and leave home...

Many of the Nicoles of her generation seem to take that easy-come, easy-go attitude regarding intimate relationships into their workaday ones: This Nicole has a history of crash-and-burn jobs that typically left her—not just her bosses—frustrated and angry. Temperamental and a loner, she has driven ambulances, welded, repaired machines, built houses... anything until the latest gig, too, leaves her burned out and leads her to walk out. In all that, where is the stability? Where is the ability to change anything, to stay with a person or a thing long enough to build a base upon which to grow something real, rich and sustaining? Where is the consistency her sons need to learn to trust the adults, especially the men in their lives? Will her misery just be passed on?

This rant is not about my daughter but about the essentially-single mothers of her generation who are raising children, particularly boys, who will have known no lasting bonds with the very role models they *need* to become adjusted, productive men and women. Like their mothers, will such children grow up to be too individualistic and welded to their own ideas of how they think a gig should go down—unable to listen to others without feeling offended by differing opinions? Will they be too busy doing their own, isolated and transitory thing to accomplish much of real greatness as adult individuals, let alone as part of any group? Will they ever learn how to "dance" with others—or only know how to run? What will they lose by not being able to stay in one place, with one person or project long enough to let relating to another person expand their soul?

My great-great-grandfather, Louis Lee Luick, "recruited" his children to be in a "family band," including: Curtis (with violin), Henry, Ethel, George, Mary (née Hunt), Albert and drummer Charles; circa 1896.

Truthfully, I do not have pat answers to such probing questions. I can only surmise—based on my difficult experiences with the one child of mine I have met to date—that such unanchored souls will continue to drift over the land, randomly searching for strands of meaning to weave into their vacuous, amorphous inner landscapes. As they do, how can they do anything other than leave wide swaths of emotional destruction behind them? Who will clean it all up—how?

Ironically, as she was establishing contact with me, Nicole began hammering together a family tree. Although she wrote in her essay regarding genealogy, that she "didn't even know the first thing about it," when I offered to send her an electronic copy of my tree, thoroughly documented back to the 1490s in England, she seemed indifferent. Instead of keenly taking that of a Ph.D. historian, she continued to root about the emerging online data she was piecing together from various sources. So, while her words chimed "I am contacting you to find my ancestors" her actions screamed "I'm only interested in what I, myself, stumble upon." For a woman feverishly seeking the names and faces of those whose DNA she carries in her body, she casually brushed aside gold nuggets of findings: In the above photo alone are faces belonging to five ancestors inhabiting her tree—as explained here.[167]

I'm a big boy; I've chewed my way through disappointment before: I'll be ok. Still, I worry about our young people, for if they only know how to sprint far rather than saunter close when the going gets less than smooth, I fear they will miss much of what they are seeking: connection, realness, substance... love. In this case, because Nicole only knew how to go but not to stay, one Millennial went away empty-handed: In her rush out the door, she left behind some of the very treasures she said she sought. Unable to concede to me the grace of letting me be all the colorful complexities that I am, she kept expecting some Indefinable Thing from some Fantasy Father that she always wanted but who I never was. (For a while, soon after we met, she asked me if I'd like "to return home, live behind a white-picket fence and be near [my] grandsons"—and her. To find me a partner who'd make me happy and thus facilitate my fashioning domestic harmony not far from her, my daughter even started combing the gay pages of printed personal ads, as well as on-line profiles; she sent me several "likely candidates," along with leads on teaching-job offers at Central Iowa universities or colleges.) Instead of learning to dance together—to purposefully select sequences of emotional as well as physical movement that would have allowed both of us to draw closer to The Other, over time, symbiotically—we stayed stuck. Too welded to our own rigid ideas of how we thought this gig should go down and too unwilling to listen to each other without feeling offended by differing opinions, we remained busy doing our own, isolated thing— and thus failed to accomplish anything of real greatness as a duo. From the moment she sprung to her feet, announced she was leaving and fled out the door, we found ourselves in stubborn stalemate—and not yet recovered our earlier, promising, lovely connecting across continents.[168]

So, as with Lucy and Linus... as with the Democrats and Republicans, the Russians and the Americans, the rich and the poor, Boomers and Millennials... as with too many mortals currently populating our weary world, Nicole and I now find ourselves incomplete and sad—each wanting sorely to find acceptance and love from the other, yet through blindness and pride are unable or unwilling to concede compassion for The Other. Were we to crack the code to breaking through toxic ancient conditioning, how would that look? Well, it might look like this suggestion for

How deadlock can be prevented:

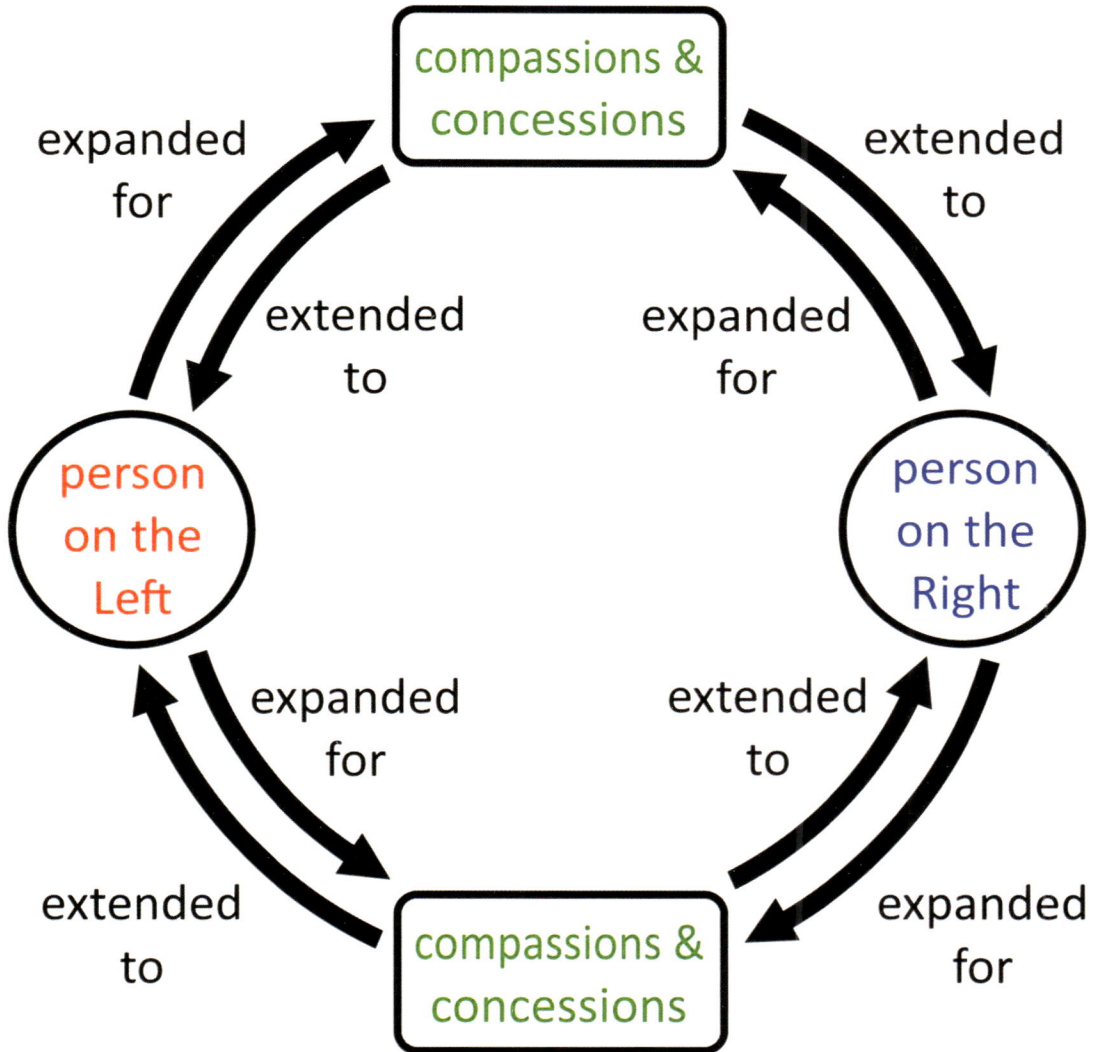

My heart so yearns for reconciliation with all other sentient beings with whom I share this assaulted planet—even as my head recognizes that the exact same wish is now more than that; it is now a requisite for survival. I *must* change, I *must* grow and become more loving, less guarded and petty—but, I am *not* alone: We must *all* evolve—and that in shortest time—*if* any of us wishes for our descendants to remember their closest ancestors with anything other than raw, searing contempt. As my Quaker-shrink hero, M. Scott Peck, reminded us in *The Different Drum*,

We know the rules of community; we know the healing effect of community in terms of individual lives. If we could somehow find a way across the bridge of our knowledge, would not these same rules have a healing effect upon our world? We human beings have often been referred to as social animals. But we are not yet community creatures. We are impelled to relate with each other for our survival. But we do not yet relate with the inclusivity, realism, self-awareness, vulnerability, commitment, openness, freedom, equality, and love of genuine community. It is clearly no longer enough to be simply social animals, babbling together at cocktail parties and brawling with each other in business and over boundaries. It is our task—our essential, central, crucial task—to transform ourselves from mere social creatures into community creatures. It is the only way that human evolution will be able to proceed.[169]

*

Celebrate Our Humanity

At present, with all that's going on in the world, isn't it easy to feel rather down on humanity? I mean, hundreds of thousands of years' evolution have led us to... *this*? Gimme a colossal break! It seems as if everything we had built, depended on and held dear is falling apart. We can't even come together enough as neighbor-citizens, let alone as political parties, to find common ground. Yes, the systems we had taken for granted are fraying: This is a crisis, even as it is an opportunity.

The German Federal Archives ("Bundesarchiv") caption reads "Berlin, refugees from the East Zone-1945." It is plausible that the woman on the right dressed as a man to evade being raped by Russian soldiers, or to distract from the other two, so that three unaccompanied women would not be in the open alone.

I live in the former German "Democratic" Republic. Most of the "*Ossis*" I live amongst have known at least three, some of them up to seven currencies! Representing sharply-contrasting systems— in some cases as many as more than a half-dozen—those competing ways of organizing a society have been: the *Weimarer Republik*, the Third Reich, US occupation (so, dollars or, rather, Hersey bars and Lucky Strikes), Soviet occupation followed by the Stalinist-puppet "GDR," then when it crumbled reunification with what at the time was the "Federal Republic of Germany," which—in turn—sacrificed its rock-solid *Deutsche Mark* (the bedrock for half a century of West Germany's *"Wirtschaftswunder,"* or "economic wonder") for the EU's Euro. And now, *voilà!*, we have a European Union under attack from far-Rightists within and Putin's sabotage from without, with its alley the United States ongoingly paralyzed by inter-partisan as well as intra-familial deadlock.

That's *only* Germany—not to mention once- or still-divided countries like Vietnam, Korea and the Sudan, or dreamed-of "Kurdistan," "Palestine" and other also-ran sovereign political entities. At the same time, some historical dinosaurs (e.g. a "United" Kingdom set to lose Scotland or Ulster, if not Wales) stumble around even as they slowly teeter, as history continues to untidily unfold. In such a chaotic era, the center cannot hold: We burrow deeper into our emotional bomb shelters, increasingly unable to face the daily social and physical beatings facing modern humans.

We do not know what tomorrow will bring—but I <u>do</u> know this: At least for the short-term future, whatever tomorrow brings, it will affect *homo sapiens*. For that reason and for the sake of social harmony—not to mention the survival of our species—I offer, for now, a last strategy for change:

15) celebrate being human.

"Why—for what?" you might quip. Well, there are practical as well as "impractical" reasons. The former should be clear by now: Either we pull together as we learn to like—or at least tolerate—each other, *or* we are <u>not</u> going to make it. The latter, however, offers much more inspiration—which, frankly, we need now more than we have for a very, *very* long time. Let me put it this way:

We humans—with all of our myriad, often stupid, destructive or simply unnecessary lines and "boxes"—have (at least seemingly) out-evolved all other species on the planet. (Up to now, anyway.) So, we're "it," Kids! That being the case, shouldn't we celebrate what *is* good about us?

We've also been almost solely the source of our Mother Earth's current climatic suffering—yet, paradoxically, only *we*, at this point, can consciously change, perhaps even reverse to some degree the present, dire trajectory. If not us, who—or what? What *is* the alternative, at present, to humans remaining the primary force for change in our world?

Well, there already *is* one—but it *ain't* a particularly pretty scenario:

Increasingly, all The Talk is of "AI," of all those applications of chic, much-touted Artificial Intelligence that "they" say is "coming" but, in reality, is already here—at least, in semi-restrained doses. Still, ya know that wall Lucy had pleaded for on July 4th, the summer that I ran for the US Senate from Iowa: You know, the one ta keep out The Other—in that case, Mexicans and Central Americans? Well, the harsh truth is, "they" are *not* the ones taking "our" jobs; rather, it's robots.

Yep, ya got that right: Already extensively in automotive plants and increasingly in hospitals, nursing homes and so many other settings, "fake humans" already have supplanted us real ones—and that is only the beginning! While the most recent wave of Latin-American migrants largely typically burp white elites' babies or mow many of our lawns or reshingle our garages, the jobs that Whitie most covets are being awarded *not* to José and Maria, but to robots—by far.[170]

Can we compete with these mechanized interlopers? Hardly. Will our losing to their competition change the most core rules of the game? *Oh-h-h*, ya!

What exactly is "AI" anyway? According to Professor Pedia, it is:

> [...] intelligence demonstrated by machines, in contrast to the natural intelligence displayed by humans. Leading AI textbooks define the field as the study of "intelligent agents:" any device that perceives its environment and takes actions that maximize its chance of successfully achieving its goals. Colloquially, the term "artificial intelligence" is often used to describe machines (or computers) that mimic "cognitive" functions that humans associate with the human mind, such as "learning" and "problem solving."[171]

See the recent *New York Times* article[172] about a robot with a human-like hand that can solve the Rubik's-Cube puzzle, according to one source, in "just 0.38 seconds."[173] Well, that's all fine and good, but there *are* still areas where computers simply can *not* compete—let alone "compute." As far as I know, as of this writing, computers:

- cannot eat and savor food that humans often consider to be "delicacies."
- do not sleep, at least in an unconscious "restorative" mode that humans and all other animals do.
- do not dream, either in the sleep state or in the sense of a "day dream," yearning for something.
- neither have nor yearn for sex, either for pleasure, emotive communication or procreation.
- do not smile, shout, hug or dance in response to internally-generated, unprogrammed stimuli.
- experience no self-generated senses of fear, jealousy, pride, satisfaction, "justice" or the like.
- neither fall in cathectic love nor extend or expand themselves on another's behalf per volition.
- do not engage in "sports" or exercise for the sake of pleasure or perceived self-betterment.
- write neither poetry or music based on self-sensed passion or empirical experience.
- do not create original visual or performance art without being asked to do so by external input.
- neither ponder religious ideals in non-rational ways nor experience spiritual senses of wonder.
- know neither intrinsic, "altruistic" loyalties nor the ability to shift allegiances based on "morality."
- never die per se, only per internal mechanical failure or externally-programmed commands.

For these and so many countless reasons, for all of our collective as well as individual screw-ups and short-comings, we humans are still unique in ways other animals are not, but moreover in a vast, cold and dark universe. It might be this appreciation of our species' worth that gives us cause to get up, dust off scraped knees and try again to walk upright, over the Earth and, perhaps someday, even among the stars. We cannot hope to get there, however, solo—solely together.

afterword

"Critics say that America is a lie because its reality falls so short of its ideals.
They are wrong. America is not a lie; it is a disappointment.
But it can be a disappointment only because it also is a hope."

— Samuel Huntington,
quoted in the *National Review*[174]

Is Present "Past" as Future?

Unable to land at clogged Heathrow, the plane from Leipzig circles endlessly over Southeast England. I stare down over sprawling London and meditate on a country where I once lived and studied, but now hardly recognize. The cabin is quiet but freezing: I shiver as I ponder what I, as a bona fide Brexit tourist, will encounter over the next surrealistic "daze" leading to 31 October.

Finally on land, I see "HSBC"[175] plastered on every surface imaginable: the airport's myriad jet bridges, glass doors and luggage-trolley handles, signs straddling baggage carousels, etc. I wonder how much Europe's biggest bank pays for this infinite advertising—omni-visible yet subliminal. *Who has bought Britain* I ask myself, followed by *and who felt they had the right to sell it?*

As I seek the way to my digs, I ask four computer geeks, returning from gaming in Düsseldorf, how to reach West Brompton best. They cannot tell me, so consult Google. I ask them if they enjoyed their time in Germany. "It's always grand" Leader Apparent says, "to return to Britain from Europe. Here, we're sovereign and free." I scratch me head as I mutely moan *Bloody hell!*

A Jewish dealer of Indian and Islamic art, my host Simon worries on both practical—"How will I sell this house to pay for 89-year-old Mum's care, when no one's buying, so prices are in free-fall?"—and philosophical levels: "How soon before disgruntled Brits blame Jews for the coming, disastrous post-No-Deal-Brexit financial woes? People will seek scapegoats; they *always* have."

On Thursday morning, 31 October 2019—commuters rushing by—I snapped these pictures of diehard Brexiteers camped out across from the Houses of Parliament's main entrance. I felt bad for the over-the-top man, whose family I presumed originated in a former British colony: What would Brexit gain <u>him</u>?

I ask Simon from where Brexit mania comes, who drives it and why. "It's part of this tiny island's decline, having lost an empire. It's all going to pieces" he says, "and Brexiteers are putting their panicky fingers in the wrong holes of all the wrong dikes. Meanwhile, general rot has set in. A Spanish engineer toured here newly and told me 'I've seen your best—but it's not very good.'"

"Our infrastructure's crumbling" he grumbles, "public works are chaotic and underfunded, with National Health possibly on the auction block for you lot to privatise. A blanket mediocrity has taken over" Simon maintains, "with crippling consequences for us all. Brexit is only accelerating and assuring our tragic end, which will result in us being irrelevant to the rest of the world."

Over tepid tea (pricey wine not being offered), Simon stews about England's demise. "I would leave" he confides, "but *where* would I go? Others, who can, are fleeing to wherever they can. It is diminishing London: What will remain here in a few years—not to mention in the North?" Bent-over Barbara nods blankly. As I depart, the mother's and son's joint depression is palpable.

As I set off to my next host, I talk with Brits I encounter along the way. All say they are stressed by "the unending misery of it all" but no one seems to be doing anything about Brexit being stalled, let alone the illegitimate child of a 1% "majority." There are still supporters, but *all* I ask report feeling sad, confused and helpless—"like waiting for a 'punishment beating' at school."[176]

Riding the Tube, I sit amidst three recent music-college graduates, each scrambling for "real," sustaining work in a deflating economy. They tsk-tsk about the "current situation" yet when I ask what they are going to do to counter it, they peer at each other dumbly, then shrug their shoulders in unison. "Is there a future for this country?" I ask. "We *hope* so" one weakly replies.

A middle-aged French father, standing nearby, slowly shakes his head and rolls his eyes, hearing this. As the deafening Tube rocks and thunders its way under a frenetic city, he and I lock gazes. As we stand to disembark, he bids "What are they doing, the Brits?" I reply "Hell if *they* know!" He forces a smile, then adds "We had loved coming to London, but it's a different place now."

At Charing Cross I change to a train to Cowford. A portly, loafer-wearing ancient-Greek scholar across the aisle swears he lives here "for the cultural resources, as I'm in cavernous archives almost daily—but *what* is coming?" He holds up a seminal English-language study of tragedian Sophocles: "I can't get this in Athens, yet now my English neighbors look at me walleyed. *Why?*"

In our twenty minutes together, we two academics talk of how a once-vast empire afforded endless annals, plus all of the pomp and circumstance, the grand buildings and ambitious canal, later rail projects central to the burgeoning Victorian era. As our train shakes and clangs its way past industrial-era dinosaurs, he and I sigh: We can smell the gravity of this historical moment.

"Ya know" I note, "the first time I came here, in 1980, the fabled 'English garden' wasn't jus' in parks. We young Iowa Methodists marveled over the immaculate gardens laid out behind prim terrace houses. But look" I point out the smudged window, "ya hardly see a well-kept one these days. What happened to those people's kids or grands that it all seems untidy, even feral now?"

As we deboard then part faking a smile, I think of translator Edi, a Kurd who has lived in London 20 years, his sister near Stuttgart for almost as long—far-flung dots in the Kurdish diaspora. I remember his answer to my question, why England looks so tattered: "The people don't have the money anymore to invest in fixing their places, as they are focused on feeding their faces."

My next host, James, awaits me at Cowford Station. As we stroll to cozy "Thorn Cottage"—built in 1855, the year my last English ancestors sailed for the New World—he reveals much. With his dad a Yank raised in the Bronx of Polish parents and his mum a "council-flats" Scot, James has lived in America's Deep South and Spain, but the longest—17 years—in Australia. Now, he frets:

"When Pat and I came back to live, just before Brexit passed—51%, which is *no* mancate—we never dreamt… [his voice fades off]. The covert politics of this place is the predictable outcome of empire, of a culture of extraction from the masses by the few. Before, it was of faraway Asians and Africans, now it's of those just beyond the City or Westminster. We're living out the past."

"We look at history peering backward" James explains, "but if we imagine being omniscient and traveling back in time a century or two, then look forward to the consequences of how we lived then, with our serial conquests around the globe squared with the social hierarchy here needed to make that possible, what's happening today would seem not only plausible, but predictable."

"For centuries, the few have herded the many, making decisions behind closed doors, then manipulating the masses to carry out those decisions on their threadbare backs. This is the land of Orwell" James warns. "We saw '1984' as a pinpointed prophecy of his but the 'moment' he portrayed has become protracted social reality: Now, the past threatens to dictate our future."

"The systems that arose when we were a different people don't work anymore, but we haven't reformed or replaced them." As James' voice lowers and his speech slows, my thoughts drift to *Tante* Herta's crammed cottage in Prussia. "The 'sheep' don't know where to jump to next, and the few shepherds left can't agree on a new direction—even as slaughter swiftly approaches."

I sit back in the sofa and look out James' window, over a valley of cramped little rowhouses. Before I can break my reflective silence, he comes out of his to add "The shit we are wading through now is really the compost of past matters, not fully or properly broken down. The process is inevitable, only a question of time. What counts is, what we make out of the muck."

*

sources of images:

1. _ML-T cover photo_: Michael Luick-Thrams' [henceforth "ML-T's"] private collection
2. "Political discord" poster by Las Laguna Gallery; https://www.sparkoc.com/classified/political-discord/
3. _deadlock graph #1_: ML-T's concept as designed by David Birkhead
4. _prairie at sunset_: ML-T's private collection
5. _BUS-eum exhibited in Iowa City_: ML-T's private collection
6. _stand of Turkeyfoot_: Friends School Plant Sale photo by Pat Thompson
7. _topography of Iowa_: © User:Billwhittaker / Wikimedia Commons / CC-BY-SA-3.0
8. _Vladimir Ilych Ulyanov Lenin_: Demetre Chinchaladze's private collection
9. _Young Pioneers poster_: Demetre Chinchaladze's private collection
10. _postcard of Satow_: ML-T's private collection
11. _Ashlawn Farm picnic_: ML-T's private collection
12. _"Life Can Be Wonderful"_: http://artheat.net/mixtape/?p=48
13. _Chuck Grassley, 2017_: public domain
14. _Chuck Grassley, 1977_: public domain
15. _Arctic Restaurant & Hotel_: image I-50656 courtesy of Royal BC Museum and Archives
16. _Arctic Restaurant ad_: image I-50657 courtesy of Royal BC Museum and Archives
17. _Heinrich Luick Jr_: ML-T's private collection
18. _Frederick Trump Sr_: public domain
19. _ML-T at meetinghouse_: Cedar Rapids _Gazette_ photo by Benjamin Roberts
20. _"Iowa Cultural Historian Seeks Senate Seat," 12 April 2016_: Heartland Parties
21. _ML-T eating "humble pie"_: Republished with permission © 2016 _The Gazette_, Cedar Rapids, Iowa
22. _ML-T in Prague, 2013_: ML-T's private collection
23. _Mitchell Schmidt, "Independent Luick-Thrams to challange Grassley", 13 April 2016_: Republished with permission © 2016 _The Gazette_, Cedar Rapids, Iowa
24. _ML-T Senate brochure inside view_: ML-T's private collection
25. _ML-T Senate brochure 3-fold view_: ML-T's private collection
26. _ML-T addressing students_: Cedar Rapids _Gazette_ photo by Benjamin Roberts
27. _LGBTQI Pride 2016 poster_: Heartland Pride Guide Poster, Omaha, NE USA 2016
28. _ML-T at Des Moines Gay Pride 2016_: ML-T's private collection
29. _Falcon bank in Mount Vernon_: ML-T's private collection
30. _"General Political-Rainbow Graph"_: ML-T's concept as designed David Birkhead
31. _Little Iowans in Manitoba_: ML-T's private collection
32. _Mason City KKK_: courtesy of Mason City Public Library
33. _article about KKK in Iowa_: courtesy of Mason City Library
34. _Dunnings Spring Park_: © User:Tomruen / Wikimedia Commons / CC-BY-SA-4.0
35. _Vesterheim Norwegian-American Museum_: © User:Jonathunder / Wikimedia Commons / CC-BY-SA-3.0
36. _"Letter to the Editor/Op-Ed Piece," 19 April 2016_: Heartland Parties
37. _Martin O'Malley and family, 2011_: Maryland GovPics - Official and Public Inauguration of Gov Martin O'Malley / Wikimedia Commons / CC-BY-2.0
38. _Martin O'Malley, 2014_: Governor O'Malley Portrait (cropped) by MarylandGovPics / Wikimedia Commons / CC-BY-2.0
39. _Obama family, 2009_: public domain
40. _Sylvester Petyt, ca.1710_: public domain
41. _Ermysted's Grammar School, March 2006_: Thomas Wales / Wikimedia Commons / CC-SA-1.0
42. _global temperatures change_: public domain
43. _Omega House, Minneapolis_: ML-T's private collection
44. _1980s "urban pioneers"_: ML-T's private collection
45. _"Little Lucy"_: ML-T's private collection
46. _Cary Grant in "North by Northwest"_: public domain
47. _Ashlawn Farm, 1950s_: ML-T's private collection

48. *Baby-Boomer-cousins collage*: ML-T's private collection (center); from upper left image clockwise: Mr. Potato Head, Gumby, G.I. Joe toy soldiers, mechanical monkey, Atomic Energy Lab, Barbie Doll No. 1, Vernon Bickford baseball card, Tonka Truck, Slinky, Tiny Tears doll, Play Doh

49. *Moorehead siblings, 1870s*: ML-T's private collection

50. *Ingalls sibling, 1870s*: http://littlehouseontheprairie.com/in-search-of-laura-about-laura-ingalls-wilder

51. *the Pompeii Forum and Vesuvius*: © Heinz-Josef Lücking / Wikimedia Commons / CC-BY-SA-3.0

52. *fresco from Pompeii*: fresco from Pompei by Gisle Hannemyr / Wikimedia Commons / CC-BY-2.0

53. *modern Pompeii map*: © User:WolfgangRieger / Wikimedia Commons / CC-BY-SA-3.0

54. *ML-T explaining exhibit*: courtesy of the *Schwäbische-Zeitu*ng in Tübingen, Germany

55. *lesson at Scattergood Hostel*: TRACES Center for History and Culture

56. *ML-T at Iowa Holocaust Memorial*: ML-T's private collection

57. *"Cow War" photo, 1931*: ML-T's private collection

58. *Iowa State Fair, 2016*: *The Register\USA TODAY* Network

59. *Scattergood's Main Building in 1930s*: TRACES Center for History and Culture

60. *refugees arriving at Scattergood, 1939*: TRACES Center for History and Culture

61. *Eisenhower's inauguration, 1953*: ML-T's private collection

62. *Eisenhower in Texas, 1916*: US Army Photography / public domain / courtesy of Fort Sam Houston Museum

63. *aerial view of Ashlawn Farm, 1950s*: ML-T's private collection

64. *aerial view of Ashlawn Farm, 2019*: Imagery ©2019 Google, Imagery ©2019 Maxar Technologies, USDA Farm Service Agency, Map data ©2019

65. *Bud Luick on combine, 1950s*: ML-T's private collection

66. *Elmer Thrams on reaper, 1920s*: ML-T's private collection

67. *Emma Goldman, 1911*: public domain

68. *"le Libertaire," 1860*: public domain

69. *Pierre-Joseph Proudhon, 1865*: public domain

70. *"Open Letter to the Des Moines Register"*: Michael Luick-Thrams and Charles Aldrich

71. *FDR and Hopkins, 1938 (flipped horizontally)*: public domain

72. *Pauline (Fiedman) Phillips, 1961*: public domain

73. *Iowa Loess Hills*: LHKW-014 © 2011 Kenneth G. West Jr.

74. *postcard of Morningside College, 1910s*: public domain

75. *Chuck Grassley and Patty Judge, 2016*: Justin Wan, AP (making contact with source failed: see "disclaimer")

76. *Merrick Garland with Barack Obama, 2016*: public domain

77. *swearing-in of Brett Kavanaugh, 2018*: public domain

78. *ML-T, summer 2016*: ML-T's private collection

79. *Philando Castile funeral procession*: ML-T's private collection

80. *memorial at the shooting site, 2016*: ©Fibonacci Blue / https://www.flickr.com/photos/fibonacciblue/27587896483/ / CC-BY-SA-2.0

81. *Diamond Reynolds speaking at a rally*: Diamond Reynolds speaking at a rally in memory of her boyfriend on the day after his death by Lorie Shaull / Wikimedia Commons / CC-BY-2.0

82. *Black Lives Matter protest in Saint Paul*: by Tony Webster/ Wikimedia Commons / CC-BY-2.0

83. *Zephyrus and Hyacinthus*: public domain

84. *Richard Puller von Hohenburg*: public domain

85. *Punch magazine cartoon*: public domain

86. *"Annual Reminder" activists*: © Kay Tobin Lahusen / Wikimedia Commons / CC-BY-SA-3.0

87. *Obama signing bill into law*: public domain

88. *ML-T in Berlin, 2016*: ML-T's private collection

89. *ML-T at Taliesin, 1998*: ML-T's private collection

90. *ML-T at Lima, 2018*: ML-T's private collection

91. *Terry Branstad and Xi Jinping, 2012*: Steve Pope/Iowa Governor's Office

92. *children at Scattergood*: TRACES Center for History and Culture

93. *Kapo in Latvia*: Bundesarchiv, Bild 101III-Duerr-054-17 / Dürr / CC-BY-SA-3.0

94. *Willard Drake Johnson: public domain*
95. *Shirley MacLaine, 1987*: © Roland Godefroy / Wikimedia Commons / CC-BY-SA-3.0
96. *Alice Miller*: credit Julia Miller (making contact with source failed: see "disclaimer")
97. *Saddam Hussein, 1956*: public domain
98. *Donald Trump, 1964*: public domain
99. *"Welcome to Fabulous Las Vegas"*: Lasvegassignflowers © User:Rmvisuals / Wikimedia Commons / CC BY-SA 4.0
100. *Quaker meeting for worship, circa 1800*: flickr// John Hall (engraving, J. Walter West)
101. *Central America, 2011*: public domain
102. *Greta Thunberg in April 2019*: European Parliament from EU - Greta Thunberg at the Parliament / Wikimedia Commons / CC-BY-2.0
103. *Morgan Scott Peck*: http://www.gurteen.com/gurteen/gurteen.nsf/id/X0004D8CE/ (making contact with source failed: see "disclaimer")
104. *Guthrie Theater, 1980s*: City of Minneapolis Archives from Minneapolis, United States - Walker Art Center / Guthrie Theater / Wikimedia Commons / CC-BY-2.0
105. *artistic portrayal of a "Schweinehund", 1993*: © Roland Godefroy / Wikimedia Commons / CC-BY-SA-3.0
106. *medieval artistic portrayal of a "Schweinehund"*: © Z thomas / Wikimedia Commons / CC-BY-SA-3.0
107. *ML-T in 1983*: ML-T's private collection
108. *20th anniversary of the March on Washington, 1983*: ML-T's private collection
109. *2017 Women's March in Washington, DC*: Mobilus In Mobili - Women's March on Washington / Wikimedia Commons / CC-BY-2.0
110. *German Green Party sunflower symbol*: © Bündnis 90/Die Grünen / http://www.gruene.de / Wikimedia Commons / CC-BY-SA-3.0
111. *East German Green Party logo, 1990*: Bundesarchiv, Bild 183-1990-0208-015 / CC-BY-SA-3.0
112. *segregated drinking fountain*: public domain
113. *restaurant window in Lancaster, Ohio*: ML-T's private collection
114. *Luick family at Ashlawn Farm, summer 1963*: ML-T's private collection
115. *deadlock graph #2*: ML-T's concept as designed by David Birkhead
116. *Luick family Christmas, 1965*: ML-T's private collection
117. *Aral Sea in 1989 (left) and 2014*: public domain
118. *abandoned ship near city of Aral, Kazakhstan*: public domain
119. *9,000-year-old paintings*: © User:Nandanupadhyay / Wikimedia Commons / CC-BY-SA-3.0
120. *Greek statuette of dancer*: © Claire H. / https://www.flickr.com/photos/8435962@N06/2508700900 / CC-BY-SA-2.0
121. *Luick family band, 1890s*: ML-T's private collection
122. *Felt Boot Orchestra, 1910s*: ML-T's private collection
123. *deadlock graph #3*: ML-T's concept as designed by David Birkhead
124. *East German refugees, 1945*: Bundesarchiv, Bild 146-1974-152-14 / CC-BY-SA 3.0
125. *"Brexit Now" poster, 31 October 2019*: ML-T's private collection
126. *Brexit supporter, 31 October 2019*: ML-T's private collection
127. *Farmers' Holiday strike in Iowa, 1932*: State Historical Society of Iowa
128. *Liz Martin, "Independent hopeful Luick-Thrams raising issues in U.S. Senate race", 11 October 2016*: Republished with permission © 2016 *The Gazette*, Cedar Rapids, Iowa
129. *George & Jennie (née Barlow) Moorehead family photo collage*: ML-T's private collection
130. *John & Ann (née Kew) Moorehead family group photo*: ML-T's private collection
131. *Kathie Obradovich, "Independent Candidates: Spoilers or Saviors", 31 May 2016*: *The Register\USA TODAY* Network
132. *Kathie Obradovich, "Even a vote for a losing candidate can have an impact", 11 August 2016*: *The Register\USA TODAY* Network
133. *Courtney Hoffman, "Historian, Former Sperm Donor Contacted by Biological Child", 4 April 2019*: Courtney Hoffman (*Mount Mercy Times*)
134. *Iowa winter landscape*: ML-T's private collection
135. *Nicole as baby*: Editor, "First birthday, Nicole", 9 November 1985: Knoxville Journal

136. *Alfred Doten, circa 1860s*: Nevada Historical Society collection
137. *Ronald Reagan working for WHO*: public domain
138. *Ronald Reagan's boyhood home in Dixon, Illinois*: User:Teemu008 / Wikimedia Commons / CC-BY-2.0
139. *Fifteen expats attended Anahita's presentation*: ML-T's private collection
140. *The Global Salon poster*: ML-T's private collection

disclaimer:

This book is published by the TRACES Center for History and Culture as: a) a historical record of A. M. Luick-Thrams' campaign for the US Senate race in 2016; and b) a record of historical events and figures, biographical sketches, travels, etc. therein. Any proceeds from the sale of this report will underwrite other projects of TRACES, a non-profit educational organization.

At the same time, publication by TRACES Center for History and Culture implies Board of Directors members' endorsement of neither the contents of this book nor any of the author's opinions expressed therein. This is a historical record, not a political treatise or broadside.

As far as possible, the author and his interns obtained consent to use any images not from the author's own collection. Three images' owners could be reached or even identified: If you or someone you know possess any unacknowledged rights, please contact staff@TRACES.org.

a hearty Thank You to proofreaders, critics and the designer:

Brent Aldrich, Ward Bauman, Timothy Bell, David Birkhead, Simon Brandenburger, Sally Campbell, Dori Collogan, Paul Cutting, Martha Davis, Tanya Demmel, Geri Falcon, Steve Feller, Elisa Guyader, Veronica Guyader, CeCeile Hartleib, Ruth Huffmann, Dana Kittel, Midge Kjome, Barry Lawson, Cliff Luke, Birgitta Meade, Marianna Nicholas, Seema Prakesh, Saul Prombaum, Karen Reimann, Frank Salomon, Pat Schultz, Gerry Schwarz, Nathan Lee Thompson, Patrick Valentine, Clark White and Jim Yates. The layout of both the paper and digital version of this book, as well as the on-line posting of the E-book version reflects Demetre Chinchaladze's flexibility, dedicated work and endless hours, diligently tinkering on this project.

See ya in my sequel,

Hawkeye:

What is to BE Done?

Part of the larger Farmers Holiday strike of 1932, picketing farmers blocked roads into Council Bluffs in a tense stand-off with law enforcement. This was a subset of a larger wave of farmer rebellions, including 1931's "Cow War" in Eastern Iowa and other forms to resistance to the Great Depression's status quo.

by Michael Luick-Thrams

copyright 2021

footnotes

[1] Both the "deadlock" graph and this example are modeled after work by the Indian-based computer-science portal GeeksforGeeks—specifically, on its webpage https://www.geeksforgeeks.org/introduction-of-deadlock-in-operating-system/, accessed 13 November 2019. The creator(s) of that webpage go on to explain (as adapted by this author) that:

> **Deadlock can arise if the following four conditions hold simultaneously ("Necessary Conditions"):**
> Mutual Exclusion: One or more of the persons is non-sharing (i.e., only one process can happen at a time)
> Hold and Wait: A person is refusing at least one expected concession, yet awaits concessions from Others.
> No Preemption: A concession is not granted unless an Other grants one, first or in agreed-upon turn.
> Circular Wait: A set of people are waiting for each other in circular form for not-forthcoming concessions.
> **Methods for handling deadlock; there are three ways to handle deadlock:**
> 1) Deadlock prevention or avoidance: The idea is to not let the system devolve into a deadlocked state. Prevention is done by negating one of above-mentioned necessary conditions for deadlock; or Avoidance is futuristic in nature: By using a strategy of "Avoidance," we need to ensure that all information about desired concessions are known to all parties prior to the execution of the process.
> 2) Deadlock detection and recovery: Let deadlock occurs, then make concessions to handle it.
> 3) Ignore the problem all together: If deadlock is very rare, then let it happen and "reboot the system," which has logical procedures in the computer world, but in the human one there is more variability.

[2] For a representative video tour of the BUS-eum, see http://usgerrelations.traces.org/Buseum_3_tour/Held%20in%20the%20Heartland%20Current/hartland-video.html. The downloadable Adobe Flash Player required to view it is free and virus-safe.

[3] Over a third of a million visitors have toured our "BUS-eums," our mini-museums in recycled school buses; we know, as we have a counter. Among others, TRACES' past exhibit topics have included refugees from Nazi-occupied Europe who found safe haven in the middle of our vast country, US rescuers of Jews, civilian internees and prisoners of war, Midwest liberators of concentration camps and pilots of the Berlin Airlift, etc. Planned mobile exhibit topics involve anti-German hysteria during World War I, the global flu pandemic of 1918-19 (which virulently arose in Kansas in March 1918), the Second Wave of the Ku Klux Klan in the 1920s, and farmer rebellions during the Great Depression. For more information, see: www.TRACES.org.

[4] The full title of the book is *Iowa, a Celebration of Land, People & Purpose,* published by the Iowa Sesquicentennial Commission, printed by Meredith Publishing Services in Des Moines, 1995.

[5] Shade-intolerant, Turkeyfoot is adapted to fire and a wide range of soil types. Depending on soil and moisture conditions, it grows to a height of 1–3 meters [3.3–9.8 ft]. As the roots are 1.8–3 m [6–10 ft] deep, and the plants send out hardy rhizomes, it forms strong sod. The stem base turns blue or purple as it matures. In Latin "Andropogon gerardi," Big Bluestem serves as the state grass of Illinois and Missouri, and Manitoba's official prairie grass. Compiled from https://en.wikipedia.org/wiki/Andropogon_gerardi, accessed 3 December 2019.

[6] Upon hearing "Marcellus'" criticism of my using Iowa as the backdrop of a larger story, one proofreader wrote: "Under-rating Iowans and our inability to change [might warrant giving] some thought to those who have engendered change. The first farmers' cooperative in the country was born right here – in Rockwell – to combat the low prices being paid by the corporations. People like Norman Borlaug did amazing things as did Edwin Hubble – we were the first state to enable same gender marriage – the first farm tile was developed in Mason City, changing farming forever. Changes do come when the motivation is high enough. Our governor [Robert Ray] at the time welcomed refugees from S.E. Asia and despite opinions like [Lucy's], they have integrated reasonably well into Iowa life. Carrie Lane Chapman Catt began her work for suffrage during the years she was in Mason City, first as a teacher and then as superintendent of schools. After Congress passed the 19th amendment in June of 1919 Iowa was among the first states to ratify - doing so in July. Students in Des Moines with their black arm bands forever made a change in rights to free expression. Two black college football players were among the earliest to be able to join teams – Jack Trice wasn't one of the first here but he may be the best known. Do these and other examples give us any ideas as to how to bring change about?

Perhaps what you missed in your campaign is that change can happen but that it takes longer to build than one campaign season. While individuals can do amazing things, does it take a ground swell to really get there? How might it have been different had you been in Iowa for ten years, slowing building a base that might swell?"

[7] Some persons' and place names in this otherwise non-fictional account have been altered, for the usual reasons. A few characters portrayed are composites of individuals I encountered along the way—as are a few real conversations, held in various contexts. "Lucy" and "Linus" are fictionalized composites of several relatives, and some family photos have been altered to insure privacy, even as the photos' use was germane to the narrative.

[8] ...followed by: standing (from the left) Marcia Hunt, Thurman Floyd, Bud Luick, Hank Bredenbeck, Phyllis (Thrams) Luick, Jack Hunt and Erma (Falcon) Thrams; seated (from the right) Elmer Thrams, Eleanor (Thrams) Hunt, Terry Hunt and Steve Floyd. The period ad embodies the domestic-bliss ethos of the time: "Life can be wonderful!"

[9] I took Cong bowling, to hunt knowledge or practical help at the Clear Lake and Mason City Public Libraries, on hikes or walks along the lake; I drove him and his family shopping or to meet with social workers or public officials. For my birthday, his mother prepared a sumptuous feast and his siblings performed ancient Laotian folk dances in my honor; Cong presented me with a handsewn shoulder bag boasting an elephant holding up the globe. I had rarely felt so connected to someone outside my own family. Helping Cong and his family enriched and swiftly altered my life.

[10] See https://www.politifact.com/punditfact/statements/2015/aug/27/nicholas-kristof/more-americans-killed-guns-1968-all-wars-says-colu/, accessed 13 April 2019.

[11] One proofreader wrote: "And yet those pioneer ancestors–and our "founding fathers"–contributed early to the gap, by owning slaves, by nearly killing off the entire native population, by decimating native food supplies, by bringing diseases, but not including women in their vision, by believing in the inherent right of Europeans to claim whatever they wanted and to disdain those who differed. What they did was both admirable and terrible. It is too easy for Trumpers to say "Make American Great Again" and ignore that our history has indeed built a great country, but not without costs. Is it possible that in this fairly young Democratic Republic we are actually still trying to mature but with disagreement about what that looks like? Whether it should be a continuation of the past we know–with all its flaws–or something new and better, a different kind of growth." She later added: "Along this country's journey to the present, we are also forgetting some of our successes. We built a strong free-enterprise system, rewarding individual incentive and hard work. But along the way we realized capitalism has some pitfalls – so we regulated monopolies and financial systems, established protected federal lands, established unions to protect workers' rights. Ironically, it seems today we are going backwards. Instead of understanding the impact of greed and desire for power and guarding against it, we are rewarding it."

[12] For details on Terry and Eric Branstad's political careers, see
https://www.desmoinesregister.com/story/news/2015/12/13/governor-terry-branstad-iowa-reaches-record-mark/77244172/ and https://www.desmoinesregister.com/story/news/politics/2016/06/15/eric-branstad-lead-trumps-presidential-campaign-iowa/85937960/, accessed 28 July 2019.

[13] A Cedar Rapids Gazette article accessed on 13 January 2020 confirmed what I had suspected already during my 2016 campaign and months before writing this originally footnote; see the
https://www.thegazette.com/subject/news/government/republicans-say-pat-grassley-builds-consensus-democrats-say-they-hope-so-20200113?utm_campaign=magnet&utm_source=entity_page&utm_medium=related_articles.

[14] One draft-reader commented: "How can people vote for people with a family name into office? There are many logical reasons. Name recognition, loyalty, comfort and predictability, tradition that is felt deeply. All virtuous impulses, really. That is something to think about."

[15] See https://www.theguardian.com/us-news/2016/nov/21/trump-grandfather-friedrich-banished-germany-historian-royal-decree, accessed 14 April 2019.

[16] Henry funded the Luick House Hotel in part with a windfall from distant Germany—as announced miles away, in the *Jackson Sentinel* on 14 November 1872, in Maquoketa, Iowa: "Mr Luick, an active and intelligent German of Eddyville [Iowa], has fallen heir to $55,000 and has gone to Germany to reap his reward." More than thirteen months later, on 19 December 1873, Cedar Falls' *Gazette* confirmed: "HJ Luick, who was one of the heirs to a large estate in Germany, has just received his portion with amount to $92,000 in gold. His name ought to be spelled without the 'i'."

Perhaps it was Vienna's stock-market crash on *Schwarzer Freitag*, the "Black Friday" of 9 May 1873, or a sudden surge in the value of the American dollar given European-rate fluctuations, that somehow transformed his earlier estimated windfall of $55,000 into a reported $92,000, but in any event Henry bagged a lot. Already a man of means—having been one of the first landowners of Wright County, a commissioner and judge—the "Mad Bobcat" invested his now-considerable worldly wealth in at least one business venture, for the 1875 edition of the *Wapello County, Iowa Business Directory* lists: "Luick, H.J., proprietor – Luick House, born Germany, came to Iowa in 1852 [sic]."

After he returned to Iowa—his pockets full of gold guilders—what had being back in Germanic lands meant to the man who brought my family to live in the heart of North America, the world in which I grew up? I can't know what it meant to him to slip between worlds but I know what it means to me. It's enriching but confusing. The above account is a compilation of information gleamed from pages 13-14 in *Chasing Restless Roots* and pages 131-132 in *Tap Roots Betrayed*, respectively volumes 2 and 3 in the pentalogy *Oceans of Darkness, Oceans of Light: Our Family's Trials and Treasures in the New World*, published by TRACES Center for History and Culture, 2015.

For additional information about the Arctic Hotel, see https://www.timescolonist.com/news/b-c/b-c-first-nations-tourist-draw-has-a-piece-of-tawdry-trump-history-1.2223889, accessed 30 November 2019.

[17] See https://www.economist.com/united-states/2015/02/05/the-silent-minority, accessed 15 April 2019.

[18] The 1900 US census documented that half of the residents of Iowa, Minnesota, Nebraska and the Dakotas were born in Germany or the children of German immigrants.

[19] Fred Trump Sr died in May 1918, one of the first victims of a flu pandemic that claimed up to 50 million lives, worldwide. Learn more about it https://www.youtube.com/watch?v=a8bWeJKJVWE&feature=youtu.be, or specifically about Fred Trump and other victims at https://www.youtube.com/watch?v=mnX_l7OiBPE&t=9s. Do note in this photo Henry's prominently-displayed gold-watch chain, likely a leftover of his short-lived wealth.

[20] The complete verse reads "Give me your tired, your poor, Your huddled masses yearning to breathe free, The wretched refuse of your teeming shore."

[21] America was not the paradise all would-be immigrants expected: By the beginning of World War I, about a third of all recent arrivals packed up after a disappointing sojourn and moved on—to South America, to Australia or back to from where they came, or...

[22] What could I say to my Czech students, after class one day in 1991, when they asked me "Why are Americans so superficial?" First, it took me aback, that they would come to this conclusion so soon after having had their only contact with Americans since the recent fall of communism. Once I refound my wits, I fumbled a moment, then offered: "You know, on the frontier, our ancestors came from 'out East' or fresh off the boat from Europe and were heading across the country in search of their American Dream. Some went all the way to the West Coast, but many more did not: They went a couple hundred miles until they reached cheap or even free land, then set down roots—at least for a while. But while on the move, they rumbled over unknown landscapes by day and camped in tight circles by night. As darkness fell the pioneers often congregated with strangers also crossing a vast continent—not just for protection from feared "Injun" attack or wolves or bandits, but for company, to share news from back home or of the lands awaiting them ahead. Whether you are moving a few dozen miles a day or a few hundred miles every generation, it's hard on the human heart to forge deep bonds, only to have those bonds brutally broken by dream-chasing departure or by death. I guess a common and understandable reaction was to keep most folks at emotional bay, to look instead to one's own family for emotional sustenance and confidence; all others were kept at a 'safe' distance lest one 'care too much' about other people populating a transitory world. Under such conditions, how much would people really reveal of their pasts or even present, of their depths or fear of death? Today you see this in everyday life: Americans form alliances in a flash but much slower genuine friendships that last. It sabotages real intimacy and makes commitment extremely hard, yet this national reflex to keep most people at an almost-unbridgeable emotional distance is plausible, even 'natural.'"

[23] For a comprehensive history of Quakers, not only in England and the US but at the local level in Iowa, see https://www.iymc.org/wp-content/uploads/2018/05/History-Iowa-Yearly-Meeting.pdf, accessed 30 November 2019.

[24] To learn more about what Washington and Adams thought about the perils of a two-party system, see https://ritholtz.com/2011/07/founding-fathers-beware-two-party-system/, accessed 20 April 2019. Adams, for one, said "There is nothing which I dread so much as a division of the republic into two great parties, each

arranged under its leader, and concerting measures in opposition to each other. This, in my humble apprehension, is to be dreaded as the greatest political evil under our Constitution."

[25] Martin, Liz (2016, October 11). Independent hopeful Luick-Thrams raising issues in U.S. Senate race. *The Gazette* of Cedar Rapids, Iowa.

See the full article at https://www.thegazette.com/subject/news/government/elections/independent-hopeful-luick-thrams-raising-issues-in-us-senate-race-20161011, accessed 30 November 2019.

CEDAR RAPIDS — Michael Luick-Thrams said he "assumed from the get-go I wouldn't win" Iowa's race for U.S. Senate.

That seems a safe bet since the Mason City cultural historian counts about 50 active supporters, had raised less than $4,000 as of June 30 and gets exposure speaking at the State Fair, striking up conversations as he travels Iowa and piggybacking on events like the University of Northern Iowa's "Indigenous People's Day."

"I'm raising issues," Luick-Thrams told The Gazette Editorial Board Tuesday. "I want to raise issues Grassley and Judge won't raise" and help Iowans see the real issues as well as understand that voting for the same old, same old isn't helping.

"We vote for people we know. We avoid risk," he said. Iowa voters "keep returning people to office who support the status quo."

So they get Republican Sen. Chuck Grassley — "Uncle Chuck" — who Luick-Thrams said is "great on Social Security and getting your brother-in-law's Iranian wife a visa."
Democratic challenger Patty Judge is the "Democratic National Committee's girl, foisted on the Iowa Democratic landscape … an old boy in a skirt."

As a historian, Luick-Thrams said he takes the long view and believes the key to Iowa's future success can be found in its past. Iowa thrived when its water was clean, before one-third or more of its topsoil had been washed down the Missouri and Mississippi rivers.

Now, 71 of 99 counties are losing population. Small towns are struggling as Wal-Marts move in and young people move out.

"We need triage," Luick-Thrams said. "We need to draw a line … like deciding county seats cannot be allowed to go under."

Too many current leaders fail to recognize the importance of rural Iowa to the state's vitality.

"It wasn't the cities that built the rest of Iowa. The rest of Iowa built the cities," Luick-Thrams said. "There is something inherently valuable in the rural experience."
That means challenging many accepted beliefs and practices.

"Why should Iowa feed the world?" he asked. Increasing row crop yields and livestock production is turning the state into a chemical dump.

"We're raising all of this food in Iowa, but it's poisoning us," he said. "There's a direct correlation between Iowa and obesity" because federal subsidies contribute to the overproduction.

It's time for a change, and neither Grassley nor Judge can or will deliver because they are "products of The Depression … too blinded by the cornstalks to see the field."

Luick-Thrams, who has lived and studied in Germany, said Iowans need a senator who can see the bigger picture, someone who has lived outside Iowa, who knows the impact of U.S. foreign policy, someone "who knows what it's like not to come from (Iowa) framework."

"We're being had," Luick-Thrams said. "I'm the real deal."

---

[26] A glance through any *Time* or *Newsweek* issues from pre-Reagan years will show how the levels of writing and of general education in the United States have decreased greatly over the intervening years—a great danger to democracy, which depends on a literate and articulate electorate in order to function well and into the future.

27 The phrase "others in order to succeed" necessarily includes non-human "Others"—flora, fauna and other Earthly creatures inescapably essential in sustaining life on the planet.

28 See http://www.quakercenter.org/quaker-quote-archive/%20and%20https:/www.azquotes.com/quote/691316, accessed 1 May 2019.

29 I came to Quakerism as a young army-registration resister. For an in-depth telling of that tale, see my sequel to this book, planned title being *Hawkeye: What is to BE Done*.

30 The alluded-to Biblical quote from Matthew 25:44 reads "Then they will reply, 'Lord, when did we ever see you hungry or thirsty or a stranger or naked or sick or in prison, and not help you?'" One proofreader treated such people more generously than I, writing: "I would not call it this, as they do not merely do 'lip service' in their communities [as they] contribute to their churches' missionary programs, not just to convert, but to provide aid. I would say instead that they have trouble looking past what they know, to the distant, to the unknown."

31 Programmed and unprogrammed Friends come from shared roots but divergent experiences, with the former resembling mainstream Protestants and the latter retaining many of the original ways of the earliest Quakers.

32 One early-draft reader wrote about this point, "I think this is a significant contributor to politics today: more money = more exposure (not necessarily expression of ideals); sheep voters vote for the one they see the most and don't really consider the issues."

33 List of overall candidates: Robert Hogg filed on 29 February; Thomas Fiegen on 3 March; Charles Grassley on 14 March; Patty Judge on 17 March; Bob Krause on 18 March; Michael Luick-Thrams on 1 August; Charles Aldrich on 3 August; Jim Hennager on 19 August; filing for the state primary was 29 February-18 March, the primary itself was on 7 June 2016.

34 Little Switzerland is a subregion of the Upper Midwest's Driftless Area—which is one of the reasons that Decorah is atypical of the larger Midwest and home to so many atypical people. Scientists revealed in 2013 that this college town rests atop a giant crater, formed by a crashing comet. Metaphysicists attribute the community's current uniqueness to its pre-human history. Partial source: https://www.washingtonpost.com/health-science%2fcrater-found-in-iowa-points-to-asteroid-break-up-470-million-years-ago, accessed 15 May 2019.

35 I often pondered why Willy is not out, not even to his "welcoming" Presbyterian-activist mother who loves me.

36 Readers interested in corollaries between personality types and political tendencies can learn more at these links: https://personalityjunkie.com/08/personality-politics-liberals-conservatives-myers-briggs-big-five/ and https://www.verywellmind.com/the-myers-briggs-type-indicator-2795583 .

37 Literally, a "simple majority" consists of one "in which the highest number of votes cast for any one candidate, issue, or item exceeds the second-highest number, while not constituting an absolute majority."

38 For a wider perspective, see https://news.gallup.com/poll/247025/democratic-states-exceed-republican-states-four-2018.aspx, accessed 28 July 2019.

39 Those waves can be approximately dated as 1865-1872, 1915-1945 and 1950 to the present.

40 I apologize for any erroneous associations—but kindly note that my mother's fading memory, wedded with a lack of known ways to connect with the subjects' surviving family members or locate telling public records made it nearly impossible for me, in the limited time available—and then mostly from Germany—to adequately research and confirm the cited individuals' recalled pasts and connections. I own any mistakes.

41 Lest the good former Governor think I hold him in low esteem, I state here that it is not the case. I respect his obviously carefully considered values, especially his schooling-derived Jesuit sensibilities regarding the disadvantaged—as evidenced in his Thanksgiving-eve 2019 driving out of modern money changers: https://www.theguardian.com/us-news/2019/nov/28/martin-omalley-slams-trump-official-immigration, accessed 30 November 2019. Oh, and I often enjoy a few good rounds of Irish music, too: "Play on, Martin!"

42 The full quote is "Where there is no vision, the people perish: But happy is he who keeps the law."

43 According to the National Assessment of Educational Progress, a.k.a. the "Nation's Report Card," "proficiency" rates in 2018 were below 50 percent for every racial and ethnic group, in both reading and math, in both 4th and 8th grade. The exceptions? Asians, in all subjects (51-64 percent) and whites in 4th grade math only (54 percent). Source at https://www.npr.org/sections/ed/2014/10/11/354931351/it-s-2014-all-children-are-supposed-to-be-proficient-under-federal-law accessed 28 July 2019.

44 Those three women were: my mother, Phyllis Ann (née Thrams) Luick, born 1935; my maternal "Grandma," Florence "Erma" (née Falcon) Thrams, 1896-†1987; or my paternal "Gramma," Charlotte Adelia (née Juhl) Luick, 1913-†1997.

[45] As the text at http://www.iptv.org/iowapathways/mypath/first-bridge-over-mississippi-and-effie-afton [accessed 21 December 2019] explains, that first rail-bearing bridge crossed the Mississippi between Rock Island, Illinois and Davenport, Iowa. Grandma Thrams' grandfather had arrived from Franken, in what's now Bavaria, the previous year. After working a year in a knife factory in Lynn, Massachusetts, Wilhelm and his fellow-Germanic-immigrant bride, Gertrude, set off for the Iowa prairies by train. As theirs would have been the first to cross the new bridge in April 1856, the crossing was granted gratis to lure would-be passengers otherwise fearful of plunging into the Mighty Miss' swift waters, below.

[46] The full passage from Genesis 1:26-28 (per the King James Version) reads "And God said, Let us make man in our image, after our likeness: and let them have dominion over the fish of the sea, and over the fowl of the air, and over the cattle, and over all the earth, and over every creeping thing that creepeth upon the earth. So God created man in his own image, in the image of God created he him; male and female created he them. And God blessed them, and God said unto them, Be fruitful, and multiply, and replenish the earth, and subdue it: and have dominion over the fish of the sea, and over the fowl of the air, and over every living thing that moveth upon the earth.."

[47] "Vestae" is said to mean "Keepers of the Hearth" according to an article at https://www.iowa4hfoundation.org/index.cfm/30678/1634/2002_cerro_gordo_county__marlene_bartlett, accessed 24 November 2019. The subject of that article, Marlene Bartlett, was a longtime co-leader of that club, with my mother. My family had long, valued ties with the families of both brothers, Bob and Bill Bartlett.

[48] See an overview of 1968 at https://www.history.com/news/the-revolution-that-was-1968, accessed 11 July 2019.

[49] My codification of these groups is based on my pre-1968 socialization. In my mind, at that time South-Asian Indian men or women would have been granted higher social standing and greater license to achieve than, say, "yellow" East Asians of either gender or any other conditions, but less than Arabs.

[50] The [hi-]story about Jefferson's motives and vision is told in depth on pages 48-54 in Tap Roots Betrayed, volume 3 in the pentalogy Oceans of Darkness, Oceans of Light: Our Family's Trials and Treasures in the New World, published by TRACES Center for History and Culture, 2015.

[51] The series consists of these titles, which focus on specific experiences: https://en.m.wikipedia.org/wiki/List_of_Little_House_on_the_Prairie_books. One reader noted: "The truth is the so-called objectionable parts should be read and discussed with the understanding that this was indeed the attitude in the Middle West – fear built on [Iowa's] Spirit Lake Massacre – one in Minnesota – etc., accompanied by no understanding of the real plight of Native Americans. I doubt they shared the concept of 'Manifest Destiny,' but were only doing their best to survive and hopefully prosper. And why Huckleberry Finn is perhaps the most important American novel ever written – Twain is not imposing racism when he writes 'Nigger,' he is being intensely critical of racism. He is also introducing a uniquely American style of regionalism that is highly admirable – asking readers of his time – and ours – to take a good look at what has shaped and motivated them. . . just as you are doing here [in Turkeyfoot]."

[52] As summarized here from many more details recorded on pages 215-217 in Chasing Restless Roots: The Dreams that Lured Us Across America (TRACES Center for History and Culture, 2015), between May and November 1889, George Moorehead lost a baby boy, toddler daughter and his first wife, Jennie (née Barlow) Moorehead. On top of that, "George had just lost four of his sisters, half of his family, to that same tuberculosis epidemic."

Above: Leila Ann (standing), Jennie (née Barlow) and baby Leslie Moorehead, last half of the 1880s; on the right, Jennie and George's wedding picture, circa Christmas 1884. Below, always left to right: Margaret (standing), Jennie, Frank, Mary, Ann; John (sitting) Bert, Ann [née Kew] and George Moorehead, first half of the 1880s

[54] The fresco includes a detail of the "Ritual of initiation into the Mysteries" at the Villa dei Misteri, painted in the "second style" of Pompeii, about 60 BC. The overview of Pompeii is based on a 1:5000 map of Pompeii by Hans Eschebach, published in: *Gebäudeverzeichnis und Stadtplan der antiken Stadt Pompeji*. Cologne: Böhlau 1993.

[55] The earliest printed citation for this quoted proverb is in John Heywood's *A dialogue conteinyng the nomber in effect of all the prouerbes in the Englishe tongue*, 1546.

[56] The puppets used in the "The Lonely Goatherd" scene in the 1965 film were created by Mason-City-raised Bill Baird and today hang in the town's Charles H. MacNider Art Museum.

[57] For details, see https://www.youtube.com/watch?v=BRAwQLi6vqY, accessed 24 December 2019.

[58] According to one source, at https://en.wikipedia.org/wiki/Civil_Liberties_Act_of_1988, $20,000 1988 dollars would be at inflation-adjusted rates about $40,000 in 2016. Many surviving internees, however, said that any sum of money meant less to them than the implicit apology: https://www.npr.org/sections/codeswitch/2013/08/09/210138278/japanese-internment-redress, accessed 28 July 2019

[59] Ibid.

[60] One of the difficulties of living on two continents is that a person does not live wholly on either: Having all TRACES records in Iowa yet writing this while sojourning in Germany, I had to reconstruct the people's names from memory, crosschecking individuals' dates of sojourning with each other. Note: As did many other "guests" at Scattergood Hostel, the Viennese couple Adolf and Lisa Beamt ["official" or "civil servant" in German] anglicized their surname to "Beam;" Adolf took "Albert" as a first name; "Lisa" perhaps came from 'Elisabeth."

[61] Find one of several related articles about the "Iowa Cow War" at http://lib.dr.iastate.edu/cgi/viewcontent.cgi?article=3298&context=iowastate_veterinarian, accessed 15 October 2019.

[62] Source: https://www.niemanlab.org/2019/07/newsonomics-its-looking-like-gannett-will-be-acquired-by-gatehouse-creating-a-newspaper-megachain-like-the-u-s-has-never-seen/, accessed 27 July 2019.

[63] Watch this candidate rather self-consciously explain "Why you shouldn't vote for me" at https://www.youtube.com/watch?v=AluZDRdcHr0, recorded 14 August 2016 at the *Des Moines Register*'s Political Soapbox, held every election year at the Iowa State Fair.

[64] Obradovich, K. (2016, May 31). *Independent Candidates: Spoilers or Saviors* in the *Des Moines Register*.

VOICES & COMMENTARY

INDEPENDENT CANDIDATES:
SPOILERS OR SAVIORS?

I f you talk to people who have tried to run for office as political independents, a phrase you'll hear often is "Catch-22."

Voter dissatisfaction with the two major political parties is off the charts, anger with the dysfunction and polarization in Congress is boiling over and the need for independent voices has rarely been so obvious. And yet, nearly every aspect of our democratic process shuts out and sidelines anyone with the gall — or naivete — to offer themselves as an alternative.

ON POLITICS

KATHIE OBRADOVICH
kobradov@dmreg.com

Michael Luick-Thrams from Mason City, running as an independent candidate for U.S. Senate, said people will criticize the Republican and Democratic parties but are "allergic" to throwing their support to an independent candidate.

He wants to reform the political system — something the major parties talk about but have little self-interest in actually doing.

Independents aren't given a forum in the media or on debate stages. Luick-Thrams, a historian who works with Traces, a non-profit educational organization, said he's been refused time to speak on college campuses because only a student political party representative can issue an invitation.

Today, a candidate can gain an audience and raise money through social media — something Luick-Thrams discounts because he says older voters aren't engaged. I think my mom and mother-in-law, who are both on Facebook, might disagree.

But if an independent candidate is wealthy or famous enough to get attention, that person is sidelined as a spoiler for whichever party is least objectionable to a voter.

"It's a Catch-22. If we keep on doing what we've been doing, we're going to get what we've always got," Luick-Thrams said.

In Des Moines, Derek Tidball is now a Republican candidate for the Iowa House in District 36. But in 2008, he ran for Congress as an independent in the district then held by Democrat Gabby Giffords.

He said running as an independent was one of the two hardest things he's ever done — and he's served combat in Afghanistan as an Army paratrooper.

Raising money was tough, he said. "That wasted vote thing comes back to you a lot. They don't give you the money and then as soon as you put out your financial reporting each term, it just validates the fact that you don't have any money and so you're not valid, but 'I can't give you any money because you're a wasted vote.' It's like a Catch-22."

Tidball said he couldn't get the Republican Party in Arizona to support his candidacy because he wasn't ideologically pure enough on some issues. He opposed the Bush administration's handling of the wars and was unhappy with the Veterans Administration's treatment of wounded veterans.

"I don't think Republicans at the national level and Republicans that you just see on the street are really on the same page," Tidball said.

Michael Luick-Thrams

Derek Tidball

Greg Orman

But he found that as an independent, it was hard for voters to understand his agenda. "As an independent, you have to create your entire platform and you have to message that each time," he said.

Greg Orman is a former independent candidate from Kansas who ran for U.S. Senate in 2014. His book, "A Declaration of Independents," asserts that electing more independent candidates is the only solution to America's political malaise.

He compared the Republican and Democratic parties to a divorcing couple who have stopped all communication. Independent lawmakers are needed to mediate, or nothing can get done.

"I do think we are at a point in time when the electorate would be ready for a credible independent candidate to run for president," Orman said in a recent interview during a trip to Iowa.

The rise of Donald Trump as the GOP nominee and self-described democratic socialist Bernie Sanders as a significant Democratic contender is an embodiment of how disconnected voters have become with the major parties, he said.

Orman said he's trying to address the sort of messaging roadblock that Tidball experienced by helping people define independent candidates. He says while independents may be on the political fringe on either the left or the right, they have in common a willingness to put their country ahead of their party, lack of obligation to special interests and party bosses, and the temperament to be a problem-solver.

His advice to would-be independent candidates is to ignore the naysayers. "Pay no attention to those who say that your campaign will only spoil the race for one of the parties," he wrote.

He urged disaffected Republicans and Democrats to re-engage in their parties if they aren't ready to become independents.

That's what Tidball did upon moving to Iowa, where he found a more inclusive attitude. He said he was able to return to the GOP because Statehouse leaders were more interested in a candidate who fit the district than one who can check every box on the platform.

He would face incumbent Democratic Rep. Marti Anderson if he wins the contested primary on June 7.

Luick-Thrams will face the winner of the Democratic Senate primary and incumbent Sen. Chuck Grassley in November. He's been doggedly persistent in trying to get mainstream media to take notice. "I'm a pain in the butt, people know it, but I have a larger goal here."

Maybe Luick-Thrams should found the Pain in the Butt Party. People might at least pay attention.

Obradovich, K. (2016, August 11). *Third-party votes aren't "wasted:" Even a vote for a losing candidate can have an impact* in the *Des Moines Register*.

wasted

Even a vote for a losing candidate can have an impact

KATHIE OBRADOVICH
kobradov@dmreg.com

The headline on an article that popped up on my news feed was enough to annoy the heck out of me: "How Not to Waste Your Vote: A Mathematical Analysis."

The top of the article by Stephen Weese was even worse. It presented a definition of a wasted vote from that great oracle of Internet accuracy, Wikipedia. It defined as "wasted" a vote that is cast for a losing candidate or a vote cast for a winning candidate in excess of the number required for victory.

What a dopey premise, I thought. First of all, voters don't always know in advance in a contested election whether they are backing the winner. Secondly, nobody knows which votes for a winning candidate came in "excess" of the exact number needed to win.

Votes for losing candidates, even those the voter can reasonably expect to lose, aren't wasted either. And to my delight, that was exactly the point that Mr. Weese would eventually make in his article. This is why we don't flame articles on social media based on the headline, by the way. But that's beside the point.

In Iowa, where the major parties are competitive, the concern about "wasted" votes comes up most often in terms of independent or third-party candidates. People may be dissatisfied with the Republican and Democrat on the ballot, but they're reluctant to "throw their vote away" on a third-party candidate.

Weese points out that third-party candidates can and do win elections, on occasion. Beyond winning, however, there are other benefits for third-party voting. "It makes a political statement to the majority parties. It helps local politicians of that party in elections. It can help change platforms to include third-party elements. And it provides recognition for the party among voters as a viable alternative," he wrote.

In Iowa, a third party only needs 2 percent of the vote for its presidential or gubernatorial candidate to be considered an official political party. There's a lot of interesting, data-based analysis in Weese's article, which you can find at the Foundation for Economic Education, fee.org.

Third-party candidates are getting more attention in this year's presidential race, in large part because of voter qualms with both of the major-party candidates. CNN just held a second town hall with Libertarian Party nominee Gary Johnson, former New Mexico governor, and his running mate William Weld, the former Massachusetts governor. Green Party nominee Jill Stein is enjoying a higher profile of any candidate from her party since Ralph Nader. And yet both Johnson and Stein will likely fall short of the poll numbers needed to qualify for offer that makes his candidacy worth voters' attention: A long-term vision for Iowa's future.

Michael Luick-Thrams

He proposes a 30-year plan aimed at the year 2046, the 200th anniversary of Iowa's statehood. Some of his goals include revitalizing county-seat towns, ensuring each has amenities needed to attract and retain residents: healthcare and recreational facilities, vibrant educational and cultural institutions, high-speed Internet, recycling and clean energy.

"I keep telling people we need to drag Iowa out of the '80s," Luick-Thrams said in an interview. He said he was in junior high when Sen. Chuck Grassley, the Republican incumbent, was elected.

"We're looking toward Iowa's third century and not to be offensive or morbid, but Chuck (Grassley) and Patty (Judge) will hardly be there in 2046," he said.

You can read his entire plan at heartlandparties.us. Some of you may think it's the wrong direction for the state but ask yourselves this: What long-term visions have you heard from the major-party candidates?

Also on the ballot for U.S. Senate is a Libertarian candidate, Charles Aldrich of Clarion. He ran in 2008 for the U.S. Senate in Minnesota and received 0.48 percent of the vote, a fourth-place finish. In Iowa, he says he's relying on radio ads to spread the word about this candidacy.

He's an engineer who has been working in farm implement manufacturing before becoming a full-time candidate. He worked on the petition drive to get Johnson and Weld on the ballot in Iowa.

Charles Aldrich

Much of Aldrich's agenda is rooted in the idea that the United States is spending too much money overseas. He wants to end this country's involvement in the current wars and military actions, including the battle against ISIS. He would withdraw from NATO, shutter foreign military bases and cut off foreign aid.

"I'm not an isolationist. I think we should have embassies and have trade with countries. But as far as going in there and dictating how they're going to run their country, which is what NATO does ... it's counterproductive to do that," Aldrich said.

I disagree with Aldrich that there's no benefit for U.S. security to fight terrorism in the Middle East or maintain military bases in allied nations. But again, this is a point of view that voters won't find from either of the major-party candidates.

You can hear from many of the candidates on this year's congressional and Senate ballot, including Luick-Thrams, at the Des Moines Register's Iowa State Fair Soapbox, starting Thursday. See the updated schedule here: Desmoinesregister.com/soapboxschedule. And remember, the only wasted vote is one not cast.

[65] At that time, those headquarters were in downtown Des Moines. The *Register*'s current location is far-removed from the city's "center." While mega-conglomerate Gannett likely rationalized the move as "cost-saving" no matter what the reasoning behind surrendering the *DMR*'s downtown presence greatly impacts its coverage.

[66] When the Thramses arrived from Kröslin in Pommern in 1855, they settled in Wisconsin; to this day, beloved Ehrhardt cousins of mine live there: I delight every time I'm in Wisconsin—America's most-German state, which former German *Bundeskanzler* Helmut Kohl made a point of visiting in May 1996, exactly for that reason.

[67] In my frustration, I failed to fully consider the day-to-day reality facing newspapers in the US today. Readership and advertising income have declined so greatly that many have shut down their presses. Survivors have cut staff as well as the number of pages. Competition from electronic media has engendered starving newsrooms. Editors must make difficult coverage decisions every day. Reporters' pay, especially in smaller communities, barely constitutes a "living wage." This likely contributed somewhat—although not entirely—to the rejection I encountered when approaching print media for campaign coverage. For example: So few newspapers in Northwest Iowa reported on US Representative Steven King's many controversial comments that only three in ten people interviewed in his district even knew he had a Confederate flag on his desk and had made strongly-racist comments. Coverage concentrated largely on local topics, with little said about political issues. I fear, this reflected not just a lack of space or reporters, but also a sense of what their readership wanted or did not want to know. In my campaign experience, the lack of space may have been somewhat to blame, but was only part of the story. See: https://iowastartingline.com/2016/07/24/why-western-iowa-keeps-voting-for-steve-king/.

[68] Further information is available at https://newsmaven.io/indiancountrytoday/archive/two-quaker-presidents-h5YOqNzXskOxFpz-tlAwww/, accessed 28 July 2019.

[69] My conclusions about Scott Simon are not unique to me: See echoing concerns by Daniel Kovalik (a labor and human rights lawyer in Pittsburgh) at https://www.counterpunch.org/2012/06/04/scott-simon-npr-the-empire/, accessed 24 December 2019.

[70] Some of those present were: local Quaker farmer and hostel volunteer Verlin Pemberton (walking toward the camera; his daughter Lillian later became the hostel's dietician—as well as married fellow staff member George Willoughby), Viennese stationer Fritz Treuer (behind the hatted woman), resident co-caretaker Walter Stanley (in front of the wheel, wearing flat cap), Viennese Kurt Rosegg (standing next to Walter), guide John Kaltenbach (with foot on front bumper), Berlin mathematician Kurt Schaefer (on extreme right), with the car that brought them from Philadelphia, the "Conestoga," being in the right background. The cited article is at https://www.thegazette.com/subject/news/80-years-ago-scattergood-hostel-took-refugees-fleeing-nazis-wwii-west-branch-cedar-county-edith-lichtenstein-morgan-froehlig-20190627, accessed 30 November 2019.

[71] The requirement on the related sheet Justin sent me read "The candidate is the nominee of a political party recognized under state law, as determined by the Iowa Secretary of State's office," but my checking with that office confirmed: The State of Iowa designates *solely* the Democratic and Republican as "recognized" parties; it sees the Greens and Libertarians, to cite two, not as "parties" but only "non-partisan political organizations."

[72] This passage was accessed 26 July 2019 at https://en.wikipedia.org/wiki/Dwight_D._Eisenhower. Note: Eisenhower did oppose the Supreme Court decision regarding the Brown vs. the Board of Education case, meant to desegregate public schools.

[73] Interestingly, the young Eisenhower was not only learning about starting a military career while at St. Louis College, but about starting an entire life: https://www.expressnews.com/sa300/article/Young-Dwight-D-Eisenhower-learned-from-12246492.php#photo-14271230, accessed 1 December 2019.

[74] This passage was accessed 26 July 2019 at https://en.wikipedia.org/wiki/Republican_Party_(United_States).

[75] The macro history of US agriculture's shift from being family-run, with mostly organic practices to being industrial and almost exclusively chemical-based is told in micro form, as experienced at Ashlawn Farm, on pages 45-51 and 102-104 in Roots of Darkness, volume 1 in the pentalogy Oceans of Darkness, Oceans of Light: Our Family's Trials and Treasures in the New World, published by TRACES Center for History and Culture, 2015.

[76] Out of Iowa's 99 counties, according to the *Des Moines Register*, data from the US Census Bureau showed that 71 counties lost population between 2010 and 2017, while 28 gained. This phenomenon in large part explains how Iowans as a state could vote for Obama, twice even, but then vote for Trump. For details, see

https://www.desmoinesregister.com/story/news/2018/05/29/map-shows-stark-reality-iowa-rural-population-loss-depopulation-metro-urban/652175002/, accessed 26 July 2016.

[77] Source: https://www.desmoinesregister.com/story/news/politics/iowa-poll/2016/10/10/iowa-poll-grassley-leads-judge-in-senate-race-by-17-points/91824228/, accessed 15 June 2019.

[78] I wrote this section while sojourning in a wooded valley near Decorah, Iowa, during the months of May, June and July 2019. Not only did the log cabin—where I had sequestered myself in order to write undisturbed—lack internet access and cellphone coverage, but documentation of my 2016 campaign remained inaccessible in storage in Germany. It could be, therefore, that some of the events described in this section are out of the chronology in which they actually took place—a regrettable state for which I take ownership and apologize.

[79] The Organization for Economic Cooperation and Development (OECD) is a forum established in 1961, where the governments of 36 democracies with market economies work with each other, as well as with more than 70 non-member economies to promote economic growth, prosperity and sustainable development.

[80] Adapted from https://en.wikipedia.org/wiki/WHO_(AM), accessed 25 December 2019.

[81] That brave man's humanitarianism changed my life forever: 'Twas my close interactions for a year or so with Cong Kam Li and his Laotian-refugee family that stretched my world and set my life down a different path from what had preceded it. And, that exposure to the plight and needs of refugees motivated me to want to become a Methodist pastor, then serve in that capacity in refugee camps in Southeast Asia—a longing to serve others in foreign settings that ultimately went unmet in that form but later got expressed differently than I ever could have expected. For that, I will be forever grateful for Robert Ray's visionary leadership, as outlined at http://www.iptv.org/iowapathways/mypath/robert-d-ray-iowa-governor-humanitarian-leader, accessed 25 December 2019.

[82] One of the acts for which I long admired Jim was his participation in the "Continental Walk for Disarmament and Social Justice" of 1976, which happened around the time of our outing to Sioux City. For additional information, see https://sojo.net/magazine/february-1976/continental-walk, accessed 1 July 2019.

[83] Source accessed 12 July 2019 at https://en.wikipedia.org/wiki/Chuck_Grassley.

[84] According to one account at https://www.desmoinesregister.com/story/news/politics/2016/10/19/grassley-judge-clash-over-supreme-court-border-security/92350594/, accessed 25 December 2019, I wasn't the only one underwhelmed by this "debate."

[85] For an update on this persistent problem, see https://www.apnews.com/d9128f4c388db34492beb040c120de3e accessed 12 July 2019.

[86] For further details, see https://www.theguardian.com/us-news/2018/jun/17/separation-border-children-cages-south-texas-warehouse-holding-facility, accessed 27 July 2019.

[87] For further details, see http://bronx.news12.com/story/34801622/minnesota-police-kill-man-in-car-video-is-widely-shared, accessed 27 July 2019.

[88] For further information about Philando, see https://time.com/4397086/minnesota-shooting-philando-castile-role-model-school/, accessed 18 July 2019.

[89] For further details, see https://www.washingtonpost.com/nation/2019/04/30/minnesota-police-officer-convicted-murder-fatal-shooting-australian-woman-who-called/?noredirect=on&utm_term=.961ddb82a6d5, accessed 27 July 2019.

[90] For further details, see https://www.npr.org/2019/07/16/742186042/nypd-officer-wont-face-federal-criminal-charges-in-eric-garner-s-death-sources-s, accessed 27 July 2019.

[91] Steve Paddock, 64, of Mesquite, Nevada, fired shot after shot from his room at the Mandalay Bay Resort and Casino into the crowd of about 22,000 attending a rock concert. His actions resulted in the worst mass murder in modern American history. For further details, see https://www.nbcnews.com/storyline/las-vegas-shooting/las-vegas-police-investigating-shooting-mandalay-bay-n806461, accessed 27 July 2019.

[92] This lack of dexterity in dealing with the modern world can have deadly consequences. Estimates hold that some ten percent of Amish children leave their closely-knit communities and either join their more modernity-embracing theological cousins (such as New-Order or Beachy Amish, or the Mennonites) or leave Anabaptist culture completely. My friend Raul Nutting has worked with several Amish young men in restoring log cabins in Northeast Iowa and Southeast Minnesota. He has encountered, firsthand and repeatedly, the limits of most of these young men's abilities to cope with modernity. One who left Amishdom struggled to integrate into non-Amish culture—only to eventually drive trucks in a fracking boomtown in the Dakotas, come to drink heavily

and enter into a relationship with a non-Amish woman, in front of whom he later shot himself dead, unable to cope any longer with his adopted life in the wider world.

[93] About the evolution of the word "gay" as illustrated by the *Punch* cartoon from 1857, which uses "gay" as a colloquial euphemism for being a prostitute: One woman says to the other (who looks glum), "How long have you been gay?"—with the poster on the wall advertising *La Traviata*, an opera about a courtesan; taken from https://en.wikipedia.org/wiki/Gay, accessed 1 December 2019. For details of gay-specific references, see https://aminoapps.com/c/lgbt-1/page/blog/zephyrus-and-hyacinthus/MQ3p_kY4HkugXQWYKozd7XE2KPY7zWjoeD5, https://en.wikipedia.org/wiki/Richard_Puller_von_Hohenburg and https://en.wikipedia.org/wiki/Annual_Reminder, accessed 1 December 2019.

In my father's family, homosexuality was such a taboo, as a child I did not even know it existed. In my mother's family, the score was different. Shown in the above photo are music teacher Willard Lovell (left) and a friend. Willard was my mother's Aunt Bernice's live-in uncle, with whom she grew up in Hampshire, Illinois. Bernice's daughter, Audrey, once told me "Mother was close to her gay uncle and didn't give a hoot who he loved." That, however, was not the only incident of same-gender love among my mother's people: Late in life, Phyllis [Thrams] Luick confided that she once found love letters that her Aunt Florence Thrams had written to a woman. When I asked, however, where they were, she admitted "I burned 'em up." When I asked her why, she only shrugged.

[94] Hoffman, C. (2019, April 4). Historian, Sperm Donor Contacted by Biological Child. *Mount Mercy Times*, p. 6

Historian, Former Sperm Donor Contacted by Biological Child

By Courtney Hoffman
News Editor

Michael Luick-Thrams was a college student in the 80s, when he became a sperm donor. Two months ago, something unexpected happened—a stranger contacted him, asking if he was her father.

Luick-Thrams' March 28 lecture, Needles and Haystacks: Finding Family "Love" in a Digital Age highlighted some recent life changes and the resulting questions about the roles and responsibilities of genetic donors.

"Eight weeks ago tomorrow I got an email," he said, and that's where his whirlwind story began. The woman who contacted him, _____ had taken a 23andMe DNA test to learn more about her ancestry and to look for siblings.

Though she found none in her search, she was able to use the genetic information to trace family trees. She narrowed down candidates for her biological father to one of five cousins, including Luick-Thrams.

"So she sent this email, and she said more or less 'I don't know what you'll do with this, but I just want you to know that I exist and I think I'm your daughter,'" Luick-Thrams said.

"At first there was shock. Confusion. It felt like the world was falling out under my feet."

Luick-Thrams also came out as a gay man in his youth and struggles to find out how and where to fit this new family into the life and identity he's built.

"I had invested all this energy in this gay identity," he said. "And it wasn't a conscious thing, it was just a natural role."

"So I invested all of this energy and some woman comes and says 'I'm your daughter,' where do I fit her in my worldview? Where does she fit in?"

Despite all of these concerns, he shocked _____ by replying back to the email, and so their connection began. DNA test results found that they were an extremely close match, and Luick-Thrams marveled at their "quite cosmic and quite unexpected" connection, along with their many similarities.

Throughout this whole ordeal, he says he's discovered three questions that he's been contemplating: who should live, how should people live, and who gets to decide?

One issue is that some donors don't want to be found or contacted. Some bring lawyers into the equation to formally cut off contact when offspring try to contact them.

But is this contact necessary in some cases? Though the application process for these programs is different now, Luick-Thrams said he wasn't required to share his medical history before joining the program. This leaves offspring without the information they need to receive proper medical care.

Such lack of regulation would contribute to the loss of _____'s 3-year-old son, who passed away from leukemia before she stumbled across any information about her father.

Another question he posed was about the extent to which donors should be held responsible as parents. How far do you take it, he wonders, when that child wouldn't be in the world without him?

Luick-Thrams doesn't claim to know the answers to these questions. Adjusting as best he can and open to the various unexpected outcomes of life, he knows only that the future is uncertain.

"I knew in the 80s that I was casting my DNA throughout and making human lives possible and I had no control."

"I don't know what's coming," he said. "It's a challenge."

Courtney Hoffman/ Times

Guest lecturer Michael Luick-Thrams shares his story as a sperm donor who was cotacted by one of his biological children in Betty Cherry on March 28.

---

[95] Patricia (née Larson) Schultz served as a Clear Lake High School journalism teacher to my family and me in the 1970s and '80s. She later served as chair of the TRACES Center for History and Culture board of directors as well

as a volunteer; several of the fifteen books TRACES has published (including this one) were edited or illustrated by Pat. As a cherished, trusted family friend as well as proofreader/editor, she advised me that I "also need to acknowledge that one of the healing elements is time. Your parents changed; they helped you; they welcomed your friends into their home; your mother came to Europe to see you. Your father not only began to speak to you, but to work with you" on various TRACES projects, such as building exhibit props and on the BUS-eum."

96 For documentation of this mostly forgotten riot in "Lake Wobegon," see https://www.mprnews.org/story/2019/07/22/photos-documenting-1967s-fiery-unrest-in-minneapolis, accessed 22 July 2019.

97 For further information, see https://onmilwaukee.com/raisemke/articles/diverse-dining-dinners-for-change.html, accessed 27 July 2019.

98 To view the entire video, see https://www.youtube.com/watch?v=Bq1kPcoo_Go, accessed 21 September 2019.

99 For further details, see https://en.wikipedia.org/wiki/Dark_energy, accessed 22 July 2019.

100 Additional material that "got cut" from inclusion is at https://www.scribd.com/document/265176852/disReality, accessed 23 November 2019.

101 The New Oxford American Dictionary recognized Sarah Palin's gaffe "refudiate" as the "Word of the Year" in 2010, according to https://en.wikipedia.org/wiki/Portmanteau, accessed 10 September 2019.

102 In his 2006 book, Forza della gentilezza [The Power of Kindness], Piero Ferrucci explores in more depth both the nature and touted benefits of kindness: "Giving kindness does us as much good as receiving it [as] kind people are healthier and live longer, are more popular and productive, have greater success in business, and are happier than others. In other words, they are destined to live a much more interesting and fulfilling life than those who lack this quality. They are much better equipped to face life in all its savage unpredictability and frightening precariousness." He maintains that "If we are healthier when we are caring, empathic, and open to others, it means we are born to be kind. If we push our way forward, cultivate hostile thoughts, or bear lifelong grudges, we will not be at our best. And if we ignore or repress our positive qualities, we may harm ourselves and others. As psychiatrist Alberto Alberti maintains, love that is not expressed becomes hate, joy that is not enjoyed becomes depression. Yes, we are designed to be kind." He goes on to say that "kindness in all its aspects can become an extraordinary inner adventure that radically changes our way of thinking and being, and moves us briskly along in our personal and spiritual growth." Ferrucci promises that "The gifts of kindness and its qualities are various. Why are grateful people more efficient? Why are those who feel a sense of belonging less depressed? Why do altruistic people enjoy better health, and trusting individuals live longer? Why is it that if you smile, you are perceived as more attractive? Why is it advantageous to take care of a pet? Why do those elderly who can talk more with others have less probability of contracting Alzheimer's disease? And why do children who receive more love and attention grow healthier and more intelligent? Because all these attitudes and behaviors, which are all aspects of kindness, bring us closer to what we are meant to do and to be. It is so elementary: If we related better with others, we feel better." Furthermore: "Kindness has to do with that what is tenderest and most intimate in us. It is an aspect of our nature that we often do not express fully—especially men in our culture, but also women—because we are afraid that if this vulnerable side comes to light, we might suffer, be offended, ridiculed, or exploited. We will find rather, that we suffer by not expressing it. And that by touching this nucleus of tenderness, we enliven our entire affective world, and we open ourselves to countless possibilities of change." Excerpted from pages 4-9 in the Tarcher/Penguin paperback edition (2007).

103 This statement comes in George Fox's 1656 letter to ministers, which he sent when he was in prison in Launceston, in Cornwall. It was transcribed for him by Ann Downer (1624–1686), who had walked from London to assist him. Source: https://qfp.quaker.org.uk/passage/19-32/, accessed 27 July 2019.

104 Founded in 1991 and renamed "Lesbian & Gay Hospitality Exchange International" ("L/GHEI") in 1993, further details are at http://lghei.org/. Iowa State University also sponsored a later tour through Australia and New Zealand, where I spoke about Out of Hitler's Reach at Quaker meetings and schools.

105 For details on Quakers owning slaves, see: https://beyondthehistorytextbooks.com/2013/09/23/quakers-as-slave-owners/, accessed 27 July 2019.

106 As accessed 27 July 2019 from its website at http://iowaprayerbreakfast.com/about-iowa-prayer-breakfast/, the event's current host organization describes its Mission Statement as: ""The Iowa Prayer Breakfast exists to glorify Jesus Christ through the public affirmation of His sovereignty over our State and our Nation. In obedience to 2 Chronicles 7:14, we pray for God's intervention in the affairs of our State and His favor and blessing on our leaders." Regnery Publishing—cited as being that of the scheduled 2020 speaker, pastor Jim

Garlow—bills itself on its website as "the leading publisher of conservative books. Bestselling authors include Ann Coulter, [Rush's brother] David Limbaugh, Dinesh D'Souza and more." The names in this passage assigned the other four ISU students who attended the 1985 event are pseudonyms for actual people at the event.

[107] For images and details, see https://www.lib.iastate.edu/about-library/art/facade-engraved-text, accessed 13 September 2019.

[108] Based on statics accessed 9 September 2019 from https://en.wikipedia.org/wiki/List_of_African_countries_by_Human_Development_Index.

[109] According to documentation entailed in https://www.nytimes.com/2019/08/02/opinion/sunday/nuns-slavery.html, accessed 9 September 2019, "as women began to enter the first [American] Catholic convents in the late-18th and early-19th centuries, some brought their human property with them as part of their dowries, historians say. [...] Wealthy supporters and relatives of the nuns also donated enslaved people to the convents. Meanwhile, Catholic sisters bought, sold and bartered enslaved people. Some nuns accepted slaves as payment for tuition to their schools or handed over their human property as payment for debts, records show." While incredible today, documents indicate it was the norm to see enslaved "chattel" as property, in capitalist terms as investments. In his piece *Observations Concerning the Increase of Mankind, Peopling of Countries, etc.*, Benjamin Franklin calculated coldly "Tis an ill-grounded Opinion that by the Labour of Slaves, America may possibly vie in Cheapness of Manufactures with Britain. The Labour of Slaves can never be so cheap here as the Labour of working Men is in Britain. Any one may compute it. Interest of Money is in the Colonies from 6 to 10 per Cent. Slaves one with another cost 30 £ Sterling per Head. Reckon then the Interest of the first Purchase of a Slave, the Insurance or Risque on his Life, his Cloathing and Diet, Expences in his Sickness and Loss of Time, Loss by his Neglect of Business (Neglect is natural to the Man who is not to be benefited by his own Care or Diligence), Expence of a Driver to keep him at Work, and his Pilfering from Time to Time, almost every Slave being by Nature a Thief, and compare the whole Amount with the Wages of a Manufacturer of Iron or Wool in England, you will see that Labour is much cheaper there than it ever can be by Negroes here. Why then will Americans purchase Slaves? Because Slaves may be kept as long as a Man pleases, or has Occasion for their Labour; while hired Men are continually leaving their Master (often in the midst of his Business,) and setting up for themselves." Source: http://www.columbia.edu/~lmg21/ash3002y/earlyac99/documents/observations.html, accessed 9 September 2019.

[110] For more information, see https://www.friendsjournal.org/slavery-in-the-quaker-world/?utm_source=friendsjournal&utm_medium=enewes&utm_campaign=Sept092019, accessed 13 September 2019.

[111] For details, see https://www.cnn.com/2016/12/07/asia/china-iowa-xi-jinping-branstad-trump/index.html , accessed 28 July 2019.

[112] For details, see https://www.britannica.com/event/Citizens-United-v-Federal-Election-Commission, accessed 28 July 2019.

[113] This and the following quote are from Peck's *The Road Less Traveled*, as cited in http://www.gurteen.com/gurteen/gurteen.nsf/id/X00090436/, accessed 4 November 2019.

[114] See the source at https://www.firstpeople.us/FP-Html-Legends/TwoWolves-Cherokee.html, accessed 27 July 2019.

[115] Edith traveled across the Upper Midwest with TRACES programs, one of which was featured by Minnesota Public Radio: https://www.mprnews.org/story/2010/04/02/edith-morgan More recently, on 27 June 2019, the Cedar Rapids *Gazette* published an in-depth article about Scattergood Hostel, including Edith's memories of her family's 9-1/2 month stay there: https://www.thegazette.com/subject/news/80-years-ago-scattergood-hostel-took-refugees-fleeing-nazis-wwii-west-branch-cedar-county-edith-lichtenstein-morgan-froehlig-20190627.

[116] This source, accessed 28 July 2019, https://quizlet.com/134766361/south-africa-flash-cards/, indicates blacks were allowed leadership roles in their own townships, especially in locations near borders, in hopes they would withdraw from South Africa—which did not happen.

[117] For a wider view of the workings of Apartheid, see https://www.facinghistory.org/confronting-apartheid/chapter-2/introduction, accessed 27 July 2019.

[118] According to https://www.snopes.com/fact-check/did-lincoln-racism-equality-oppose/ accessed 23 July 2019, the quote from the Lincoln-Douglas debates documented therein shows that Lincoln did not believe in the equality of the races. The source accessed on the same date at

http://www.loc.gov/teachers/classroommaterials/connections/slavery/history.html confirms that all abolitionists did not believe in equal justice, integration, etc. The source at https://www.history.com/news/slavery-american-colonization-society-liberia verifies that some abolitionists as well as slaveholders favored "returning" African Americans to Africa, including the multitudes who had been born in North America or were descended from generations of enslaved persons held in America.

[119] The source accessed 28 July 2019 at https://theintercept.com/2018/02/06/lie-after-lie-what-colin-powell-knew-about-iraq-fifteen-years-ago-and-what-he-told-the-un/ documents that Powell lied—and that ISIS is, indeed, a "love child" of his shameful deceit.

[120] Taken from https://en.wikipedia.org/wiki/Alice_Miller_(psychologist), accessed 14 September 2019; for more information see https://www.nytimes.com/2010/04/27/us/27miller.html, accessed on the same date.

[121] One reader pointed out: "And yet this does not explain all 'evil.' Those who owned slaves were not acting out of childhood abuse but out of human greed. Thus are there not varying causes for evil? Take Trump – does his desire for absolute power and inability to accept even constructive criticism come from having no power and too much criticism in his youth or from being so coddled and assured of his own importance that he believes he is entitled to do just what he wants?"

[122] The quoted text goes on to reveal that "Later in [Saddam Hussein's] life relatives from his native Tikrit became some of his closest advisors and supporters. Under the guidance of his uncle he attended a nationalistic high school in Baghdad. After secondary school Saddam studied at an Iraqi law school for three years, dropping out in 1957 at the age of 20 to join the revolutionary pan-Arab Ba'ath Party, of which his uncle was a supporter. During this time, Saddam apparently supported himself as a secondary school teacher. Ba'athist ideology originated in Syria and the Ba'ath Party had a large following in Syria at the time, but in 1955 there were fewer than 300 Ba'ath Party members in Iraq and it is believed that Saddam's primary reason for joining the party as opposed to the more established Iraqi nationalist parties was his familial connection to Ahmed Hassan al-Bakr and other leading Ba'athists through his uncle." This material comes from https://en.wikipedia.org/wiki/Saddam_Hussein, accessed 15 September 2019.

[123] I wrote this before Donald Trump gave his family's "friend" and business partner (see the 12 November 2019 *New York Times* article at https://www.nytimes.com/2019/11/12/us/politics/trump-erdogan-family-turkey.html?action=click&module=Top%20Stories&pgtype=Homepage) Recep Erdoğan a free hand to invade and annex the northeast corner of Syria—a move which resulted directly in the deaths of hundreds, if not thousands of people, thereby rendering my wish, stated here, moot.

[124] During his TEDxFindhornSalon talk captured at https://www.youtube.com/watch?v=4-vxUtmtKKc and accessed by this author on 29 September 2019, Alastair McIntosh warned "We have to face our psychological history if we are not going to repeat these things."

[125] Peck's full quote in his *The Road Less Traveled* begins: "There really are people and institutions made up of people, who respond with hatred in the presence of goodness and would destroy the good insofar as it is in their power to do so. They do this not with conscious malice but blindly, lacking awareness of their own evil—indeed, seeking to avoid any such awareness. As has been described of the devil in religious literature, they hate the light and instinctively will do anything to avoid it, including attempting to extinguish it. They will destroy the light in their own children and in all other beings subject to their power. [… The quote later resumes with] My second conclusion, then, is that evil is laziness carried to its ultimate, extraordinary extreme [and concludes:] Ordinary laziness is nonlove; evil is antilove." Excerpted from http://www.gurteen.com/gurteen/gurteen.nsf/id/X00090436/, accessed 3 November 2019.

[126] See https://www.good.is/articles/rick-santorum-thinks-carbon-dioxide-isn-t-harmful-to-plants-tell-that-to-a-plant, accessed 25 September 2019.

[127] For a description of this personality archetype of analytical-psychologist Carl Jung's twelve, see https://thoughtcatalog.com/brianna-wiest/2016/01/12-signs-you-are-the-wounded-healer-personality-archetype/, accessed 21 January 2020.

[128] Strikingly, Jan and I had a "radio date" to discuss some Midwest-history topic live on-air on the morning of 11 September 2001. Soon after the second jet flew into the World Trade Center, a staffer of his called to cancel that interview, citing "We have more important events to cover this morning."

[129] It is also sad what suffering can befall also those whom one finds "challenging"—as seen in an update on Jan Mickelson's health at https://eu.desmoinesregister.com/story/news/local/columnists/kyle-

munson/2016/08/17/whos-jan-mickelson-returns-iowa-state-fair-live-broadcast/88889264/, accessed 25 September 2019.

130 For further information, see https://www.monticello.org/sallyhemings/, accessed 14 September 2019.

131 See https://www.huffpost.com/entry/noahs-ark-dinosaurs_n_577d9ff8e4b0344d514dea93?guccounter=1&guce_referrer=aHR0cHM6Ly93d3cuZ29vZ2xlLmNvbVb S8&guce_referrer_sig=AQAAAJ0xtPSbhGrpHUDoqioWsXTbqgcYnhgLfPNcl_E0aOA-kb2UyrmhZarMa3E0kn001By_5SEtzkWmlrhCz3-UhxKxoCBL7xWgRakSZmE-hW-NUgYGy6Nek6zTwGCnzJyEOkEd5Os0OPO4PPPMjzDC1fx-ghFEyleifni0cfcjawDz or https://en.wikipedia.org/wiki/Ken_Ham for possible explanations, as accessed 24 September 2019.

132 For the full transcript of Greta Thunberg's address to the United Nations General Assembly, see https://www.npr.org/2019/09/23/763452863/transcript-greta-thunbergs-speech-at-the-u-n-climate-action-summit?t=1569324226301 accessed 24 September 2019.

133 See https://www.huffpost.com/entry/michael-knowles-greta-thunberg_n_5d898513e4b0c2a85caffdaa, accessed 26 September 2019.

134 For this and other definitions in this section see https://www.lexico.com/en/definition/conviction, accessed 6 October 2019.

135 The above two paragraphs are synthesized from https://en.wikipedia.org/wiki/Eskimo_words_for_snow, accessed 17 October 2019.

136 From the word root "lowly" at https://www.merriam-webster.com/dictionary/lowly, accessed 17 October 2019.

137 Morgan Scott Peck is buried in Quaker Cemetery, Duchess County, New York: https://www.findagrave.com/memorial/13156708/morgan-scott-peck , accessed 18 October 2019. Another icon of that era, natural-foods advocate Euell Gibbons, was not born a Quaker but had become one. Other notable Americans or Brits with Quaker connections have included: flag sewer Betsy Ross, First Lady Dolley (née Payne) Madison, poet John Greenleaf Whittier, dogs-playing-poker painter Cassius Marcellus Coolidge, exhibition shooter Annie Oakley, sexually-ambiguous actors Montgomery Cliff [buried in Brooklyn's Quaker cemetery] and James Dean [interred in a Quaker cemetery in Indiana], sci-fi-writer Piers Anthony [Jacob] and musician David Byrne; in Britain, chocolatier John Cadbury, Listerine-inventor Joseph Lister and actress Judi Dench. See https://www.thevintagenews.com/2018/10/21/quakers/, accessed 3 December 2019.

138 Lon Shapiro (at https://medium.com/@lonshapiro/m-scott-peck-wrote-the-best-definition-of-love-i-ever-found-a2386babaf08, accessed 15 October 2019) commented on the emotional risks involved: "If you truly love someone, regardless of where the relationship goes, your desire for their happiness and growth won't ever change. But that doesn't mean you won't feel grief or loss."

139 Lissa Rankin wrote on 17 July 2013 (accessed 15 October 2019 at https://www.facebook.com/lissarankin/posts/while-reading-m-scott-pecks-the-road-less-traveled-i-came-across-a-definition-of/655964521099639/) "While reading M. Scott Peck's The Road Less Traveled, I came across a definition of love that is perhaps the best I've ever read. Dr. Peck differentiates between "falling in love" and "genuine love." Falling in love he defines by the psychiatric term "cathexis," which he defines as "being attracted to, invested in, and committed to an object outside ourselves." We can "cathect" a beloved, a child, or even a hobby, like writing or painting. But according to Dr. Peck, the state of cathexis is temporary, both in romance and in friendship, an illusion that in romance often tempts us to consummate our affection sexually and ultimately propagates the species by luring us into marriage vows that we might never agree to were we not cathecting the one we "love." While cathexis is necessary - and almost always precedes genuine love - it is short-lived, wearing off not only in romances but in friendships as well. Only when this phase wears off do we have the opportunity to mature into genuine love, which he defines as "the will to extend one's self for the purpose of nurturing one's own or another's spiritual growth." Dr. Peck says love is not dependency or self-sacrifice or lust or even a feeling of love - that someone can feel "love" - cathexis - can "fall in love," and experience the euphoria of such a feeling, but that it's not truly genuine love unless the feeling is accompanied by action, that genuine love is defined by loving action. Love is conscious attention, a time investment, a commitment to nurturing the spiritual growth of one another, the willingness to take risks even when it's scary, the risk of opening the heart, even with the knowledge that the heart is likely to get broken, if not right away, then one day in death. Dr. Peck goes on to say that we do not offer genuine love with the expectation that it will be returned, but that after enough expenditure of energy fails to elicit loving action, even when it is clear that loving feelings are present, one's energy simply needs to be conserved. He writes, "Because genuine love

involves an extension of oneself, vast amounts of energy are required and, like it or not, the store of our energy is as limited as the hours of our day. We simply cannot love everyone. True, we may have a feeling of love for mankind, and this feeling may also be useful in providing us with enough energy to manifest genuine love for a few specific individuals. But genuine love for a relatively few specific individuals is all that is within our power. To attempt to exceed the limits of our energy is to offer more than we can deliver, and there is a point of no return beyond which an attempt to love all comers becomes fraudulent and harmful to the very ones we desire to assist. Consequently, if we are fortunate enough to be in a position in which many people ask for our attention, we must choose among them whom we are actually to love. This choice is not easy; it may be excruciatingly painful, as the assumption of godlike power so often is. But it must be made. Many factors need to be considered, primarily the capacity of a prospective recipient of our love to respond to that love with spiritual growth. People differ in this capacity... It is, however, unquestionable that there are many whose spirits are so locked in behind impenetrable armor that even the greatest efforts to nurture the growth of those spirits are doomed to almost certain failure. To attempt to love someone who cannot benefit from your love with spiritual growth is to waste your energy, to cast your seed upon arid ground. Genuine love is precious, and those who are capable of genuine love know that their loving must be focused as productively as possible through self-discipline."

[140] That tree-planting action took place at the Strategic Air Command headquarters at Offutt Air Force Base outside Bellevue, Nebraska. I was not arrested that day, but some Ames Friends were. As for the base: Offutt's history began with the commissioning by the War Department in 1890 of Fort Crook, a dispatch point for conflicts with Native Americans on the Great Plains. Troops from the fort fought in Cuba during the Spanish–American War; its regiment suffered heavy casualties: Only 165 of the 513 regiment members survived, with most succumbing to tropical diseases after the battle. At the close of World War I in 1918, the 61st Balloon Company of the Army Air Corps, which had performed combat reconnaissance training, was assigned to Fort Crook. In the spring of 1921, construction allowed for an airfield suitable for frequent takeoffs and landings, and as a refueling stop for mail and transcontinental flights. The first permanent hangars were completed in 1921; in 1924, the airfield was officially named "Offutt Field". In 1940, the Army Air Corps chose it as the site for a new bomber plant, where in 1944 production switched to B-29 Superfortresses, among which were the *Enola Gay* and *Bockscar*, the B-29s that dropped the first atomic weapons to be used in a military action, against the cities of Hiroshima and Nagasaki, Japan. When our ragtag crew of demonstrators protested the SAC at Offutt Air Force Base, we also were rejecting the legacy of the organized stealing of the prairies from its aboriginal inhabitants, the sham Spanish-American War and the wholesale bombing of civilian targets. At the time we planted our Peace Tree on base property (which we assumed was immediately ripped out), we never could have imagined that less than two decades later, on 11 September 2001, President George W. Bush would conduct one of the first major strategy sessions for the response to the September 11 attacks from a bunker at the base. This information was compiled from https://en.wikipedia.org/wiki/Offutt_Air_Force_Base, accessed 4 December 2019.

[141] The trip organizers called together participants to attend orientation at Minneapolis' Central Lutheran Church, which formed in 1919 in part in response to anti-immigrant sentiment following World War I; for details see https://pages.stolaf.edu/locluth/project/central-lutheran/, accessed 20 October 2019. In 1988, the American Lutheran Church fused with the more conservative Evangelical Lutheran Church in America.

[142] For "live" coverage of that march, see https://www.c-span.org/video/?88744-1/20th-anniversary-march-washington, accessed 20 October 2019.

[143] To access that study, go to http://traces.org/pdf/Rural_Iowa_Study_by_ML_1984.pdf.

[144] Though factually representing actual people, the names of those in the cited activists' group have been altered.

[145] I use the word "disproportionate" here solely in relation to the proportion of Jews present at that conference, in marked contrast to the percentage of Jews in the United States' population, as seen as an ethnic group, demographically; I do not use it as a value judgement or indication of political views, held by myself or others.

[146] See https://www.npr.org/2019/11/03/775818666/protests-around-the-globe, accessed 5 November 2019.

[147] Technically, "hats" are free-standing, due to having a brim or bill and typically a "pinched" firm-sided crown; in contrast, "caps" have soft-sided crowns and usually no brims, bills, peaks or visors, so cannot stand upright. One proofreader of an early draft of this text protested "My hat, or cap, as you are calling it, didn't cost me time, energy or money. People were handing them out to us as we headed to the march site. I think we all went out because we were so disgusted and shocked that he was actually the president. Lots of men were

there too! Not just women. [Husband] Terry went." For details about the "Pussyhat Project" and the Women's March itself, see https://en.wikipedia.org/wiki/2017_Women%27s_March, accessed 22 October 2019.

[148] According to Wikipedia entries about the march, others of those cited as having present include: Dianna Agron, Christina Aguilera, Jane Alexander, Maryum Ali, Gillian Anderson, Jacinda Ardern, Patricia Arquette, Rosanna Arquette, Kevin Bacon, Joan Baez, Lance Bass, Jennifer Beals, Samantha Bee, Maria Bello, Melissa Benoist, Tom Bergeron, Mayim Bialik, Rowan Blanchard, Mayor Muriel Bowser, Jennifer Finney Boylan, Benjamin Bratt, Connie Britton, Roslyn Brock, Rabbi Sharon Brous, Steve Buscemi, Sophia Bush, Peter Capaldi, Mary Chapin Carpenter, Jessica Chastain, Chris Colfer, Courteney Cox, Laverne Cox, Darren Criss, Jackie Cruz, Jamie Lee Curtis, Miley Cyrus, Laurie David, Rosario Dawson, Adam Dell, Laura Dern, Fran Drescher, Lena Dunham, Eliza Dushku, The Edge, Edie Falco, America Ferrera, Josh Gad, Ana Gasteyer, Gina Gershon, Joseph Gordon-Levitt, Ariana Grande, Clark Gregg, Jennifer Grey, Rebecca Hall, Chelsea Handler, LaDonna Harris, Melissa Harris-Perry, Vanessa Hudgens, Helen Hunt, Angelica Huston, Donna Hylton, Jidenna, Leslie Jones, Ashley Judd, Kesha, Carole King, Stephen King, Madeleine Kunin, Joshua Kushner, Padma Lakshmi, Brie Larson, John Legend, Juliette Lewis, Blake Lively, Julia Louis-Dreyfus, Demi Lovato, Natasha Lyonne, Macklemore, Rami Malek, Julianna Margulies, Ed Markey, Debi Mazar, Mary McCormack, Frances McDormand, Rose McGowan, Ian McKellen, Idina Menzel, Debra Messing, Lin-Manuel Miranda, Helen Mirren, Moby, Janet Mock, Janelle Monáe, Julianne Moore, Mandy Moore, Chloë Grace Moretz, Kacey Musgraves, Kathy Najimy, Thandie Newton, Cynthia Nixon, Lupita Nyong'o, Chris O'Dowd, Nick Offerman, Rosie Perez, Pink, Amy Poehler, Ai-jen Poo, Natalie Portman, Laura Prepon, John C. Reilly, Patricia Richardson, Rihanna, Jason Ritter, Chris Rock, Michelle Rodriguez, Gina Rodriguez, Seth Rogen, Samantha Ronson, Tracee Ellis Ross, Kristin Rowe-Finkbeiner, Paul Rudd, Mark Ruffalo, Taylor Schilling, Amy Schumer, Ilyasah Shabazz, Jenny Slate, Willow Smith, Regina Spektor, Kristen Stewart, Barbra Streisand, Amber Tamblyn, Chrissy Teigen, Charlize Theron, Bella Thorne, Marisa Tomei, Lily Tomlin, Aisha Tyler, Jenna Ushkowitz, Rufus Wainwright, Kerry Washington, Emma Watson, Naomi Watts, Randi Weingarten, Ming-Na Wen, Olivia Wilde, Jessica Williams, Raquel Willis, Evan Rachel Wood, Alfre Woodard, Bonnie Wright, Zendaya, Dolph Ziggler and David Zuckerman.

[149] This hard-to-trace saying is said to be an African proverb, its use attributed to Al Gore at https://jezebel.com/on-the-origin-of-certain-quotable-african-proverbs-1766664089, accessed 6 November 2019.

[150] See https://en.wikipedia.org/wiki/Greens/Green_Party_USA, accessed 23 October 2019.

[151] Stockman, Farah (23 December 2019). "Women's March Roiled by Accusations of Anti-Semitism." *New York Times.*

[152] What author-historian is not gratified to discover, later, that her or his research—or interpretation of same— was not, ultimately, borne out by subsequent developments? Such was the case in this case—as documented in a New York Times article accessed 18 January 2020: https://www.nytimes.com/2020/01/18/us/womens-march.html.

[153] Distilled from https://en.wikipedia.org/wiki/Right-wing_politics, accessed 24 October 2018. That article goes on to say that "The political terms 'Left' and 'Right' were first used during the French Revolution (1789–1799) and referred to seating arrangements in the French parliament: Those who sat to the right of the chair of the parliamentary president were broadly supportive of the institutions of the monarchist Old Regime. The original Right in France was formed as a reaction against the 'Left' and comprised those politicians supporting hierarchy, tradition, and clericalism. The use of the expression la droite ('the right') became prominent in France after the restoration of the monarchy in 1815, when it was applied to the Ultra-royalists. The people of English-speaking countries did not apply the terms 'right' and 'left' to their own politics until the 20th century."

[154] Distilled from https://en.wikipedia.org/wiki/Left-wing_politics, accessed 24 October 2019.

[155] Taken from https://www.nytimes.com/2019/10/17/world/europe/france-far-right-environment.html, accessed 17 October 2019.

[156] One example of her uncanny ability to see what others often cannot or do not wish to see: In a later email "Bug" sent to me on 11 November 2019, she wrote "Every rule has exceptions and this isn't even a rule but just a frequently corroborated observation on my part: 'Inheritances make your children stupid, and they make your grandchildren stupid and mean.'" An earlier quote of hers, from during my 2016 campaign, gave me great pause: "Leaders lead by loving their followers/constituents as they currently, imperfectly are. They don't lead by being contemptuous of them. That's what makes being a leader so hard."

[157] See pages 253-254 of Elena Aguilar's manual, The Art of Coaching Teams: Building Resilient Communities that Transform Schools (2016, Jossey-Bass).

[158] I do not use here the adjective "domesticated" to describe the human "animal" casually. While I cringed at the low-level advertising marring their left on-screen borders, I did find two related articles of particular interest and relevance to my cautiously-chosen wording at https://io9.gizmodo.com/7-signs-that-humans-are-domestic-animals-1586580895 and https://io9.gizmodo.com/yes-humans-are-animals-so-just-get-over-yourselves-1588990060, accessed 16 November 2019. Also, regarding "perfectly"-round lines: Neither Earth nor its moon is a perfect sphere—and, while eggs are "natural" ovals they are not "perfect" ones, in the sense of having an exactly symmetrical, uniform radius from their center, all the way around that center. Regarding the fine hairs of fine lines, as I wrote this section I took into careful consideration the precise wording of contributors at https://www.quora.com/Is-it-redundant-to-say-straight-line-Are-all-lines-not-by-definition-straight, accessed 16 November 2019.

[159] As Newitz puts it: "Beavers build dams that utterly transform the way water moves through forests, flooding some areas and parching others. Ants build massive underground cities, full of farms where they 'milk' aphids for food and grow fungus to eat. So we are not the only polluting life forms, and we are not the only ones to transform landscapes with building and farming."

[160] And—stretching a bit here, grasping for grounds for our kind's collective moral redemption—as Newitz puts it: "[We] aren't the only species to spread all over the planet either. Humans share that honor with other invasive species, including extinct animals like trilobites, as well as living ones like rats, crows, cockroaches and more. Invasive species have roamed across the Earth since life began. Humans are about as special as dirty little rodents, scampering between walls in search of some garbage to eat." Still, we can attribute (or fault) our artificial [i.e., human-generated or "non-natural"] creation—this parallel "universe" we have created within the cosmic one provided to us by Life itself—to our unique ability to create boxes.

[161] From Latin, literally "made by hand."

[162] E.g., made from cloth woven on boxlike looms, sectioned by angular cutting machines and flattened by frame-borne mangles, packaged into cardboard boxes then shipped around the globe in rectangular containers, etc.

[163] Taken from https://www.vmdtoday.com/news/american-pet-spending-reaches-new-high, accessed 18 November 2019.

[164] In the process of learning how to manufacture things on mass scales, along exact lines, we realized that handmade rifles—for example—all vary, even if a decisive little. If, however, we tooled each component of a certain kind of rifle to be exactly the same, then these new, interchangeable parts would enable us to fabricate zillions of weapons—and, voilà!, today the world is wracked by incessant warfare... weapons being only one of the most extreme examples of what can happen when parts are emphasized over their sum contra the whole they form.

[165] A BBC feature on 6 December 2019 about "language extinction" maintained that of the 7,000 or so languages in the world today, likely half will become extinct by the end of this century. Some of the speakers stressed the importance of preserving at least some of the endangered languages, or spoke of lingual diversity on a virtual par with biodiversity in terms of importance for humans. For details see https://www.bbc.co.uk/programmes/w3csyddy, accessed 7 December 2019.

[166] Social "safety valves," however, were built-in: Watch old Jane Austen films and note how in public dance scenes two people might come together through dance, but then a changing roster of other partners gave them time apart—something one or both might have welcomed, depending on the degree of mutual attraction or interest. The higher the social strata, the more strictly obligatory dance cards assured that two people could not dance an entire evening together and would be forced to dance with others. Usually only engaged couples danced with each other for repeated sets, yet another man (never a woman) might ask to relieve the man—a courtesy seldom denied.

[167] The boy in front of the window, George, was my great-grandfather and namesake. His father, Louis, and mother, Mary, would be two more of my daughter Nicole's direct ancestors. In addition, between the two solo portraits over the mantle (or is than an organ?)—on its left a colored tintype of Louis at about sixteen, right likely an image of Mary as a girl, circa 1865–rests (or hangs?) a photo of Louis' father, Henry Luick Jr (seated, center), accompanied by his siblings: (standing) William, Catherine (née Luick) Elder, David; John (seated left) and (right) Frederick. The photo was taken during John's visit from Michigan to his Iowa family, likely as it became clear [note both seated brothers' hands lain on him] that Henry had not long to live, circa 1898. The

fifth, suspected ancestor of mine and Nicole's would be the likeness of the woman captured in the (charcoal?) image, thought to be of Mary's mother, Martha Jane (née Toler) Hunt. Mary's mother, who had lost her mother while riding in a covered wagon from Missouri to California in 1848 during the Gold Rush, became the unrequited—and apparently one-sided—love interest of one of Mark Twain's later drinking buddies, the adventurer-journalist-womanizer-drunk Alfred Doten. Having sailed from his home in Plymouth, Massachusetts to California via the sea route around the farthest tip of South America, Doten's diary entries involving his fascination in and relentless pursuit of Martha Jane Toler offer rare, colorful, often disturbing glimpses into life on the Western frontier—as published in detail in pages 17-36 in *Chasing Restless Roots: The Dreams that Lured Us Across America*, volume 2 in the pentalogy *Oceans of Darkness, Oceans of Light: Our Family's Trials and Treasures in the New World*, published by TRACES Center for History and Culture, 2015.

Your friend.
Alf Doten.

[168] One proofreader, my trusted, treasured friend Pat Schultz, wrote on 7 December 2019 a "dissenting view:"
There are other signs of our decreasing "Dancing together."

1. Church membership has declined. The social value of church over the years has been as valuable as its religious value: meals shared, happy occasions celebrated, sad occasions shared, many things done together that developed deep friendships and personal commitments often lasting several generations.

2. Our greater mobility: As we seek jobs, marry outside our communities, give more leisure time to travel, families today tend to live more geographically separated. Families with three generations living close enough to interact regularly are far fewer than they once were. High school friends move on, aunts, uncles and cousins often hardly know each other.

3. Increase in divorce rates, which you've indirectly referenced.

4. Women's clubs have trouble maintaining membership, many becoming white-haired, as younger women have jobs and much less time to devote to such social circles. Men, too, in Lions Clubs, etc., at least around here, seem to have fewer younger men in their ranks. I don't think it is so much because people just don't care anymore.

5. Technology which allows us contacts but without face to face relationships - and often keeps us from engaging in those relationships - i.e. the couple in the restaurant paying more attention to their phones than each other.

(I'm not sure capitalism has as much to do with it as you purport. I believe in capitalism, but also believe history has clearly show us that unrestrained capitalism is a problem - thus Pure Food and Drug legislation, labor laws, anti-trust legislation. What worries me right now is this administration's intent to get rid of some of those important regulations.)

And yet, we do still seek our dance partners, as Maslow's needs haven't disappeared. But, it is harder to do than it was before the changes I've noted above. It leaves those like Nicole looking for roots but not really knowing how to connect once one is found or even how to successfully create a relationship. It means kids without role models at home - most often male role models - join gangs. People do still join teams - sports teams, art clubs, photography clubs, the list goes on. However, those groups are usually short-term, not long-term relationships.

And some join groups with a commonality that unites them - indigenous groups, environmental protestors - right now young people in the Middle East - fundamentalist Christian or Muslims. Groups like these have for centuries competed with each other, abused each other, even warred with each other.

However, today it is indeed harder to find the "We." The divisions between us and even the increased ability to live "alone" with less reliance on others have are much starker today - in part because of political conflicts not based on uniting us but on "winning."

What drives our "we-ness" is that basic Maslow need for belonging and acceptance - and thus we are Republicans or Democrats and so forth, in other groups that compete. And that's one thing Maslow did not address. Human beings seem to have an inherent need to compete and to classify themselves and each other. We like to "classify" everything - which serves us better perhaps in understanding biology, cells and matter than it does in classifying each other, where it has become destructive instead of constructive. Maslow knew we had to come to "love" and accept ourselves, but he said little about any need for loving and accepting others - even though he did urge us to understand that others act in order to meet their own needs.

Another factor at work in our divisions is fear of change - for many another very normal response. And things are changing so quickly today (not just technology and the availability of more things but also in a greater feeling of being part of a global community instead of a simple, closely knit community), that fear drives some people deeper into the disparate groups where they are comfortable. When groups we easily learn about from enhanced communication are asking for change, perhaps the easiest thing to do is to crawl into our turtle shells and just avoid it. The world IS striving for greater equality and better ways to work together - but the idea is so foreign to us and so resisted by some parts of it, we honestly don't know how to do it. How much easier it was when colonialism could wield power to get the world to shape to its wants - at least for those who benefited. The current drive for nationalism by many countries, I think, is part of that fear.

The key has to be – it has to be - focusing on commonalities. You've suggested at this throughout this second part of the book. You and "Lucy" have come together, even if not very successfully, on the common ground of love for your mother. The problem is how to get disparate groups to come together to find their commonalities - to find dances they are comfortable sharing. Tragedy proves we can do it - farmers still gather to harvest the crops of a neighbor who is seriously ill - whether they are Republicans or Democrats ceases to matter. The children of the tragedy of a mass shooting in their school have come together to work for change with their former cliques mattering much less than they once did. Tornados, floods - those working at the site of the crumbled towers - people in such situations suddenly don't care about race, religion, etc. We have to find commonalities that aren't focused on disasters. However, those make good starting points and I believe the climate crisis is beginning to fill that function. While there are those in their turtle shells, more and more of the world's population is becoming impacted and growing in understanding.

Both you and Nicole share a commonality in terms of not having that sense of familial belonging. But other differences have driven you apart. Lacking you, she has turned to your sister in her need - which you should not resent but understand.

I, too, am impacted. Since my husband's death, "things" have become more important to me - possessions, other ways of identifying myself. I have never been a natural joiner - unless there was a cause involved - my fellow teachers, volunteering at Opportunity Village, making the restoration of the Park Inn a reality. Losing two close friends, of which I really do not have many, has made me feel even more "alone" and isolated. But, I have that one wonderful thing that keeps me "safe" - my family and extended family. We "dance together" wonderfully.

In short, I guess what I'm saying is that you haven't given this last topic the full thought and investigation that have gone into the rest of the book. By focusing on your daughter for a very large part of it, you have ignored much.

The obvious answer is to find the "we" - our commonalities from which to build a base. But how to do that is far, far from easy and I would maintain that in part, it always has been.

[169] Taken from http://www.gurteen.com/gurteen/gurteen.nsf/id/X00090436/, accessed 6 December 2019.

[170] See https://www.nytimes.com/2019/11/14/opinion/andrew-yang-jobs.html, accessed 23 November 2019.

[171] See https://en.wikipedia.org/wiki/Artificial_intelligence, accessed 23 November 2019.

[172] See https://www.nytimes.com/2019/10/15/technology/robot-hand-rubiks-cube.html?searchResultPosition=1, accessed 23 November 2019.

[173] The citation at https://www.bbc.com/news/technology-50064225—accessed 23 November 2019—read: "Using machine-learning and robotics to solve a Rubik's cube has been achieved before. Notably, in March 2018, a machine developed by engineers at MIT managed to solve a cube in just 0.38 seconds."

[174] American political scientist Samuel Phillips Huntington, as quoted in an article published by Rich Lowry in the National Review, 8 October 2019.

[175] "HSBC" stands for the "Hongkong and Shanghai Bank Corporation," founded by Scot Thomas Sutherland in 1865. It is not only Europe's largest bank, but—depending on the year of the report and the source of the estimate—the world's sixth or seventh. The author found this page on HSBC's website https://www.us.hsbc.com/financial-wellness/coming-to-america/ of personal interest—accessed 4 November 2019.

[176] During my short sojourn in tense London town, a general sense of uncertainty and stress felt palpable. While most people with whom I spoke seemed helpless to know what to do, a few had been trying for some time to cope with the situation as it arose moment to moment—as seen in a video at https://www.facebook.com/scientistsforeu/videos/3111952288877302/, accessed 12 October 2019.